The Fracturing of the
American Corporate Elite

The Fracturing of the American Corporate Elite

Mark S. Mizruchi

HARVARD UNIVERSITY PRESS
Cambridge, Massachusetts
London, England
2013

Library of Congress Cataloging-in-Publication Data

Mizruchi, Mark S.

   The fracturing of the American corporate elite / Mark S. Mizruchi.

     pages   cm

   Includes bibliographical references and index.

   ISBN 978-0-674-07299-2 (alk. paper)

     1. Corporations—Political aspects—United States—History.   2. Chief executive officers—United States—History.   3. Business and politics—United States—History. 4. Social responsibility of business—United States—History.   5. United States—Social policy.   6. United States—Economic policy.   I. Title.

HD2785.M574   2013

322'.30973—dc23   2012044933

For
Mom and Dad,
Josh,
and Gail

Contents

Acronyms

AARP	American Association of Retired Persons
AEI	American Enterprise Institute
AFL	American Federation of Labor
AHIP	America's Health Insurance Plans
AMA	American Medical Association
APHA	American Public Health Association
BRT	The Business Roundtable
CED	Committee for Economic Development
CIO	Congress of Industrial Organizations
EPA	Environmental Protection Agency
GE	General Electric
GM	General Motors
HIAA	Health Insurance Association of America
HMO	Health Maintenance Organization
HR	Human resources
KKR	Kohlberg Kravis Roberts
LBO	Leveraged Buyout
NAM	National Association of Manufacturers
NCF	National Civic Federation
NFIB	National Federation of Independent Business

NLRB	National Labor Relations Board
NRDC	National Resource Defense Council
NWLB	National War Labor Board
NYT	*New York Times*
OECD	Organization for Economic Cooperation and Development
OSHA	Occupational Safety and Health Administration
PATCO	Professional Air Traffic Controllers Organization
PhRMA	Pharmaceutical Research and Manufacturers of America
SEIU	Service Employees International Union
TWA	Trans World Airlines
UAW	United Auto Workers of America
USCAP	United States Climate Action Partnership
WBGH	Washington Business Group on Health
WPA	Works Progress Administration
WSJ	*Wall Street Journal*

Preface

Like many Americans, I have become increasingly distressed by the state of our politics. In part this is because I am unhappy with the action (or lack of action) that our elected officials have taken. In part it is because of the content of political debate, in which neither side seems willing to address the pressing issues of the day. Perhaps most of all, I am troubled by the stalemate, the inability to accomplish even the most routine tasks of government, and the intransigence of those who have managed to hold the nation hostage to their extreme views.

In trying to understand the roots of this predicament, as well as a way to extricate ourselves from it, I have come to see the problem as a lack of leadership at the national level. This lack of leadership resides not in the absence of visionary political figures, however, but rather in the abdication of responsibility by a group that in earlier decades played a constructive role in both presenting solutions to national problems and in maintaining a moderate cast to our politics: the leaders of large American corporations, the group I call the American corporate elite. This group, which arose in the period after World War II, was far from perfect; books can (and have) been written about its shortcomings. Yet the American corporate elite of the post–World War II period, despite its faults, was able to offer a moderate and pragmatic approach that helped the society flourish, both economically and politically, especially compared to what we observe today. This book represents an effort to understand how this elite arose, what sustained it, what led to its undoing, and the consequences of its demise.

It is ironic that I would be writing about the postwar American corporate elite as a model for responsible leadership. I spent the early part of my career characterizing these people as the "bad guys," and there certainly was plenty about which to complain. This is the group that helped to usher the United States into the Vietnam War. Its members presided over a system rife with poverty, racism, repressive social norms, and a smug, uncritical attitude in which they refused to acknowledge the problems they had created or exacerbated. History can play strange tricks, however. What looks one way at one point may look very different when viewed with distance and a different perspective, and in retrospect it is evident that the postwar corporate elite did much that was good.

In telling this story I have treaded over some very controversial material. I have tried to be as fair as possible to all parties involved. I have not tried to hide my views, but I hope that I have given every side a sufficient hearing. If there are any positions to which I have not done justice, I hope that proponents of those approaches will make their views heard.

Authors of books frequently offer the cliché that book writing is a collective process, in which others had as much or more to do with the final product than the author him or herself. Some cliches survive because they are true, however, and at the risk of perpetuating this overworked notion, I am honored to be able to say that a broad array of individuals and organizations played an indispensible role in the production of this book.

I want to begin by thanking my colleagues at the University of Michigan. In fact, I want to thank the university itself, for providing the facilities, the resources, and an intellectual atmosphere that represent all that is great about the academic enterprise. My former and current department chairs, Howard Kimeldorf and Alford Young Jr., have provided intellectual, moral, and institutional support for this project. Howard also proved to be a valuable sounding board on Chapter 4, as did Greta Krippner on Chapter 6. Jerry Davis was a constant source of support in ways too numerous to mention. I am also grateful to Jason Owen-Smith, Renee Anspach, and Elizabeth A. Armstrong. My dean, Terrence J. McDonald, generously allowed me to defer my impending administrative duties so that I could complete the manuscript, and Jason Owen-Smith selflessly and artfully performed those duties in my absence. The University of Michigan also provided numerous sources of financial support. Units that contributed to this project include the Department of Sociology; the College of Literature, Science, and the Arts; the Rackham School of Graduate Studies; the Barger Leadership Institute; the Interdisciplinary Committee on Organizational Studies; the Ross School of Business; and the Office of the Vice President for Research.

I also want to thank the National Science Foundation, whose support through grant SES-0922915 allowed me to collect the data on which the book is based. And I would like to thank the John Simon Guggenheim Memorial Foundation for the fellowship that allowed me to complete the writing of the manuscript. It is especially necessary to point out that the views expressed in this book are mine, and do not necessarily reflect the views of either of these agencies.

In addition to my colleagues at the University of Michigan, I was fortunate to have a highly skilled and committed group of research assistants, whose support was invaluable. Anne Bowers (formerly Fleischer) was my first RA on the project, and her painstaking research and constant encouragement helped me get the study off the ground. During various stages of the project I received valuable help from Jonathan Atwell, Helena Buhr, Natalie Cotton-Nessler, Dan Hirschman, Connie Hsiung, and Alwyn Lim. I am especially indebted to Maria Farkas, Mikell Hyman, Todd Schifeling, and Lotus Seeley. Mikell, Todd, and Lotus provided detailed written comments on the entire manuscript, and Lotus did a fabulous job of editing. Todd's role was closer to that of a colleague than a student.

Several colleagues at other universities also provided numerous forms of support. I am almost certainly going to omit some people here, for which I apologize, but I want to especially thank (in alphabetical order) Steve Barley, Robert Boyer, Bruce Carruthers, Tony Chen, J. Adam Cobb, Bill Domhoff, Mark Granovetter, Howell John Harris, Bruce Kogut, Nelson Lichtenstein, Chris Marquis, Beth Mintz, Victor Nee, Eric Neuman, Don Palmer, Woody Powell, Monica Prasad, David Stark, Wolfgang Streeck, and Mike Useem. I would also like to thank the colloquium and conference audiences at the more than twenty universities in both the United States and Europe at which I presented earlier versions of my argument. It is because of your generosity that there are too many of you to mention.

My editor at Harvard University Press, Michael Aronson, deserves special thanks. Not only did Mike support this project from the start, but he helped jump-start the writing process by telling me to "just write it," and he followed that up by providing detailed comments on the entire manuscript, as well as on multiple drafts of individual chapters.

I am especially indebted to four people: Michael Schwartz did not read the manuscript, but he was a constant sounding board, especially during the early stages of the project. His influence, as it always has been, is evident on virtually every page of the book. Frank Dobbin, Richard Lachmann, and Charles (Chick) Perrow provided an extensive, stimulating, and challenging set of comments on the entire document. Whatever is good about this work can be attributed to their efforts. I especially want to single out Chick Perrow. For nearly four decades, Chick has been a role model for me of how to conduct sustained, hard-hitting, engaged scholarship. He was an early supporter of this project—in fact, he was present when I first ad-libbed the idea at a conference panel on which we participated nearly a decade before I completed the book. He has been a constant source of support during the entire project, pestering me to "get on with it" while refusing to let me get away with careless arguments and unsupported claims. If I have spent too much time "sounding the violins" rather than "blasting the trumpets," as he complained in his review, it is because few writers can accomplish the latter the way Chick can.

My academic colleagues are not the only ones who provided important feedback on the manuscript. My sister, Susan L. Mizruchi, offered valuable comments on the first chapter, as did my stepdaughter, Karen Schwartz. My brother-in-law, Sacvan Bercovitch, and my nephew, Sascha Bercovitch, helped me in the search for a title. Equally important, though, was the moral support that they, and other members of my family, provided. My brother, David, his wife, Marcia, my niece, Mikayla, and my stepson, Steven Schwartz, were all there when I needed them.

My most important personal debts are to four people. My parents, Ruth and Harold Mizruchi, taught me to appreciate what was good in the world and to care about what was not. My son, Joshua A. Mizruchi, has given me more happiness than any parent could ever have hoped to experience. I only hope that I have given him a fraction of what he has given me. My wife, Gail, is the light of my life. It seems strange, yet oddly fitting, that as one who lives by the written word, I should become tongue-tied when trying to express what she means to me. In this public forum, I just want to say thank you for everything you've done.

Things fall apart; the center cannot hold; . . .
The best lack all conviction, while the worst
Are full of passionate intensity.

—William Butler Yeats, "The Second Coming"

1 ||| Introduction

In October 1957, the Soviet Union successfully launched the first artificial satellite to orbit the earth. The American public reacted in panic at the possibility that the Communist power was poised to surpass the United States in space technology and, by extension, possibly military technology as well. Intelligence reports had already suggested that the Soviets were about to launch their satellite, and President Eisenhower had been duly forewarned. Most policy makers, members of the media, and the public were taken by surprise, however.

Shortly after this episode, an organization of business leaders, the Committee for Economic Development (CED), sprang into action. The group held a high-level meeting with government officials. It prepared reports on the need for increased government efficiency, coordination of defense expenditures, economic performance, and a massive upgrading of American education, all of which the group saw as essential to fighting the Cold War with the Soviets. Within a year, government officials had begun to address these issues. Congress passed the National Defense Education Act, which increased federal education funding to more than six times what it had been earlier in the decade. President Eisenhower signed the bill that created the National Aeronautics and Space Administration (NASA). In the following decade, federal funding for scientific research increased tenfold. The

United States, living up to President Kennedy's call, put a man on the moon.

It is possible that this massive effort would have occurred without the input and support of these business elites. Presidents Eisenhower and Kennedy were both committed to it, as were members of Congress. The public, clearly alarmed, was supportive as well. Yet the business support was crucial. The CED, several of whose members had been appointed to President Eisenhower's cabinet, played a significant role in developing the ideas behind these policies, as did organizations such as the Council for Aid to Education and the Rockefeller Brothers Fund, both of which participated in the debates over the expansion of American education.[1] This episode was far from anomalous. A decade earlier, the CED had helped form a plan for the postwar reconversion of the American economy. The group was instrumental in convincing a skeptical Congress and public of the need for a massive aid plan to Europe, what became the Marshall Plan. A few years later, the CED's members serving in Eisenhower's administration were instrumental in the Republican president's decision to not only maintain the core elements of the New Deal but to increase them. And in the 1960s, a group of business leaders provided the key support for an element of President Johnson's Great Society—the building of new, low-density public housing for the poor. Even as many, perhaps the majority, of American businessmen continued to hold to the traditional views of laissez-faire, the leaders of the largest American corporations were in the vanguard of moderate, pragmatic solutions to pressing economic and social problems.

The twenty-first century has presented the United States with problems of a similarly grave nature. The nation has experienced two major financial crises. The system of public education is in disarray in many parts of the country. The cost of health care has become so debilitating that it threatens economic catastrophe. Although seemingly blunted by the financial crisis, the nation continues to experience cultural divides that threaten its long-term health, including elements that resist the teaching of evolutionary biology in the schools. The nation's infrastructure is in disrepair, its roads, bridges, air, and rail systems in need of massive upgrading. And years of denial and inaction on the nation's energy needs have resulted in serious, and potentially irreparable, damage to the environment. These problems have occurred during a period of record-setting deficits that threaten the nation's future. They are exacerbated by a gridlocked political system that seems to ensure that virtually nothing can be done to address them. All of these concerns threaten to leave the United States further behind the other developed countries, as well as the rapidly advancing Chinese.

Unlike in the mid-twentieth century, however, there has been a noticeable lack of action from the leaders of large American corporations as these problems have mounted. Many large companies have supported health care reform as a means of addressing the cost issues with which they are increasingly burdened, but the corporate community has been unable to provide a solution to the crisis. Despite occasional voices from individual business leaders calling for greater attention to the society's infrastructure and its educational system, no group of corporate officers has developed a comprehensive plan that has attracted serious attention from elected officials. The leaders of big business have also done little to break the gridlock in Washington. During the debt ceiling crisis in the summer of 2011, the Business Roundtable, a group of chief executive officers from large firms, was reduced to offering a vacuous plea to the president and Congress to fix the problem. Unlike the business leaders of the earlier era, the leaders in 2011 made their appeal without proposing a single specific recommendation.

The problems that the United States has experienced in the early twenty-first century are not necessarily of greater magnitude than those of earlier decades. Even the apparent golden age of American economic strength, in the post–World War II era, witnessed severe crises, including involvement in a devastating war and enormous social and political turmoil. Yet there is a significant difference between the postwar era, which dates from 1945 to roughly 1973, and the period since then, in the willingness of American business leaders to mount a systematic effort to address the problems of our age. Some commentators have described the change in terms of the rise of what they call "neoliberalism," an ideology that emphasizes the virtues of free markets and is critical of the relatively high level of government involvement in the economy that characterized the postwar period (Harvey 2007; Crouch 2011). Others have discussed the shift in corporate orientation from a focus on powerful professional managers to a system in which the capital market now determines corporate behavior and managers are reduced to mere pawns in the service of "shareholder value" (Fligstein 2001; Zajac and Westphal 2004). Others have viewed the change as a shift from a "Fordist" mode of production toward "post-Fordism," in which mass production in large manufacturing firms has given way to a disjointed system in which smaller, service-oriented firms predominate (Piore and Sabel 1984; Boyer 1990). And still others have focused on the shift from an economy based on the production of goods to one driven by financial instruments that generate revenue by converting funds from one form to another (Davis 2009; Krippner 2011).

All of these views are related—in fact similar—and all identify significant changes that have occurred in American society since the early 1970s. Whatever differences I might have with the specific components of these arguments, I do not take issue with their general thrust. My concern in this book is with what I believe is a neglected aspect of the changes others have described, and that may in fact constitute the root cause of those changes: the changing nature of leadership in the United States, in particular the leadership within the community of large corporations. I argue that the leaders of the largest American corporations, to whom I refer as the American corporate elite, once played an important role in addressing, if not resolving, the needs of the larger society. Since the 1970s, the members of this group have largely abandoned their concern with issues beyond those of their individual firms. This abandonment, I suggest, is one of the primary causes of the economic, political, and social disarray that American society has experienced in the twenty-first century. In earlier decades, the United States had a corporate elite that, however imperfect, was willing to see beyond the short-term interests of the firms that its members directed. Today this is no longer the case. The corporate elite that exists today is a disorganized, largely ineffectual group. Paradoxically, I argue, individual American corporations have more political power in the early twenty-first century than at any time since the 1920s. As a group, they are fragmented, however. Unlike their predecessors in earlier decades, they are either unwilling or unable to mount any systematic approach to addressing even the problems of their own community, let alone those of the larger society.

In this book I examine the rise and fall of the American corporate elite, from its pinnacle in the 1945–1973 period, through its period of turmoil and transition in the 1970s and 1980s, to its present state, in which the group is only a shadow of its former self. I argue that the decline of this elite is a significant source of the current crisis of American democracy and a major cause of the predicament in which the twenty-first-century United States finds itself.

In making this claim, I do not want to imply that the corporate elite of the postwar period was uniformly altruistic or public spirited. On the contrary, business leaders during that age were strongly protective of their interests, as they have been in every historical era. Nor am I suggesting that postwar America was a society that we should attempt to emulate in every respect. Social and cultural norms have become far less oppressive since that time. Our society today is far more tolerant and accepting of difference than it was half a century ago. Innovation, especially in the area of information technology, has improved peoples' lives in many, albeit not all, respects. Consumer products in general are more plentiful and less expensive than in earlier years. There is no returning to the past, nor should this be an ideal to pursue. Yet for all its problems, the postwar United States had a number of qualities that are lacking today: an expanding economy with a high level of upward mobility, declining inequality, a relatively high level of security, a well-functioning political system, and a widespread belief that problems were solvable. And underpinning these forces was a corporate elite that provided a degree of leadership and vision that are not in evidence today. My goal in this book is to explain how this elite emerged, what sustained it, how it declined, and the consequences of the group's demise.

The Rise and Fall of the American Corporate Elite

In the postwar period, a small segment of leaders emerged in the American business community. This was not the first time that American business leaders had organized. In the early 1900s, a group of business leaders formed the National Civic Federation, in which they developed a series of suggestions for dealing with some of the deleterious consequences of the rise of corporate capitalism at the turn of the twentieth century (Weinstein 1968). The postwar effort to address major national concerns was equally serious. The leaders of this group sat atop the largest firms and held positions in multiple organizations, which allowed them to see the world from a relatively cosmopolitan perspective. This breadth led these elites to exhibit a moderate approach to politics that included limited acceptance of both labor unions and government regulation. They participated actively in policy-making organizations, such as the CED, and they played a significant role in formulating ideas that were later adopted as national policy, in both Republican and Democratic administrations. These people were not liberals. Like the heads of smaller firms, they too were largely opposed to organized labor and had major reservations about government intervention in the economy. The heads of the leading firms tended to hold a more pragmatic approach toward strategy, however. They also believed that it was in their long-term interest to have a well-functioning society.

Three forces, I argue, contributed to the moderate, pragmatic approach adopted by the postwar corporate elite: a relatively active and highly legitimate state, a well-organized and relatively powerful labor movement, and the financial community, which served as a source of interfirm consensus. The state provided regulation of the economy through its taxing and spending policies, its provision of welfare expenditures (which helped it create effective demand for the products of American industry), and its regulation of business with agencies such as the Federal Trade Commission and the Securities and Exchange Commission. Because of the enormous success that the American economy experienced during the postwar period, a Keynesian consensus emerged among national political leaders and economic policy makers. As we shall see in Chapter 3, the corporate elite largely accepted this consensus. The labor movement provided a series of constraints on firms' actions as well as benefits for the firms. The unions' industry-wide presence in core sectors of the economy helped maintain a relatively stable price structure, which prevented destructive competition. Union leaders also worked with corporations to ensure that more radical elements within their ranks were kept at bay. Management assisted in this effort by agreeing to provide relatively high wages and benefits in exchange for labor peace, an agreement that has been referred to as the postwar "capital-labor accord." The banks, meanwhile, because of their concern with the economy as a whole, played a role in mediating disputes across sectors. Bank boards of directors became meeting places for the chief executives of leading nonfinancial corporations, which helped to generate and maintain a broad consensus on issues of business-wide concern. The banks also occasionally played a role in disciplining individual capitalists who engaged in erratic or deviant behavior.

This situation prevailed from the mid-1940s until the early 1970s. Although this period was characterized by significant social turmoil, it was also a time of sustained economic growth, the expansion of the middle class, and an increasing level of economic equality. The relative strength and legitimacy of both organized labor and the state was not only a consequence of the moderate orientation of the corporate elite. These institutions, along with the financial community, also acted as constraints on business, compelling them to maintain their accommodationist perspective. Corporate leaders fought with unions and government during this period, sometimes fiercely, but they accepted the existence and permanence of these institutions, deciding it was better to work with them than to mount a full-scale assault. This approach was reflected in the attitudes of the corporate elite. By 1971, a majority of top corporate executives expressed support for both Keynesian deficit spending and the idea that the government should step in to provide full employment if the private economy was incapable of doing so (Barton 1985).

This system began to unravel during the 1970s. High government spending levels, the emergence of foreign competition, and the energy crisis of 1973 created an unprecedented combination of high inflation and unemployment, which called into question the Keynesian economic orthodoxy of the time. The aftermath of Vietnam and Watergate created a legitimacy crisis among major American institutions, including business. The emergence of new regulatory agencies, most notably the Environmental Protection Agency and the Occupational Safety and Health Administration, which were instituted over the opposition of many corporations, turned many businesses against regulation.

As a result of these crises, corporate elites saw business as embattled, and vulnerable. In response, they mounted a counteroffensive, a full-scale mobilization in which corporations, large and small, found an increasingly unified voice. Business organizations, including the newly formed Business Roundtable, began to attack government regulation. They also became increasingly aggressive in fighting unions. By the time of Ronald Reagan's election as president, labor was already in significant retreat, and after Reagan's inauguration in 1981, regulations were more loosely enforced.

As we moved into the 1980s, however, a paradox became evident. Corporate interests had been extremely successful in weakening the labor movement and thwarting government regulation. In winning this war, however, it became apparent that organized collective action within the business community was no longer necessary. As a result, the corporate elite began to fragment. This fragmentation was hastened by the decline of commercial banks, a group whose boards of directors had served as meeting places for the heads of the leading nonfinancial corporations. As the banks dropped from the center of the corporate network, the cohesiveness of the elite began to decline as well. Companies began to go their own way, increasingly pursuing relatively minor firm and industry-specific issues, as exemplified by the Tax Reform Act of 1986, in which a plethora of individual and small groups of firms lobbied separately for specific provisions to the law. By the late 1980s, the relatively cohesive, relatively pragmatic character of the American corporate elite had begun to disappear. The corporate elite had, ironically, been "killed" by its own success. In later years, this decline would become evident in the elite's inability to act collectively to address issues with which its members were concerned.

Meanwhile, in response to a chronically undervalued stock market and a state that had become negligent in enforcing antitrust laws, a massive acquisition wave emerged, which led to the disappearance of one-third of the Fortune 500 during the decade. Corporate CEOs, who, although subject to pressures from government and labor during the postwar period, had been insulated from pressures from stockholders and Wall Street analysts, began to see themselves as increasingly vulnerable. As executive tenure declined—average tenure among Fortune 500 CEOs dropped nearly 25 percent between the early 1980s and 2000—sitting CEOs were no longer thinking about the long-term interests of the business community but rather about their own short-term survival. The increasing turnover also led to a further decline in group cohesion, as long-term ties were severed.

The consequence of these developments, I argue, is that there was no longer a relatively cohesive group of moderate, pragmatic leaders at the top of the American business community. Patrician, statesmanlike CEOs such as H. J. Heinz II and Reginald Jones gave way to more colorful but single-minded executives like Albert J. Dunlap Jr. and John F. Welch Jr., known, respectively, as "Chainsaw Al" and "Neutron Jack" for their willingness to slash jobs in an effort to increase shareholder value. This generational shift left the society with a collection of large corporations that, while increasingly able to realize their firm-specific interests through lobbying, were increasingly less able to provide collective solutions to issues of concern to the business community, and the society, as a whole.

The decline of the American corporate elite has played a major role in the crisis of twenty-first-century American democracy, I argue. The gridlock in Washington, the prominent role of extremist elements who in earlier decades would have been considered outside the realm of legitimate political discourse, the inability to address serious problems such as health care, the deficit, financial reform, and global warming are all due in part to the absence of a committed, moderate elite capable of providing political leadership and keeping the destructive sectors of the American polity in check.

These claims require substantiation, of course, especially considering that to some extent they run counter to established wisdom. After all, as Kim Phillips-Fein (2009) has argued in a widely acclaimed book, from its inception in the 1930s, powerful American capitalists worked tirelessly to undermine, and even fully repeal, the policies from the New Deal that provided a social safety net for the larger population. And yet to focus only on those who attempted to dismantle the New Deal provides only a partial account. It is true that there have always been corporate interests in the United States that have fought to prevent, or reverse, virtually all legislation designed to protect the public from the ravages of capitalism. It is even fair to say that this view has represented the center of gravity of business opinion in the United States. But it also misses something very important. The leaders of the corporate world—the heads of the largest corporations— were not always preoccupied with reversing the New Deal. On the contrary, in the postwar period this group exhibited moderation and pragmatism. Its members made their peace with strong government and organized labor. They exhibited an "enlightened self-interest," in which they believed that their own privileges would be secure only to the extent that the society rested on a strong foundation. This meant full, or nearly full, employment. It meant sufficient means to purchase the products that were so massively and rapidly produced. It meant protections from the dangers of economic downturn, as well as old age. And it meant concern for the most vulnerable members of the society. Beyond this was a recognition that, however distasteful, the right of workers to organize and bargain collectively was an established fact of American life, one that required acceptance, however grudging.

This position was driven by several forces. Certainly the Cold War, in which the United States saw itself challenged by an alternative conception of social organization, played a role. If America was to compete, the society could not squander its human resources, including those mired in poverty. Certainly the strength and legitimacy of the government among the larger population, and the strength and legitimacy of labor unions, placed constraints on what was politically feasible for business to seek. And certainly the strength of the corporations themselves—who enjoyed an environment in which American capitalism reigned supreme, free from global competition, with the largest among them awash in profits—allowed business leaders the slack to focus on issues beyond mere market survival. And yet the American corporate elite was driven by more than pure pragmatics. These forces may have been necessary conditions for the role that corporations played. But the corporate elite was also driven by an ethic of responsibility—that as leaders of the society, they had an obligation to that society. This ethic may not have been evident to most Americans at the time. It was surely not evident to the thousands who protested the actions of American elites during the Vietnam War. And yet with the hindsight provided by several decades of history, it is now possible to see that, by comparison, the elite of the postwar era indeed did display a level of collective responsibility that, I argue, is missing in the twenty-first century.

My goal in this book is to demonstrate the basis for this argument. But first, it is necessary to explain why it is worth focusing on corporate elites in the first place.

Why Corporations?

Americans have been suspicious of concentrated power dating back to the nation's founding. This suspicion was based initially on the power of the state, a result of the Colonists' experience with Britain. By the late nineteenth century, however, the rise of large corporations created another potential source of concentrated power. Debates over the proper role of large corporations became a central component of American politics at the turn of the twentieth century. Although the extent of anticorporate sentiment ebbed and flowed through the course of that century, the corporation remained a continuing source of controversy.

There is little debate about the corporations' size and potential impact on American society. In 1933, the 500 largest nonfinancial firms accounted for nearly 60 percent of all nonfinancial firm assets in the United States. This figure held at 55 percent in 1945, 54 percent in 1970, and, despite the downsizing wave of the early 1990s, 50 percent in 1997 (Tan 2008). Given the size of the largest corporations, any action they take is likely to have an impact on the larger economy, especially if they act collectively. In two works that appeared simultaneously in the 1970s, Charles Lindblom (1977) and Fred Block (1977a), writing from two very different perspectives, reached almost identical conclusions. The national government, they argued, is largely compelled to act in the interests of business because the state's revenue depends on taxes, which depend on a high level of economic activity. The best way to ensure a high level of economic activity is to stimulate private investment. For companies to invest, however, they must have confidence that the economy will continue to grow, and such confidence depends in part on the government's economic policies.

Large corporations are influential for another reason. Their leaders, who sit at the command of organizations with assets in the billions of dollars, are members of society's elite. Their views are important, as is their expertise. This significance is reflected in the historically high representation of corporate leaders in both government positions and government advisory committees (Freitag 1975; Domhoff 2006). Some authors, including Domhoff, have suggested that this high level of participation by corporate elites is an indicator of business domination of the government. Others, including Judis (2001), suggest that it reflects a genuine commitment to public service. There is some truth in both of these claims. Paul Hoffman, cofounder of the CED, a group about which we will hear much in this book, used the term "enlightened self-interest" to describe the views that he believed should motivate the participation of corporate elites in his organization. By referring to "self-interest," Hoffman acknowledged that factors other than altruism should motivate those who choose to serve. On the other hand, there is an important distinction between "enlightened" self-interest and "short-term," or "naked," self-interest. Even if one views enlightened self-interest as simply a broader, more long-term manifestation of the latter phenomenon, the difference between the two has real consequences for those affected by the strategy. Hoffman explicitly mandated that his group, which formed in 1942, would be motivated by a concept of the "national interest," and that it would not be a forum for the expression of mere individual, or even class, interest.

One could of course argue, and several scholars have, that what elites viewed as the national interest was conveniently analogous to their own class interest, however unintentional such coupling may have been. Still, an approach that is based on service to the national interest is likely to lead to policies quite different from one that is narrowly self-interested. Only in the most general sense could Jay Rockefeller, the long-time Democratic senator from West Virginia, be said to be serving his class interest. Similarly, the actions of the late Senator Edward Kennedy could be viewed as motivated by class interest only if we adopt an almost hopelessly expansive definition of the term. Yet regardless of whether corporate elites were operating in an entirely altruistic fashion (which virtually no one, even their strongest supporters, suggests) or in an entirely self-interested one, what matters for my thesis is simply that their views and actions are centrally important and their influence disproportionately high. Corporate leaders, to paraphrase F. Scott Fitzgerald, really are different from the rest of us, regardless of how self-interested, or selfless, they are.

Who Are the Corporate Elite?

Given the importance of the corporate elite to my story, it would seem wise to make clear exactly to whom I am referring. By corporate elite, I mean a particular subset of the presidents, chairmen (and women, where applicable), and what are now called chief executive officers (CEOs) of the largest American corporations. The population of large corporations has traditionally been defined as the 500 largest manufacturers in terms of sales, as ranked by *Fortune*. For its first four decades of rankings, *Fortune* also listed the fifty largest companies in six other sectors: commercial banks, insurance companies, diversified financial firms, transportation firms, retailers, and utilities. This group was therefore sometimes referred to as the "Fortune 800." In 1995, *Fortune* dispensed with its seven-sector classification scheme and began to rank the 1,000 largest companies in a single group, regardless of sector. Although its outlines have varied over time and were not clearly discrete in either period, I will use the Fortune 800 and 1000 as a starting point from which to identify the elite.

Even within this group, I am interested in a particular subset of actors. Michael Useem (1984) identified what he called the "inner circle" as those who sat on two or more corporate boards, and thus possessed what he called "business scan," the ability to see the world from a broader perspective than one could do from the perspective of only one's primary employer. He argued that this vantage point gave the inner circle two distinct characteristics: On one hand, it contributed to the ability to see, and act in, the interests of the larger group, as opposed to the interests of one's own firm. On the other hand, it contributed to a relatively moderate, pragmatic perspective, as firm officials were able (or compelled) to see things from multiple viewpoints. The result was both a collective orientation and a willingness to compromise, and thus a rejection of the extreme conservatism that has often characterized significant elements of the American business community. The fact that Useem saw the inner circle as simultaneously collectively oriented as well as moderate is one of the reasons that subsequent observers tended to conflate the two (an issue that I address shortly).

The group that I call the corporate elite is analogous to Useem's inner circle, although I do not use the criterion of multiple board membership to identify its members. The postwar elite that I use as the starting point for my discussion shared the two basic characteristics identified by Useem, both of which distinguish it from its post-1990 counterpart: First, its political views were moderate and its political strategy was pragmatic in its dealings with government, labor, economic policy, and social issues. Second, it was unified—that is, able to act collectively to advance its interests, which were above and beyond those specific to the individual firms with which they were affiliated. It is within this group, as opposed to business as a whole or even large corporations as a whole, that I argue that a relative degree of unity existed in the postwar period.

The suggestion that the postwar corporate elite was both relatively unified and politically moderate raises a question: Are unity and moderation necessarily coupled? The answer is that they are not. A group can be unified yet practice a highly conservative (or highly liberal) form of politics. I shall argue, consistent with Useem, that both traits—unity and moderation—characterized the American corporate elite of the postwar period. I also suggest, however, that the elite has exhibited neither quality since at least the early 1990s. The decade in which the two characteristics became disconnected was the 1970s, during which the elite became significantly more conservative. Despite some fissures, primarily between moderate and conservative forces within the CED, the corporate elite retained—and may have even increased—its unity in the 1970s. It was after the group succeeded in weakening government regulation and defeating organized labor, combined with the decline of the banks and the takeover wave of the late 1980s, that it began to lose its unity. The top of the corporate world in the twenty-first century lacks the ability to act collectively that its predecessors of the postwar period exhibited. How the corporate elite reached this state is the focus of this book.[2]

The Role of the Elite

Concurrent with discussions about the role of large corporations, a spirited and often contentious debate on the nature of power in American society arose in the postwar period. On one side was a set of scholars, primarily in political science, who viewed power as widely dispersed among a broad range of groups (Truman 1951; Dahl 1961). In this view, known as pluralism, any of these groups—whether business (or sectors of business), organized labor, consumer and environmental groups, or organizations supporting various social initiatives—could gain disproportionate influence at particular points, but none was able to consistently maintain this influence over time. On the other side was a set of scholars, primarily in sociology, who viewed power as concentrated among a relatively small group of elites (Hunter 1953; Mills 1956). In this view, known as elite theory, members of the elite, through their control of major societal institutions, were able to regularly achieve political outcomes in accordance with their interests, even if those interests ran counter to those of the majority.

This debate occupied political theorists for years, but it ultimately stalled, due in part to its high level of abstraction. Pluralists were able to demonstrate that elites often failed to get their way, but they were unable to address the criticism that the issues they selected represented only those that were permitted to reach the public arena in the first place. Elite theorists were able to demonstrate that elites were often able to prevent issues from reaching the public arena, but they had difficulty addressing the criticism that once an issue did reach the public arena, the elites sometimes failed to get their way. Ironically, proponents of each perspective eventually moved closer to the other, as they began to acknowledge the tenability of the others' claims. Pluralists became increasingly willing to admit that American politics did not take place on an equal playing field—that some groups had built-in structural advantages that gave them disproportionate power (see, for example, Lindblom 1977; Dahl 1982). Elite theorists were increasingly willing to admit that elites were not always unified nor did they always get their way. On one issue, however, the two groups remained apart.

In a 1958 essay, the distinguished political scientist Robert Dahl argued that for a group to exert power, two things are necessary: the group must have a high level of resources, and it must have a high level of unity. The one group in American society that virtually all observers acknowledged had a high level of resources was large corporations. It was in part this high level of resources—their enormous size and their access in the postwar world to seemingly limitless sources of capital—that formed the basis of the public's fear of big business. By themselves, however, these resources, no matter how immense, were not necessarily a source of power. Whether they could be converted into power, Dahl reasoned, depended on whether corporations could achieve a unified stance on political issues. If this unity were not possible, he argued, then these different resource-rich sides, through their opposition, would merely battle each other to a standstill. John Kenneth Galbraith (1952a) made a similar claim, suggesting that the built-in conflicts of interest across sectors of the business community—as well as between business and other sectors such as organized labor—created a system of "countervailing power," in which no one sector was able to dominate.

Examples of such conflicts within the business world were not difficult to find. Automobile companies might prefer to purchase the less-expensive steel produced by non-American firms, while steel manufacturers might prefer tariffs on imported steel to reduce the incentives for such purchases (Bauer, Pool, and Dexter 1963; Milner 1988; Prechel 2000). Firms that produce pollution control equipment might support the strengthening of the Clean Air Act, while firms that pollute might prefer to weaken it (Mizruchi 1992). Regions that depend on tourism might oppose the efforts of a chemical company to build a plant in their midst. And firms that depend on low-cost labor might oppose the efforts of real estate interests whose goal is to increase both commercial and residential rents (Lowi 1969).

Yet there were also instances in which large corporations managed to forge a unified position on issues, or at least avoid opposing one another. Whitt (1982), for example, showed that financial interests and oil companies— two groups with seemingly opposing views toward mass transit—were able to come together to support the building of the Bay Area Rapid Transit system in metropolitan San Francisco. Clawson, Neustadtl, and Bearden (1986) showed that although corporations frequently pursued different strategies in their campaign contributions—contributing primarily either to incumbents on one hand or to conservatives on the other—they rarely engaged in direct opposition in individual congressional races. And I showed, in an earlier study (Mizruchi 1992), that in their testimony before congressional committees, corporations that testified at the same hearing agreed with one another more than four times as frequently as they disagreed.

The fact that instances of business unity were plentiful and easy to locate raised a serious problem for pluralism. If the corporate world is fraught with political conflict, as pluralists suggest, then business, or rather, particular sectors of business, represent just another interest group. To the extent that corporations are able to reach a unified perspective, on the other hand, then in Dahl's formulation, business as a group will hold a unique level of political power. Yet the work by Bauer, Pool, and Dexter and others, which showed different sectors of business in seemingly perpetual conflict, raised serious questions for elite theory as well. For every study that suggested that business was able to achieve a unified perspective, another appeared that suggested irreconcilable differences.

Subsequent work has called into question the entire basis of the debate over business unity. Useem (1984) argued that both sides of the debate were correct, but at different levels of analysis. From the perspective of all corporations, large and small, business is far from a unitary political actor. The diversity of interests and perspectives suggested by pluralists accurately captures this complexity, Useem suggests. On the other hand, there was, according to Useem, a relatively small group of leaders at the top of the corporate world, among the very largest firms, that had in fact succeeded in forging a roughly, if not completely, unified position. This "inner circle," as he called it, behaved in a way generally consistent with elite theory. In a subsequent study (Mizruchi 1992), I pushed Useem's point in a different direction. The question was not whether business was unified, at any level, but rather, when—that is, under what conditions did business unity occur? In other words, business was neither unified nor divided, but exhibited varying degrees of unity depending on the situation.

The question of unity at the top of the business world has reappeared in recent years, especially since the onset of the 2008 financial crisis. Authors such as Simon Johnson and James Kwak (2010) have spoken of the "new financial oligarchy," conjuring up images of the Gilded Age in the late nineteenth century. Others (Rothkopf 2008) have suggested the emergence of a worldwide "ruling class." I am suggesting that something else is at issue. Historically speaking, the small elite at the top of the American corporate world was relatively unified in the postwar period, through the 1970s, at least compared to its twenty-first-century counterpart. This group became less unified beginning in the 1980s, however, and has become increasingly fragmented since that time. Moreover, this fragmentation is not necessarily a positive development for American democracy. As we have seen, proponents of pluralism and elite theory debated over the extent to which a small, unified elite existed at the top of developed capitalist societies. All of these thinkers shared the view, however, that the existence of this type of elite would be a uniformly bad thing for a democratic system. The past half-century has raised questions about this claim. American democracy has actually fared more poorly, I argue, as the elite has become increasingly fragmented, and I will suggest in the chapters that follow that this is not a coincidence. In making this point, I am touching on claims made decades ago by E. Digby Baltzell (1959, 1979), as well as in somewhat different form more recently by John Judis (2001). Both authors argued that an informed, moderate, and responsible elite is essential for the optimal functioning of a democracy. We can set aside the question of whether an elite of any kind is a necessary element of a society; elites populate virtually every existing society. To the extent that an elite exists, however, the society will benefit to the extent that the elite exercises moderation and responsibility. I argue that American democracy worked more effectively in the post-war period, when the society had a relatively cohesive, moderate elite than it has since the elite's dissolution.

Does Success Create Fragmentation?

The alternatives to the pluralist and elite theory approaches may have moved us beyond the simple, abstract debates over whether business was a unified actor. It is worth asking, however, whether the assumption that unity increases a group's power is even warranted. On one hand, the claim seems self-evident. Scholars and political actors in a range of areas have for decades treated the unity-power relation as a fundamental dictum, and examples are plentiful. Political parties fear hotly contested primary elections, out of concern that such divisiveness will lead to weakness in the general election. Disputes among factions have forged the downfall of many social movements. Highly competitive industries have lower profit margins than do highly concentrated ones. Dahl's original claim that unity, if it exists, will increase a group's power has become an almost taken-for-granted assumption among students of politics.

A closer look, however, suggests that there are reasons to question this assumption. Evidence on the relation between cohesion and performance among military units is equivocal (Mullen and Copper 1994). As long as unit members understand their tasks and can predict what their peers will do, then unit performance does not depend on social cohesion among group members.[3] Other researchers have argued that diversity is beneficial to a group, even if it is accompanied by a certain degree of conflict. March (1994) suggested that too much homogeneity of ability can prevent group members from asking questions that, even if apparently ill informed, will not be asked by the more competent members, to the group's detriment. Page (2007) provides numerous examples of the benefits of a diverse set of views. In a study of bankers (Mizruchi and Stearns 2001), Linda Stearns and I showed that deals in which bankers gained approval from a diverse set of superiors were more likely to successfully close than those that gained approval from a more homogenous group. Ansell (2001) showed that conflict among factions in the French labor movement actually contributed to the movement's success. These findings are rooted in an argument made by Georg Simmel (1955) nearly a century ago. His idea that internal conflict can become a source of group strength served as the basis for one of the most important works of sociological theory in the mid-twentieth century, Lewis Coser's *The Functions of Social Conflict* (1956).

Even if unity does lead to power, it raises a question that appears to have received little attention: To what extent does the successful acquisition of power enable a group to maintain its unity? In other words, does power, or the successful attainment of a political goal, lead to unity in the same way that unity leads to power? There are reasons to believe that success leads not to unity but rather to division or fragmentation. Groups come together in part because they have a goal that they can best achieve through collective action. Once the actors have succeeded, the rationale for the collective organization no longer remains. In fact, having achieved their goal, the group's members might even find themselves squabbling over the proceeds. This is sometimes observed when individual members of a championship sports team begin complaining after their victory of being underappreciated or undercompensated. There does not appear to be a large body of work on this question. A literature in social psychology suggests that "self-efficacy" may, contrary to widely held belief, lead to a decline in performance (Vancouver, Thompson, and Williams 2001) and that success in task performance can lead to "coasting" (Mizruchi 1991; Carver 2003). In a study within the social movements area, Meyer (2008) showed that a group of socially homogenous, densely connected autoworkers who successfully organized a union in their shop emerged from the episode with a relatively low level of solidarity. An old literature in organizational sociology suggests that some organizations do not even want to accomplish their goals, because it would undermine the justification for their existence (Perrow 1986, chapter 5).

The suggestion that individual actors, once they have achieved their political goals, respond by drifting off in different directions, is what, I argue, occurred with the American corporate elite in the 1980s. Simmel (1955), in another of his classic formulations, suggested that when faced with an external threat to their existence, the members of a group will forge a cohesive bond to fight off the threat. It follows from this, however, that once the threat has been removed, the basis for the cohesion disappears, and the separate agendas of the group's individual members become more prominent. In the postwar period, the American corporate elite faced the dual pressure of a relatively strong and legitimate federal government and a relatively powerful labor movement. In addition to the mediating role of the financial community, these pressures helped create a level of unity among the leading elements of the business community. As business faced what it saw as a threat to its existence in the 1970s, corporations, both large and small, forged an even broader unified front that resulted in an offensive against government and labor. By the early 1980s, government and labor were no longer capable of exercising their previous level of constraint on business. Business had won the war. In winning this war, however, the corporate elite undermined the basis of not only its unity but ultimately its effectiveness as well. This process was furthered by the decline of the banks and the massive takeover wave, both of which occurred later in the decade. By the 1990s, the forces that had allowed the corporate elite to maintain its moderation and its ability to act collectively were no longer present. In throwing off the constraints it had faced in earlier decades, the American corporate elite had rendered itself incapable of addressing a series of increasingly vexing issues.

Plan of the Book

In the chapters that follow, I trace the rise and fall of the American corporate elite. In Chapter 2 I discuss the roots of the elite that emerged in the post–World War II period. I describe the precursor to the postwar elite that arose at the turn of the twentieth century in response to concerns about the threat of labor militancy and socialism. I then discuss the elite's role during the Great Depression and the rise of the postwar elite during World War II. I follow this discussion with separate chapters on each of the three constraints that contributed to the postwar elite's unity and moderation: In Chapter 3 I discuss the role of the state in managing the economy and the role of the corporate elite in both influencing and reacting to the government's actions. I also discuss the elite's role in supporting various policies of social amelioration during the 1960s and early 1970s. In Chapter 4 I discuss the relations between the corporate elite and organized labor, focusing on management's ambivalent response to the unions, as well as the uneasy peace that the two sides reached in the postwar period. In Chapter 5 I discuss the role of the banks as a source of consensus within the corporate elite. I deal with the debates over the extent to which financial institutions exercised power over nonfinancial corporations. I conclude that although such episodes were rare in the postwar period, the banks did act as a constraint on the actions of nonfinancial firms, as well as a source of interfirm unity. I then turn, in Chapter 6, to the crucial decade of the 1970s, in which a series of exogenous forces—a deteriorating economy, increasing foreign competition, the energy crisis, and the crisis of legitimacy of major American institutions—led corporate leaders to believe that the free enterprise system was experiencing a serious threat. I discuss the corporate elite's response to this situation, focusing on the group's offensive against government regulation and organized labor. Following this discussion, I turn in Chapter 7 to the 1980s, when, having accomplished virtually all of its long-term goals in terms of the weakening of government and labor, the corporate elite began to experience increasing internal conflict, a situation that was exacerbated by the decline of the commercial banks as meeting places for leading chief executives—and thus facilitators of corporate cohesion—as well as the massive takeover wave that drastically altered the environment within which corporate CEOs operated. The consequence of these changes, I argue, was a gradual decline in the ability of the corporate elite to act collectively to address issues of concern even to its own members, let alone the larger society. I describe these consequences in Chapter 8, in which I show how by the 1990s, the American corporate elite had been rendered ineffective. I illustrate this lack of efficacy by examining the elite's response to two important issues: tax policy and health care. Finally, in Chapter 9 I discuss the implications of the decline of the corporate elite for the problems that the United States has experienced in the twenty-first century. In doing this, I raise a question: In the absence of a mass-based, progressive social movement, is a commitment to responsible leadership by corporate officials our best hope for addressing these problems? The following chapters provide what I hope is a basis for answering this question.

2 ||| The Rise of the American Corporate Elite

The origins of the American corporate elite can be traced at least as far back as the Founding Fathers. There are clear ideological affinities between the group that emerged in the twentieth century and early leaders such as George Washington and Thomas Jefferson (Judis 2001, 16). The corporate elite as a collective entity was a product of two historical events, however: the rise of industrial capitalism in the late nineteenth century and the reaction of business leaders to the consequences of this development.

The period from 1870 to 1900 witnessed a revolution in American economic life. Spurred on by the expansion of the railroads and the development of the telegraph, the United States experienced a period of rapid industrialization, as well as the rise of a new organizational form—the large corporation (Chandler 1977). Corporations had emerged as legal entities in the early nineteenth century (Roy 1997), but it was only after the Civil War that the privately owned joint stock company came to dominate. The initial surge occurred among railroads. Many of the leading businesspeople of the era—Jay Cooke, Jay Gould, and Cornelius Vanderbilt among them—were railroad magnates, although John D. Rockefeller in oil and Andrew Carnegie in steel were also major figures. By the 1890s, a significant financial system had arisen, led by J. P. Morgan, and financial interests remained the centers of power into at least the second decade of the twentieth century.

The American corporate elite got off to a somewhat rocky start in the late 1800s, a period characterized by significant conflict and turmoil. Morgan began to consolidate his empire during the Depression of 1893, when several railroads faced bankruptcy. He was able to reorganize and gain control of several major carriers, including the Erie, the Reading, and the Baltimore & Ohio, and he participated in the creation of the Southern Railway System as well (Cochran and Miller 1942). The watershed event, however, was the creation of the United States Steel Corporation in 1901—a combination of Carnegie Steel, Federal Steel, and several other firms (Corey 1930, 262–276)—followed by International Harvester in 1902 (ibid., 319). Morgan extended his control over these firms not through ownership of the firms' stock but rather through his control of capital and his placement of associates on their boards of directors (Corey 1930, 284; Mizruchi 1982, 97–99). In his testimony before the Pujo Committee investigation of the "Money Trust," Morgan revealed that he had approved the entire board of U.S. Steel (U.S. Congress 1913, part 15, 1025).

Morgan was the preeminent figure of the early twentieth-century business world. He and his firm, J. P. Morgan & Company, established control over several financial institutions, including Central Trust, the National Bank of Commerce, and the New York Life and Mutual Life insurance companies (Mizruchi and Bunting 1981, 483). He was also a close ally of George F. Baker, cofounder and president of the First National Bank of New York. Morgan was only one of several powerful individuals, however. A rival group that included John and William Rockefeller, Jacob Schiff of the investment bank Kuhn, Loeb & Company, James Stillman of the National City Bank, and railroad magnate Edward H. Harriman also held control over a number of firms, including U.S. Trust, Amalgamated Copper (forerunner of Anaconda), and Equitable Life Assurance (ibid.).[1]

The rivalry between these two groups came to a head in 1901 during a contest for control of the Great Northern Railroad, which ran from St. Paul to Seattle near the border with Canada.[2] The road had been controlled by a group that included Morgan and the road's chief executive, James J. Hill. Both Hill and Harriman, president of the Union Pacific, had hoped to gain control of the Chicago, Burlington, and Quincy Railroad, which would provide access to Chicago. Unable to persuade the owners of the Burlington (as it was called) to sell, Harriman aborted his effort and shifted his focus to the Western portion of his line. Hill, however, managed to convince Burlington's owners to sell. Angered by this, Harriman (backed by Schiff) made a surreptitious attempt to gain control of the Northern Pacific—a railroad running parallel to the Great Northern in which both Morgan and Hill had an interest—an effort made possible by the fact that the Morgan–Hill interests owned only 20 percent of Northern Pacific's common (voting) stock. By the time Hill discovered that someone had been buying Northern Pacific's stock, Harriman's share exceeded 46 percent. This led to an intense battle, which increased the price of Northern's stock from $100 a share to as high as $1,000, creating a panic on Wall Street as the value of other stocks plummeted. A truce was eventually reached: the Morgan-Hill interests maintained control, but Harriman, Schiff, and William Rockefeller (a Harriman–Schiff ally) gained seats on the Northern Pacific board, and Harriman gained a seat on the Burlington board as well.

For Morgan, this episode represented a failure of his earlier attempts to minimize what he believed was destructive competition. In reorganizing the railroads during the 1890s, Morgan sought to ensure the existence of a "community of interest"—a term that Morgan himself used—to facilitate cooperation (Corey 1930, 303; Cochran and Miller 1942, 196–197). This involved either the combining of firms through mergers or, where that was not possible, joint control, through a combination of stock ownership, voting trusts, and representation on the firms' boards (Corey 1930, 284). Morgan was able to achieve this community to the extent that his power was uncontested (ibid., 293–294). The one group capable of mounting an effective challenge to Morgan was the alliance of the Rockefellers (whose control of Standard Oil gave them enormous wealth), Schiff of Kuhn Loeb, James Stillman of the National City Bank, and Harriman (ibid., 294–295; Mizruchi 1982). The battle over the Northern Pacific demonstrated that Morgan had not fully succeeded in establishing the community of interest. But the resolution, with joint representation of Morgan and Rockefeller interests on the boards of the Burlington and Northern Pacific, suggested the possible end of debilitating proxy fights between them.[3] Over the next several years, the interests of the two groups increasingly merged. By 1907, Morgan had become a major stockholder in the bank, and Stillman joined with Morgan and Baker to purchase shares in the National Bank of Commerce (Allen 1935, 175–176). By the time of the Pujo Committee hearings in 1913, Stillman was viewed as an ally of Morgan and Baker.

There is a widespread belief among social scientists and business historians that this group represented a relatively cohesive and dominant corporate community. Contemporaries wrote of the "financial oligarchy" (Pratt
1905) and the "money trust" (Noyes 1909). Concerns about the concentration of economic power were at the root of the muckraking journalism of
Ida Tarbell (see, for example, her writing on Standard Oil [1905]) as well as
the academic writing of Anna Youngman (1907a, 1907b). Historians writing decades later referred to the period as an era of "finance capitalism"
(Cochran and Miller 1942) and spoke of the power exercised by the leading
bankers of the day. This group, led by Morgan, Rockefeller, Baker, Stillman, Harriman, and Schiff, among others, could be described as the first
American corporate elite.[4] Whether the members of this elite were able to
see beyond their immediate short-term interests, or saw themselves as responsible for the well-being of the larger society, was another matter.

On one hand, there is evidence that this group did exhibit concern for
the larger financial system. A good example of this was Morgan's role in the
panic of 1907. The American economy was in the midst of a serious downturn in 1907, and stock prices dropped significantly in March.[5] Meanwhile,
a group that included Charles W. Morse, Edward R. Thomas, and the
Heinze brothers (Augustus and Otto) attempted to manipulate the market
for shares of United Copper, a firm controlled by the Heinzes. The group
miscalculated, and the share price collapsed. Because the Heinzes also controlled the Mercantile National Bank (of which Morse was a board member), depositors panicked and made a run on the bank. The Heinzes ap-
pealed to the Clearing House, a group of New York banks that provided
help for institutions in distress, and the Clearing House provided the funds
to save the bank, but only on the condition that the Heinzes and Morse
resign. Meanwhile, Knickerbocker Trust, which had provided funds to the
Heinze-Morse group (its president, Charles T. Barney, was an ally of Morse),
began to experience a run of its own. In this case, the Clearing House refused to step in, and the bank failed.

The Wall Street community was in a panicked state when Morgan went
into action. Over a period of eleven days, he saved the Trust Company of
America, which had experienced a run, by convincing the secretary of the
treasury, George Cortelyou, to deposit federal funds into the bank and by
selling off the bank's assets to provide further cash. He convinced bankers
to infuse funds to shore up the stock market, which was in danger of

collapse. He persuaded local clergy to reassure their congregations that the financial system was sound. And, most impressively, he holed up in his library with a group of bankers, locked the door (with the key in his pocket), and refused to let them leave until they had agreed to provide $25 million to save a group of failing banks. One of Morgan's key decisions had been to rescue the imperiled brokerage house Moore & Schley, by having U.S. Steel purchase Tennessee Coal & Iron, a company that Moore & Schley had used for collateral. To do this, Morgan risked violating the Sherman Antitrust Act, since the two firms operated in the same market. Morgan managed to convince President Roosevelt to refrain from invoking the Sherman Act, however. In what many observers believe was his finest hour, Morgan had put an end to the panic.

Although Morgan was able to virtually single-handedly rescue the financial system, this episode drove home the need for a federal agency to provide a mechanism for preventing or resolving similar situations in the future. Morgan had supported the idea of a federal bank, as did several other leading figures of the period, and a group of bankers, including Morgan partner Harry Davison and Frank A. Vanderlip, Stillman's successor at National City Bank, met with Senator Nelson Aldrich in 1912 to draft a bill for its creation (Allen 1935, 198–199; Wiebe 1958). By the time the bill was pushed through by President Wilson in 1913, it had been significantly altered—to the consternation of the bankers, who had preferred to control the bank themselves (Corey 1930, 418). Still, the bankers did achieve one major goal: they now had a federal institution capable of putting a stop to panics, thereby absolving private bankers from the responsibility to do so themselves.

Although Morgan and his allies were able to overcome their immediate interests to save the financial system, there is less evidence of their concern for the larger society. As Allen (1935, 198) put it, "The bankers had disclaimed obligation for the general social welfare, but they had frequently stated that many social benefits would result from their financial deals." The captains of industry displayed little regard for the rights of their workers. Working conditions nationwide were by all accounts abominable in the late nineteenth and early twentieth centuries. Jobs were "monotonous and dangerous" (Cochran and Miller 1942, 231), with accidents reaching a peak between 1903 and 1907. In 1913 alone, more than 25,000 workers died in accidents and more than a million were injured on the job (ibid.). In 1911,

78 percent of U.S. Steel workers worked twelve-hour days (Corey 1930, 277). And workers often lived in company towns, in which they were charged high rents in company-owned housing and high prices in company-owned stores.

Workers, in attempting to organize, faced severe obstacles as well. Most employers were fiercely opposed to unionization of any kind. Morgan was willing to intervene to force a compromise in the coal miners' strike during the presidential election of 1900, but he resisted intervening during a similar strike in 1902, until pressured by President Roosevelt (Corey 1930, 212–213, 278). He also strongly opposed the unionization of U.S. Steel, stating, during a strike in 1901, that "there has been no settlement and there can be no compromise" (ibid., 279). Morgan's views and actions on these issues were representative of those of most of the leading business figures of the day. The workers, ethnically diverse, and weakened in their efforts to unionize by a constant influx of immigrants, faced great odds. Even the government typically took the side of the employers. The Sherman Antitrust Act, designed to limit corporate concentration, was often invoked instead against unions, on the ground that collective action by workers amounted to a restraint of trade (Allen 1935, 146).

The Emergence of Moderates

Not all corporate leaders of the period were as singularly unconcerned about the consequences of their actions. Running parallel to the domination of Morgan and Rockefeller was a group of leading businessmen that was explicitly concerned with ameliorating the most destructive aspects of the newly emerging corporate capitalism. This group came together in an organization established in 1900: the National Civic Federation (NCF). The NCF was not the first major organization of businessmen. The National Association of Manufacturers (NAM) had been formed in 1895. The NAM, made up primarily of small businesses, adopted a traditional laissez-faire approach to capitalism, however, one that has continued almost without interruption to the present day. The NCF had a very different perspective. Founded by journalist and former activist (and Republican) Ralph Easley, the goal of the organization was to serve as a moderating force between business and labor, to project a vision of "responsibility," in which "all classes [would work to] maintain and increase the efficiency of the existing social order" (Weinstein 1968, xi). The organization did this by sponsoring conferences, publishing books, and circulating position papers among its membership (Mitchell 1989, 13–14). The group was also involved in proposing both legislation and regulatory proposals to government officials (Weinstein 1968, 7).

Unlike the NAM, the NCF's members included labor leaders, academics, and other public figures as well as businessmen. Reminiscent of the "corporatist" model in Europe (Streeck and Kenworthy 2005), the group was organized into three divisions, representing business, labor, and the "general public." The NCF's early members included its first president, Marcus Hanna (a powerful Republican senator from Ohio and campaign manager for President William McKinley), Cyrus McCormick (president of what became the Chicago farm equipment giant International Harvester), Chicago utilities magnate Samuel Insull, Andrew Carnegie, Frank Vanderlip (future president of National City Bank), and several partners of J. P. Morgan & Company, including George W. Perkins, although not Morgan himself. Other members included American Federation of Labor president Samuel Gompers, former president Grover Cleveland, and the new (but ultimately long-time) president of Columbia University, Nicholas Murray Butler.

In contrast to the NAM, which was vehemently opposed to unions in any form, the NCF attempted to mediate between business and labor, much as its philosophical successor, the Committee for Economic Development (CED), tried to do several decades later. The approach adopted by the NCF was termed "corporate liberalism" by one of the group's leading chroniclers, historian James Weinstein (1968).[6] The term is ironic, and perhaps a bit misleading. Classical liberalism, of course, was the doctrine associated with followers of Adam Smith, who supported a laissez-faire policy toward business. Smith himself was reacting to the tyranny associated with the old feudal monarchies, to which the free market (and its associated political freedoms) was an alternative. In that sense, classical liberalism was a progressive force, standing in contrast to the traditional conservatism of the aristocracy. Even today, the term "neo-liberalism" is used to describe an ideology based on limited government intervention in the market, a throwback to the earlier laissez-faire approach.

By the twentieth century, however, the term liberalism, at least in the United States, came to stand for something else: an attempt to balance the interests of competing groups in the society, most notably business and labor. This policy came to full fruition under Franklin Roosevelt in the 1930s, as the state stepped in to address the devastation caused by the Great Depression. It had already begun to emerge among corporate elites at the beginning of the century, however. This so-called corporate liberalism, according to Weinstein, was based on "an awareness on the part of the more sophisticated business and political leaders that the social order could be stabilized only if it moved in the direction of general social concern and social responsibility" (1968, 3). Given the ambiguity associated with the term liberalism, I shall eschew the label in favor of one that I believe more accurately captures the spirit of the world-view: corporate *moderation*.[7] What distinguished the members of the NCF from the more militant NAM was their willingness to compromise, to accept the workers' needs and (in later years) state intervention in the economy, as legitimate. In fact, some members of the NCF viewed the NAM as radicals, or, as Easley called them, "anarchists among capitalists" (ibid., 11).

The NCF saw itself as a neutral party, playing a moderating role in the competition between classes. Easley "started with the assumption that problems were essentially technical, that the framework of the political economy need only be rationalized and that 'experts' applying their skills in the assumed common interest could best do the job" (Weinstein 1968, 30–31). Hanna, the group's first president, hoped to create "a relation of mutual trust between the laborer and the employer," and Perkins spoke of the need to allow workers to share in the benefits of the trust system. John Mitchell of the United Mine Workers wrote of the need to "bring into closer and more harmonious relation these two apparently antagonistic forces" (ibid., 9).

The NCF experienced a significant amount of success in its early years. It was instrumental in establishing child labor laws and the regulation of utility companies, and it played a role in establishing the Federal Reserve Bank (Jensen 1956; Wiebe 1958; Judis 2001, 20). The group was less successful in persuading significant numbers of business leaders to support unions. In fact, several of its own members, although they supported the idea of conservative unionism, were strongly antiunion when it came to their own firms (Weinstein 1968, 11–12). Elbert H. Gary, for example, who as the president of U.S. Steel played a significant role in preventing the unionization of the company, was a member of and generous contributor to the NCF.

By 1905, having failed in their efforts to gain support for unionization, the NCF turned to firm-sponsored programs, or what later became known as "welfare capitalism," as an alternative. These programs contained a broad array of services, including housing, subsidized company eating facilities, and in some cases pensions and health care. Among the early adopters of these programs were the two Morgan-controlled companies with which Perkins was affiliated—U.S. Steel and International Harvester—as well as National Cash Register (the forerunner of NCR) and Sears (Weinstein 1968, 19–21). By 1910, more than 60 companies had instituted pension plans, a number that grew to more than 300 by 1925, and by 1920 more than 100 had instituted employee stock ownership plans (Mitchell 1989, 15). Henry Ford introduced the five-dollar day in 1914, and General Electric in 1922 adopted a comprehensive plan that included health care, disability, and paid vacations as well as an employee stock ownership plan (ibid., 12–13). The workers saw such plans as paternalistic, however, and in some cases supported government programs as alternatives to the company-financed plans. The NCF itself was not entirely averse to state-run programs. In one case, dating back to 1909, organized labor and the NCF joined forces to support a government workers' compensation plan (Weinstein 1968, 48–50). By 1920, all but six states—all of which were in the South—had a workers' compensation law, and according to Weinstein, the NCF was largely responsible (ibid., 61).

Two issues present themselves regarding the NCF. First, who were its members? And second, to what extent were their actions motivated by a genuine concern for the larger well-being as opposed to expedience? Regarding the first point, Weinstein (1968, 4–5) argues persuasively that moderation among corporate leaders was primarily a function of the amount of slack a firm had, in terms of being insulated from the most severe forms of competition. Small firms had little room for maneuver, given the market pressures they faced and their consequently small profit margins. The larger firms, which experienced less immediate constraint from the market, were in a stronger position to observe both the societal-wide threat posed by the radicalization of the workforce and the danger that a confrontational approach to labor entailed.

That small size and intense competitive pressures contributed to a strongly antilabor perspective is undeniable. On the other hand, large size, while perhaps a necessary condition for moderation, was not a sufficient one. Among business leaders associated with large firms, those from financial institutions were more likely to adopt a moderate perspective, while those directly engaged in manufacturing held more confrontational views (Weinstein 1968, 11). This is reflected in an exhaustive study of the Federation by Jensen (1956). Among the six businessmen listed by Jensen as founding members of the organization, five were bankers. Still, the business leadership of the Federation drew from a broad range of industries. Among those listed by Jensen were officers of such nonfinancial firms as Bethlehem Steel, the Southern Pacific Railway, and R. H. Macy, as well as a number of leading bankers. Weinstein (1968, 8) noted that nearly one-third of the 367 largest corporations (based on capitalization) had representatives in the organization, as did nearly one-quarter of the 67 largest railroads.

As for the degree to which members of the NCF were sincere in their desire to improve the lives of workers, this is a difficult question to answer. There is no question that the group's members were driven in part by fear, in particular that if workers were treated badly under capitalism, they would eventually support an alternative system. Indeed, support for socialists increased significantly during the first decade of the twentieth century, with the Socialist Party electing more than 1,000 candidates nationwide and Eugene V. Debs drawing nearly one million votes in the 1912 presidential election. The organization's officials were up front about these concerns. The liberal lawyer, future Supreme Court justice, and crusader against the Money Trust Louis Brandeis noted that the trade unions represent "a strong bulwark against the great wave of socialism" (Weinstein 1968, 17). Those firms that established corporate welfare plans were also well aware of the instrumental benefits such programs might hold. As Perkins put it in referring to the workmen's compensation program at International Harvester, the firm "'did not do this out of pure philanthropy,' but was motivated by a 'purely business spirit'" (ibid., 46).

An example of the extent to which businesspeople of the time saw the necessity of addressing labor issues is illustrated by the formation of the Special Conference Committee, organized in 1919 by an International Harvester human resources official, Clarence J. Hicks. Hicks had been employed by John D. Rockefeller in 1914 to help establish a company union at Colorado Fuel and Iron in response to the 1913 Ludlow Massacre, in which nineteen of the company's striking coal miners were shot by National

Guardsmen. Four years later, Rockefeller asked Hicks to help respond to a series of strikes at Standard Oil of New Jersey, which led to the implementation of a series of welfare measures at the firm. In 1919, Hicks assembled a group of ten business leaders, representing firms such as Goodyear, General Electric, Bethlehem Steel, U.S. Rubber, and Westinghouse, as well as International Harvester and Standard Oil, to form the Special Conference Committee (Nelson 1982). The group subscribed to the principle that "the maintenance of harmonious and helpful relationships throughout the organization ranks in importance with production, distribution, finance, and other major functions of management" (ibid., 345). This statement illustrates the instrumental nature of firms' attempts to placate their workers. Similar views were adopted by the emerging field of management, which became prominent along with welfare capitalism in the 1920s.

Yet to treat these efforts as exclusively cynical, devoid of any sincerity, seems itself an exaggeration. In a 1913 speech to the Chicago branch of the American Institute of Banking, A. C. Bartlett, president of the Hibbard, Spencer, Bartlett Company (the predecessor of True Value Hardware), told the audience that people of modest means, those "short of time and not long on purse," were those most involved in human betterment. "The rich," Bartlett suggested, "are not our best citizens" (*New York Times,* January 19, 1913, 1).[8] Although presumably not a result of this speech, the period shortly after he spoke witnessed a wave of corporate philanthropy, from John D. Rockefeller to Andrew Carnegie. Much of this charitable work, Rockefeller's in particular, was undoubtedly driven as much by public relations as authentic concern. It would be unfair to assume a complete absence of humane motives, however. There was also, among at least some firms, a genuine desire to make life better for their workers. Neil J. Mitchell (1989, 112–142) has uncovered a series of statements from the 1920s—by corporate officials as well as business journalists of the period—that suggest a shift in orientation from what predominated at the end of the nineteenth century. "The narrowly individualistic attitude toward business and social problems that formerly prevailed is being outgrown," suggested a study by the National Industrial Conference Board (later known as simply the Conference Board). "Businessmen generally are adopting a broader approach to such questions and are recognizing their responsibilities to other groups in society as well as to their own employees" (quoted in Mitchell 1989, 113). As an example of this, Charles M. Schwab, president of Bethlehem Steel, suggested that "cooperation requires leadership in industry that regards itself not as a partisan but as a trustee, striving to guide the efforts of both capital and labor into profitable channels" (ibid., 118).

These views were also reflected in the new academic field of management, known today as organizational theory. Frederick Winslow Taylor had pioneered his theory of scientific management in the early part of the century, culminating in his *Principles of Scientific Management* (1911). This approach, which removed virtually all discretion from line workers and replaced it with extremely close supervision, proved ineffective, however, as workers engaged in relatively fierce resistance (Braverman 1974). By the 1920s, management theory had taken a more humanistic turn, as theorists such as Chester Barnard and Elton Mayo wrote of the corporation as an "organic" entity, in which management and workers each strove toward a common goal (Bendix 1963; Perrow 1986). Clearly, corporate leaders were, by the 1920s, directing their firms with a softer edge, and they certainly expressed more conciliatory attitudes toward their employees than in earlier decades.

Did these views represent a genuine change of heart by the business elite, as writers such as Mitchell and Judis suggest, or were they merely the voices of expedience, as argued by Weinstein and Domhoff? In one sense the question is unanswerable, if not irrelevant. Even in otherwise private communications, it is difficult to read into the minds of those offering the statements. Motivation, as psychologists have long known, is a complex matter. Whether the threat posed by the workers triggered a softening of attitudes or whether the expressed attitudes reflected an accommodation to a changed reality is almost impossible to disentangle. Most likely, both were at work to varying degrees among individual businesspeople. What we can observe is tangible behavioral evidence that the growth of unionization precipitated a moderate, conciliatory response among a certain segment of the corporate elite.

And yet this response went only so far. The threat of unionization declined after the "Red Scare" period following World War I, and the average wages of American workers remained low during the 1920s. A study published in 1929 (before the stock market crash) by the Brookings Institution revealed that more than half of the American population earned less than the Bureau of Labor's floor for a "decent standard of living" (Venn 1998, 9). And even welfare capitalism essentially disappeared with the onset of the

Depression. After having nearly doubled between 1915 and 1920 to more than five million workers, union membership declined continuously through the early 1930s, reaching a low of fewer than 2.7 million workers in 1933 (Mayer 2004). Meanwhile, the National Civic Federation, although it continued to exist, had faded from the national scene by the 1920s.

The 1930s

The debates over the role of business during the 1930s involve the extent to which an organized group of moderate corporate leaders, representing their class, helped to construct and provided support for key legislation. Scholars have debated the origins of several New Deal–era programs, but the issue that has received the most attention is the Social Security Act of 1935. Although there are several accounts of the role of business in the shaping and passage of this bill, they can be classified into two broad approaches: a business-centered model, in which relatively enlightened members of the corporate community played a significant role in formulating and generating support for the bill, and a state-centered model, in which the peculiar structure of the American government (including, for example, the seniority system in Congress that gave Southern Democrats disproportionate power), played the greatest role in the outcome, while business leaders, even the few mavericks who supported the program, played little role. The business-centered model is identified primarily with G. William Domhoff (see, among his many works, 1970, 1990) and Jill Quadagno (1984, 1988). The state-centered model is identified primarily with Theda Skocpol (1980) and several of her collaborators (Skocpol and Ikenberry 1983; Skocpol and Amenta 1985). Manza (2000) provides an excellent review of these and other perspectives on the policy provisions of the New Deal.

What can we make of this debate, and what relevance does it have for my argument? That most American businessmen were opposed to Franklin Roosevelt's New Deal reforms, including Social Security, is not in doubt. The debate has focused on whether those who supported it represented a significant and influential segment of the corporate community, as Quadagno and Domhoff suggest, or whether they were simply a handful of unusually liberal businesspeople who had little influence within either the larger business community or the government, as Skocpol argues. It is not necessary for us to resolve this debate here. Skocpol is certainly correct that there were many factors other than support from business that went into the development of Social Security. And Domhoff and Quadagno perhaps go too far in suggesting that the support of some capitalists for Social Security reflected the interests of a class, or even a class segment. Yet corporate support for Social Security clearly went beyond the actions of a handful of idiosyncratic capitalists.

It is true that no list of individual business leaders, no matter how prominent, can serve as proof of general corporate support—or even the support of a class segment. At the same time, Quadagno (1985, 1988) offers persuasive evidence of systematic business support, as well as a compelling discussion of the basis of this support. The willingness of business leaders to consider the need for a government-administered program had its roots in an inexorable fact: the corporate welfare programs that proliferated in the 1920s were becoming increasingly expensive and unmanageable by the middle of that decade. Under these circumstances, many companies began to have second thoughts about the viability of these programs. The idea of a government pension system to relieve firms of the burden of providing retirement income became increasingly attractive to company leaders by the late 1920s. The National Industrial Conference Board, which had strongly supported corporate welfare in earlier years, had by 1929 proposed a government-managed system, albeit one that would remain under the control of employers (Quadagno 1985, 576).

After Social Security was passed, many employers who had opposed it began to realize its benefits. Some firms reduced their own pension payments by the exact amount that Social Security was now accommodating. A survey conducted by *Fortune* in 1939 found that although 57 percent of the executives who were interviewed recommended changes in various aspects of the system, only 17 percent favored repeal (*Fortune* 1939, 52). In fact, several of the opinions expressed in this survey were remarkable for the moderation they exhibited.[9] Even the Wagner Act, which greatly expanded the rights of workers to organize unions, was believed to warrant repeal by only 40.9 percent of the respondents, while the Works Progress Administration (WPA), which created government-sponsored jobs, was said to warrant repeal by 44.4 percent. Meanwhile, several other New Deal policies were even less likely to generate opposition than the Social Security Act. These included the Civilian Conservation Corps (7.4 percent), the Banking Act of 1933 (otherwise known as Glass-Steagall), which required

the separation of investment banking from commercial banking (3.8 percent), and the Securities Exchange Act (3.6 percent). Remarkably, 42.9
percent of the businesspeople surveyed believed that "business would be
better off if the unions were to merge into one big powerful union," compared to only 38.5 percent who believed that business would be worse off
(ibid., 53). It is true that the lack of support for repealing the various New
Deal measures did not necessarily translate to complete agreement with the
policies. Although 78 percent of the respondents supported keeping the
Civilian Conservation Corps, 65 percent supported the Banking Act, and
57 percent supported the Federal Housing Administration, sizable proportions believed that other programs should be modified, including 41.9 percent for the Wagner Act, 41.7 percent for the WPA, and 57.9 percent for
the Social Security Act. Yet it is striking that the majority opinion was to
either keep as is or modify the existing programs rather than to repeal them
outright.

If by 1939 a majority of businessmen had made their peace with the New
Deal, opposition had been strong in the early stages and remained strong at
least through the 1936 election. Franklin Roosevelt was aware from the
start of his presidency in 1933 that his policies were likely to generate opposition from business. To stem this anticipated reaction, Daniel Roper,
FDR's secretary of commerce, suggested the formation of a group of business leaders to promote "a more harmonious relationship between government and business" (Collins 1978, 371). A 1933 meeting of this group,
which became known as the Business Advisory Council, was attended by
several important business leaders, including Gerard Swope of General
Electric, Alfred P. Sloan of General Motors, Walter Gifford of AT&T, and
Alexander Legge of International Harvester. Some of these people, most
notably Swope, were known to be relatively liberal and generally supportive
of the New Deal. Swope went well beyond standard New Deal thinking.
Among his proposals was an idea to organize leading industries into cartels,
under government supervision. The state would permit price fixing and restrictions on supply, while firms would guarantee relatively high wages and
employment levels (McQuaid 1978, 353). Other members were more traditional, and more skeptical of New Deal programs, however. In fact, an attempt by Roosevelt to claim Business Advisory Council support for an extension of the National Recovery Act, against the wishes of the Chamber of
Commerce, led to a severe backlash and a series of resignations (Collins

1978, 372). Although the council subsequently gained new members and offered support for some New Deal policies, including Social Security, the group remained critical of Roosevelt. This included putting pressure on FDR to balance the budget in 1937, an effort that, in the view of many economists, was the source of the downturn that occurred soon after (Krugman 2010).

In some respects the Business Advisory Council could be said to be the forerunner of the Committee for Economic Development. Council members supported the idea of national planning and regulation of industry, as Swope's idea for industry cartels illustrates. Some of its members went even further, supporting the idea of Keynesian deficit spending (previously an anathema to business leaders, who were strongly wedded to the concept of a balanced budget) and full employment (itself a controversial position given its potential for upward pressure on wages). This latter group consisted of a relatively small number of liberal businessmen, including Lincoln Filene, owner of the Boston department store, and Morris Leeds, president of Leeds and Northrup, a Philadelphia electrical instrument manufacturer (Collins 1978; Licht 1992). Although these people were able to sway few other business leaders, they did manage to gain support from attendees at a 1939 conference organized by *Fortune,* and they were successful in convincing President Roosevelt to engage in deficit spending (Collins 1978, 379). Among those most responsible for influencing FDR was a foundation director, academic, and businessman named Beardsley Ruml. Ruml would later play an important role in a new and highly influential group, the Committee for Economic Development.

The Formation of the Committee for Economic Development

The group that epitomized the moderate postwar corporate elite was an organization known as the Committee for Economic Development (CED). The CED was established by two people associated with the University of Chicago: William Benton, an advertising executive who had retired at age 36 and become the vice president of the university, and Paul Hoffman, the president of the automobile manufacturer Studebaker and a member of the university's board of trustees. As Karl Schriftgiesser, a public relations officer at the CED, put it in his comprehensive history of the organization's first two decades, most American businessmen at the dawn of World War

II "still seemed to live in an atmosphere of McKinleyism" (1960, 3), adhering to a laissez-faire view of economic policy. Benton and Hoffman aimed to provide a counterweight to this view. The pair had three goals in mind as they formed their organization. First, they hoped to "rescue the businessman from his own intellectual neanderthalism, to wash the clichés of an outworn ideology from his mind." Second, they aimed to bring business leaders together with academics, in part to "wipe the theoretical cobwebs from the thinkers' minds." And third, they hoped to provide a forum in which the academics could help guide the business leaders toward supporting a sound economic policy (ibid., 7).[10]

In 1939, Benton approached a friend, Lewis Brown, the president of the Johns Manville Company, with an idea for bringing together a group of academics and the presidents of the 100 largest corporations (Schriftgiesser 1960, 10–11). Benton and Hoffman subsequently approached the heads of (among others) Scott Paper, General Foods, General Electric, and Procter and Gamble, as well as Henry Luce, the publisher of *Time,* and Ruml, by then the treasurer of Macy's (Schriftgiesser 1960, 13; Collins 1978, 386). They called their group the American Policy Commission.

Meanwhile, in 1941, the Business Advisory Council formed a Committee on Economic Policy, led by Marion Folsom, the treasurer of Eastman Kodak. Similar to the Benton-Hoffman group, the committee members believed that an economic policy based on the principles of laissez-faire was obsolete, and they supported a program of "intelligent planning" to regulate the economy (Collins 1978, 386). Although the United States had not yet entered World War II, this group was already concerned about the need to plan for the postwar economy, in particular to avoid a return to the conditions of the 1930s. Aware of the similarities between Folsom's Committee on Economic Policy and their American Policy Commission, Hoffman and Benton approached Folsom with the idea of merging the two, but Folsom was not receptive to the idea of including academics in the organization (Schriftgiesser 1960, 23–24). Instead, Hoffman and Benton met directly with Jesse H. Jones, the head of the Commerce Department in the Roosevelt administration. Jones, a conservative Texas businessman, had never been a strong supporter of the New Deal, and Benton and Hoffman were not optimistic that he would support their plan. To their surprise, however, Jones agreed to support the new organization that they had envisioned and to provide funds sufficient to establish a significant research component

(Schriftgiesser 1960, 24–26; Collins 1978, 387). Jones believed that an organization devoted to postwar planning should consist entirely of businessmen and, unlike the Business Advisory Council, be completely independent of the government.

A statement culled by Schriftgiesser from the minutes of the meeting establishing the new organization provides a good illustration of the role that the committee had set for itself. It was emphatically not to be an interest group advocating for the needs of business. It was expected "to avoid assiduously any tendency towards promoting the special interests of business itself as such." On the other hand, it was not expected to speak for the national interest above and beyond the interests of business. It was "to refrain from any implication that the Committee seeks to speak for the nation, or even to deal with, the public responsibilities or special interests of other groups in the economy, such as labor, agriculture, or government." Instead, its major goal was "to promote commerce after the war" (Schriftgiesser 1960, 26). This charge may have resulted from a compromise that Jones had reached with the National Association of Manufacturers and the U.S. Chamber of Commerce. These far more conservative organizations were highly suspicious not only of government involvement in the economy but also of the idea of economic planning, which to them smacked of socialism. Yet as well-established probusiness organizations, they had legitimate questions regarding why the Commerce Department had not selected them to lead this effort, and they were equally concerned about the idea of a new business group that would not only constitute a rival to them but would also have the support of the government. Their agreement with Jones stipulated that the new organization would exist only for the duration of the war (Schriftgiesser 1960, 22). As we shall see, the Committee for Economic Development—as it was subsequently named—not only continued to exist after the war, but its members began to speak with explicit concern for what it viewed as the larger national interest.

Who Was in the CED?

The new Committee on Economic Policy named Hoffman as its chair and Benton as vice chair. The other original members of the board of trustees were either selected by Secretary Jones, who chose one person from each of the twelve Federal Reserve districts, or recommended by Hoffman, with

Jones's approval. Schriftgiesser (1960, 227–228) provided a list of the eighteen original members of the board, including Hoffman and Benton. Of these eighteen, three were originally recommended by Hoffman and Benton, seven (including Hoffman) were recommended by Jones, and the remaining appointments were of indeterminate origin.[11] According to Collins (1981, 84), of the twenty individuals who served as trustees at some point in 1942, fourteen were or had been associated with the Business Advisory Council.[12] The organization, which was eventually named the Committee for Economic Development, was formally incorporated on September 3, 1942. By July 1945, seven of the original eighteen individuals mentioned by Schriftgiesser, including Beardsley Ruml and General Electric chairman Owen D. Young, were no longer associated with the organization, and the board had grown to twenty-seven individuals. Table 2.1 lists the board members as of July 1945, drawn from the CED publication *American Industry Looks Ahead* (Committee for Economic Development 1945a, 62).

What can we make of the composition of the CED? In speaking of the early figures in the formation of the CED, including Filene, Ruml, Benton, and Hoffman, Collins (1978, 390) notes that they "were not themselves big businessmen in the traditional sense of that imprecise designation." This is true. Filene was a department store owner, Ruml had been a foundation director, and both Ruml and Benton had academic backgrounds. Even Hoffman was president of a relatively minor automobile manufacturer. On the other hand, a look at the CED's board of trustees suggests a different picture. Of the twenty-seven trustees listed in Table 2.1, twenty-one were primarily affiliated with corporations, not including Eric Johnston, who was the president of a business association—the U.S. Chamber of Commerce. Of those twenty-one, fourteen represented corporations that were in the Fortune 500 in its initial year (1955) or a subsequent year, and two others represented a major retailer (Federated Department Stores) and a major investment bank (Goldman Sachs), respectively. Moreover, these fourteen were not the only individuals representing major corporations. The organization's marketing committee included officers of Firestone Tire & Rubber, Carrier, Pillsbury, Western Electric, Westinghouse, General Motors, Lever Brothers, Armour, and Standard Oil of New Jersey, along with Metropolitan Life Insurance and the investment firm Smith Barney. The Field Development Committee included officers of Wachovia Bank, Burlington Railroad, and Sinclair Oil.

Table 2.1 CED Trustees and Positions as of July 1945

Name	Position	Firm	City
Paul G. Hoffman[a]	President	Studebaker	South Bend, IN
William Benton[b]	Chairman	Encyclopedia Britannica	New York
Marion B. Folsom[b]	Treasurer	Eastman Kodak	Rochester, NY
W. Gibson Carey Jr.	President	Yale & Towne Manufacturing	New York
Frank A. Christensen[c]	Vice president	Continental Insurance	New York
W. L. Clayton		Anderson Clayton & Co.	Houston
Chester C. Davis	President	Federal Reserve Bank	St. Louis
Milton S. Eisenhower	President	Kansas State College (subsequently University)	Manhattan, KS
Ralph E. Flanders	President	Federal Reserve Bank	Boston
Clarence Francis	Chairman	General Foods	New York
Walter D. Fuller	President	Curtis Publishing Co.	Philadelphia
Lou Holland	President	Holland Engraving Co.	Kansas City
Charles R. Hook	President	American Rolling Mill Co.	Middletown, OH
Jay C. Hormel	President	George A. Hormel Co.	Austin, MN
Reagan Houston	Industrialist, merchant		San Antonio
Eric A. Johnston	President	Brown-Johnston Co. and U.S. Chamber of Commerce	Washington, DC
Harrison Jones	Chairman	Coca-Cola	Atlanta
Fred Lazarus Jr.	President	Federated Department Stores	Columbus
Thomas B. McCabe	President	Scott Paper	Philadelphia
Reuben B. Robertson	Executive vice president	Champion Paper and Fibre	Canton, NC
Harry Scherman	President	Book-of-the-Month Club	New York
Robert Gordon Sproul	President	University of California	Berkeley
Elmer T. Stevens	President	Charles A. Stevens & Co.	Chicago
John Stuart	Chairman	Quaker Oats	Chicago
Wayne C. Taylor	President	Export-Import Bank of Washington	Washington, DC
Sidney J. Weinberg	Partner	Goldman Sachs & Co.	New York
Charles E. Wilson	President	General Electric	Schenectady, NY

a. CED chairman
b. CED vice chairman
c. Subsequently became president of Continental
Source: Committee for Economic Development (1945a).

Although it seems clear that the businessmen associated with the CED in its early years were drawn primarily from large corporations, detecting a pattern in terms of which corporations is more difficult. This becomes easier in later years, as the size of the board expanded rapidly, but the small numbers in the group's initial stages render systematic conclusions difficult. Only two financial institutions (and no commercial banks) were represented among the sixteen major firms. The group included four companies in the food industry, two in paper, and a third in publishing. Heavy industry was underrepresented, with only one automobile manufacturer and one steel company. Given the small size of the board, however, it is difficult to infer the extent to which the CED represented the views of large corporations in general. Certainly judging by the corporate response to the New Deal and the CED's roots in the Business Advisory Council, one might view the CED as representing a relatively small group of liberal businessmen. Two things suggest otherwise. First, most of the early leaders of the CED, including Hoffman, were Republicans. Subscribing to moderate views about the role of the state in economic planning was therefore not confined to either Roosevelt supporters or Democrats in general. In fact, Wendell Willkie, the Republican nominee for President in 1940, was himself a proponent of government-business cooperation and an internationalist foreign policy, both anathema to the NAM and the Chamber of Commerce, and he received support from even liberal business leaders such as the successive presidents of General Electric, Gerard Swope and Owen D. Young (McQuaid 1978, 365).[13] Second, during the war many corporate leaders accepted positions in the government to help with the effort. At the time the United States entered the war in December 1941, business opinion of government remained overwhelmingly negative. The experience in government appears to have led to a softening of business attitudes toward the state, however. As Folsom put it in his memoirs, "The war did an awful lot to business people. Many of the top business advisory people had government jobs during the war, you see, and realized what a tough job it is to run a government. So the businessmen got to appreciate the government and not be so critical of it" (quoted in Jacoby 1993, 545).[14]

Ironically, then, the representation of businesspeople in the government, so often decried by radical critics of American society (for the classic statements, see Mills 1956; Domhoff 1967), may, whatever its consequences for American democracy, have helped liberalize, or at least moderate, the views of American business leaders. Finally, it is worth noting again that despite their general antipathy toward government, by the end of the 1930s, as indicated by the *Fortune* survey, American businesspeople had come to grudgingly accept, albeit not without criticism, most of the New Deal policies enacted earlier in the decade. The CED reflected these views. The CED was not by any means interested in strengthening the welfare state, nor were its members wholehearted supporters of the New Deal. They were pragmatic, however. The CED's members understood that the government was going to play a significant role in postwar economic policy. Given this inevitability, they reasoned, it was better for business to be able to shape that policy than to oppose any government role altogether, thereby confining oneself to irrelevance.

Conclusion: A Pragmatic Corporate Elite

By the end of World War II, a moderate, pragmatic corporate elite had emerged, based primarily in the largest American corporations. This group was not a discrete entity with clear boundaries. Its views were well articulated by the CED, but the members of this moderate elite were not necessarily affiliated with that organization. The elite that emerged in this period was historically unique, but its roots were evident in the elite groups and actions of earlier decades.

At the turn of the twentieth century, the NCF represented a group of moderate corporate leaders who displayed a degree of pragmatism not unlike that of the later CED. The problems that the NCF faced—a working class experiencing draconian working conditions and near starvation—were different from those faced by the CED, although labor militancy was certainly a significant issue in the post–World War II period. Just as the CED acknowledged the importance of government and pledged to work with the state, the NCF initially acknowledged the role of unions and pledged to work with them. When that failed, the NCF's members turned to welfare capitalism—a private solution—in an effort to keep the state and labor unions out of their businesses. In its focus on private solutions to socioeconomic problems, the corporate elite of the early 1900s may have had more in common with that of the early 2000s than with the post–World War II elite.

On the other hand, the early twentieth century did have an organized and significant contingent of moderate business leaders who believed in the need to address the problems of contemporary capitalism. Moreover, although the businessmen of the period ultimately rejected independent unionism, they were willing to support government involvement in the economy, including the establishment of the Interstate Commerce Commission, the Federal Trade Commission, and the Federal Reserve. After focusing primarily on privately based welfare capitalism in the 1920s, some business leaders were willing to support various elements of the New Deal, including Social Security. Others, most notably Gerard Swope, the president of General Electric, proposed even more radical ideas about government planning and management of industries. If the corporate elites of the early twentieth century did not exhibit the overall level of organization and moderation that characterized the postwar period, they did provide glimpses of what would subsequently emerge.

The development of this moderate corporate elite was driven in part by pressure from workers. Organized labor grew rapidly in the late 1930s and 1940s after the passage of the Wagner Act. It was in part due to the growth of the state in response to the Great Depression and the corresponding increase in the government's legitimacy and power. It was also due, however, to a view among segments of the corporate elite that they were responsible for the well-being of the larger society. As Weinstein (1968, x) put it, in describing the early NCF, "The key word in the new corporate vision of society was responsibility." To be sure, as Weinstein noted, the word had different meanings to different people. To social reformers it meant the need to improve the conditions of workers and the poor, while to businessmen it meant "the responsibility of all classes to maintain and increase the efficiency of the existing social order" (ibid., xi). Still, in its acknowledgement of responsibility to the larger society, along with its goal of cooperation between classes, the corporate elite of the NCF approached that of the postwar elite.

The postwar elite was unique nonetheless. Its members expressed a degree of moderation—especially with regard to the role of government in the economy—that was not approached either before or since. But as with the elite of the early twentieth century, its moderation was not born in a vacuum. It was a response to a set of conditions that, even if they originated in the actions of business, were now external to business itself. Three forces helped create and, especially, maintain the moderation that the corporate elite exhibited in the period from 1945 through approximately 1973: an increasingly large, relatively powerful, and relatively active state; a growing and increasingly strong labor movement; and a financial community centered in the largest commercial banks. The rise of the state and the labor movement precipitated the moderate reaction of the corporate elite, but the elite's accommodation to these forces further legitimated and strengthened them. It is to the role of these institutions that we now turn.

3 ||| The State and the Economy

It is widely assumed that government began to play a significant role in the American economy only in the 1930s. In fact, as a number of scholars have shown, the American state had already become an active force in the early nineteenth century (see, for example, Hartz 1948; Goodrich 1960). The government developed the corporation as a public institution, using it to build canals and to facilitate the expansion of the railroads (Dobbin 1994; Roy 1997). Later in the century, it became increasingly active in regulating the economy—establishing the Interstate Commerce Commission and the Federal Trade Commission, and passing the Sherman Antitrust Act (Cochran and Miller 1942; Weinstein 1968). By the beginning of the 1900s, the state even became involved in social amelioration, establishing programs for workers' compensation and soldiers' pensions. And the government's role in economic activity reached a peak not in the 1930s but during World War I.

It is therefore incorrect to suggest that massive state involvement in the American economy began with the New Deal. Government spending increased to be sure, nearly doubling as a percentage of gross domestic product between 1930 and 1940.[1] The most important development of the 1930s was not state involvement per se, however, but rather the conception of the state's proper role, as protector of both the economy and the citizenry. If the majority of American corporations rejected this new view, a sizable number (especially among the largest firms) made their peace with it and instead tried to influence its character. The growing legitimacy of the state's role in the economy—the idea that government had an obligation to manage the business cycle, to provide employment, and to protect the poor and underprivileged—was a new force with which business had to contend. And many of the leading firms decided to accept the new reality and to deal with it in a pragmatic fashion, much as the National Civic Federation had accepted the obstacles faced by business three decades earlier. By the end of World War II, most leaders of the largest firms had come to accept this enlarged government role. The moderate wing of the American corporate elite that had emerged during the 1930s reached increasing prominence during this period. In its willingness to accommodate to the state, its members developed a sophisticated brand of pragmatic politics.

This need to deal with a strong government was a new experience for American corporations. Certainly the state had been a presence, especially in its efforts to rein in the trusts during the Progressive Era. Yet the federal government at that time was also heavily under the sway of business, with relatively little ability to respond. Corruption was widespread, as leading businesspeople offered financial contributions without restraint (Josephson 1962 [1934]). By the 1930s, this business domination of government had changed. Corporations were powerful to be sure. Had they not been, it might not have been necessary for President Franklin D. Roosevelt to establish the Business Advisory Council. It became increasingly evident during the decade, however, that Roosevelt was determined to pursue his own agenda, regardless of whether he antagonized corporate leaders in the process. Yet by the end of World War II, an increasing number of business leaders had come to accept the new reality: the state was now a permanent fixture in economic policy making, and its role included a concern with maintaining high levels of employment, as well as providing a safety net under the society's most vulnerable members.

The Ideology of American Business

Although there has always been a significant amount of ideological diversity among American businesspeople, there have also been certain broadly held positions. Most American businesspeople have adhered to an ideology of laissez-faire capitalism. The central idea underpinning this view is the virtue of the autonomous individual, free from the constraints of external authority, especially that of the state. This personal freedom is focused primarily on the operation of one's enterprise, however. Freedoms outside the realm of business, such as those outlined in the Bill of Rights, have typically been seen as less important than those involved with commerce. It is not that American businesspeople oppose freedom of speech, assembly, and the press, but only that they have been more concerned with the freedom to run their business as they see fit.

Behind the emphasis on freedom was a belief in the value of free markets. There is some controversy about whether Adam Smith ultimately believed in the idea of an "invisible hand" that would ensure that the pursuit of one's self-interest would automatically result in a beneficial outcome for the larger society. But regardless of what Adam Smith believed, this was certainly the view of the majority of American businesspeople. If the free market was the optimal means of organizing the production and distribution of goods, then any interference in this process by the government had to be viewed with suspicion. Attempts to regulate commerce—to place a floor on wages or a ceiling on prices, to limit a firm's pursuit of market share, or to impose restrictions on a firm's packaging of its products or its treatment of its workers—were all seen as interfering with the efficient functioning of the free market. They were thus viewed as counterproductive not only for the firm but also for the society as a whole. Among the greatest evils that the state could permit was the ability of workers to organize, which businesspeople saw not only as an attempt to artificially restrict competition (unions were seen as cartels) but also as creating unfair constraints on a firm's decision making. These views—belief in the value of free markets, minimal government intervention in the economy, support for low levels of both business and personal taxes, and opposition to organized labor—are considered conservative in early twenty-first-century political discourse, and the association of business with these ideas is reflected in their general (albeit not unanimous) support for the Republican Party.

Although there is considerable truth in these stereotypical views of the ideology of American business, the reality is more complicated. First, although there has always been a degree of ideological purity in some segments of the American business community, there has been a level of pragmatism as well. American business leaders have often been willing to suspend ideological doctrine when conditions warranted it. This has re-sulted in a history of complex, and frequently contradictory, attitudes and behavior. Members of the coal industry discovered in the late 1800s that free market competition was leading them to ruin. Attempts to construct a cartel that would maintain a profitable industry-wide price repeatedly failed. Ultimately, members of the industry came to accept not only unionization—which, paradoxically, allowed them to profit by forcing them to maintain an above-market, industry-wide price—but also to accept a degree of government regulation (Bowman 1989). Members of several other indus-tries eventually welcomed regulation as well. In the 1880s, railroad inter-ests came to see the benefits of federal regulation as a means of preventing destructive competition (Kolko 1965; Fligstein 1990, 86–87). Producers in the sugar industry supported the Sugar Act of 1948, which reallocated previously established quotas on production (Berle 1954, 50). Oil company executives supported the limits on production stipulated in the Interstate Oil Compact of 1935 (Leach 1957). And the airline industry supported the regulations of the Civil Aeronautics Board that provided a steady stream of profits from the 1940s into the 1970s (Lawrence 2004). Moreover, despite concerns about interference in the market, American business leaders ex-pressed considerable support for a broad-based antitrust policy (Krooss 1970, 313–314) as well as the need for the Federal Reserve Bank (as we saw in Chapter 2).

Business Ideology and the Depression

If American businesspeople occasionally allowed pragmatism to trump ideology, their ideology remained overwhelmingly in support of the free market through the 1920s. The Depression led to a reassessment, however. How, if the free market was a self-correcting system, could such a massive breakdown occur? Business leaders were not the only ones asking this ques-tion, of course, and to this day economists have not come to an agreement on the Depression's causes. There was no shortage of attempts to explain this event. Interestingly, however, American businesspeople appeared to adopt a crude form of Keynesian economics in the 1920s, before Keynes's ideas had even begun to influence American thinking.

There are two components of the Keynesian position that concern us here. First, Keynes argued that the downturn was caused by insufficient spending. A corollary to this, although not argued directly by Keynes himself, was the idea that a lack of demand among the consuming public as a whole was the primary cause of the Depression. Although bankers were focused primarily on monetary policy as the main cause of the crisis, industrialists and merchants were focused primarily on the relation between production and consumption. Some saw the problem as overproduction. The Chamber of Commerce, for example, produced a report in 1931 suggesting that excessive speculation created a situation in which production had outstripped consumption (Krooss 1970, 144). Others focused on the flip side of the problem, a lack of sufficient demand and thus spending. The reasons offered for this "underconsumption" were varied. Paul Mazur of Lehman Brothers attributed it to an inadequate supply of money, which led to high interest rates. Edward Filene and Henry Dennison, in contrast, blamed excessive saving and inadequate wages, suggesting the need for a more equitable distribution of income (ibid., 145). One goal of the New Deal, which became a rationale for government intervention in support of disadvantaged segments of the society, was to increase the purchasing power of the general population. Because the wealthy tended to save a much higher percentage of their income, while the working class and the poor by necessity had to spend virtually all that they made, it made sense to provide support for lower-income families.

The second key component of Keynes's argument involved the consequences of what he viewed as excessive saving. In a downturn, families tend to tighten their belts to conserve whatever income they have. By neglecting to spend, however, consumers actually exacerbate the problem, a phenomenon referred to by Keynes as the "paradox of thrift." With little prospect of profits, it made little sense for businesses to invest, Keynes argued, even when interest rates were low. Under these circumstances, the only entity with sufficient power to break this cycle was the government. Keynes thus advocated significant government spending, even if it meant running a deficit. At the time, most economists and businesspeople were strongly committed to a balanced federal budget, which was seen as a necessity in almost religious terms. The idea that deficit spending could actually benefit the economy faced strong opposition from virtually all quarters. The combined local branches of the Chamber of Commerce, for example, voted 1,173 to 6 in favor of a balanced budget during this period (Krooss 1970, 155). Roosevelt himself was so strongly committed to a balanced budget that in 1937 he inadvertently created a spike in unemployment by attempting—prematurely in the views of Keynesian economists—to balance the budget. Even Gerard Swope, who (as we saw in Chapter 2) was among the most liberal members of the business community, stressed the importance of a balanced budget (ibid.). The state's role, in this view, amounted to little beyond balancing the budget and regulating the money supply.

As Roosevelt's popularity continued to increase, the power of the state relative to business began to shift, however. It reached a peak as the United States entered the war in 1941. At this point, the restriction of federal spending, deficit or no deficit, was no longer an option. Keynes had remarked that only in war would there be an opportunity to provide a genuine test of his argument. "It is, it seems, politically impossible for a capitalistic democracy to organize expenditure on the scale necessary to make the grand experiment which would prove my case—except in war conditions," Keynes stated in a *New Republic* article (1940, 158) published more than a year before the United States entered the war. Once the U.S. entered the war, the government did spend, to a greater extent than at any point in history, and the Depression rapidly disappeared, as Keynes had predicted.

Postwar Keynesianism

How, then, did American business leaders deal with the growing role of government in the economy and with Keynesian ideas in particular? In a study detailing the ways in which American business leaders responded to the government's use of Keynesian economics, Robert Collins (1981) notes that there was a range of possible applications of Keynes's ideas. On one side there were liberals, such as Harvard economics professors Alvin Hansen and, later, John Kenneth Galbraith, who advocated increased expenditures on social programs, including infrastructure, education, and unemployment insurance (a position that Galbraith eloquently advanced in a 1952 article in the *New York Times Magazine;* see Galbraith 1952b). On the other side there were more conservative spokespersons, such as the leadership of the Chamber of Commerce, who preferred that the spending be directed toward national defense, with a minimum earmarked for social needs. Most business leaders who accepted Keynesian ideas preferred the latter approach.

Keynes himself, as evidenced by the above quote, had expressed pessimism that business forces would accept a serious government effort to meet social needs, because such programs would make inroads into areas that might otherwise provide opportunities for private profit. Writing in the 1960s, neo-Marxist economists Paul Baran and Paul Sweezy (1966) echoed a similar theme, arguing that such spending would be impossible within an advanced capitalist economy. The opposition by health insurance companies to Democratic proposals for a "public option" in the 2010 health care bill provides a recent example consistent with this argument. Baran and Sweezy may have overstated the impossibility of significant social spending under capitalism in general. Several countries in Western Europe, most notably in Scandinavia, have maintained such systems, albeit with increasing difficulty in recent years. Still, in the United States it was clear that social welfare spending faced a level of intense and effective opposition, even in the relatively moderate postwar period.

Yet even in the United States there were significant elements within the corporate elite that did exhibit support for, or at least acceptance of, a modest level of social spending. This included support for the Employment Act of 1946—its full-employment mandate watered down to be sure, but supported at least in principle. It included acceptance of New Deal programs, including the expansion of Social Security, even under Dwight Eisenhower's presidency. And it included outright support for elements of Lyndon Johnson's Great Society programs in the 1960s. Even business support for John F. Kennedy's 1963 tax cut represented a major new turn in corporate economic ideology: a willingness to accept deficit spending.

In the remainder of this chapter I will illustrate the role played by the moderate corporate elite in economic and social policies during the postwar period, dating from the war's end into the early 1970s. My focus will be primarily on the Committee for Economic Development (CED), which remains the clearest organizational expression of this pragmatism. As we shall see, however, the moderation exhibited by the American corporate elite extended well beyond the CED. Even the otherwise extremely conservative National Association of Manufacturers (NAM) moderated its positions at certain points. As I have suggested, this moderation among the American corporate elite was a function of three significant forces: the state, organized labor, and the financial community. In this chapter, the focus will be on the first of these forces: a state that, in the wake of the Great

Depression, played an increasingly active role in ameliorating the excesses of the free market. In pursuing these policies, the state acquired a high level of legitimacy, creating a significant presence of what Galbraith (1952a) called "countervailing power," with which the corporate elite was forced to contend.

The Corporate Elite after the War

In the period leading up to America's entry into the war, the NAM actually flirted with the possibility of embracing some aspects of Keynesianism. In papers produced in 1940 and 1941, the group admitted the possibility that deficit financing might be a feasible strategy (Collins 1981, 87). Ironically, according to Collins, the NAM was able to envision deficit spending only on New Deal–type programs, however, and was thus unable to see the possibility that military spending might play a similar role in stimulating the economy. Ultimately, the group reverted to its traditional conservatism on fiscal policy, rendering it increasingly irrelevant in policy circles (ibid., 88).

The Chamber of Commerce, in contrast, moved in a different direction. The passage of New Deal legislation in the 1930s had created conflict within the group and resulted in the appointment of a new leader, Eric A. Johnston, in 1942. Frustrated with the group's apparent inability to be heard during the debates over the New Deal, Johnston advocated a more moderate approach to the state (Collins 1981, 88–93). This included a search for "areas of accord" between the Chamber and the government, as well as a general willingness to accept change and to work to influence its direction rather than continuing to offer wholesale resistance, as the NAM had done. Among the changes under Johnston's leadership was an increased acceptance of Keynesian thought, albeit in a relatively conservative form. This accommodation was a direct consequence of the growing power and legitimacy of both the government and organized labor. As Collins put it:

> Foremost among the changed conditions confronting the Chamber were the increased stature and power of labor and government; recognition that these rivals had valid roles to play in the political economy constituted another element in the Chamber's new *Weltanschaunng* [worldview]. Believing firmly that the old free-booting laissez faire of the nineteenth century was

dead, [Johnston] advocated a "new capitalism" which, while resolute in its opposition to "super-statism," recognized nonetheless that "the role of government must keep pace with change—the game has become so complicated that government in its legitimate character of umpire has vastly more to do." (Collins 1981, 91)

Johnston also aimed to move the Chamber beyond its traditional hostility toward labor, which he viewed as a "primitive stage," characterized by "illogical prejudices and blind opposition." Instead, he advocated acceptance of "collective bargaining as 'an established and useful reality'" (ibid., 91–92).[2]

Part of the Chamber's motivation for this position was that it wanted to avoid being completely left out of the discussion, as had occurred with the NAM. The Chamber's view at the time, not unlike that of the CED, was that it could accomplish more, including reining in the more liberal proponents of Keynesianism, by accepting government's role in the economy and then attempting to place limits on it.

Among the most important issues for business leaders in the postwar period was the fate of the American work force. There was widespread agreement that the massive spending effort on the war had lifted the nation out of the Great Depression. Now that the war was over, business was faced with two enormous concerns. On one hand, as military spending wound down, there was concern that the consequent absence of government stimulus could result in a return to depression. On the other hand, the return of troops from overseas threatened to exacerbate an already precarious employment picture.

Business was not of a single mind on what could be done to stave off the anticipated downturn. Paul Hoffman, the chairman of the CED, made a case for government intervention to ensure a high level of employment: "Private business has little to do with maintaining high levels of employment, and . . . there is little that local government can do. It follows, therefore, that the government must take certain steps if we are to achieve high levels of employment" (Collins 1981, 86). Still, when Senator James Murray (D-Montana) introduced a full-employment bill in 1945, the Chamber of Commerce, despite its recent moderate turn, opposed it on the ground that it was not the government's role to guarantee a right to employment. The Chamber did support an alternative version of the bill, however, closer to the one that eventually passed. This bill did not ensure full employment, but it did at least affirm that the idea of full employment was a good one in principle.[3] The bill that passed established the Council of Economic Advisers and institutionalized the idea that the government had a role in at least helping facilitate full employment, if not mandating it. Moreover, the Chamber's Committee on Economic Policy proposed a series of countercyclical measures for government to take during recessions, including public works, tax reductions, and a willingness to engage in deficit spending to meet these needs (Collins 1981, 110).

Despite Hoffman's early support for government-sponsored employment, the CED's views on the bill as it emerged were more complicated. Although the CED had made clear that it was not a lobbying group (and therefore did not try as an organization to directly influence the passage of bills), individuals within the group often testified before Congress, and they were willing to express public views on particular legislation, as well as propose ideas. Some members of the group initially expressed support for Senator Murray's bill, despite reservations (Schriftgiesser 1960, 87–92). Noting that "government expenditure is one of the most important weapons in the arsenal for fighting unemployment," Ralph Flanders expressed enthusiastic support:

> This is an epoch making bill. . . . This right to a job is a right which I myself have come, after much thought, to accept as an objective which our society may attain. . . . The man or woman out of work has the right to expect that all responsible elements of society, and particularly the government, will use all appropriate and effective means to assist his own best effort in finding productive and profitable work. (Schriftgiesser 1960, 94–95)

Ruml was more reluctant to support the bill, as were Hoffman and even Flanders, both of whom pulled back from their earlier positions. Hoffman, in hearings before the Senate Committee on Banking and Currency, spoke in favor of government public works employment:

> Through public services and public works, we the people, acting through our Government, protect and strengthen our natural resources, human and material; lift up the standards of health, education, and welfare for ourselves and our children at all levels of individual income; mitigate individual

misfortune; and execute projects not appropriate to private action. Even when the general level of business activity is satisfactory, public works and other public services may be helpful in coping with temporarily depressed conditions in a local or regional area. (U.S. Congress, Senate 1945, 707)

Although Hoffman testified that "there were many and varied types of government action that could contribute to full employment" (U.S. Congress, Senate 1945, 713), he suggested that the government stop short of issuing an iron-clad guarantee. The "most vital function of government," he argued, "is to establish conditions under which the free enterprise system can operate most effectively and to counteract the tendencies in the system toward booms and depressions" (ibid., 708). Drawing on a CED publication that appeared around the same time, *Toward More Production, More Jobs, and More Freedom* (1945b), of which he was the principal author, Hoffman proposed establishing a President's Commission on Full Employment. The establishment of the Council of Economic Advisers, which became the primary accomplishment of the final bill, was, according to Schriftgiesser (1960, 99), "inspired to a great extent by the CED commission plan."

The Chamber's (Partial) Right Turn and the CED's Continued Moderation

As for the Chamber of Commerce, the group's relatively moderate views during the postwar period were largely a result of Johnston's leadership. In his farewell speech in 1946, Johnston made a final plea to the Chamber to support the new capitalism, "stripped of the ancient prejudices against organized labor, government activity, and community planning." "We in business must liberalize," he stated, "or face the threat of economic liquidation" (Collins 1981, 121–122). After Johnston resigned under pressure from the organization's rank-and-file, the Chamber reverted to its more traditional antigovernment stance, closer to the position of the NAM. But it did not retreat fully to this position. Instead, the economists in the Chamber's research department continued to accept the basic tenets of Keynesian economics. Although Johnston's replacement, William Jackson, moved the group in a more conservative direction, he did not return the group to, as Collins puts it, the "sullen negativism of the late thirties" (ibid., 118–122).[4]

As the Chamber returned, at least partially, to its traditional conservatism, the CED maintained its moderation. The group issued several documents near the end of the war that evinced its willingness to accept a benevolent role for the state. In *A Postwar Federal Tax Plan for High Employment* (Committee for Economic Development 1944)—to which Hoffman referred in his Senate testimony—the organization's Research Committee argued that taxes would have to remain high—between two and three times any previous peacetime high—to achieve high postwar employment. Although the committee recommended a reduction in taxation of business and a reduction of the top income tax rate to 53.6 percent (well above the current top rate of 35 percent, but well below the 90 percent that prevailed at the time), it also advocated an income tax that would rise "progressively with ability to pay" (ibid., 7) and a reduction in sales taxes (which, as the group stated, are notably regressive). Moreover, in a 1945 document that anticipated the final version of the Employment Act of 1946, the CED's Research Committee expressed a clear willingness to support deficit spending as an appropriate government policy under particular conditions. Although the document made clear that an increase in the public debt should be avoided, the group also "generally agreed that attempting to balance the budget *every* year is impractical," and that "an attempt to balance in a depression year might work against recovery" (Committee for Economic Development 1945b, 32; emphasis in the original). Hoffman expanded on this position in a 1946 article in the *New York Times,* as well as a 1947 speech at a convention of the insurance company New York Life. In the former, he argued, in Keynesian-like fashion, that instability in capitalism is due to insufficient demand. To increase demand, Hoffman suggested that government should strengthen unemployment compensation, spend on public works projects during economic downturns, and promote research and education. It was essential that government and business cooperate, Hoffman argued, and he saw no contradiction between free market capitalism and a significant government role in the economy. "The major emphasis which capitalism places on the individual does not preclude collective activity," he stated. "As a matter of fact, the interests of the individual can be advanced only through a wide range of collective actions, both governmental and private" (Hoffman 1946, SM3). In the 1947 speech, Hoffman advocated unemployment compensation, public spending, and tax cuts as mechanisms that government could use to counter downswings in the business cycle (*New York Times* [hereafter *NYT*], April 11, 1947, 33).

The CED's efforts as a nonlobbying group standing "above the fray" were reflected in the support it gained from academic, government, and even labor officials. According to an article in the *New York Times* (May 26, 1946), the group's ability to generate this support was to a great extent a result of its effort to place the national interest above the interests of the business community per se. This broad support was matched by intense opposition from traditional segments of the business community, as reflected in the frequent scathing editorials attacking the group in the *Wall Street Journal*.[5] That the group was highly influential was apparent in a number of ways. Hoffman was the sole nongovernment official in a meeting with President Truman and Treasury Secretary John W. Snyder devoted to strategies for combating inflation (*NYT*, July 3, 1946, 1). So many CED members joined Truman's administration that the group was forced to call a meeting to replenish its ranks (*NYT*, January 13, 1947, 28).

In addition to its crucial role in the Employment Act of 1946 and its role in promoting deficit financing, the CED was heavily involved in the formation of the International Monetary Fund and the development of the Marshall Plan. In a 1947 speech, Marshall, President Truman's secretary of state, had proposed a major reconstruction program for Western Europe. In response to this, Truman appointed nineteen individuals to a Committee on Foreign Aid (Schriftgiesser 1960, 127–128). Nine of the nineteen members were businessmen, and five of those nine were CED trustees. An issue that immediately divided the committee was whether to condition aid to Western European countries on their renunciation of European Welfare State programs such as Britain's national health care system, which the committee viewed as "socialist." Playing a mediating role in the controversy, Hoffman insisted that American aid should not be dependent on the governments' economic and social policies, as long as those policies were "consistent with basic democratic principles" (quoted in Schriftgiesser 1960, 128–129). Hoffman did find it necessary to add (and undoubtedly believed) that "the American system of free enterprise is the best method of obtaining high productivity," but he also maintained that the proposed foreign aid should not "be used as a means of requiring other countries to adopt it" (ibid.). Hoffman became the administrator of the program after the Economic Cooperation Act (the Marshall Plan) was passed.

The End of the CED?

When the CED was established, many members of both the NAM and the Chamber of Commerce viewed the organization as a threat, a rival business group with an alternative (and to many, unacceptable) perspective. In response to this, the CED had reached an informal agreement with the NAM and the Chamber that it would disband after the war (Schriftgiesser 1960, 71). Once the war was over, however, the CED's trustees were reluctant to close down the organization.[6]

In addition to its board of trustees, the CED was organized in two divisions: the Research Division and the Field Development Division (Schriftgiesser 1960, 35). The Research Division, led by Ralph Flanders, was concerned primarily with drafting position papers suggesting possible policy initiatives, as exemplified by the 1944 *Federal Tax Plan for Postwar Employment.* The Field Development Division, led by Marion Folsom, consisted of local affiliates of the national organization. To organize these affiliates, Folsom recruited Cyril Scott Fletcher, a salesman and assistant to Paul Hoffman at Studebaker, to run the operation. Fletcher led a drive that ultimately created nearly 3,000 local branches of the CED. These branches, which were typically led by prominent local businesspeople, engaged in a mutual dialogue with the national headquarters in developing ideas for postwar economic conversion. As the CED described it in a 1946 report:

> The Field Development Division, a task force organized to encourage bold and realistic postwar planning by businessmen, set up approximately 2,900 local CED committees—in most communities of 10,000 population or over as well as in many smaller towns and villages. Over 60,000 individual businessmen, volunteer members of these local CEDs, were in contact with an important segment of the nation's 2,000,000 business employers. Each CED community committee had complete autonomy in developing its own program for more production, sales, and jobs after victory. In all cases local CEDs worked in close cooperation with other organizations. . . . Nationally, the Field Development Division acted as a clearing house for the best ideas on company planning. It sought to provide CED community committees, and through them individual businessmen, with all possible assistance in working out sound plans for expanded peacetime operation. This assistance took the form of handbooks, sound slidefilms, charts, etc., suggesting step-by-step

planning procedures. To prepare this material, CED mobilized the nation's outstanding experts in various phases of business activity—management, sales, advertising, marketing, etc. These experts, formed into twenty-seven Action and Advisory Committees, pooled their "know-how" for the benefit of all businessmen. (Committee for Economic Development 1946, 17; see Schifeling 2011 for a more detailed discussion)

As the war came to a close, the CED's leadership was forced to confront its original agreement to disband. With regret, the organization concluded that it would be necessary to close down the Field Development Division. Fletcher suggested that the division be absorbed into the Chamber of Commerce, an idea deemed feasible because of the Chamber's moderate leadership under Eric Johnston. Both Fletcher and Hoffman held a series of meetings with the Chamber in an attempt to work out an agreement. Opposition within the Chamber led to the eventual failure of this plan, however, and the Field Development Division was dissolved.[7] In contrast, Hoffman was reluctant to end the work of the Research Division. As he put it, "There are still a number of important studies under way dealing with long-range problems—*maintaining* high employment. We cannot solve our problems by ignorant change or ignorant opposition to change" (quoted in Schriftgiesser 1960, 75; emphasis in the original). Encouraged by a letter from Harrison Jones (the chairman of Coca Cola), the CED's trustees voted unanimously to maintain the Research Division. The initial decision was to continue for between eighteen months and three years (ibid., 75–76). As it turned out, the organization forged ahead, publishing eighty research reports between 1950 and 1970 alone (Schifeling 2011). Although the CED is no longer a significant force in the national policy arena, it continues to exist more than six decades after the reading of Jones's letter.

The 1950s

One might argue that the moderate elements within the business community were able to exercise influence in the 1940s because of the presence of Democratic presidential administrations. This suggestion would be an overstatement, however. As we have already seen, most of the leading moderate businesspeople were in fact Republicans. Hoffman was a Republican, as was Folsom, who later served as President Eisenhower's secretary of health, education, and welfare (Derthick 1979, 68). Ralph Flanders, the pioneering CED official, was elected to the U.S. Senate from Vermont in 1946 as a Republican. Moreover, the political ascendancy of the moderate elite continued in the 1950s, during a Republican administration.

President Eisenhower had been a trustee of the CED in the years prior to his election, and his early appointments included numerous CED members. As *Business Week* noted, there was "a marked similarity between CED and the new administration." "Both," the magazine continued, "represent the views of a particular type of forward-looking businessmen, a sort of progressive conservatism" (quoted in Schriftgiesser 1960, 162; see also Griffith 1982). As it turned out, the CED's subsequent influence in the administration never approached what its members had hoped. Still, the group had its moments of success. In 1953, in the midst of a recession, the administration announced its intention to balance the budget and reduce the national debt (ibid., 165). The Chamber of Commerce and the NAM supported the idea of a balanced budget, but only if it was accompanied by a reduction of both the personal income tax and an excess profits tax that was on the books at the time. The CED, on the other hand, was willing to support the tax reductions proposed by the Chamber and the NAM, but only if Congress was able to reduce expenditures sufficient to balance the budget while simultaneously retaining a high level of employment. President Eisenhower supported the CED's position, against the wishes of both the Chamber and the NAM. The *New York Times* took note of the CED's willingness to exercise responsibility in this regard. As the *Times* put it in an editorial:

> No one familiar with the views of CED doubts that it detests the excess profits tax quite as thoroughly as do the NAM and the Chamber of Commerce. But the CED has not permitted either its detestation or its zeal for tax relief to blind it to the central issue involved. (*NYT,* June 10, 1953, 28)

Although by Schriftgiesser's own admission the CED appeared to lose influence with the Eisenhower administration over time, it would be a mistake to assume that this reflected a decline in the moderate orientation of the corporate elite. On the contrary, the influence of the moderates in the national political discourse, even if not directly reflected in the CED's power as an organization, was evident in a number of ways. Eisenhower's own policies were, to the disappointment of many more traditional elements in the business community, continually moderate. This included an increase in Social Security payments, as well as the expansion of the program to include agricultural workers, a move advocated by Folsom (Jacoby 1993, 525).[8] Eisenhower's treasury secretary, George M. Humphrey, himself a former CED trustee, went so far as to suggest the possibility of a "broad public works program" if the economy failed to recover during the 1953 recession, a policy consistent with the CED's recommendations (Schrift-giesser 1960, 169–171). Eisenhower was also willing to entertain the possibility of deficit spending, despite his own distaste for the idea.[9] Meanwhile, even if the CED had lost some of its power over time, the group's influence remained substantial. The organization's chairman, Donald David, noted in 1957 that "at every major economic watershed of these past 15 years you will find a reservoir of CED research and recommendations" (quoted in Collins 1981, 142). However self-serving David's comment may have been—he was speaking to a meeting of the organization's trustees—it is still notable, in that the powerful are in so many cases either unaware of or reluctant to acknowledge their influence.[10] Whether located within the CED or elsewhere, the moderate views within the corporate elite were the ones that prevailed during this period.

A 1956 article in *Time,* which was reprinted as a full-page advertisement for the magazine in the *Wall Street Journal* two weeks after President Eisenhower's reelection, illustrates the extent to which moderate ideas dominated in the corporate discourse of the time. Commenting on what it called the "new conservatism," the article hailed the rise of moderate thinking by the corporate elite. Portions of this revealing article are worth quoting at length:

> Though ultraconservative businessmen (and many liberals) thought in 1952 that a G.O.P. victory would be a triumph for reaction, they sadly misjudged the temper of the times. By conserving and enlarging the social programs inherited from the New and Fair Deals, the Eisenhower Administration helped set a course for the new conservative. Instead of returning to a dog-eat-dog economy, Administration trustbusters have vigilantly policed big business. The Administration has expanded social security, federal aid to hospitals, low-cost housing subsidies, and other programs that were once anathema to the standpat [*sic*] conservative. (*Wall Street Journal* [hereafter *WSJ*], November 21, 1956, 13)

Numerous business leaders are quoted in the article, all of whom express support for the kind of moderation noted above, as, for example, in the following:

> Though businessmen fought a long delaying action against the growth of labor unions, against Government intervention in economic affairs, against social legislation, the majority now realize that welfare programs help store up purchasing power in the hands of the consumer. Says Gaylord A. Freeman Jr., vice president of the First National Bank of Chicago: "I think social security is good. I think unions are good. Unemployment compensation is desirable. Social legislation can add to the totality of freedom, increase the dignity of the individual." (*WSJ*, November 21, 1956, 13)

This support of government activism extended to regulation as well:

> Businessmen who once decried Government meddling in the economy also recognize that most federal police powers, e.g. regulation of the stock market, benefit business as well as the consumer. Most businessmen today agree with Du Pont Chairman Walter S. Carpenter Jr. that the anti-trust laws, under which his company has been haled [*sic*] into court 22 times, "are fair and should be vigorously enforced." Though some businessmen still argue publicly that the Federal Government should stop regulating business, the majority agree privately that Government intervention is preferable to the economy of the jungle. (*WSJ*, November 21, 1956, 13)

The authors of this article make no pretense to having conducted a scientific study, and they may have exaggerated when they claimed that a majority of business figures supported the kind of government activism that the article describes. Yet Herman Krooss (1970), in a more scholarly examination of business opinion, provided evidence consistent with the magazine's conclusions: "What was different about the post-1954 era," Krooss argued, "was that a great many more businessmen freely accepted the so-called 'New Economics' [by which he meant Keynesian ideas] with its compensatory fiscal policy and among businessmen in general there was less reluctance to espouse the notion that the government should run a deficit in times of depression" (1970, 250). Some of this was a result of President Eisenhower's acceptance of (or at least unwillingness to repeal) the policies of the Roosevelt and Truman administrations, Krooss argued. "Some of the things that had been abhorred in the New Deal and the Fair Deal, notably deficit spending, an unbalanced budget, and more government regulation, were accepted by most of the business community when they came wrapped in a different package, tied with different intellectual string" (ibid., 251). Although there were some public expressions of dissatisfaction with Eisenhower, most notably in a speech by H. E. Humphreys of United States Rubber, Krooss indicates that Humphreys "was definitely in the minority of business leaders. The majority, having watched Ike's administration and having found it to their liking, resigned themselves to the fact that big government was here to stay" (ibid., 251–252).

Sputnik

A telling event that highlights the differences between the postwar corporate elite and its twenty-first-century counterpart was the elite's response to the Soviet Union's launching of the Sputnik satellite in 1957. As we saw in Chapter 1, this event caught American officials, the news media, and the public by surprise and shocked policy makers into concern that the United States was being eclipsed by its Communist rival. Although President Eisenhower seemed less concerned, others, including Senators Lyndon Johnson and Mike Mansfield, saw the situation as grave and recommended a significant national response. In the following year, the government increased support to the National Science Foundation by nearly 300 percent (and by nearly an additional 300 percent over the next decade). Funding for education in general was also increased. During this period, the CED issued a report, *Paying for Better Public Schools* (1959), in which the group advocated increased funding, including federal support, for primary and secondary education. This was an important, and even courageous, step for the CED to take at the time, given that conservatives had long held that the federal government should not be involved in the funding of primary and secondary education. The group's position on this issue reflected its concern for the well-being of the broader society, in that its focus was not only on the expansion of education in science and technology (the fields most closely associated with direct military application) but with education broadly conceived. On one hand, as one might expect, the report notes:

The whole nation has been shocked into awareness of a great threat to our national security. That a connection exists between our precarious security position and our educational system has become widely appreciated. This connection is sometimes found in the training of scientists and engineers. It is sometimes found in high rates of draft rejection for illiteracy and the inadequate background of many who are accepted into the military services. But the connection between education and security is even more general and basic than this. (Committee for Economic Development 1959, 10)

On the other hand, the report goes considerably beyond the need for training scientists and military personnel:

We have not sufficiently valued intellectual achievement—either in what we paid for it or in the respect and freedom we gave it. This applies to all fields of intellectual endeavor, and not merely to the sciences. Education's responsibility for national security extends far beyond the training of scientists and servicemen. It extends to the influence that education exerts upon the ability of people to understand the alternatives before them and choose wisely among the real alternatives. The real danger to our security arises from the fact that we are not using our resources as wisely as we could. (Committee for Economic Development 1959, 10–11)

Here we see, similar to the views expressed in the *Time* article, an understanding that a democratic society requires well-rounded citizens, educated in a variety of fields, with an understanding of the social as well as the physical world. In contrast, even when contemporary elites acknowledge the importance of education, as in a 2006 report by the Business Roundtable, *Tapping America's Potential,* the focus is exclusively on science and mathematics education. The CED's effort in 1960 to forge a compromise solution to expand federal funding for education was unsuccessful. Yet its views ultimately prevailed, as funding at both the K–12 and university levels increased rapidly during the 1960s.

It is evident, then, that the Eisenhower administration, despite its traditional conservative constituency, displayed a degree of pragmatism consistent with (and supported by) the moderate corporate elite that prevailed during the postwar period. Eisenhower's economic adviser, Arthur Burns, had noted in a 1955 speech that "today there is substantial agreement among Americans that the Federal government cannot remain aloof from what goes on in the private economy, that the government must strive to foster an expanding economy, and that the government has definite responsibility to do all it can to prevent depressions" (quoted in Collins 1981, 14). The eight years of his presidency indicated that Eisenhower had fully accepted this view.

The 1963 Tax Cut

Although it is difficult to imagine in the political climate of the twenty-first century, there was a time when American corporations were so concerned with balanced budgets that they were regularly willing to either support tax increases or oppose tax cuts. Although business leaders preferred that the government cut spending before raising taxes, the need for a balanced budget was taken as virtually an article of faith. Even Franklin Roosevelt, the president most historically identified with increasing the role of government, was committed to a balanced budget. As we have seen, this commitment was so strong that Roosevelt was willing to reduce spending in 1937 to the point that, according to many analysts, he triggered a recession just when it appeared that the United States was emerging from the Great Depression (Stein 1969, 115–116).

Yet as we have also seen, Keynes's great innovation was the idea that government, by spending—even to the point of running a deficit—could stimulate economic activity sufficiently to resuscitate a recession-afflicted economy. Although corporate leaders began to slowly accept this idea, as Roosevelt himself ultimately (albeit grudgingly) had, they remained reluctant to advocate a significant tax cut as an explicit government policy. Herbert Stein, the CED's primary economist (and later the chairman of the Council of Economic Advisers under Richard Nixon), had raised the possibility of deliberate deficit spending in a 1954 report, but the idea of a significant cut in the personal income tax had not, during Eisenhower's presidency, made its way into the policy arena.

Like his predecessors, John F. Kennedy was a proponent of balanced budgets. Kennedy assumed office in the midst of a recession, and his advisors had suggested a tax cut to stimulate the economy. Kennedy was reluctant, in part because he believed that the idea ran counter to his larger call for Americans to sacrifice for the good of the nation (Collins 1981, 179), but also because of his concern about running a deficit. According to both Collins (ibid.) and Stein (1969, 74), it was only after the business community, including the Chamber of Commerce and even the NAM as well as the CED, made it clear that it was willing to support the cuts, even with the resulting deficits, that Kennedy was convinced to proceed. As Stein put it, "The changed attitude of the business community is an important part of the story of the revolution in fiscal policy from the 1930s to the 1960s" (ibid.).

The degree of unity among these different business groups was notable. As we have seen, it was the CED, rather than the NAM and the Chamber (except briefly, during Johnston's term as chair), that represented the moderate wing of the business community on economic policy. Yet all three groups supported the tax cut. One could argue, of course, that it is easy for businesses to support reduced taxes, something we know from twenty-first-century American politics. After all, as Stein pointed out (1969, 74), the idea of tax cuts could be viewed as fully compatible with—perhaps even identical to—the concept of spending cuts that had prevailed in earlier decades. It was not only on taxes that business unity had increased, however. By the 1950s, Krooss argues (1970, 248), business political opinion in general had become more homogenous, although divisions remained on government fiscal policy.

The Corporate Elite and the Great Society

As the 1960s progressed, the corporate elite broadened its focus from economic concerns and education to a wider social agenda. Some of this was reflected not in anything that business leaders did but in what they did not do. As Lyndon Johnson launched the most ambitious set of social legislation since the New Deal, there was virtually no public opposition from large corporations (Vogel 1989, 24–25).[11] If businessmen were not significantly involved in the War on Poverty or the establishment of Medicare (whose only significant organized opposition came from the American Medical Association, a conservative group at the time), neither did they speak out against these programs. Moreover, in some cases corporate leaders actively supported the Great Society. In 1966, for example, a group of twenty-two chief executives drafted a statement in support of President Johnson's "Demonstration Cities" bill. The goal of this bill was the rehabilitation of urban slum areas, primarily through the building of new housing. The bill passed in the Senate but faced a series of attacks by Republicans in the House. In response to this, the businessmen, led by Edgar F. Kaiser of Kaiser Industries and Ben Heineman of the Chicago and North Western Railway (both of whom were members of the presidential task force on the bill), drafted a statement expressing strong support for the project. "The most pressing domestic problem of our time is the problem of the American city," the letter states. "Our cities are being submerged by a rising tide of confluent forces—disease and dispair [sic], joblessness and hopelessness, excessive dependence on welfare payments, and the grim threats of crime, disorder, and delinquency." After describing the Demonstration Cities Act, the authors stated that "as responsible and deeply concerned citizens over the future of American cities, we urge prompt passage of this, the single most important domestic proposal before the Congress."[12] The twenty-two signers of the letter appear in Table 3.1.

As is evident from the table, the signers of this letter represented some of the most respected and visible chief executives of leading American firms. Eleven of the twenty-two were at various points trustees of the CED; among those who were not CED members were such distinguished figures as David Rockefeller of Chase Manhattan Bank, Thomas S. Gates Jr. of Morgan Guaranty Trust, and Kaiser. Nor were these people associated with corporations that stood to gain an immediate advantage from urban renewal projects. Certainly banks can benefit from an increase in urban real estate values, as J. Allen Whitt (1982) showed in his study of the Bay Area Rapid Transit System, and slum clearance projects not only promised to improve land values but also to potentially enrich the coffers of the companies that secured government contracts to build. Yet it seems unclear how companies such as Ford, General Electric, IBM, and Chevron (Standard Oil of California) could have had a major stake in these contracts. If they did stand to benefit it was primarily indirectly, through whatever reductions in poverty might have ensued. The support of these businessmen for the Demonstration Cities Act is difficult to reconcile with a motive of short-term self-interest. It serves instead as evidence of a sense of responsibility for the larger society that revealed itself in the postwar era but rarely surfaced by the twenty-first century.[13]

Housing was not the only social issue on which the postwar corporate elite took a moderate stand. The CED continued to press for increased fed-

Table 3.1   Businessmen Who Signed Letter Supporting the Demonstration Cities Act

Name	Position	Firm
Stephen D. Bechtel	Chairman	Bechtel Corporation
Fred J. Borch	President and CEO	General Electric
Howard L. Clark	President and CEO	American Express
Donald Cook	President	American Electric Power Service Corporation
Justin Dart	President	Rexall Drug and Chemical Company
R. Gwin Follis	Chairman	Standard Oil of California
Henry Ford II	Chairman and CEO	Ford Motor Company
Thomas S. Gates Jr.	Chairman and CEO	Morgan Guaranty Trust
Ben Heineman	Chairman and CEO	Chicago and North Western Railway
Edgar F. Kaiser	President	Kaiser Industries
David Kennedy	Chairman and CEO	Continental Illinois National Bank & Trust
Robert Lehman	Chairman and CEO	Lehman Brothers
John McCone	Investment banker	
Cyril J. Magnin	President	Joseph Magnin Company
Stanley Marcus	President	Neiman-Marcus
Alfred E. Perlman	President and chief administrative officer	Pennsylvania New York Central Transportation Co.
Herman H. Pevler	President	Norfolk & Western Railway Company
David Rockefeller	President and chairman of the executive committee	Chase Manhattan Bank
Stuart Saunders	Chairman and CEO	Pennsylvania Railway
Herbert R. Silverman	Chairman and CEO	James Talcott Inc.
Jack I. Straus	Chairman	R. H. Macy Inc.
Thomas J. Watson Jr.	Chairman	International Business Machines Corporation

Source: Edgar F. Kaiser Papers, Bancroft Library, University of California, Berkeley.

eral aid to education. In 1963, T. V. Houser, the group's chairman, addressed a conference of public school officials and called for $600 million in federal aid to needy schools. Marion B. Folsom, the original member of the CED and secretary of the Department of Health, Education, and Welfare (now Health and Human Services) under President Eisenhower, also called for increased spending on education (*NYT,* April 10, 1963, 24). Two years later, the CED called for an increase in support for mass transit as a

means of countering urban decay. Although the CED acknowledged the
rise in property values that would likely accompany an expansion of com-
muter railroads, the group was willing to advocate property taxes on both
commuters and businesses, with rates pegged to proximity to the system
(*NYT*, April 19, 1965, 1).

The broadening business support for government social programs was
not lost on the press at the time. In a 1966 article reminiscent of the *Time*
story from a decade earlier, *New York Times* reporter James Reston described what he referred to as "big business progressives" (*NYT*, October
12, 1966, 42). Although Reston focused on the Kaiser letter expressing
support for the Demonstration Cities Bill, he provided other examples as
well. In one case, Reston noted, a substantial minority of corporate executives, including the heads of AT&T, Campbell Soup, and the Pennsylvania
Railroad, gave their support to President Johnson's bill to suspend a 7 percent tax credit for capital investment. In another, John A. McCone, a California investment banker and supporter of Ronald Reagan's 1966 guberna-
torial campaign in California (as well as a former director of the Central
Intelligence Agency), proposed a $100 million program to invest in the
impoverished Watts area of Los Angeles.

Interestingly, Reston emphasized the fact that these corporate leaders
continued to support Republicans. "There seems to be a growing difference these days between how the big business leaders vote and how they
talk and act," Reston wrote. As we saw regarding the Eisenhower presidency, however, and as we shall see in our discussion of Richard Nixon's
administration, the Republicans during the postwar period exhibited very
different perspectives and behavior from those of the twenty-first century.
Although they were considerably more conservative than the Democrats,
even Republican politicians, especially at the national level, were compelled to deal with the existence of a powerful and active state, whose role
in addressing both economic and social issues had attained a high degree
of legitimacy. In engaging in this behavior, both Republican and Democratic officials were responding in part to the pressures they faced from the
corporate elite.

One could argue, as Vogel (1989, 25) has, that business leaders could afford to be moderate during the mid-1960s, given the favorable economic
conditions of the period. As we have seen, however, this moderation dates

from at least the end of World War II, and it persisted through the several recessions that occurred in the meantime. It is true nevertheless that despite the recessions, the United States maintained a position of unquestioned dominance in the global economy during this period. This provided a level of "slack," to use a term from organizational theory (March and Simon 1958), that allowed major corporations to support (or at least tolerate) more moderate policies.

The corporate elite's growing involvement in social issues continued into the later part of the decade. A 1967 report by the CED called for tax reforms to ameliorate poverty (*NYT,* June 8, 1967, 32). A speech the same year by Robert W. Sarnoff, president of RCA, to the Los Angeles Chamber of Commerce called for an increased effort by government to educate urban youth, who made up a high proportion of the unemployed (*Vital Speeches of the Day,* October 10, 1967, 94–96). "Quite apart from the cost in human distress," Sarnoff stated, "the extent of joblessness and subemployment bears a shocking price tag," which he placed at more than $28 billion. The solution, Sarnoff stated, was in a partnership between business and government:

> During the past three decades, this nation has completed its divorce from Locke's concept of government as an instrument intended solely for the preservation of property. In its place, we have evolved a new relationship based upon growing cooperation between government and business in the achievement of national goals. These goals can be solved only with efforts so large that the active partnership of industry and government is essential to their success. (*Vital Speeches of the Day,* October 10, 1967, 96)

In April 1968, a panel convened by Governor Nelson Rockefeller of New York, a moderate Republican, recommended a federal commitment of $11 billion to support a negative income tax that would bring all thirty million impoverished Americans to an income equal to or above the poverty line. The panel, chaired by Joseph C. Wilson, chairman of Xerox, included executives of such major corporations as Metropolitan Life Insurance, Marine-Midland Bank, Ford, Mobil, and Pepsico (*NYT,* April 30, 1968, 1). And the CED, in a report on post–Vietnam War economic conversion, recommended that the government "review and bring up to date a shelf of public programs deferred because of the war," so that increased federal domestic spending could be used to maintain a high level of total demand" (*WSJ*, April 18, 1968, 18).

The corporate moderation on economic issues also continued during this period. Facing a projected budget deficit of $10 billion (a remarkably small figure by twenty-first-century standards, but one considered substantial at the time), the CED in 1966 called for a one-year tax increase combined with spending cuts sufficient to create a $3 billion surplus (*NYT*, December 2, 1966, 24). Although the CED was clear that it preferred spending cuts to a tax increase, the group believed that "it would not be realistic" to expect cuts alone to eliminate the deficit. The interesting feature here is the group's willingness to acknowledge that spending cuts could not be viewed as the sole solution to the deficit without at least some level of tax increase. Again, this contrasts with the American business community of the post-2000 period, which has been unwilling to even raise the possibility of a tax increase, despite a deficit of far greater magnitude than that experienced during the 1960s.[14]

In August 1967, Treasury Secretary Henry H. Fowler organized an informal group of 113 business leaders in support of a wartime tax increase, as a means of reducing the deficit. Fowler, who had organized a similar group in support of the 1964 tax cut, was able to enlist the support of fifty-six members of the Business Council. Among the companies whose heads agreed to support the tax hike were AT&T, Campbell Soup, Chase Manhattan Bank, Ford, General Electric, General Motors, IBM, Mobil, and U.S. Steel (*NYT*, August 25, 1967, 1; Martin 1991). Consistent with its historically moderate approach, the CED, which had already called for a tax increase, added its support to this group. In line with its more conservative approach, the Chamber of Commerce opposed it. Interestingly, the National Association of Manufacturers, which experienced a brief foray into moderation during the 1960s, also expressed its support for the increase. Here, too, it is instructive to contrast this episode with the absence of similar activity during the Iraq War four decades later. Facing a far greater deficit and wartime conditions, as well as the recent September 11th attacks, there was no call from corporate leaders for a tax increase, even to pay for the war effort, let alone to address the more general issue of the deficit.

The Nixon Presidency

The election of Richard Nixon in 1968 promised a rightward turn in both economic and social policy. In fact, however, Nixon's economic policies turned out to be moderate in character, and even liberal in some cases. Nixon's legacy included the establishment of the Environmental Protection Agency and the Occupational Safety and Health Administration, as well as the first wage and price controls in the American economy since World War II.[15] Although he engineered an economic slowdown at the beginning of his presidency, Nixon also supported a negative income tax for the working poor and presided over the emergence of affirmative action programs in hiring on federal contracts.

Nixon's policies were a reaction in part to the growth of social movement activity—especially around environmental issues—as well as challenges from Democrats, but they also reflected the continuing moderation of the corporate elite during the late 1960s and early 1970s. This corporate elite moderation was, of course, itself a response to the social turmoil of the period. Its consequences were significant, however.

Perhaps the culmination of the moderate social orientation of the corporate elite in the postwar period occurred with the publication of the CED's 1971 document, *Social Responsibilities of Business Corporations*. This document had its roots in the work of the Research and Policy Committee's Subcommittee on Business Structure and Performance. According to the full committee's cochairman, Emilio G. Collado, executive vice president of Standard Oil of New Jersey (subsequently Exxon), the subcommittee, which was originally formed in 1966 to address economic issues, became increasingly concerned with the social problems facing American society as well as the role that large corporations might play in addressing these problems. This view reflected, according to Collado, "the growing consensus in our society that higher priority than ever before must be given to the nation's social problems" (Committee for Economic Development 1971, 8).

In some respects, this fifty-five-page document (which contained an additional thirteen pages of commentary and dissent) was a classic plea for what is today known as corporate social responsibility, or "CSR." It was more than just a screed for CSR, however. First, the document was distinct in the range of social issues that its authors addressed. The issues that the document viewed as central included

> elimination of poverty and provision of good health care; equal opportunity for each person to realize his or her full potential regardless of race, sex, or creed; education and training for a fully productive and rewarding participation in modern society; ample jobs and career opportunities in all parts of society; livable communities with decent housing, safe streets, a clean and pleasant environment, efficient transportation, good cultural and educational opportunities, and a prevailing mood of civility among people. (Committee for Economic Development 1971, 13)

One might argue that the above constitute what Charles Perrow once called "motherhood items." Just as no one opposes the idea of motherhood, few reasonable people would be opposed to the elimination of poverty, the provision of good health care, or the opportunity for rewarding participation in modern society. Yet it would be unfair to dismiss this document as a simple exercise in public relations. Rather, the authors frankly emphasized what they called "enlightened self-interest." As they explained:

> There is a broad recognition today that corporate self-interest is inexorably involved in the well-being of the society of which business is an integral part, and from which it draws the basic requirements needed for it to function at all. . . . This body of understanding is the basis for the doctrine that it is in the "enlightened self-interest" of corporations to promote the public welfare in a positive way. (Committee for Economic Development 1971, 27)

Among the behaviors included in this doctrine were contributions to charitable organizations, gifts to universities, and investments in urban housing, educational, and recreational facilities. A major rationale for the concept was that if corporations did not take the initiative to address these social problems, government would be forced to increase its own involvement. In that sense, the document could be viewed as a conservative plea to corporations to limit the role of government. In fact, in a dissenting comment to this section, Robert R. Nathan, a CED trustee, explicitly spoke to this issue, arguing that "enlightened self-interest is a highly desirable objective for business but it is not a major alternative to the role of government."

"It must be recognized," Nathan continued, "that the very nature of a competitive economy renders governmental intervention and regulation not only inevitable but proper" (Committee for Economic Development 1971, 69).

And yet the authors of the document acknowledged Nathan's point. Despite their insistence that corporate attention to social issues could help stave off a more extensive level of government intervention, the authors also noted the need for government to play an active role. In speaking to the issue of stockholder rights, for example, the document noted that since the business community as a whole has an interest in a well-functioning society, it is in the stockholders' interest for their firms to pursue policies that help further this goal. "Indeed," the authors state, "this long-range stockholder interest would justify governmental regulation to bring about improved environmental operating conditions . . . if corporations singly or as a group cannot achieve such results on their own" (Committee for Economic Development 1971, 30).

In fact, as important as private philanthropy and attention to social responsibility were, the authors of the document believed that private efforts alone would ultimately not be sufficient to fully address the social problems of the age. In most cases, the suggested role for government involved the creation of incentives (and in some cases subsidies) that would allow corporations to directly pursue solutions. But the authors acknowledged an important and necessary role for government, above and beyond the provision of incentives. This included support for nondiscriminatory hiring, as well as pollution controls. The authors noted the potential free-rider problems that could occur in the absence of a clearly enforceable set of rules and supported regulatory measures "to insure that *all* businesses, not only the financially strong and more socially responsible ones, act in accordance with the public interest" (Committee for Economic Development 1971, 58; emphasis in the original).

Perhaps the most remarkable aspect of this document, however, was its acknowledgement that private philanthropy alone was insufficient to fully address such a broad range of problems. Instead, the authors recommended a business-government partnership, including the idea of combined public-private corporations that could take advantage of the government's resources and the private sector's expertise. Amtrak, the National Railroad Passenger Corporation, was listed as an example of such a hybrid organization.

Government's suggested role included, in addition to financing, "overall planning," as well as "public accountability," through a public board of directors, partly elected and partly appointed. In addition, the list of recommended corporate activities included support for both fiscal and monetary policies as a means of facilitating economic growth (Committee for Economic Development 1971, 37).

As in the 1950s, support for moderate policies among the corporate sector was not limited to the CED. Even the historically conservative *Fortune* magazine expressed support for measures to clean up the environment. "To reverse environmental deterioration will be one of the main goals of the next generation, involving all the major functions of society," the publication's editors noted in their introduction to a special issue on the environment (*Fortune* 1970a, 93). "It will not be enough to cope with each environmental atrocity as it reaches the point of clear and present danger to life and health" (ibid.). The editors were of course not recommending environmental measures so radical that they significantly weakened the American economy, but they were serious about the need for action. This view was echoed by Fortune 500 chief executives. In a survey of 270 Fortune 500 CEOs conducted by Daniel Yankelovich, Inc., the executives exhibited a set of attitudes that would be almost unthinkable by the standards of the twenty-first century. In response to the question "Would you like to see [the federal government] step up its regulatory activities, maintain them at the present levels, or cut them back?," 57 percent of the executives believed that the government should step up its regulatory activities, while 29 percent said it should maintain them at present levels. Only 8 percent believed that the government should cut back its regulatory activities (Fortune 1970b, 119). Fifty-three percent of the executives favored a "single national agency to establish standards on air and water pollution control," while only 35 percent preferred that the standards vary by locale. Even more remarkably, 85 percent of the CEOs believed that "the protection of the environment should be taken into consideration even if it [meant] reducing profits," and 88 percent agreed that protection of the environment should be taken into account even if it meant "inhibiting the introduction of new products" (ibid.). In the midst of these views, the corporate CEOs did express some negativity toward organizations in the environmental movement, but even here the level of opposition was far from universal. Although a plurality

(47 percent) viewed conservationist groups as "simply a pressure group," nearly as many (38 percent) believed that the groups represented "general public opinion."

The results of this survey suggest that the many individual examples we have seen of moderation among American corporate leaders were not simply isolated cases. Instead, they represented the general view of the American corporate elite during the late 1960s and early 1970s. This is further illustrated by the results of a survey conducted in 1971 by Allen Barton (1985), who, in interviews with 130 leading corporate executives and wealthy individuals, asked a series of questions about their views on economic and social policy. All of the executives in the study—80 percent of the sample—represented Fortune 800 firms.[16] The remaining 20 percent were classified by Barton as wealthy individuals. Barton grouped his respondents into four broad categories based on their responses to a series of questions about economic policy. "Keynesian liberals" were those who expressed support for deficit spending during recessions, support for federal antipoverty programs, and support for redistribution of income and/or wealth. "Keynesian moderates" were those who expressed support for deficit spending and federal antipoverty programs but not for redistributive measures. Fourteen percent of the 95 corporate executives fell into the Keynesian liberal classification, and 43 percent were Keynesian moderates. In other words, 57 percent of the leading corporate executives in Barton's survey were classified as either Keynesian liberals or moderates. An additional 22 percent of the executives supported deficit spending during recessions but not the two other policies, and were thus classified by Barton as "Keynesian conservatives." This means that nearly 80 percent of Barton's corporate respondents were at least partial supporters of Keynesian economics. Only 10 percent of the executives were classified as "anti-Keynesian conservatives" (Barton 1985, 63–66), a view that would be most closely associated with American corporate leaders in the twenty-first century.[17] Equally remarkable were the responses to some of Barton's individual items. Sixty percent of the executives expressed agreement with the statement that "the federal government should support the creation of jobs in the public sector for those for whom the private sector does not provide employment" (ibid., 85). And 41 percent of the respondents expressed support for an even more radical idea, that "The political power of the poor should be increased by encouraging community organization and participation in control of government programs" (ibid.).

Conclusion

From the 1940s into the early 1970s, the American corporate elite established itself as a moderate, and in some cases even liberal, force in national politics. The leaders of large corporations had extended their concerns far beyond that of a full-employment economy, to support for civil rights for disadvantaged minorities, for measures to eradicate poverty, and for cleaning up the environment. But this moderation, as prominent as it became in later years, had already emerged on a significant scale in the 1940s, and it maintained its presence well before the turmoil (and general liberalism) of the 1960s.

These moderate views on the role of government in American life were driven in part by the high degree of legitimacy, and thus power, that the American state enjoyed during this period. There was a consensus in the larger society that the government, although far from perfect, was in general a force for good. This is reflected in polling data, which reveal a level of positive sentiment toward government that would be unimaginable in more recent years. One way in which these positive views manifested themselves during this period was in the absence of negative sentiment. The Inter-University Consortium for Political and Social Research at the University of Michigan conducted a series of surveys in which its pollsters asked the question "How much of the time do you think you can trust government in Washington to do what is right—just about always, most of the time, or only some of the time?" The proportion of Americans suggesting that one could trust government only "some of the time" was only 23 percent in 1958, 22 percent in 1964, and only 25 percent in 1968, despite the social turmoil of the period (Lipset and Schneider 1983, 16–17). The level of distrust did increase by 1972, to 32 percent, and it rose sharply during the 1970s, reaching 47 percent in 1980. An indicator of "antigovernment sentiment," based on a mean of four items administered by the Survey Research Center at Michigan, revealed a level of only 28 percent in 1958 and 32 percent in 1964. This indicator did show an increase in hostility toward the government by 1968—to 40 percent—but even this negativity paled compared to subsequent years, in which antigovernment sentiment increased to 50 percent in 1972 and to 67 percent by 1980 (ibid., 32–33).

Writing about Americans' attitudes toward government in the early 1960s—a period that he termed the "age of affluence"—political scientist Robert Lane speculated that not only were working-class Americans likely to continue to support the welfare state, even as they became increasingly secure economically, but also that "the middle class will associate its own increasing welfare and security with the policies of the welfare state, including flexible fiscal policies, and will be in no mood for change" (1965, 880). Meanwhile, he suggested, "many industrialists and businessmen will come increasingly to perceive that the fight against a limited management of the economy is not in their interests because these 'liberal' policies provide the basis for the prosperity and growth in which they share" (ibid.).

As Lane's discussion suggests, the high degree of power and legitimacy held by the state during this period created constraints within which business was compelled to operate. The positions that the corporate elite could take were limited by what was politically possible, and the idea that the United States would return to a largely laissez-faire economic policy was simply no longer feasible. Moreover, the enormous success of the American economy in the postwar period and the role of the state in facilitating this success not only further strengthened the state but also convinced many leading businesspeople that government intervention actually was a positive force in the economy. In fact, the economic success of the era made it possible for many large corporations to accept the expanded role of the state, knowing not only that they would continue to profit but that the state had helped create the conditions for this success. Yet despite the state's power, the American corporate elite did not *have* to react in the accommodating way that it did. It could have gone the way of the NAM and other opponents of the New Deal and continue to act in a contrary and confrontational manner. Instead, the group compromised and took on a role of leadership rather than the pursuit of narrow self-interest. In doing so, the American corporate elite developed a worldview that recognized the value of addressing societal as well as economic problems.

Meanwhile, regardless of the problems that American society experienced during this period—and there were many—the nation continued to be the world's leading economic power. This situation would not last, however. Economic problems that surfaced in the late 1960s, most notably inflation, became increasingly severe as we moved into the 1970s. The nation's economic dominance began to fade, as the economies of Japan and Germany, among others, recovered from the ashes of World War II or emerged from underdevelopment. The changes of the 1970s would have far reaching effects, leading to a gradual but distinct shift in the orientation and actions of American business. Before discussing this shift, however, we turn to another factor behind the corporate moderation of the postwar period: the strength of organized labor.

4 ||| Labor as Uneasy Partner

If the state created one constraint on the autonomy and actions of business, organized labor provided another. Just as the growing power and legitimacy of the government contributed to the moderate perspective exhibited by the American corporate elite in the postwar period, so too did the growing power and legitimacy of labor. The elite's attitudes toward organized labor may have been less accommodating than those toward the state. Business, even its most moderate elements, was opposed to collective bargaining at virtually all points. But as it did with the government, the corporate elite made its peace with the labor movement in the postwar period, however uneasy this peace may have been.

The postwar period was not the first time that American business leaders had attempted to reach an accommodation with their workers. As we saw in Chapter 2, at the turn of the twentieth century, members of the National Civic Federation (NCF) made significant efforts to convince their fellow business leaders to accept the concept of independent labor unions. When this failed, many companies turned to welfare capitalism as a means of absorbing potential (and actual) disruption. It was not until the 1930s, however, especially after the passage of the National Labor Relations Act (now known as the Wagner Act) in 1935, that labor unions became a major force in the American workplace. The law created the National Labor

Relations Board (NLRB), whose role included the supervision of secret-ballot elections for unionization, and it legalized collective bargaining, in effect providing state protection for workers to organize into unions.

Unlike the Social Security Act, which at least experienced some support from business and had become broadly (albeit grudgingly) accepted by the end of the 1930s, the Wagner Act initially faced virtually universal opposition from American corporations. Yet even with the Wagner Act, a certain degree of acceptance, or at least resignation, had set in by the end of the decade. It is true that only 17 percent of the executives surveyed by *Fortune* in 1939 favored repeal of Social Security. But only 41.7 percent favored repeal of the Wagner Act, a far higher proportion to be sure, but still a minority. Another 41.9 percent of respondents believed that the Wagner Act should be modified, and 3.7 percent believed that it should remain unchanged, so there was clearly a high level of dissatisfaction with the act among corporate executives. On the other hand, it is interesting that as many executives favored modification or maintenance of the law as favored repeal. As *Fortune* put it, in summarizing the overall results of the survey:

> It can be argued that so far as major principles of reform are concerned, the New Deal has produced nothing that business is not willing to have stand, at least with modifications. . . . The impressive fact remains that whatever changes business might demand in such laws as the Wagner Act, Social Security, and the Wages and Hours Law, business seems to embrace the principles of this legislation—collective bargaining under federal supervision, federal provision for old age, and a federal floor to the wage and ceiling to the hours of the country's working week. (*Fortune* 1939, 52)

Perhaps even more remarkably, more than 78 percent of the executives responded "yes" when asked whether they agreed with the idea of labor unions (*Fortune* 1939, 90). It is true that the respondents believed that unions had "hurt" rather than "helped" the United States as a whole (48 to 32 percent, respectively). Yet even among those who believed that unions had hurt the country, approximately two-thirds still supported the concept of unions in general (ibid., 92). Interestingly, as we saw in Chapter 2, by 43 percent to 38 percent, the businesspeople surveyed believed that business would be better off with "one big powerful union" (ibid., 53). The reason for this appeared to be concerns about unreliable union leadership, corruption (including the presence of organized crime), and interunion conflict (ibid., 92). Overall, these views, according to *Fortune,* "seem to refute the idea that employers have a reactionary view of labor."

In the Senate hearings on the formation of the NLRB, three consecutive representatives of Kentucky-based tobacco companies extolled the virtues of their relations with the Tobacco Workers Union, an affiliate of the American Federation of Labor (AFL) (U.S. Congress, Senate 1935, 212–218). Edwin J. Helck, vice president of Axton-Fisher Tobacco, noted that the firm's founder "recognized the benefits accruing to business through collective bargaining" (ibid., 212), and had even requested the union to organize the plant. "We have dealt with the union for nearly 36 tranquil years," Helck stated, and "not once have we had any labor disturbance. . . . My experience in dealing with organized labor proves to me that it is a force for good" (ibid., 212–213). Wood F. Axton, the company's president, offered similar praise of the union:

> I firmly believe that the organization of workers under the American Federation of Labor plan leads to better wages, fewer hours, and improved working conditions; that vast benefits can accrue to the employer, that it develops character, fosters justice and tolerance, and makes for better economic conditions in the Nation. My experience has convinced me that organized labor is a great constructive force in the betterment of economic growth, as applied to industrial relations. (U.S. Congress, Senate 1935, 215)

According to Kochan, Katz, and McKersie (1994, 26), some companies even signaled their willingness to accept the idea of organized labor on Keynesian grounds: that it would lead to higher wages and thus an increase in purchasing power. As an example, they referred to the testimony of H. M. Robertson, general counsel to Brown and Williamson Tobacco:

> It became obvious to the management of our company that no mass production could long be carried on unless there was increased purchasing power by the great masses of people. To us this meant there must be increase [*sic*] in wages and shortening of hours. This became the very fixed conviction of our management. The more difficult question was as to how this should be accomplished, and we arrived at the conclusion that collective bargaining by employer and employee, with both of these elements dealing

at large length and yet fairly with each other, was the only means by which, under our system, any adjustment in the equitable distribution of income could be accomplished. We realized the difficulties of this method, but we felt that if this method did not accomplish the desired end, then the present capitalistic system would collapse. (U.S. Congress, Senate 1935, 218)

These progressive views toward organized labor were clearly the exceptions rather than the rule, and the majority of companies, especially at that stage, continued to oppose the unionization of their firms. In fact, even the support from these two tobacco companies might have been motivated by the hope that the passage of the National Labor Relations Act would compel their competitors in the industry to unionize as well, thus helping to level the playing field. A similar process had occurred in the coal industry in earlier years (Bowman 1989).[1]

As for the stronger opposition to the Wagner Act compared with Social Security, this may not have been surprising given the important differences between the two measures. Social Security, although in part funded by the employers, was also funded by the government, thus relieving firms of at least a portion of their obligation to provide company-sponsored pensions. The Wagner Act, on the other hand, struck directly at what employers saw as their most fundamental prerogative: the ability to have full control and flexibility with respect to their workforce. Still, the views of the managements at Axton-Fisher and Brown and Williamson did presage an approach that, although perhaps more out of necessity than choice, became far more common in later years.

There is considerable debate over whether the Wagner Act was the actual cause of the surge in union membership that occurred after its passage. Regardless of whether the act was causal, however, the proportion of non-agricultural workers in the American labor force who belonged to unions increased rapidly—from 11.5 percent in 1934 to 27.6 percent in 1939. By 1945, this figure had increased to 34.2 percent (Freeman 1998). The labor economist Richard Freeman has argued that a rise in union membership would likely have occurred even in the absence of the Wagner Act. He shows, for example, that in the two years after the passage of the Wagner Act (1936 and 1937), nearly three times as many workers (74 versus 26 percent) were organized as a result of "recognition strikes" than through elections supervised by the NLRB—despite the fact that the Wagner Act was designed in part to eliminate the need for recognition strikes (ibid., 282).[2] By 1938, the percentages had reversed themselves: 76 percent were organized through NLRB-supervised elections, which might suggest that the act had become the primary basis for union organization. Freeman argues, however, that the law merely changed the way that unions were organized, to a more orderly, less disruptive system. In fact, recognition strikes continued to be a significant source of unionization. Between 1941 and 1945, more than half a million workers were organized through this practice (ibid.).

Even as most businesses opposed the Wagner Act and unions in general, by the end of the 1930s most had adopted a perspective that the labor historian Howell John Harris (1982) has referred to as "realism." In fact, the rudiments of the postwar arrangement between management and labor were already in place by this time. In a 1944 article in *Fortune*, William Benton of the Committee for Economic Development (CED) offered the following principle:

> To compensate for the weakness of their individual bargaining position, wage earners need the right to combine into organizations for collective bargaining. Provided that the power of these organizations is not permitted to stifle technical progress, or unduly to limit access to jobs, or in other ways to be abused, labor unions can serve the common good. (*Fortune* 1944, 162)[3]

This does not mean that companies had come to completely accept unions. One group, termed by Harris the "belligerents," most of whom were closely affiliated with the National Association of Manufacturers (NAM), was willing to resort to overt oppositional approaches, including violence, to stem the tide of unionization. These companies, which included two members of the group known as "little steel"—National Steel and Republic Steel—never made up a majority of firms, and this approach ultimately proved to be counterproductive, in that it turned public opinion against the companies. As a result, it soon fell out of favor (Harris 1982, 24–25). A second group, termed by Harris the "sophisticates," which included International Harvester, Goodyear Tire and Rubber, and Ford, was also willing to use violence when they deemed it necessary. For the most part, these companies tended to be more subtle in their antiunion activities, however, by discriminating against union supporters in hiring and firing, and engaging in surveillance and antiunion propaganda. The most common response, especially among those in "core" manufacturing industries (Averitt 1968), was a grudging acceptance of unions, Harris's "realism." As Harris terms it, these companies did not "welcome" unions, but they resigned themselves to the unions' existence as a necessary evil, even as they continued to issue antiunion propaganda and lobby against the Wagner Act. As one unnamed executive put it:

> We signed up for two reasons. First, we believe the union has come to stay in our industry; and second, we knew we were the next citadel for assault by the CIO [the Congress of Industrial Organizations], and, in point of fact, we *had* to sign. Financially, we were in no position to stand a two or three months' shutdown of production or to carry the ball for the rest of the industry. (quoted in Harris 1982, 26; emphasis in the original)

General Motors was viewed by Harris as the prototypical realist firm, whose management was sufficiently pragmatic to reach an accommodation with the United Auto Workers (UAW) prior to the war. In response to a brief 1939 strike, in which future union president Walter Reuther's CIO-affiliated branch of the UAW consolidated its support from GM's workers, GM's management realized that "it was going to be troubled by the UAW for a long time" (Harris 1982, 29). In an early version of what later became known as the "Treaty of Detroit," GM's management decided to no longer oppose the union's attempt to organize its workforce, insisting instead that the union help the company maintain discipline. Unlike General Motors, most realist firms tended to be reactive rather than proactive, however, responding to union demands only when a crisis occurred that threatened to shut down production.

Even as firms began to acquiesce under pressure to the existence of unions, a handful of companies stood out for their proactive, progressive stance. Most notable among these companies were United States Rubber and General Electric. U.S. Rubber's director of industrial and public relations, Cyrus S. Ching, made a strong plea for the use of "fair tactics" and "friendly attitudes," in the belief that by treating the unions well, the company would receive the same in return. Ching worked out an agreement with Sherman Dalrymple, the leader of the United Rubber Workers, in which the company accepted the union and the union agreed to work to prevent wildcat (unauthorized) strikes (Harris 1982, 32–33). This agreement allowed U.S. Rubber to avoid the strikes that plagued its rival Goodyear. GE, on the other hand, was able to accept the United Electrical Workers due to its domination of its industry. Both U.S. Rubber and General Electric (along with General Motors) also made use of industrial relations experts from universities, whom they brought in to serve as mediators. These academics shared the view of the progressive management spokespersons that unions could contribute to the stability and efficiency of production. Although this approach never became the dominant one among large American companies, it became increasingly prevalent by the 1950s. Yet the differences between these progressive firms and the realists may have been largely one of degree. Even if they were less proactive than the progressive firms in encouraging the formation of their unions, the realist firms grew increasingly able to see the benefits of unions, especially as the latter became more bureaucratized after the war. By 1939, the essentials of a postwar "capital-labor accord" were already in place, although they were interrupted by the war and a postwar surge of militancy. Even the NAM recognized that "reaction and belligerency were no longer a sufficient response to challenges to business hegemony" (ibid., 39).

By the start of the war, a corporatist-style approach to bargaining had emerged—a tripartite system involving management, labor, and government officials (Streeck and Kenworthy 2005). Although union membership continued to grow during World War II, the degree of worker militancy declined. Two government agencies, the National Defense Mediation Board during 1940 and 1941 and the National War Labor Board (NWLB) from 1942 through 1945, gained assurances from unions not to strike. Although the pledge was technically voluntary, the possible sanctions that unions faced for violating it were sufficient to keep most of them in line. The pledge was not airtight, however. Wildcat strikes were common during this period, especially in the heavy manufacturing industries such as auto and steel (Harris 1982, 61). Other strikes were actually called by unions, most notably the United Mine Workers, in response to the frustrations involved in dealing with private and government-led arbitration (ibid., 44–47). In 1944 there were 4,956 strikes, the highest number ever recorded by the

Bureau of Labor Statistics (1945, 1–2). Although these strikes were relatively short in duration (averaging just 5.6 days), more than two million workers were involved. Workers were aided during this period by the existence of virtually full employment, as all of the nation's resources were directed toward the war effort. Even women and minorities made significant inroads into the labor force during this period, although minorities often faced substantial resistance not from employers or union leadership but from other workers (Freeman 1978).[4]

At the war's end, the CIO had been hoping to continue the corporatist form of bargaining that had prevailed over the previous several years. To further this goal, the presidents of the CIO and AFL, Philip Murray and William Green, cosponsored a "Labor-Management Charter" with the Chamber of Commerce's Eric Johnston (*New York Times* [hereafter *NYT*], March 29, 1945, 16; Lichtenstein 1989, 128–129). The labor officials agreed to support management's right to "direct the operations of an enterprise," as well as to support capitalism in general ("the rights of private property and free choice of action"). Johnston agreed to support "the fundamental rights of labor to organize and engage in collective bargaining," as well as "employment at wages assuring a steadily advancing standard of living" (*NYT,* March 29, 1945, 16). The group proposed to create a committee consisting of representatives of business and labor. The six business representatives included Henry Kaiser of the Kaiser Company, E. J. Thomas of Goodyear Tire and Rubber, J. D. Zellerbach of Crown-Zellerbach, and Paul Hoffman of Studebaker (and cofounder and president of the CED).

Although this agreement among the AFL, the CIO, and the Chamber of Commerce received praise from an editorial in the *New York Times,* it was criticized by Ira Mosher, the president of the NAM, as overly vague (*NYT,* March 29, 1945, 16). Mosher also argued that the management side of the group needed to be more broadly representative of business. Lichtenstein (1989, 130) suggests that the union officials specifically targeted the most liberal elements of the business community, ones whom they believed would be most sympathetic to their position. Kaiser, for example, had not only made his fortune on New Deal construction projects and war contracts, which predisposed him toward support for government spending on both domestic and military concerns, but he was also known for having good relations with his unions, as well as for having established the health care plan for his workers for which he later became famous. Johnston, as we have seen, was an uncharacteristically moderate leader of the Chamber of Commerce, who stepped down soon after this pact was announced. On labor issues, Lichtenstein suggests, this group was a minority within the business community and had limited influence (1989, 130). The more central figures, he suggests, were the "practical conservatives" in the core manufacturing industries—steel, electric, auto, and rubber—and transport. Included in this group were John A. Stephens of U.S. Steel and Charles E. Wilson of General Motors. "These industrialists," Lichtenstein notes, "recognized the potential usefulness of the new industrial unions as stabilizers of the labor force and moderators of industrial conflict, but they also sought the restoration of managerial prerogatives that wartime conditions had eroded in the areas of product pricing, market allocation, and shop-floor work environment" (ibid.).

This argument by Lichtenstein is indicative of an ambiguity that pervades the labor histories describing the postwar period. On one hand, management is seen as vehemently antiunion: after the war, managers sought to reclaim the rights of firm-level decision making that they believed had been weakened by the pressures of war production; they also sought to reduce the rights of workers codified in the Wagner Act—such as sympathy strikes—that they believed had gone too far; and they were almost uniformly opposed to the social democratic reforms advocated by labor. On the other hand, management is seen as moderate and pragmatic: despite their opposition to organized labor, even the so-called practical conservatives recognized that there were leaders of major unions who were willing to cede to management the right to "direct the operations of an enterprise," as the Labor-Management Charter made clear. The solution to this dilemma is to recognize that both views of management are accurate: managers were indeed prepared to fight unions at every step, but they were also able to see the silver lining in the cloud—that unions could have positive aspects as well. The fact that these businessmen were willing to accept, however grudgingly, the existence of collective bargaining, the fact that they were able to see the potential value of unions for disciplining their workforces, and the fact that they were willing to acknowledge the legitimacy of unions in the first place represented a major change relative to the situation at the end of World War I.

The Postwar Push and Reaction

The end of World War II saw a continued high level of strike activity, with the strikes becoming larger and of greater duration. In 1945, there were 4,750 strikes, averaging 9.9 days and involving nearly three and one-half million workers. By 1946, there were a record 4,985 strikes, averaging 24.2 days and involving 4.6 million workers. In this context, labor leaders had reason to believe that now that the war was over, conditions were good for continued improvements. This turned out to be only partly true, however. As we saw in the previous chapter, the high hopes for a law rendering employment a right of citizenship—the Employment Act of 1946—were tempered by resistance from multiple quarters. The bill passed, and the idea of high employment was recognized as an important goal of economic policy, but the law contained no specific provision for providing it. Meanwhile, unions began to face more strident opposition from management.

The UAW struck General Motors in 1946 as part of its effort to secure a wage increase of thirty cents per hour. This was deemed necessary because of the lost purchasing power the workers had experienced after the reduction of overtime pay at the end of the war. To bolster public support for its goal, the union based its argument not on self-interest but on the Keynesian principle that wage increases were necessary to maintain consumption levels, thus preventing a return to the depression of the 1930s. The UAW, led by Reuther, and the CIO in general, did succeed in gaining a significant wage increase of 18.5 cents, but the union was thwarted in its effort to prevent GM from passing on these wage gains to consumers through price increases (Lichtenstein 1989, 132–133). The end of government-administered price controls led to further inflation, which led the unions to repeatedly strike for increased wages, which in turn led to further price increases. According to Lichtenstein, the hostility to the unions that resulted from these strikes played a major role in the election of a Republican Congress in 1946 and the passage a year later (over President Truman's veto) of the Taft-Hartley Bill, a bill that led to a partial rollback of the Wagner Act. The existence of a Republican Congress also derailed the attempts by labor to push through social democratic reforms, including national health insurance. Even the CED, in a 1947 report, expressed surprisingly conservative views on labor issues (Committee for Economic Development 1947). The unions were further weakened when management pressured the CIO and other groups to expel Communists from their ranks, since the latter had been among the most militant of the union's members.

In November 1945, President Truman had brought together leaders from business and labor to discuss postwar reconversion issues. Unlike the tripartite meetings during the war, or the committee named by the 1944 Labor-Management Charter, the business representatives at this meeting were overwhelmingly conservative, consisting primarily of large and mid-size manufacturers. Of the thirty-six businesspeople on this committee, only one—Eric Johnston—was a moderate, according to Harris (1982, 112–113).[5] The others were from firms strongly associated with the NAM. Labor representatives came from the AFL, the CIO, the United Mine Workers, and the Railway Brotherhoods (Warren 1948, 352). The businessmen brought with them a document that had been written by a think tank, the Industrial Relations Counselors, Inc., and approved by the Labor Policy Committee of the Business Advisory Council. Although Harris notes that the Business Advisory Council had traditionally been viewed as a relatively moderate group, six of the committee's eight members were active in the NAM.

What is striking, however, is not that the group was well organized, that it was dominated by conservatives, or that its members shared a strong abhorrence of the Wagner Act. Rather, it is that the group's proposal was not only detailed but, in Harris's words, "pragmatic." The group's suggestions pointed not to repeal of the Wagner Act but "towards an attainable, realistic goal of labor law reform" (Harris 1982, 113). And interestingly, the discussions between business and labor leaders, taking place in the midst of a wave of strikes and lockouts, resulted in a surprising level of agreement, which showed "how far American business and labor leaders had moved toward one another in the ten crowded years since unions began to invade the mass-production industries" (ibid.). The business representatives agreed to accept the idea that employers bargain in good faith with a union chosen by the workers, a central premise of the Wagner Act. They also agreed to accept the idea of worker grievances as natural and legitimate, and to accept the legitimacy of the NLRB as an independent mediator (ibid., 114–116). Labor representatives agreed to issue grievances only within the parameters specified in the contract and to turn to the Conciliation Service—a mediating board that existed at the time under the Department of Labor and later reappeared as a separate agency after the passage of the Taft-Hartley Act (Bernstein 1947, 408)—in lieu of strike activity.

In response to the agreements from this meeting, the NAM developed a set of principles that became the basis of the Taft-Hartley Act. In drafting these principles, the NAM, in an implicit acknowledgement of the power and legitimacy of organized labor, formally adopted a moderate approach to the unions. Even with the benefit of the Republican control of Congress after the 1946 elections, "moderation prevailed," and the NAM "resisted the temptation to 'go for broke'" (Harris 1982, 119; Judis 2001, 69–70). This strategy was adopted, according to Harris, for two reasons. First, an effort to entirely dismantle the Wagner Act would have run counter to the image of moderation that American business was trying to project. Second, the NAM's members believed that even a full repeal of the Wagner Act would not have been sufficient to address their problems, which, they believed, stemmed from the existence of unions themselves, which they saw as monopolistic. The solution, they argued, was to modify the nature of government intervention, moving the balance of power toward management (Harris 1982, 119–120). After proposing a list of prescriptions seemingly every bit as platitudinous as those hammered out by Green, Murray, and Johnston in the Labor-Management Charter—including high wages, working conditions "that safeguard the health, dignity, and self-respect of the individual employee," stable employment, and a spirit of cooperation—the NAM proposed seven principles that contained a more specific set of recommendations. Among the most important of these principles was the right of workers to decline to join a union (the principle now known as the "right to work"), the obligation of unions to bargain in good faith, the requirement to act in accordance with collective bargaining agreements (including a prohibition on strikes that violated the contract), and the stipulation that bargaining should occur only at the level of the individual employer and its local union (ibid., 121–122).

Interestingly, the debate in Congress featured positions both more and less promanagement than those proposed by the NAM. The House version of the bill, which had the support of Republicans and Southern Democrats, included provisions that had been promoted by right-wing members of the NAM but rejected by the NAM's board. The Senate version was generally more moderate (although not completely so), perhaps because of a more even split between the parties in that chamber (Harris 1982, 124). The bill that ultimately emerged and was passed over President Truman's veto contained several provisions that weakened labor's bargaining position, includ-

ing the exclusion of supervisors (meaning that shop foremen were prohibited from organizing), a ban on sympathy strikes, the legalization of state
right-to-work laws, and a requirement that union leaders sign affidavits at-
testing that they were not members of the Communist Party (Tomlins
1985, 284–285; McDonough 1994, 120). It did not contain all of the policies supported by the NAM. In fact, Senator Taft himself ultimately decided to not pursue a ban on industry-wide bargaining that had been written into the House version of the bill, possibly in deference to the members
of the oligopolistic core industries, who actually benefited from this system
(Tomlins 1985, 302–303; Lichtenstein 1997–1998, 786).[6] If the bill that
passed met with the general approval of the NAM and other conservative
elements within the business community, this approval was not without
qualification. Some elements of the law (such as the antifeatherbedding
provision) were relatively weak and were seen as likely to have little effect.
The complexity of the law suggested the possibility of increased bureaucracy and heavy reliance on the courts (Harris 1982, 126). Most businesspeople believed that the law would have little effect on their dealings with
workers (ibid.), and, according to two members of the Senate, many of the
law's provisions had already been put into practice in the years since the
passage of the Wagner Act (Tomlins 1985, 299).

There is no doubt that the Taft-Hartley Act was bitterly opposed by organized labor and denounced by some as a "slave labor law" (Lichtenstein
1989, 134). Some observers have argued that this law played a significant
role in leading American labor away from its earlier goal of a universal system of economic rights and privileges, toward an increasingly narrow focus
on self-interest and advancement (McDonough 1994; Lichtenstein 1997–
1998). This may or may not be true. The overall conservative mood of the
early Cold War period and the weakness of the labor movement itself were
probably more significant, rendering Taft-Hartley as much a symptom as a
cause. Still, if Taft-Hartley, the failure to enact national health care legislation, and other developments of the period represented a major, perhaps
fatal, setback for the cause of social democracy, these events also led to
something that barely a decade earlier would have been almost unthinkable: a broad acceptance by large corporations of the legitimacy of independent, organized labor unions as a central institution in American life.
Unlike the period after World War I, in which the unions were largely
dismantled or greatly weakened, the unions in the post–World War II

period were operating from a position of strength and had the formal support of the state (Harris 1982, 7; Judis 2001, 63–70). As businessmen tried
to roll back the progress of unions during the 1940s, "their objective was
realistic, not utopian. . . . They wanted to make the labor movement toler-
able and manageable, and then to live with it, not to destroy it" (Harris
1982, 8).

The Treaty of Detroit

Despite the significant setbacks of the immediate postwar period, then, the
unions remained a considerable force, and collective bargaining was becoming an increasingly taken-for-granted phenomenon. Not all bargaining
was successful for the unions. The United Steelworkers were unable to convince U.S. Steel to move on wage increases in 1947, and the United Electrical Workers settled for a relatively small wage increase in the same year. But
as Walter Reuther consolidated his control of the UAW, General Motors'
Charles Wilson believed that the potential existed for a long-term accommodation with the union (Lichtenstein 1995, 276–277). As a sign that the
company was willing to take a more moderate stance, Wilson removed his
combative industrial relations chief, Harry Coen, whose background was
in the production wing of the firm, and replaced him with more the more
temperate Harry Anderson and Louis Seaton, whose backgrounds were in
law and marketing, respectively (ibid.). The conditions were now in place
for the historic agreement that was soon to be achieved.

The UAW had tried in its postwar bargaining to prevent the company
from passing on wage increases to the public in the form of price increases.
Many corporate spokespersons were hoping that the government would
make significant cuts in spending to reduce inflation, but this would have
required a rise in unemployment. Increased unemployment, in turn, would
likely have precipitated an angry reaction from unions that, as Lichtenstein
notes, had the ability to shut down production, as the strikes during the
period suggested. Meanwhile, GM was making huge profits, and given the
firm's expansion plans, Wilson determined that it would be counterproductive to support a strong anti-inflationary policy, especially since he now
believed that inflation was likely to become a continuing feature of the
postwar economy (Lichtenstein 1995, 278).

A fortuitous confluence of forces had thus emerged at the beginning of 1948. GM was expanding and was making large profits, which meant that the firm could afford to increase wages. Wilson continued to view the union as a formidable opponent. His primary goal was to ensure the stability and predictability of production. Under these circumstances, the conditions were favorable for making a relatively generous offer to the union. The company's offer that year included a cost of living adjustment, to be implemented quarterly, along with a 2 percent annual wage increase, which was contingent on an even higher rate of productivity increases. Reuther was willing to accept this deal but was skeptical of the cost of living component, since if the consumer price index were to drop, the company would be able to reduce wages. This is exactly what happened early in 1949, and Reuther was caught having to defend the deal against a restless rank-and-file. Anderson acknowledged the value of the union, noting that the UAW's leadership "did a remarkable job of administering the contract" (Harris 1982, 151). "The experience through the period from 1948 to 1950 was very, very good," Anderson continued. "On the basis of this performance, we were satisfied that if we could put a five-year agreement across, which was something new, something unheard of, it would be the right thing to do."

The stage was thus set for the historic deal, which the UAW and GM reached in May 1950 (*NYT*, May 24, 1950, 3). The agreement ran for a virtually unprecedented five years and included, in addition to guaranteed wage and cost of living increases, a pension of up to $117 a month (when combined with Social Security payments), a guaranteed annual wage increase of four cents an hour, half the cost of health insurance, and more than thirty additional concessions, including a requirement that new employees join the union. The wage guarantee ensured that the workers would receive a 20 percent increase in real wages over the length of the contract (Lichtenstein 1995, 280). Daniel Bell (1950, 53), writing at the time for *Fortune,* coined the term the "Treaty of Detroit" to describe the agreement. It was hailed by virtually all members of the press, by government officials— including Labor Secretary Maurice Tobin and Cyrus Ching (who had become the director of the Federal Mediation and Conciliation Service), who called it "a milestone in the progress of collective bargaining" (*NYT*, May 24, 1950, 3)—and by Reuther himself, who called it "the most significant development in labor relations since the mass production industries were organized" (Lichtenstein 1995, 280). Reuther contrasted GM's behavior during these negotiations with that of Chrysler, whose intransigence had led to a 100-day strike. "General Motors decided to live with our union," Reuther said. "It is our considered opinion that Chrysler has not. Chrysler is still living under some delusion that by some miracle it can get rid of the union" (*NYT,* May 24, 1950, 3). Yet, as Harris noted (1982, 154), Chrysler, was more the exception than the rule among the giant firms by that point. The firm "had not balanced the costs of concession and resistance, and had clearly miscalculated its own bargaining power and the depth of the UAW's determination." "Such ineptitude," Harris suggested, "was increasingly rare amongst large corporations."[7]

As if to reinforce this point, University of Chicago labor economist Frederick H. Harbison noted that the accord showed "how deeply the roots of collective bargaining have grown into the institutional structure of the American enterprise system" (1950, 407). "From a practical political standpoint," he continued,

> the corporation has accepted collective bargaining as a necessary condition for its survival. GM recognizes that it would be impossible as well as undesirable to get rid of unions in its plants. . . . As the union so correctly points out, the 1950 contract reflects a maturing relationship with GM. In a less striking, though nonetheless certain, manner collective bargaining throughout all the mass-production industries is maturing in the same way. (Harbison 1950, 407)

An indication of just how important a figure Reuther was, in a national political sense as well as within his union, occurred in December 1950, when Reuther learned that the Truman administration was preparing a freeze on auto wages in response to the Korean War. Reuther flew to Washington and met with Alan Valentine, Truman's economic policy maker who had proposed the freeze. Reuther warned Valentine that a government attempt to freeze wages would likely generate "unrest and instability" (Lichtenstein 1995, 281). Valentine quickly backed down and exempted the UAW's wage increases from this freeze. GM also supported maintaining the contract. In a statement to the War Stabilization Board in May 1951, Harry Anderson defended the contract.

The agreement did have its more sobering consequences. As Bell put it (1950, 53), "GM may have paid a billion for peace. It got a bargain." The contract allowed GM to regain full control of the work process, including production scheduling, model changes, and plant investment, and it forced the union to concede that wage gains could be achieved only through advances in productivity (ibid., 53–54). Perhaps more importantly, at least in terms of its political implications, the agreement set the United States down the path of a private welfare state, and in that sense it represented a resounding blow to Reuther's dream of a social democratic United States (Cobb 2011, 25). Union leaders had typically opposed private benefits, preferring those provided by the state (Lichtenstein 1995, 282). Private benefits smacked of the corporate welfare programs of the 1920s, which were viewed as paternalistic. But efforts to expand the welfare state stalled after the war when the Republicans captured Congress in the 1946 elections. President Truman had hoped to pass a national health insurance program, but the plan failed. Social Security payments declined during the 1940s as well. When it became clear after the 1946 elections that an expansion of the welfare state was unlikely, at least in the near future, union leaders decided that their best hope for gaining these benefits for their workers was by making them a component of collective bargaining. The corporations were initially resistant on these issues, but a strike by mine workers and a 1949 Supreme Court decision requiring management to bargain over fringe benefits turned this into a major area of bargaining.

The Treaty of Detroit has often been viewed as the prototypical representative of what historians have termed the postwar "capital-labor accord" (Bowles, Gordon, and Weisskopf 1983). As Bowles and his colleagues put it:

> Corporations would retain absolute control over the essential decisions governing enterprise operations—decisions involving production, technology, plant location, investment, and marketing. . . . In return, unions were accepted as legitimate representatives of workers' interests. They were expected to bargain on behalf of labor's immediate economic interests, but not to challenge employer control of enterprises. . . . Unions would help maintain an orderly and disciplined labor force while corporations would reward workers with a share of the income gains made possible by rising productivity, with greater employment security, and with improved working conditions. (Bowles, Gordon, and Weisskopf 1983, 73)

In other words, corporations were willing to accept the existence of unions, along with higher wages and benefits, in return for labor peace and control of the work process.

In recent years, some labor historians have begun to question whether the capital-labor accord ever existed. Several scholars have argued that business not only continued to fight labor aggressively during this period, but that American corporations never accepted the legitimacy of unions in the first place (Fones-Wolf 1994; Kochan, Katz, and McKersie 1994, 9; Gross 1995). Rather, as McIntyre and Hillard (2008) suggest, business at most reached a partial truce rather than a genuine accord. As we have seen, there are indeed reasons to doubt the extent to which employers internalized ideas about the acceptance of labor unions. Yet whether this accord reflected deeply held attitudes toward unions may be beside the point. Just as the corporate support for certain Keynesian economic policies reflected a pragmatic adaptation to a seemingly immutable reality, the acceptance of collective bargaining also reflected an understanding that unions were a basic, even if undesirable, component of business life. Certainly unions could be fought, just as government redistributive economic policies could arouse opposition. Given their existence, however, many corporate leaders reasoned that it was preferable to make their peace with them.

The (Supposedly) Quiet Years

During the 1950s, relations between management and labor remained largely stable. As we have seen, most of the large corporations in the industrial Northeast and Midwest had by 1950 accepted the existence of unions and the necessity of collective bargaining. Unions continued to win increased pay and benefits for their workers. In 1955, for example, the UAW was able to gain supplemental unemployment insurance, first from Ford, then from General Motors, and eventually from several other companies, including farm equipment manufacturers such as John Deere and Caterpillar (Barnard 2004, 284–288; Kochan, Katz, and McKersie 1994, 38). And given the strong economic conditions during much of the decade, management was able in some cases to relax its supervision of workers on the shop floor.

Realism, according to Harris, had become viewed as an effective way to maintain a satisfactory level of efficiency and order (Harris 1982, 155).[8] In fact, the conflicts between labor and management had become so routinized that even strikes were often conducted in a nonconfrontational manner. Lester (1958, 33) noted, for example, that in strikes during the 1950s it was common for management to provide picketing workers with hot coffee and coal (for heat) or, as in the case of U.S. Steel during a 1956 strike, portable toilets. He also suggested that the continuing process of collective bargaining contributed to a muting of conflict, as company and union negotiators came to know one another and their negotiations became increasingly characterized by joint problem solving (ibid., 41). These developments were indicative of what Ralf Dahrendorf (1959, 64–67) called the "institutionalization of class conflict."

The disagreements that occurred during this period reflected this routine character. This was especially the case in the political arena, in which organized labor often found itself at odds with the CED. In 1953, for example, the CIO sparred with the CED over a proposal in Congress to approve a standby wage-price control law. The CIO strongly opposed a measure to allow the president to declare a ninety-day freeze, while the CED gave partial support to the idea (*NYT*, March 14, 1953, 31). At a House-Senate Economic Committee meeting in 1954, the CED joined the Chamber of Commerce in suggesting that no government action was needed to spur the economy. George Meany (of the AFL) and Walter Reuther (then the head of the CIO) disagreed, urging the government to stimulate the economy to reduce unemployment (*Wall Street Journal*, February 18, 1954, 4). During the 1958 recession, the AFL-CIO (the two organizations having merged in 1955) issued a statement calling for an immediate tax cut of six to eight billion dollars, with the majority of the cut going to taxpayers with incomes below $5,000. The CED had called for a similar cut of $7.5 billion but had argued for an across-the-board cut of 20 percent (*NYT*, March 25, 1958, 1). In a report later that year, the CED raised the possibility that organized labor might be responsible for inflation, a view long held by the Chamber of Commerce and the NAM. Even here, however, the CED noted that the question was "still open," and the group suggested that business might also play a role in inflation (*NYT*, July 23, 1958, 16). And in a 1961 report, a CED study group—albeit one consisting solely of economists—recommended a series of labor-friendly proposals, including granting unions permission to collect fees (in lieu of dues) from nonmembers whom the union represented in bargaining, providing protection for farm workers against employer antiunionization activities, and federal aid for job retraining for workers displaced by automation (*NYT,* December 10, 1961, 1).

This is not to say that everything ran smoothly during the 1950s, or that serious management-labor conflict was a thing of the past. When an economic downturn occurred in 1958, management began to pull back from its relatively accommodating approach to shop-floor relations. One industry in which this occurred was steel. American steel manufacturers had, by the late 1950s, begun to implement new technology in the face of their first postwar experience of significant foreign competition, and this led firms to attempt to reduce workers' control over working conditions (Harris 1982, 155). According to Brody (1980, 195–198), prior to 1959, U.S. Steel had adopted a generally "conciliatory" approach to bargaining, as well as to work rules. In its 1959 negotiations, however, the company's new management took an unusually hard line, focusing primarily on an attempt to gain control over the crew size involved in particular operations. The union believed that management already had the ability to remove these inefficiencies under the existing contract, but management held firm, leading to an eight-month industry-wide strike, in which the production of steel in the United States virtually ceased. At this point, American consumers of steel, most notably the automobile manufacturers, began to turn to foreign steel to fill their needs. This precipitated a crisis in the American steel industry from which it never fully recovered, although the full force of this crisis was not felt until the 1970s. The industry did appear to learn from this experience, however. As Brody put it, after the strike was settled, the management of U.S. Steel "increasingly dealt with productivity issues through 'objective problem solving' in an ongoing joint effort with the union. To a large degree, the industry ultimately accomplished by the cooperative route . . . what it had failed to win by force in 1959" (ibid., 197).

The steel strike illustrated another benefit that unions provided to management: a justification for raising prices. In an opinion piece in *Commentary,* published in 1960 after the end of the steel strike, Daniel Bell (1960) argued that companies used collective bargaining outcomes as a justification for raising prices and then blamed the price increases on the unions. As Bell noted, few economists, not even conservatives such as Milton Friedman, believed that the wage increases for the hourly workforce was the cause of the price increases. Rather, as was later argued by John Kenneth Galbraith in *The New Industrial State* (1967), large firms in the core industries such as auto and steel had sufficient market power that they were virtually free to set their own prices. Hearings on economic concentration chaired by Senator Estes Kefauver had revealed that company price increases were typically far greater than the wage increases that preceded them. Walter Reuther had estimated that between 1947 and 1956, every one dollar increase in labor costs from American auto manufacturers was accompanied by a price increase of $3.75 (Bell 1960, 188). According to Bell, "The net effect of union pressure—apart from the gains which have been won for the small group of highly organized workers—has been to help install a mechanism whereby the large corporation is able to strengthen its price position in the market" (ibid.). Labor had thus become a "junior partner" with the company, albeit an unwilling one.

This accommodation by labor was itself a product of the unions' increasing integration into the societal mainstream as well as their growing bureaucratization. Even during the militant mid-1940s, many unions had already begun to focus on their own narrow interests rather than society-wide ones. Yet even the more socially oriented unions, in particular the UAW, found their efforts to move American society in the direction of social democracy foiled by the political climate of the late 1940s. The Treaty of Detroit represented the culmination of this process, an example of what the organizational sociologist Philip Selznick (1949) referred to as "cooptation," a term that became popular among student activists in the 1960s as a more formal word for "selling out." As Grant McConnell (1966, 326–329) suggested, a series of agreements resulted in unions accepting mechanization in their industries in exchange for significant wage and benefit improvements, despite the fact that it led to significant layoffs of union members. This occurred among the United Mine Workers, the Teamsters, and even in the otherwise radical International Longshoremen's Association, whose legendary leader, Harry Bridges, conceded that the union's decision was "pretty selfish" (ibid., 327). The steelworkers provided an exception to this rule, remaining steadfast in their refusal to accept significant layoffs regardless of wage gains. Yet for most unions, the relative ease with which agreements were reached was in part a consequence of their growing bureaucratization. The surge of new members in the 1940s and early 1950s brought workers into the fold who had little knowledge or experience with the struggles of the 1930s and thus lacked the political consciousness of the earlier generation. Meanwhile, those who had been through the solidarity-inducing early years and achieved leadership roles had either grown cynical or exhausted, or had simply decided, as Reuther had, that one had to make the best of a less-than-ideal situation. In that sense, the unions were very much like the managers with whom they tangled. Each had accepted the existence of the other, and the need to make the best of a situation not of their own choosing.

The Return to Militancy, and Management's Response

With John F. Kennedy's election as President in 1960, the White House was again occupied by a more pro-labor administration. Shortly after taking office, Kennedy appointed the Advisory Committee on Labor-Management Policy. This committee included labor officials Meany, Reuther, Thomas Kennedy of the United Mine Workers, and David McDonald of the United Steelworkers, as well as leading CEOs, including Henry Ford II, Thomas J. Watson Jr. of IBM, Joseph Block of Inland Steel, and J. Spencer Love of Burlington Mills (*NYT*, February 17, 1961, 1, 7). The group issued a report in 1962 with a conciliatory tone much like that of the 1945 Labor-Management Charter among the heads of the AFL, CIO, and the Chamber of Commerce (*NYT*, May 2, 1962, 20; Judis 2001, 79). Similarly, shortly after his election to a full term as president in November 1964, Lyndon Johnson created the fourteen-member National Commission on Technology, Automation, and Economic Progress. Among this group's members were Reuther, Joseph A. Beirne of the Communications Workers, and Albert J. Haynes of the Machinists, along with Patrick E. Haggerty of Texas Instruments, Edwin Land of Polaroid, and John I. Snyder Jr. of U.S. Industries. The group also included three academics—Daniel Bell, economist Robert M. Solow, and legal scholar Benjamin Aaron (*NYT*, November 15, 1964, 64; Judis 2001, 82).[9] In a 1966 report, this committee recommended that the government step in as an employer of last resort and expressed support for the institution of a negative income tax (Lekachman 1966, 67–68).[10]

However harmonious relations between labor and business were in the larger political arena—and even here there were problems—things were less sanguine on the shop floor.[11] At this level, the bureaucratization of the unions began to catch up with them in the 1960s. As we have seen, although the Treaty of Detroit led to greater wages and benefits for auto workers, these gains came at a price. As Bell noted (1960, 53–54), the agreement gave General Motors full control of the work process, including production scheduling, model changes, and plant investment. The length of the agreement—five years—also meant that union members were no longer engaged in frequent debate and discussion of contract provisions. Lichtenstein (1985, 365–366) has described some of the consequences of this decision: "As an institution, the UAW increasingly came to resemble a combination political machine and welfare bureaucracy which 'serviced' the membership and 'policed' the national contract." In addition, the focus on broad bargaining objectives left the national union ill equipped to deal with working conditions at the local level. Reuther was aware of these problems, noting, in a 1955 speech to Ford officials, the importance of issues such as the conditions of lockers, toilets, and parking lots, as well as safety and health concerns (ibid., 369). Yet almost immediately after the UAW and Ford signed their 1955 contract, more than 80 percent of Ford's workers engaged in a work stoppage in protest against a range of plant-level issues (ibid., 370).

One problem that emerged as a consequence of the growing bureaucratization of not only the UAW but the large unions in general was a rationalization of grievance procedures, as union leaders encouraged the rank-and-file to file grievances formally rather than stopping production (Brody 1980, 202). In the auto industry, the frequency of formal grievances increased sharply beginning in the 1950s (Lichtenstein 1985, 374), taxing the system and leading to long backlogs of complaints. At General Motors, the number of unresolved grievances increased more than threefold between 1958 and 1970 (ibid., 370). But the proliferation of formal grievances was not the only response by workers to their shop-floor concerns. Contract rejections, which, according to Fairris (1994, 203), were virtually "unheard of" prior to the 1960s, rose to 8.7 percent in 1964 and to 14.2 percent by 1967. Strike activity also increased sharply during the 1960s, a growing proportion of which (40 percent between 1968 and 1973) were wildcat strikes, most of which were due to working conditions (ibid.). The total number of strikes, which had dropped to 3,333 in 1960 (a postwar low) and stood at 3,362 in 1963, began to increase sharply by 1964, rising to 4,405 in 1966, to 5,045 in 1968, and to 5,700 (a postwar high) in 1969 (Bureau of Labor Statistics 1982). A similar pattern occurred for strikes involving at least 1,000 workers. This figure reached a postwar low of 195 in 1961 and dropped to 181 in 1963. By 1967 the number had more than doubled, however, to 381, increasing to a high of 412 in 1969 (Bureau of Labor Statistics 2011).[12]

One argument that has been made for the growing incidence of strikes in the late 1960s was the changing nature of the unionized workforce, in particular the increase in young and African American workers. Lichtenstein (1985, 375) notes, however, that the unionized workforce (at least in the auto industry) was relatively stable during that period, with more than 65 percent of the membership as of 1967 having had ten or more years of experience. Both Lichtenstein and Fairris (1994) argue that the deterioration of working conditions is what precipitated the increase in strikes in the late 1960s. For Lichtenstein (1985, 375), this was a consequence of the failure of the union to address local shop-floor issues. As Reuther's own survey of the union's members showed, worker hostility was directed primarily at their local unions rather than the national organization. For Fairris, it was a consequence of technological changes in the production process that increased management's power (1994, 196–200). An alternative explanation, one that Fairris rejects but that I believe may have been a more likely (or at least more fundamental) cause, is the tight labor market that existed in the late 1960s. Although the correlation is far from perfect and the issue remains controversial—labor militancy was high during the Great Depression, for example—strike activity tends to increase during periods of economic expansion, when unemployment is low and labor is thus scarce (Rees 1952). This was certainly the case in the late 1960s, as a booming economy combined with the massive deployment of soldiers in Vietnam created virtually full-employment conditions. Tight labor markets give workers power because they are difficult to replace (Kimeldorf 2011). In this account, the increase in strike activity in the late 1960s was a function of the high level of worker power. This is supported by the fact that the ratio of quits to layoffs between 1966 and 1973 was nearly twice as high as in the previous seven years (Weisskopf, Bowles, and Gordon 1983, 385). The simple fact of worker power does not ensure that strikes will occur, of course. Presumably at least some level of discontent had to have been present. It would have been far more difficult to act on this frustration, however, had unemployment been high. Fairris (1994, 206–207) contends, on the contrary, that worker power had actually declined by the late 1960s as a result of the shop-floor developments described above. He acknowledges that the tight labor markets "no doubt allowed workers to vent their anger and frustration over the loss of shopfloor [*sic*] power in ways . . . that they could not have otherwise." He argues, however, that these were acts of desperation rather than the "calculated moves of the increasingly empowered rank-and-file."

Yet this argument represents a distortion of the position that tight labor markets increase the propensity to strike. It is not necessary to assume that workers were engaging in "calculated moves" when deciding to strike during periods of low unemployment. Social actors are not always conscious of their motives, and even if some of them are, strikes, especially wildcat strikes, are instances of collective action. It is likely that participants in strikes experience a broad range of motives and awareness, and there is no reason to assume that the late 1960s were unusual in this respect. In any case, the data appear to support the suggestion that low unemployment played a major role in the late-1960s strike wave. The correlation between unemployment and strike activity in the postwar period was strongly negative. Between 1948 and 1973, the correlation between the unemployment rate and the incidence of strikes involving 1,000 or more workers was −.66.[13] If the tight labor market was not a unique cause of the high level of worker militancy in the late 1960s, it was certainly strongly associated with it.

Management Responds

Although the managers of large American corporations might have been relatively accommodating to organized labor during the postwar period, the strike activity and general turmoil of the late 1960s could not be easily dismissed. Instead, labor's strong push during the decade led to a reaction from management that resulted in a renewed offensive against labor, a movement that gained full force in the 1970s. This ultimately led to the dissolution of the postwar accord.

Much of the expansion in wages and benefits in the 1950s was fueled by increases in worker productivity. In fact, a central element of the Treaty of Detroit was the measure to tie wage increases to productivity. Auto company managements were willing to do this in part because productivity was rising at a higher rate than were wages, leading to enormous profits (Bell 1960). By the mid-1960s, however, the economy-wide growth in productivity began to slow, and one source of this decline appears to have been driven by worker shop-floor resistance, including a proliferation of wildcat strikes (Weisskopf, Bowles, and Gordon 1983; Norsworthy and Zabala 1985). As productivity growth began to slow, profit margins declined as well, especially between 1966 and 1969 (Nordhaus et al. 1974). It was probably inevitable, given this situation, that business would respond.

The focus of this response was not the auto industry, however, but the construction and steel industries (Judis 2001, 120). Construction is a unique industry in that unlike most manufacturing jobs, which can be shipped overseas, building construction takes place in a particular location. The location of new construction can be shifted to locales with more employer-friendly environments—so a company can decide to construct a plant in Mississippi rather than New York because of weaker unions in the former—but this option is less feasible if one is constructing residential or commercial buildings. Although the construction unions had been restrained in pushing for wage increases during the late 1950s and early 1960s, when their unemployment rate ranged from 12 to 18 percent, by 1965 concerns about labor shortages were already beginning to appear (Linder 1999, 10). By 1968, unemployment had dropped so low (1.6 percent for electricians, for example) that companies were often forced to engage in bidding wars for skilled craftsmen (ibid., 16). This situation gave workers an enormous degree of leverage. As one worker put it, "If a foreman looked at you cross-eyed . . . you'd pick up your tools and go to another job down the street" (quoted in ibid., 17).

The steel industry, meanwhile, was, by the late 1960s, experiencing the effects of the increasing foreign competition that had emerged during the 1959 strike. In addition, steel, like other manufacturing industries, was affected by labor relations in the construction industry, since it relied on the former for building its plants. A particularly dramatic illustration of this occurred in 1967, when U.S. Steel decided to stop one of its own construction projects in Pittsburgh during a strike against local contractors, so as not to provide an alternative employer for striking workers. The company did this, according to its president, Leslie Worthington, "to exert pressure on the unions" as a means of holding down the overall costs of construction labor (Linder 1999, 24). U.S. Steel was also concerned that high wage increases in construction would motivate steelworkers to push for similar gains (ibid., 25).

In most cases, however, manufacturing companies were more concerned with having their plants constructed quickly than they were about reducing the costs of construction labor. "A long-standing contractor complaint is that owners often worry more about finishing a project on time than higher cost caused by expensive labor settlements," a 1968 article in the trade publication *Engineering News-Record* noted. "So owner pressure—if any—is on the contractor to settle, and finish the job" (quoted in Linder 1999, 183). By 1969, construction unions had received wage gains averaging 10 percent, and the cost of newly constructed industrial plants had increased by as much as 25 percent over the previous year (*Time*, August 29, 1969). Yet the manufacturers were often operating under considerable pressure themselves. At the new General Motors plant in Lordstown, Ohio, for example, construction workers were working seventy-hour weeks (and receiving double pay for every hour beyond forty) because GM needed to get its new Vega into production to compete with Ford, which had recently introduced the Maverick (ibid.).

A group of construction industry executives began to meet with some of their manufacturing customers in the summer of 1968, and by May 1969 an organization of corporate officers had formed at a meeting of the Business Council (the descendant of Franklin Roosevelt's Business Advisory Council), at which Roger M. Blough, the recently retired CEO of U.S. Steel, had agreed to be its chair. The group, which Blough termed the Construction Users Anti-Inflation Roundtable, included the CEOs of several leading firms, among them Fred Borch of General Electric, J. K. Jamieson of Standard Oil of New Jersey, Birny Mason Jr. of Union Carbide, and Frank Milliken of Kennecott Copper (Linder 1999, 190). Four years later this group merged with two other groups of executives, including the Labor Law Study Group, to become the Business Roundtable.

There is no doubt that the members of the group were extremely concerned about inflation, and that they saw rising labor costs as a serious problem.[14] And given the labor shortage of the period and the willingness of the construction unions to take full advantage of it, it is difficult to deny that there was some justification for the companies' views. Unlike the 1950s, in which productivity in the auto industry significantly exceeded the workers' wage gains, it seems likely that by the late 1960s the situation may have been reversed. And it is evident that the unions, especially in construction, were seen as the primary offenders, as contractors complained about "an industry dominated by unions . . . protected by a government that unions hold captive" (Linder 1999, 186).

Yet despite this situation, and despite the presence of a nonunion labor force in construction, the Construction Users Anti-Inflation Roundtable was careful not to attack unions as an institution. R. Eric Miller, a vice president at Bechtel, the nation's largest construction firm and a fully unionized company, argued that labor "certainly has to become a partner." In response to this, Miller suggested the formation of a council—the National Construction Industry Council—that would include representatives from construction firms, manufacturers, government, and labor, a corporatist approach much like the councils that existed during World War II, as well as in Western Europe (Linder 1999 189). This view was further reflected in Blough's statement that the Roundtable was "in no sense a union-busting group," and that "many intelligent union leaders are as concerned as we are" (quoted in ibid., 192).

Conclusion

By the end of the 1960s, then, the American labor movement had failed to achieve many of its goals. Its more radical elements had been virtually eliminated. The American welfare state paled next to its European, and even Canadian, counterparts. Union leaders had withdrawn from virtually all of their attempts to secure worker control on the shop floor. And labor still faced public opposition, a result of strikes in the 1940s and 1950s and of inflation in the late 1960s. In other respects, however, organized labor was as strong as it had ever been. Its members earned higher wages with more generous benefits than earlier generations could have imagined. Labor leaders were regularly consulted by government and the news media for their views on major issues of the day. And perhaps most important of all, unions had become fully institutionalized—certainly not loved, but taken-for-granted—in the eyes of corporate management. In this sense, the postwar American corporate elite was very different from its predecessors and, as later became evident, from its successors as well.

Although there have always been corporations that actively encouraged and supported their unions, this group has in every period been a minority. It would therefore be inaccurate to claim that the American corporate elite, even its most enlightened elements, could be characterized as "prounion" in a philosophical sense. On the contrary, just as the threat of socialism led the businessmen of the National Civic Federation (NCF) to support the idea of independent unions at the turn of the twentieth century, it was the power and militancy of the labor movement that led the corporate elite to adopt a pragmatic, moderate approach in the postwar period. Labor unions were not the only forces that created this moderation. Certainly the civil rights and antiwar movements set in motion a series of forces that required a response, and here, too, the response they received, at least from elites, was often one of accommodation rather than direct confrontation. But the disruption of labor came earlier, well before the 1960s, and hit directly at the elite's core—the process of production.

A result of these early battles, most of which occurred during the 1930s and 1940s, was the so-called capital-labor accord, an informal truce in which management agreed to accept the idea of collective bargaining and independent unions while workers agreed to focus their demands on wages and benefits rather than control of firm decision making. That this accord had existed was for many years a widely held view among sociologists and labor historians. More recently, a number of scholars have called into question whether such an accommodation ever took place. There was never a formal agreement, and it is clear that conflict between management and labor was pervasive during the postwar period, peaking, as we saw, in the late 1940s and again in the late 1960s. Proponents of the idea that an accord existed did not claim that management saw unionization as the best of all possible worlds, of course, nor did they deny that management fought actively against union demands and practices. They did, however, argue that management came to grudgingly accept the reality of unions, in part as a necessary evil and in part as a potentially useful mechanism with which to maintain worker discipline and maintain compliance. Even in the works of those critical of the idea of an accord, including those cited in this chapter, one can find copious evidence that, in this sense, management had accepted its end of the bargain.

In rejecting the idea of the capital-labor accord, many of the new labor historians argue that the assault on organized labor that occurred in the late 1970s and beyond demonstrates that business had never accepted labor unions and that company managements would seize the first opportunity they had to destroy their unions (see, for example, Gross 1995; Lichtenstein 1997–98; Phillips-Fein 2009). This argument involves reading history backward, however. It is based on the assumption that corporations in the 1970s did what they would have done in earlier years had similar conditions existed. This may or may not have been true, but similar conditions did not exist in the postwar era. Both organized labor and the government were relatively strong and had a high degree of legitimacy in the larger society.[15] It is true that business fought labor at every step, often aggressively. As we have seen, even in the early 1960s companies were working to undermine unions at every opportunity. But there has never been any dispute about the fact that management and labor have opposing interests, nor did post-war observers ever deny that class conflict in the traditional sense was rampant. Even Dahrendorf's (1959) concept of the "institutionalization of class conflict," however benign, was based on the acknowledgment that worker-management opposition was a fact of life in the postwar period.

In making a case for the existence of the accord and for management's acceptance of organized labor, I do not mean to claim that business "loved" unions. Lichtenstein may have been correct when he stated that "despite much wishful historiography to the contrary, no well-organized 'corporate liberal' body of enlightened businessmen supported either the Wagner Act or the Social Security Act" (1997–98, 769). Examples of prounion firms such as the Louisville tobacco companies that testified before Congress in the 1930s undoubtedly were exceptions, just as the pro-union businessmen from the early days of the NCF were. But even without organized corporate support for the Wagner Act and Social Security Act, there were plenty of businessmen, perhaps a majority of those from the largest firms, who exhibited a pragmatic response to unions and refrained from attempts to repeal them. Even the "sharp curbs" (ibid., 770) on union activism sought by these realists in support of the Taft-Hartley bill were modest compared with the positions businesses had taken in earlier years.[16]

The modal response of the postwar corporate elite to organized labor, then, was what Harris (1982) calls "realism," the pragmatic acceptance, however grudging, of the fact that unions were here to stay, and that management had better deal with them the best they could. Along with this pragmatism was the realization that in many cases, unions actually did serve the interests of business. This is a far cry from the attitudes that emerged in the antilabor onslaught of the late 1970s and beyond, and it is a far cry from the attitudes that exist in the twenty-first century. These earlier views would probably not have developed had workers, backed by a sympathetic state, not compelled management to adopt them. The evidence suggests that they were genuine, however. The extent to which these views were authentic will become increasingly apparent as we observe the ways in which they changed in subsequent years.

5 ||| The Banks as Mediators

Beyond the government and organized labor was a third force that contributed to the moderation of the postwar corporate elite: the financial community. That the banks would be a significant player in the postwar era, at the height of the managerial revolution, seems paradoxical. Banks are acknowledged by many observers to have been powerful in the early part of the twentieth century, and they are widely believed to be powerful in the twenty-first as well. In the post–World War II period, however, most observers assumed that the large nonfinancial corporations were so strong, with so much capital, that they did not need the banks. Instead, the banks were seen as playing a primarily advisory role—similar to lawyers and accountants—at most a site of mediation rather than a source of power.

This view is largely correct, I shall argue; bank power over nonfinancial corporations was relatively low in the postwar period. This does not mean that the banks were unimportant, however. The role that they played was a function not of their power over other firms—although this did occasionally manifest itself—but rather their centrality in the social networks created by ties among the leaders of the largest American corporations. Financial and nonfinancial firms were mutually dependent on one another during this period, and thus they acted as sources of countervailing power. Banks occasionally stepped in to discipline recalcitrant firms or individuals—as in the case of Howard Hughes and Trans World Airlines (TWA)—and nonfinancial corporations were sometimes able to dictate the terms of their loans or avoid the banks altogether. In most cases, however, neither group was able to exercise power over the other. Rather, the banks' position was a result of their unique character. Because of their interest in the entire economy, irrespective of industry, the banks became a center for the discussion of system-wide concerns that transcended those of particular companies or industries. Bank boards of directors became meeting places for chief executives of the leading corporations, who both transmitted and gained access to broad, general information about economy-wide trends. This role of bank boards, reflected in their central positions in the networks within the corporate community, rendered financial institutions a source of normative consensus among leading firms in a wide range of industries, facilitating a view that transcended the perspectives and interests of individual firms. In this way, the banks contributed to the moderate, pragmatic approach adopted by the American corporate elite in the postwar period.

Not all observers of the postwar period saw the banks as mediators. Several scholars argued that the major banks either controlled corporations or were disproportionately powerful, even in the mid-twentieth century. We shall have a chance to examine their arguments and evidence, as well as the criticisms they faced. I am not going to make this argument myself, however. On the contrary, I shall suggest that the banks played an important role in the postwar period, but not a controlling, or even hegemonic, one. Bank power did increase beginning in the late 1960s, but it began to sharply decline during the 1980s. The importance of finance capital in the postwar period was in its role as a mediator, a site at which the various segments of the business community could address issues of concern to the overall economy, and not simply to their specific firms or industries.

Of necessity, this chapter will be more theoretical than the previous two. Evidence does exist for the role that I am assigning the banks, but it is less plentiful than that demonstrating the role of the state and labor in the formation and maintenance of corporate moderation. Perhaps the strongest evidence for the idea of banks as mediators is the fact of their subsequent decline—a topic that we will visit in Chapter 7. To understand the role of the banks in the postwar era, it will be useful to discuss the various arguments about the role of finance capital, dating back to the turn of the twentieth century. In discussing this role, I will be covering what may appear to be a series of esoteric debates over arcane issues. I hope to show, however, that these debates over the role of financial institutions are relevant not only for understanding the postwar period but also for understanding the changes that the financial community experienced in the subsequent decades.

I begin the chapter with a discussion of the decline of bank power, from its heights in the early twentieth century to its apparent nadir in the post-war era. I then discuss the arguments by critics who claimed, beginning in the late 1960s, that the banks had reasserted their imperial role, and the debates that these arguments triggered. After an assessment of the evidence for and against the thesis of bank control, I develop a synthesis in which I make a case for the contingent nature of financial power. I then use this synthesis to discuss the role that the banks played in helping to maintain the moderate, pragmatic strategy adopted by the postwar corporate elite.

The Era (and Fall) of Finance Capital

Early in the twentieth century, the Austrian Marxist economist Rudolf Hilferding (1981 [1910]) discussed the dominant role of German banks, which were highly concentrated and exercised enormous influence over German industry. This view of bank power was later popularized by Lenin, in *Imperialism* (1975 [1917]). That German banks were powerful at the time (and have remained powerful) is widely acknowledged by scholars (see, for example, Roe 1994). Yet as we saw in Chapter 2, the banks were also major players in the United States in the early twentieth century. Led by J. P. Morgan, George F. Baker, James Stillman, and Jacob Schiff, the major investment and commercial banks of the period exercised effective control over a number of leading nonfinancial corporations (Mizruchi and Bunting 1981). In administering this system, Morgan—the dominant figure of the period—sought to create a "community of interest" to minimize what he saw as destructive competition, as reflected in the 1901 battle for control of the Northern Pacific Railroad that we discussed in Chapter 2 (Corey 1930, 284; Cochran and Miller 1942, 196–197; Mizruchi 1982, 98, 146).

Several factors are believed to have led to a decline in the power of financial institutions over time. First, in part as a result of the Pujo Hearings,

Congress passed the Clayton Antitrust Act of 1914, which outlawed the sharing of directors by companies operating in the same market. Prior to the Clayton Act, it was common for officers of major New York banks, even those presumed to be in direct competition, to sit on one another's boards. In 1912, the twenty largest commercial banks in the United States maintained a total of 124 director interlocks among themselves. In other words, the average bank shared approximately six directors with other banks. In 1919, five years after the passage of the Clayton Act, direct interlocks between commercial banks had virtually disappeared; only nineteen remained (Mizruchi 1982, 124). There has been a long-running controversy over the precise meaning of interlocking directorates (Mizruchi 1996). Most observers acknowledge, however, that in the early twentieth century the relatively dense network of ties among the largest firms reflected the high concentration of power during this period (see Mizruchi and Bunting 1981 for references). The disappearance of interlocks among banks in the years following the passage of the Clayton Act does not prove that their power declined, but it does suggest that it may have been more difficult for them to coordinate their activities (Mizruchi 1982).

A second factor in the decline of bank power was the Banking Act of 1933, more commonly known as the Glass-Steagall Act. This law required commercial and investment banks to separate their functions. Prior to its passage, commercial banks occasionally participated in the placement of securities for their corporate customers, while investment banks were able to hold deposits. As a result of Glass-Steagall, investment banks were forced to relinquish their deposits, which had been a major source of capital, rendering them dependent on commercial banks for financing. Commercial banks, meanwhile, were no longer able to participate in securities offerings, which had been a contributing factor in their power over nonfinancial firms (Kotz 1978, 54).[1]

Third, although the Great Depression significantly weakened all corporations, the number of bank failures and the sharp declines in size took an especially hard toll on the banks (Kotz 1978, 52–53; Herman 1981a, 115). Fourth, and perhaps most important, was the increasing ability of nonfinancial corporations to finance their investments with internal funds, that is, their reduced dependence on financial institutions for capital. This last point, which later became the most controversial of the factors said to have led to a decline in bank power, requires discussion.

Capital Dependence and Corporate Control

The place to begin for an understanding of the role of internal funds is the classic work on the large corporation, Adolf A. Berle Jr. and Gardiner C. Means's *The Modern Corporation and Private Property* (1968 [1932]). Although Berle and Means were concerned primarily with the concentration of economic power in American society, *The Modern Corporation* is best known for its thesis of the separation of ownership from control among large American corporations.[2] Berle and Means began by noting the increasing size of American companies in the early decades of the twentieth century. This size, along with the associated concentration within industries, vested a relatively small number of companies with enormous power, they argued. As these firms grew, it became increasingly difficult for the original owners to maintain their majority stockholdings, and stocks became dispersed among a large number of small shareholders. American Telephone and Telegraph, for example, had approximately 10,000 stockholders in 1901 but more than 642,000 three decades later. United States Steel's stockholders increased more than tenfold during the same period (Berle and Means 1968 [1932], 52). Along with a growing number of stockholders was a decline in the proportion of stock held by the largest owner. In both U.S. Steel and the Pennsylvania Railroad, for example, the largest stockholders held less than 1 percent of the shares (ibid., 47).

As stock became increasingly dispersed, Berle and Means suggested, the stockholders, even relatively large ones, became increasingly unable to exercise control over the firm. Instead, they viewed their holdings as an investment, for which their concerns were limited to dividend payouts and the value of their equity. As a consequence of this, Berle and Means argued, power passed to the company's managers, those who ran the day-to-day affairs of the firm. The managers, in turn, became increasingly insulated from the influence of stockholders.

If the managers who now ran the large corporation behaved exactly as the owners who preceded them, then the separation of ownership from control might have had no effect on firm behavior, and thus might have been of limited scholarly interest. Berle and Means expressed concern, however, that the managers' interests were not necessarily in line with those of the stockholders. Whereas owners preferred that profits be returned to them in the form of dividends, for example, managers preferred to either reinvest the profits or, in more sinister interpretations, to further their own privileges in the form of higher salaries or "perks." Removed from the pressures of stockholders, managers, for Berle and Means, were now viewed as a self-perpetuating oligarchy, unaccountable to the owners whom they were expected to represent.

More important for our present discussion, however, was a second presumed consequence of managerial control. Because of the growing concentration of industry, not only did corporate managers have control over the distribution of revenue within their firms, but the revenue itself became increasingly large. This control allowed the managers to reduce dividends, which increased the firms' retained earnings (Berle and Means 1968 [1932], 112–116). Two decades later, Berle, writing alone, explicitly described the consequences of this trend: the greater availability of retained earnings, he argued (1954, 35–40), freed corporations from their prior dependence on financial institutions. This led to a decline in the power of banks over nonfinancial corporations.

Several scholars in the postwar period agreed with Berle's assessment about the increasing (and crucial) role of internal financing. One of the strongest claims was made by John Kenneth Galbraith, who argued in *The New Industrial State* (1967, 92–93) that the corporation "accords a much more specific protection":

> That is, by providing it with a source of capital, derived from its own earnings, that is wholly under its own control. No banker can attach conditions as to how retained earnings are to be used. . . . Few other developments can have more fundamentally altered the character of capitalism.

Paul Baran and Paul Sweezy, two leading Marxist economists, made a similar argument:

> Each corporation aims at and normally achieves financial independence through the internal generation of funds which remain at the disposal of management. The corporation may still, as a matter of policy, borrow from or through financial institutions, but it is not normally forced to do so and hence is able to avoid the kind of subjection to financial control which was so common in the world of Big Business fifty years ago. (Baran and Sweezy 1966, 16)

The view that nonfinancial corporations were no longer dependent on banks was noted as far back as the 1940s, in a classic study by Robert Aaron Gordon. As Gordon (1945, 215) put it:

> The increased financial self-sufficiency of successful large corporations has lessened their dependence on commercial banks as well as investment bankers. The marked downward trend in the commercial loans of banks is well known. . . . With the decline in dependence on commercial bank loans, there is less chance for large firms to become subject to marked banker influence through temporary financial embarrassment.[3]

Although, or perhaps because, the idea of corporate independence from financial institutions was so widely accepted, there was little systematic study of the topic. The most widely cited study was produced by Harvard Business School finance professor John Lintner (1966 [1959]). Examining data from the 1920s through 1955, Lintner found an "extraordinary stability in the broad patterns of financing used" by American corporations (ibid., 177). This was contrary to what Berle and Means predicted, Lintner argued, given their emphasis on firms' increasing use of internal funds. One might argue, in response, that the corporations' increasing use of internal funds had already established itself by the mid-1920s and that one would not necessarily have expected to observe a continued increase after that point. Or one could suggest, as Berle (1966 [1959], xiii–xiv) himself did in the foreword to the volume in which Lintner's essay appeared, that the stability in the ratio of internal financing masked its far greater magnitude in the postwar period, given the spectacular growth in size of the largest nonfinancial corporations. Of course, the increasing size of corporations also meant a significantly greater magnitude of external financing as well.

Kinder to Berle and Means's thesis, although only partly so, was a subsequent study by Stearns (1986). Examining data from 1946 through 1980, Stearns found that firms' use of internal funds was relatively high from 1946 through 1964 but declined sharply beginning in 1965. In the former period, corporations received approximately one-third of their funds from external sources, while in the later period nearly one-half of their funds came from external sources (Stearns 1986, 53). Moreover, Stearns shows (ibid., 54) that firms' average debt ratios were at century-wide lows during the 1946–1964 period, the height of the era in which nonfinancial corporations were assumed to be relatively independent of banks. The average debt ratio ranged from 0.42 to 0.46 between 1900 and 1944, dropped to 0.33 in the 1946–1964 period, and then increased to 0.43 from 1965 through 1980. Viewed in this context, nonfinancial corporations in the postwar period, at least through 1964, did appear capable of maintaining a relatively high degree of independence from financial institutions.

The mere fact that external financing was relatively low in the early post-war period and rose after 1964 does not necessarily mean that firms became more dependent on financial institutions in the later period or that they were less dependent in the earlier one. Corporations may decide to use external funds when interest rates are low, for example, even if they might otherwise have sufficient levels of cash. Companies may also choose to borrow for the tax benefits, and they may choose to invest, or even hold, their internal resources. To examine the extent to which corporations' use of debt financing was discretionary, Stearns and I examined the borrowing behavior of twenty-two large American corporations from 1955 through 1983. We found that even taking into account a series of financial variables (including the cost of capital), the single largest predictor of firms' use of debt was the availability of retained earnings. When retained earnings were high, borrowing was low, and vice versa (Mizruchi and Stearns 1994). These findings suggest that when cash is available, corporations will use it. This means, consistent with Berle and Means's original formulation, that managers will attempt to maintain their independence from banks.

A Resurgence of Bank Control?

Given Stearns's findings, as well as the claims of postwar observers of large American corporations, it is not surprising that banks were seen as relatively unimportant during this period. To my knowledge, only one work published in English between the end of the war and the mid-1960s made a case for the power of banks: a book by a Marxist economist, Victor Perlo (1957). This situation began to change by the end of the 1960s, however, as a result of two factors. The first was the release of a study by the House Banking and Currency Committee, chaired by Wright Patman, that documented the increasing role of institutional investors in corporate ownership. The second was a massive merger wave as well as a downturn in corporate profits, which led to an increase in the use of external financing and a lessening of the seeming invulnerability of large American corporations. A third factor was the rise of the New Left, inspired by the civil rights and antiwar movements, which spawned a group of scholars and activists who offered a critical perspective on a number of broadly accepted assessments of American society. One aspect of this upsurge was a reassessment of the Berle and Means thesis. Some critics, most notably Philip Burch (1972) and Maurice Zeitlin (1974), suggested that the separation of ownership from control had been exaggerated. Others, most notably Robert Fitch and Mary Oppenheimer (1970a, 1970b, 1970c) and David Kotz (1978), argued that the banks had reasserted their power. The work by Fitch and Oppenheimer in particular triggered a fierce debate. A discussion of this debate will help shed light on the role that the banks played in the postwar corporate community.

The origins of the debate over bank control stem from the 1966 book *Monopoly Capital*, by two noted Marxist economists, Paul A. Baran and Paul M. Sweezy. This book was an attempt to provide an updated, Marxian-inspired theory to account for the changes that had occurred in capitalism since Marx's time. In laying out their model, Baran and Sweezy began by asserting that corporate control was no longer lodged in either the old capitalist families or in the financial community (Baran and Sweezy 1966, 15–20). Instead, consistent with Berle and Means's thesis, control was now in the hands of the managers who ran the day-to-day affairs of the firm. Baran and Sweezy were aware of the fact that this claim was likely to arouse the ire of traditional Marxists, many of whom believed, based on Lenin's *Imperialism*, that the banks were the centers of corporate power. They argued, however, contrary to Berle and Means, that although managers now ran the corporation, this change had no effect on the functioning of the firm. Managers could effectively be thought of as the representatives of capital, just as the earlier capitalist owners had been. Whether managers, families, or even banks controlled the firm was irrelevant to their functioning, Baran and Sweezy argued. As indicated by the passage quoted earlier in the chapter, Baran and Sweezy were willing to acknowledge that the banks played an important role in the system, since corporations "may still, as a matter of policy, borrow from or through financial institutions" (1966, 16). Because of their high level of retained earnings, they were "not normally forced to do so," however, and were therefore "able to avoid the kind of subjection to financial control which was so common in the world of Big Business fifty years ago" (ibid.).

It did not take long for this argument to evoke the reaction that Baran and Sweezy had perhaps feared. In a spirited, near-book-length article that appeared in three installments in a small left-wing publication, Robert Fitch and Mary Oppenheimer (1970a, 1970b, 1970c) provided a scathing critique of Baran and Sweezy, arguing that the banks in fact exercised continued dominance over even the largest nonfinancial corporations. Although Fitch and Oppenheimer were not always clear about the specific source of bank power, their focus was on three separate but intertwined factors: nonfinancial corporations' lack of capital and their consequent dependence on financial institutions; the increasing presence of stockholdings by bank trust departments, as revealed by Representative Patman's Banking and Currency Committee; and the representation of banks on the boards of nonfinancial firms, although this representation was itself seen as a consequence of the banks' control of capital and their stockholdings rather than an independent source of power (Fitch and Oppenheimer 1970a, 100).

In taking the first position, on the increasing reliance on external financing, Fitch and Oppenheimer directly confronted the managerialist assumption that corporations were able to finance their investments through retained earnings. Using data from the Federal Reserve, the authors showed what Stearns later documented over a longer period: the proportion of financing drawn from external funds, after remaining stable for a decade, began to increase sharply around 1965 (Fitch and Oppenheimer 1970b, 73).[4] The authors also provided numerous examples of bank trust department stockholdings, drawn from the Patman Report, as well as examples of banker representation on the boards of nonfinancial firms. The result of this system of dependence, Fitch and Oppenheimer argued, was that banks regularly intervene in the affairs of nonfinancial corporations, not only in crisis situations, but also in situations in which the firms are engaged in ordinary expansion, for which internal sources of capital are insufficient. Because the banks' interests do not necessarily coincide with those of their customers, the banks' policies may actually lead firms to engage in self-destructive behavior.

Although Fitch and Oppenheimer provided some systematic data, most of their evidence was drawn from descriptions of individual cases in which banks appeared to exercise power. In the 1970 Penn Central case, for example, two weeks before the firm declared bankruptcy, with the railroad unable to meet its debt payments, thirteen outside directors, most of whom were affiliated with commercial banks, held a meeting in which they dismissed the firm's management and agreed to seek government help for the firm (Fitch and Oppenheimer 1970a, 74–76). James Ling was ousted by the banks after his company, LTV, made an ill-fated attempt to acquire Jones and Laughlin Steel (ibid., 63). Standard Oil of New Jersey (later Exxon, now Exxon-Mobil), long a highly profitable firm that had managed to remain independent of outside influence, was forced to double its long-term debt after 1965 despite high interest rates, as profits slowed (ibid., 70–71). Howard Hughes was forced to place his majority stockholding in TWA in a trust fund administered by a group of banks and insurance companies after he was unable to generate sufficient internal funds to finance the purchase of the new generation of jets (ibid., 86–91). And Gulf and Western, a rapidly growing conglomerate in the 1960s, was not only assisted in its acquisitions by funds from the Chase Manhattan Bank, but congressional testimony indicated that Chase had participated in Gulf and Western's choice of target firms (Fitch and Oppenheimer 1970c, 68–74).

Lively as it was, and compelling as some of its examples appeared, Fitch and Oppenheimer's article soon attracted critiques of its own, from economists James O'Connor (1972) and Edward S. Herman (1973) as well as Sweezy (1972). Sweezy argued, for example, that Fitch and Oppenheimer failed to provide evidence that the representatives of bank trust departments actually use their stockholdings to influence the companies. To clarify the issue at stake here, banks in the United States are prohibited by law from directly owning stock in nonfinancial corporations. Among the divisions of many of the major banks, however, are trust departments that manage pension funds for corporations and individuals. These trust departments have invested heavily in both financial and nonfinancial corporations. They do so for the same reason that pension funds such as CREF, the College Retirement Equities Fund, do: to maximize the return on the funds they manage.

Although a number of observers, including Adolf A. Berle Jr. (in his 1954 book cited earlier), Representative Patman, and even David Rockefeller, chairman of the Chase Manhattan Bank (whose position was cited by Fitch and Oppenheimer), raised concerns about the potential power of the financial institutions whose trust departments held significant blocks

of corporate stock, a detailed study of bank trust department officers conducted by Herman and Safanda (1973) suggested that these trust departments are generally reluctant to use their holdings to influence corporate
management, or at least that they were during the 1960s. For one thing, as
Herman (1973, 21) noted in a critique of Fitch and Oppenheimer, trust
departments of banks are bureaucratically separated from the banks' commercial wings and are in competition with other investment companies
whose goal is to maximize returns for their clients. The trust departments
occasionally experience pressure from the bank's central administration,
but according to Herman, such pressure is resented because it often conflicts with the goals of the trust investors (who are in competition with
other fund managers for the accounts that they manage) and is therefore
generally rare. Second, Herman suggests, an attempt by a bank trust department to use its holding to gain control of a company could be seen as a
violation of its fiduciary obligation as a trustee, especially if, in establishing
such control, the bank were to act in a way that jeopardized the performance of the account. Third, Herman argues (ibid., 23–24) that rather
than seeing bank trust department holdings as a threat to their autonomy,
corporate managements in fact welcome the trust department purchase of
large blocks of their stock. They view this as a vote of confidence and a
means of cementing a business relationship with the bank. Based on their
own interviews, and a study of institutional investors conducted by the Securities and Exchange Commission, Herman and Safanda concluded that
most institutional investors at the time of the study (the late 1960s) were
"disinterested, lethargic, passive, and uncritically pro-management in their
use of proxies" (1973, 93).

Critics of Fitch and Oppenheimer also challenged their interpretation of
specific cases. In the episode involving Penn Central, Sweezy (1972, 137–
139) suggested that, if anything, the banks were "hoodwinked" by the
company's managers, who had succeeded in hiding the firm's losses through
clever accounting. As Herman (1973, 17) put it:

> One of the most significant aspects of the Penn Central failure was the abil-
> ity of management to dominate the board and to maintain control up to a
> few weeks before the actual bankruptcy, despite proven managerial inepti-
> tude, a high degree of dependence on bank credit, and substantial banker
> representation on the board of directors.

Sweezy described the Howard Hughes-TWA case (1972, 136) as an exception that received publicity precisely because it was so unusual. In the case of Gulf and Western and Chase Manhattan, according to Herman (1973, 28), Chase's plan to have Gulf and Western sell its shares in Pan American Airways so that Resorts International could acquire the firm was seen by Chase officials as an opportunity to gain a financial advantage for the bank's pension fund accounts, exactly what a bank trust department would be expected to do. Fitch, for his part, responded by providing examples from the SEC's institutional investor study suggesting that some bank trust department officials did believe in the necessity of intervening in the affairs of the companies in which they had invested, at least under some conditions (1972, 118–120).

A few years after the Fitch and Oppenheimer–Sweezy–Herman debate, David Kotz (1978) published a book in which he sought to systematically examine the extent of bank control. Drawing heavily on the Patman Report as well as the SEC's institutional investor study, Kotz attempted to classify the locus of control among the 200 largest U.S. nonfinancial corporations in 1969. Using bank trust department stockholdings as his primary indicator, Kotz argued that 34.5 percent of these firms were under either the full or partial control of one or more financial institutions. Kotz suggested from this finding that bank control of nonfinancial corporations was a significant and growing phenomenon. Responding to this study much as he had to the earlier work by Fitch and Oppenheimer, Herman (1979) criticized Kotz for his emphasis on stockholdings rather than credit relations as the basis of bank control.[5] My own tabulation of Kotz's data (Kotz 1979, 161–169) indicates that in only nine of the sixty-nine firms that Kotz classified as under full or partial financial control did he list a lending relation between the bank and the nonfinancial as the basis for the control. Given Herman's earlier findings on the generally passive role played by bank trust departments in governing the corporations in which they had holdings, this would seem to indicate that bank control was considerably less pervasive than Kotz suggested.

An Assessment

The debates between Fitch and Oppenheimer and Kotz on one side and Herman and Sweezy on the other left in their wake a substantial amount of confusion, not only on the facts—to what extent did banks actually control nonfinancial corporations?—but also on why such a question might matter. Regarding the extent of bank control, on the basis of my reading, I draw three conclusions about the nature of financial power and control in the postwar period.

First, although there may have been isolated examples of bank trust departments actively attempting to influence corporations—either through direct intervention or sale of their stock—there appears to be little systematic evidence that these trust departments were regularly viewed as a threat to management. Certainly these bank trust holdings were perceived as a potential threat by some observers, including members of Representative Patman's Banking and Currency Committee. There appear to have been few cases in which corporate managers themselves viewed these holdings as a threat, however, at least in the postwar period.

Second, although the representation of bankers on the boards of nonfinancial corporations may have occasionally either reflected the power of banks or served as a correlate of power, all of the parties to this debate agree that bank board representation did not by itself provide the basis for bank control. Bankers are often invited onto boards to provide financial advice, to lend prestige to the firm, or to help secure access to capital (Mizruchi 1996). Even in the latter case, however, this board presence is unlikely to provide the bank with control over the firm.

On the issue of external financing, however (the third point), the bank control theorists were on stronger ground. Based on the data presented by Stearns (1986)—who showed that the use of internal funds was relatively high from 1946 through 1964—Fitch and Oppenheimer's claim that the use of external financing increased after 1965 does appear to be consistent with the facts. Combined with the study that Stearns and I conducted showing that firms tend to rely on internal funds when they have the opportunity to do so (Mizruchi and Stearns 1994), it seems likely that the dependence of nonfinancial corporations on financial institutions increased beginning in the late 1960s. Whether this indicates a more general presence of bank control is less clear. It does suggest the possibility that bank power did begin to increase by the late 1960s.

As for the question of why this debate matters, recall that I have argued that the financial community provided a third source of constraint that contributed to the moderate, pragmatic orientation of the American corporate elite during the postwar period. The question is, what provided the basis of this constraint? One possible answer is that the banks performed this function through their control of nonfinancial corporations. I suggested at the outset of this chapter that I did not share the view that banks typically, or even frequently, exercised this control, and in the previous sections I have attempted to provide support for this claim. If the banks did not control nonfinancial corporations, however, then what exactly was their role, and how did they exercise constraint? I shall argue that the banks fulfilled this role in three ways: as sources of information, normative consensus, and what I call "cognitive range," the ability to see issues from multiple perspectives. They did this not by controlling nonfinancial corporations, however, but rather by occupying a central position in the social networks among them. The banks' centrality was a function of the fact that they possessed a universal resource—capital—as well as their neutral standing and their resulting concern for the well-being of the business community as a whole. In the following section, I develop a contingency theory of the relative power of the financial community. I then use this perspective to discuss the three processes by which the banks acted as a source of constraint for the corporate elite in the postwar period.

A Contingency Model of Financial Power

Although the banks may not have typically "controlled" large nonfinancial corporations in the postwar period, they were not without influence. In two important works, Herman (1981a) and Mintz and Schwartz (1985) moved beyond the earlier debates by replacing the idea of bank control with alternatives, in Herman's case the concept of "constraint" and in Mintz and Schwartz's case the concept of "hegemony."

In his 1981 book Herman noted, as he had done earlier, that the banks occasionally exercised power over nonfinancial corporations, primarily through their role as creditors. For Herman, actual bank control, by which he meant "the power to make the key decisions of a company" (1981a, 19), was a relatively rare event. What was not rare, however, was the ability of banks to constrain the activities of nonfinancial firms, by which he meant "the power to limit certain decision choices, as in a ceiling on dollars that may be spent on new facilities or paid out in dividends, or a power of veto over personnel choices" (ibid.). Although Herman classified only 1 of the

200 largest U.S. nonfinancial corporations in 1975 as under outright financial control, he counted 40 others as subject to "significant influence" by financial institutions (ibid., 159). As he put it:

> Direct bank intervention and virtually unilateral displacement of management . . . are rare among very large companies. But management changes under the pressure of creditors—with the creditors, if not choosing a successor, at least insisting on veto power—are not uncommon in cases where the large company is in acute distress. (Herman 1981a, 125)[6]

Herman's suggestion that the banks, although not often involved directly in firm decision making, are often able to exercise constraints on management, presents an opportunity for a resolution of the contentious debates over bank control. His approach allows for the incorporation of dramatic cases of bank intervention such as those described by Fitch and Oppenheimer. It also allows us to acknowledge the possibility that banks can (and do) regularly exercise power, without having to make the additional leap required to posit the widespread bank "control" of corporations. This is especially important in analyzing the postwar period, when American nonfinancial corporations were in a relatively strong economic position.

Another approach to the issue of bank power was presented by Mintz and Schwartz (1985). Mintz and Schwartz argued that although banks do not typically control individual corporations, they do exercise a broad "hegemony" over them, in that they create a set of conditions, primarily the requirement for capital, under which nonfinancial firms are compelled to operate. In Mintz and Schwartz's usage, hegemony exists when one firm "makes decisions that directly and significantly affect the business conditions of another firm . . . thus forcing changes in company strategy" (1985, 13). Although this often involves intervention into corporate affairs—the authors identified forty-two cases of bank intervention between 1977 and 1981 (ibid., 77–80)—it more often involves situations in which the managers of nonfinancial firms consciously act in ways that they believe will accord with the banks' wishes. Mintz and Schwartz thus shared with Fitch and Oppenheimer and Kotz the position that bank intervention "is an important factor in determining corporate behavior" (ibid., 76), but they believed that such intervention tends to be short term and episodic. They shared with Sweezy and Herman the view that long-term bank control relations "are not a major feature of the corporate landscape," but they believed that financial institutions do "play a unique, dominant role in intercorporate affairs" (ibid.).

As with Herman, the primary basis of bank power for Mintz and Schwartz, where it occurs, is in their role as creditors. Where Mintz and Schwartz differed with Herman was in the extent to which this bank power is built into the system. Whereas Herman viewed constraint by financial institutions as a contingent phenomenon, in which relations between financial and nonfinancial corporations are largely symmetric, Mintz and Schwartz saw the relations as tilted toward the banks. Both arguments are persuasive, but one can accept much of Mintz and Schwartz's position without taking the additional step of positing a structurally essential hegemony. The reason that banks hold hegemony over nonfinancial firms, according to Mintz and Schwartz, is that their responses to disturbances are asymmetric. Banks frequently intervene in the affairs of borrowers when the latter experience difficulty, Mintz and Schwartz note (1985, 32–35). Nonfinancial firms, in contrast, rarely if ever intervene in the affairs of a lending bank, even when banks face a capital surplus that renders them dependent on the former. The nonfinancial firm may compel the bank to provide more favorable terms, or it may avoid borrowing from the bank altogether, but it does not become involved in the bank's decision making.

This is a compelling argument. Although, as we saw earlier, Mintz and Schwartz provided forty-two examples of bank intervention in nonfinancial corporations over a four-year period (1985, 77–80), one would be hard pressed to find a single case of a nonfinancial corporation intervening in the affairs of a bank. Herman does present one such case (1981b, 62), in which Ben Heineman, the CEO of Northwest Industries, emerged as the most powerful individual on the board of the troubled First Chicago Bank, but that appears to have occurred not because Northwest Industries had an interest in the bank, but only because of Heineman's presence on the board's executive committee. It is the only such case I have seen in this literature. This asymmetry does suggest that Mintz and Schwartz have identified an important phenomenon.

There is an alternative interpretation of Mintz and Schwartz's argument, however, that I believe raises questions about whether the asymmetry of intervention constitutes financial hegemony. When a bank lends money to a corporation, it is risking its capital in the hope that it will be repaid with interest. Given the funds that are at stake, the bank has a necessary interest in monitoring the customer to ensure that the loan is repaid. If the company is in danger of defaulting, the bank has good reason to want to intervene, in order to maximize its probability of securing its investment. When a nonfinancial corporation is in a position of financial strength, however, it can either command a bank loan on terms favorable to itself or it can avoid dealing with a bank altogether. In either case, the company has nothing invested in the bank, and therefore it has no reason to be concerned about the bank's internal affairs. Whether the bank faces financial difficulties of its own is irrelevant to the nonfinancial firm, except insofar as it might be a poor source of funds in the future. There is thus no reason for a nonfinancial corporation to have to intervene in the affairs of a bank. The presence or absence of intervention may therefore tell us little about the relative power of the two units. A bank in need of a company's business may be as dependent on its nonfinancial customers as a nonfinancial firm in need of capital is on a bank.

In the absence of a clear resolution, the best strategy for understanding the relations between financial and nonfinancial corporations in the postwar period is to suggest that both groups had significant levels of power, that the relative power between the two was likely to fluctuate over time, and that neither was in a position to consistently dominate. As Herman (1981a, 123) suggested, although the largest financial institutions were often extremely powerful, they shared with their large borrowers "a long-lived, reciprocal relationship in which the power equation is not normally one of financial institution superiority." As support for this latter point, Herman noted that in 1975, "Citibank's top bank net income of $350 million was exceeded by 17 industrial companies. The two largest profit makers among industrials, Exxon and IBM, had net incomes ($2.5 and 2.0 billion respectively) not far short of the aggregate net incomes of the 50 largest commercial banks together ($2.9 billion)" (Herman 1981a, 367). This suggests that it is difficult, if not impossible, to establish an incontrovertible structural basis for bank hegemony. It is also undeniable that large financial institutions did play an extremely important role, even in the period in which their power may have been relatively low.

The approach that I believe best captures the existence and role of financial power is the resource dependence model, developed most comprehensively by Pfeffer and Salancik (1978) and applied to the issue of corporate financing by Stearns (1986). In this view, the relative power of financial and nonfinancial corporations fluctuates over time based on the level of dependence. When nonfinancial dependence on banks was relatively low, as in the 1946–1964 period, the power of banks, although by no means absent, was relatively low. When nonfinancial dependence on banks began to increase beginning in 1965, the power of banks, although by no means absolute, began to increase as well. Mintz and Schwartz reject the resource dependence model on the ground that it fails to recognize the unique value of capital as a resource. This is not the case, however. Not only is the resource dependence model agnostic with regard to the significance of particular resources—which are assumed to be determined by the organizations themselves—but the model is fully consistent with Mintz and Schwartz's argument about firms' dependence on external financing. Given Herman's similar focus on the importance of the credit relation, the resource dependence model is compatible with his account as well. We can conclude this long discussion of the debates over bank control, then, by suggesting that the power of banks is a contingent phenomenon, based on the degree of dependence on external financing that nonfinancial corporations face. Yet even when their power was relatively low, the banks played a significant role in the postwar business community. It is to this issue that we now turn.

What *Was* the Role of the Banks?

If the banks did not regularly control nonfinancial corporations, and did not even exercise hegemony over them, then what exactly did they do? I argue that the banks played three important roles. First, they served as centers through which information of relevance to the entire corporate community was exchanged and transmitted. Second, they served as a source of normative consensus and stability among the leaders of the largest corporations, in part by helping to forge similar worldviews and behavior and in part by sanctioning deviant and/or irresponsible actors. And third, they served as a source of cognitive range—or breadth in outlook—in terms of concern for the larger business community as well as the larger society. These roles—information, normative consensus, and cognitive range—were accomplished largely, although not exclusively, through bank boards of directors.

A key to understanding these functions is to understand the changing role of bank boards.

Our earlier discussion of financial power and control focused primarily on the banks' credit function as well as their trust department stockholdings. We saw that representation on firms' boards of directors was not an independent source of bank power. Boards of directors play other important roles, however. In particular, the fact that many corporate officers sit on the boards of multiple firms creates an extensive network of ties among large corporations. From the turn of the twentieth century through at least the mid-1970s, one fact about these ties remained constant: the most central corporations in the networks—that is, those that were connected to the largest number of other firms—were in every period the major financial institutions (Mizruchi 1982, 120–138). In the period after World War II, these financial institutions consisted primarily of the leading commercial banks. These findings indicate that there was clearly something important about the banks. In the early twentieth century, this bank centrality almost certainly reflected the power of financial corporations at the time. Using a modified measure of centrality on a network of 166 firms in 1904, David Bunting and I found that the most central corporations corresponded closely with what observers of the period believed were the most powerful firms (Mizruchi and Bunting 1981).[7] Chief among these was J. P. Morgan and Company, which was ranked as the most central firm, as well as James Stillman's National City Bank (ranked sixth), George F. Baker's First National Bank of New York (seventh), and Jacob Schiff's Kuhn, Loeb, and Company (twelfth).

Although financial institutions remained the most central firms throughout the seventy-year period of my study, an important change occurred between the 1930s and the 1960s. In the earlier part of the century (1904, 1912, 1919, and 1935), the majority of financial interlocks, between 60 and 64 percent, involved a representative of a financial institution sitting on the board of a nonfinancial firm. Although there is no assurance that financial representation on a firm's board is indicative of a control relation, these "sending" interlocks were widely believed to have reflected such relations in the early 1900s. By the postwar period, however (1964, 1969, and 1974), the proportion of financial interlocks involving a financial representative on a nonfinancial board had dropped on average more than 20 percent from the early twentieth century, to between 46 and 52 percent.[8] Some of this decline was a result of the reduced presence of investment banks after the 1930s (due presumably to the passage of the Glass-Steagall Act). Because all investment banks were partnerships at the time, they did not have boards of directors, and all of their interlocks thus involved their partners sitting on the boards of other firms. Even if we exclude investment banks from the calculation, however, the proportion of financial sending interlocks declined, from an average of 60 percent between 1912 and 1935 to an average of 44 percent between 1964 and 1974.[9]

This shift in the direction of financial interlocks after World War II is consistent with claims that the power of financial institutions declined during the period. Yet despite the fact that the banks were now more often the hosts of leading nonfinancial officers rather than vice versa, they remained in the center of the network. This suggested a change in the role of the banks over time. Instead of constituting the centers of power, as they had been earlier in the century, the banks now became examples of what I called, in an earlier work (Mizruchi 1992, 22), a "mediating mechanism"; that is, an organization or institution that serves as a meeting place for leading members of an organizational field and that provides a forum for the discussion of issues and resolution of conflicts. In other words, the boards of the leading banks now functioned as arenas in which the chief executives of the largest nonfinancial corporations, representing a broad range of industries, had an opportunity to discuss the status of various industries, the business world in general, and the larger society.[10]

The importance of these bank boards can be seen by looking at their composition. They tended to be substantially larger than the boards of nonfinancial corporations, and they typically consisted of the CEOs of the leading nonfinancial corporations, what James Bearden (1987, 50) called the "corporate all-stars." To take one example, in 1972 the outside directors on the board of Chemical Bank, one of the six major New York money market banks, consisted of officers from seventeen leading corporations, including AT&T, DuPont, Standard Oil of New Jersey, Mobil, Sears, and U.S. Steel (ibid., 53). The board of the Chase Manhattan Bank in 1982 included the chief executive officers of fourteen Fortune 500 companies (Davis and Mizruchi 1999, 217–218). This unique character of bank boards, reflected in the presence of these leading chief executives from multiple industries, allowed them to play the three important roles—noted above—in maintaining the cohesion and moderation of the postwar

American corporate elite: information, normative consensus, and cognitive range.

Before discussing these roles, it is important to mention that they are not entirely discrete phenomena. The establishment of both normative consensus and an increased cognitive range were facilitated by the transmission of information, for example, and the achievement of an increase in cognitive range was facilitated by collective efforts to reach a normative consensus. Each of the three factors is best viewed as a particular angle viewed through a single lens rather than a series of substantively distinct images.

Information.   The British sociologist John Scott (1979, 103) suggested many years ago that the structure of director interlocks between financial and nonfinancial corporations represented a "constellation of interests," "the main significance of which is the communication of business information." Useem (1984, 45–48) noted, based on his interviews with American and British executives, that multiple board memberships increased an individual's "business scan," the ability to monitor developments in business practices as well as national and world events. As one American executive explained to Useem:

> You're damned right it's helpful to be on several boards. It extends the range of your network and acquaintances, and your experience. That's why you go on a board, to get something as well as give. You get a more cosmopolitan view—on economic matters, regional differences, and international questions these days. It just broadens your experience, the memory bank that you have to test things against. (quoted in Useem 1984, 47–48)

Interlocks among large corporations have indeed been shown to provide a significant source of information for both the individuals who create them and the other members of the boards on which these individuals sit. Davis (1991), for example, showed that firms that shared directors with other firms that had recently adopted antitakeover legislation known as "poison pills" were disproportionately likely to adopt such practices themselves. Haunschild (1993) showed that firms whose CEOs sat on the boards of firms that had recently engaged in acquisitions were disproportionately likely to subsequently engage in acquisitions themselves. A study that Linda Stearns and I conducted (Mizruchi and Stearns 1994) indicated that firms with bankers on their boards tended to use relatively high levels of debt. Given the size and industry representation on bank boards, they were well-positioned to be especially valuable sources of information exchange and transmission.

Normative Consensus. In addition to the simple transmission of information, network ties among firms have also been shown to facilitate the development of a normative consensus within the corporate community, some of which was reflected in the diffusion of similar practices. Galaskiewicz (1985) found, for example, that Twin Cities–area firms that shared directors were disproportionately likely to contribute to the same charities. He attributed this finding in part to the normative pressures within the regional corporate community to give liberally and suggested that these pressures were communicated in part through mutual contact on corporate boards. My study of corporate political behavior (Mizruchi 1992) not only provides similar evidence of the role of board interlocks but also shows the unique role played by financial institutions. Examining the 1,596 dyadic (firm-to-firm) relations among fifty-seven large American manufacturing firms in 1980, I found that firms that shared directors were disproportionately likely to contribute to the same political candidates and to take the same positions in their testimony when appearing simultaneously at congressional hearings. Interestingly, however, I found that the effect of direct interlocks between manufacturing firms on the similarity of contributions was only marginally statistically significant. The effect of indirect ties through financial institutions, on the other hand, was a considerably stronger predictor of the similarity of both contributions and testimony than were the direct ties. In other words, two firms that both had interlocks with the same financial institution were more likely to engage in similar political behavior than were two firms that had a direct interlock to one another (ibid., chapters 6 and 7). This finding suggests that ties with financial institutions played a particularly important role in forging political consensus among large American corporations.

Another means by which financial institutions helped to maintain a normative consensus in the postwar period was through their sanctioning of deviant behavior. Cases in which individual companies or capitalists attempted to "buck the system" were relatively rare in the 1950s and 1960s (although they became more common during the 1970s), but the response of the banks to these cases helped reinforce the normatively prescribed behavior. One excellent example of this was the case of Howard Hughes, who, as president of TWA (and owner of 78 percent of the firm's stock), attempted in the late 1950s to fund the purchase of a new fleet of jets without the assistance of the group of financial institutions that was funding most major airlines at the time (Fitch and Oppenheimer 1970a, 86–89; Mintz and Schwartz 1985, 28–29). Hughes had been successfully financing his purchases by drawing on profits from Hughes Tool Company, which he also controlled. When the 1959 recession made it impossible for Hughes to repay a loan to Hughes Tool, the firm's lenders—which included Morgan, Chase Manhattan, Citibank, and leading insurance companies such as Equitable, Metropolitan, and Prudential—forced Hughes to place his 78 percent TWA stockholding in a trust fund, which they administered.

In an even more dramatic case, Saul P. Steinberg, the president of Leasco, a computer leasing firm, attempted to acquire Chemical Bank in 1968 by offering Chemical shareholders a return of greater than 50 percent above the firm's stock price at the time (Mintz and Schwartz 1985, 1–3; Glasberg 1989, 102–118). In February 1969, a group of institutional stockholders that included the trust departments of the five other major New York banks (all of which held stock in Leasco) began selling their Leasco stock.[11] Within two weeks, the value of Leasco's stock dropped from $140 a share to $106. Despite being a highly profitable company, Leasco's stock continued to drop, reaching $6 a share the following year.[12] Although there are multiple possible interpretations of what led to Steinberg's demise, the most plausible account appears to be that the financial community rallied to Chemical's defense in an effort to thwart a seemingly erratic "upstart."[13] The sanctioning of both Hughes's and Steinberg's deviant behavior provides examples of one of the means by which the financial community maintained normative consensus among members of the corporate community in the postwar era.

Cognitive Range. A third consequence of the network ties among firms and the central role played by financial institutions was their facilitation of a broad perspective that contributed to the moderate, pragmatic orientation within the corporate elite, a phenomenon that I call cognitive range. We have seen that multiple board positions provide a relatively broad worldview that tends to transcend that of a director's individual firm. As with the transmission of information and the development of normative consensus, this breadth should be especially available to those who sit on the boards of banks. Useem suggested that the more cosmopolitan orientation that accrues to those who sit on multiple boards produces a tendency toward moderation. As he put it, members of the inner circle "have a stronger understanding of the complexities and intricacies of the political environment in which business operates" (1984, 108). A consequence of this, Useem argued, is that the inner circle members who are the most active in policy organizations and in representing business in its dealings with the government (of which the members of the postwar Committee for Economic Development constitute a good example) "often share centrist opinions that transcend their own company's immediate welfare, and their perceptions reflect a deeper sense of how the political process works" (ibid.).[14] This argument is consistent with the findings from Barton's study (1985) cited in Chapter 3, which suggested a high degree of moderation on economic issues in 1971 among the chief executives of the largest corporations. Useem's point is also consistent with the idea that bank boards were uniquely important, since it is in these settings that directors are likely to be exposed to the broadest range of views.

There are additional findings that also provide support for the idea that firms that are central in interfirm director networks are relatively moderate. In a study of the campaign contributions of corporate political action committees in 1980, Clawson and Neustadtl (1989) found that heavily interlocked firms were disproportionately likely to contribute to incumbents (who, at the time, tended to be Democrats) and also had contribution patterns that were relatively dissimilar to the political action committees of conservative interest groups. One possible reason for the tendency of interlocked firms to contribute to incumbents might have been narrow self-interest. Even if a firm was ideologically opposed to an incumbent, the firm might have contributed to that person if he or she chaired an important committee. This pragmatic behavior is fully consistent with the moderation of the postwar corporate elite that I have described in the past three chapters. Moreover, Clawson and Neustadtl included as control variables factors such as a firm's capital intensity, its presence in a highly regulated industry, and whether it was a defense contractor. These are factors that, if a firm was operating purely in its narrow self-interest, we would expect to affect their contribution pattern. The fact that heavily interlocked firms were

disproportionately likely to contribute to Democrats and to nonconserva-
tives even after controlling for these variables is consistent with the notion
that these firms were relatively moderate as well as pragmatic.[15] Again,
given their prominent role in the interlock network and the diverse nature
of their boards, the political moderation associated with high levels of interlocking suggests that the banks played a particularly important role in
facilitating this moderation.

Conclusion

The major banks, then, provided a third source of constraint that helped to
maintain a moderate, pragmatic perspective among the American corporate elite in the postwar period. They did this not by controlling nonfinancial corporations, although they were occasionally able to exercise influence
over them. They did this by serving as a mediating mechanism, providing a
forum in which leading figures throughout the corporate community could
meet to discuss issues of concern to the business world as a whole, as well as
the larger world beyond. In serving as this mediating mechanism, the banks
performed three roles for the corporate elite. They contributed to the exchange
and diffusion of information, the maintenance of normative consensus,
and the facilitation of a broad perspective that contributed to a moderate
approach to both economic and political behavior. An example of the role
played by the banks was cited by Daniel Bell in *The Coming of Post-Industrial
Society* (1973, 292), drawing on a quote from a 1971 article in *Fortune* describing the views of Alden W. Clausen, the CEO of the Bank of America
(the nation's largest bank at the time). The article was published during a
period in which the social movements of the 1960s and early 1970s were at
their most militant, but it reflects the broader perspective that was common
among leading corporations at the time. As the author of the *Fortune* article, John Davenport, put it: "[Clausen's] thoughts turn often to: how to alleviate if not cure the blight now spreading at Hunter's Point and south of
Market Street [in San Francisco]; how to crack the city's hard-core unemployment; how to cope with student unrest at Berkeley or down the penin-
sula at Stanford."

For Bell, this was an example of the ways in which the large corporation
in general (and the nation's largest bank in particular) had, in the postwar
period, become an institution whose management was compelled to con-

sider the institution's role in the larger society. As Davenport noted in describing the difference between Clausen's approach and the views of the distinguished free market economist Milton Friedman,

> Friedman sees the corporation as fundamentally an "artificial person" and the corporate manager as simply an agent of individual shareholders. Clausen sees the corporation as having a kind of life of its own, and hence having a certain freedom of choice in balancing its contribution to the long-range needs of the community against the immediate demands of owners. (quoted in Bell 1973, 292–293)

This corporate role described by Bell and Davenport may not have been one of altruism. But it was more than simply a tool of shareholders concerned with little beyond the price of the firm's stock. I will have more to say about this latter question in Chapter 7, when I discuss the changing role of shareholders in the 1980s. For now, it is important to note the breadth and moderation exhibited by the head of the nation's largest bank during the waning days of the postwar consensus.

The banks, then, occasionally exercised power, even in the postwar period, but more often they provided a forum for moderation and consensus. Although the corporate elites who sat on multiple boards of directors sometimes discussed the pressing issues of the day, there was no "conspiracy." These people were, first and foremost, trying to run their firms, and trying to understand the best course of action for their companies. In doing so, however, they were aware of, and concerned about, the business community as a whole and the needs of the larger society. And in considering these needs, they were willing to operate pragmatically, having made their peace with the existence of a strong, active government and a well-organized labor movement.

The End of the Postwar Era

Despite the many problems, the postwar years, from 1945 into the early 1970s, were relatively good ones for the United States. Rather than slipping back into depression after the war, the United States emerged as the most dominant economic and military power in the world. Its industries produced in abundance and faced little international competition. Millions of

Americans, including many members of the working class, were able to experience a middle-class existence—including home ownership—that had previously been unimaginable. Income inequality, however high it might have been by international standards, was reduced to its lowest level in history. Despite the persistence of poverty and racial disadvantage, progress, especially on the legal side, began to occur, however slowly. As productivity continued to increase, wages increased as well, leading to an almost universal improvement in the standard of living of average people. Institutions such as government, unions, and even corporations experienced a high degree of legitimacy with the larger public, with large majorities viewing them in a favorable light (Lipset and Schneider 1983). And those at the top of the society, the corporate elite, for all of their many flaws, appeared genuinely committed to the continued improvement of the society, even if not in a manner or at a pace preferred by all of their constituents. Despite increasing pressures from the late 1960s into the early 1970s, this basic outline remained.

As we moved into the 1970s, however, this was about to change.

6 ||| The Breakdown of the Postwar Consensus

The problems that crested in the 1970s were all present in one form or another in the 1960s, and even the 1950s. The inflationary spiral that became the central economic problem of the decade actually began in the mid-1960s, a consequence of President Johnson's decision to pursue an ambitious set of social programs while conducting the war in Vietnam. The foreign competition that severely hampered American manufacturing in the 1970s had already begun to raise its head in the late 1950s during the strikes in the steel industry. The crisis of legitimacy among major American institutions—triggered in part by the Watergate scandal—was apparent in the 1960s as well, driven by opposition to the Vietnam War and frustration with continuing racial conflict. The emergence of the Environmental Protection Agency (EPA) and the Occupational Safety and Health Administration (OSHA) were outgrowths of the social movements of the 1960s. Even the energy crisis, which first hit in 1973, was the culmination of what can now be seen as the excessive consumption of a critical natural resource without regard for the consequences. The plentiful supply of inexpensive gasoline, selling for as little as twenty-five cents a gallon in the 1960s, could not continue indefinitely.

Still, although all of the problems of the 1970s were present in the 1960s, they had not yet had a major impact on the American economy. Pressures were evident. As we saw in Chapter 5, nonfinancial corporations had begun to experience a shortage of cash by 1965, and profits began to decline later in the decade, even leading to a recession in 1970. Unemployment remained low, however, and growth continued through the decade. It was not until the 1970s that a protracted economic crisis emerged. As it moved through that decade and encountered this series of shocks—both exogenous and endogenous—the American corporate elite began to turn against the forces that had constrained it during the postwar period, in particular the federal government and organized labor. In launching its campaign against these constraints, the leaders of the American business community began a retreat from the moderation they had exhibited over the previous three decades.

In this chapter I describe the American corporate elite's shift in the 1970s toward a more conservative orientation and strategy. I discuss, among other things, the factors that precipitated this conservative turn, as well as its consequences: the rise of conservative foundations and think tanks, the formation of the Business Roundtable, the decline of the Committee for Economic Development (CED), and the frustration of liberal efforts at consumer, labor, and tax reform. By the end of the decade, as the nation was poised to elect Ronald Reagan as president, the postwar consensus among business, labor, and the state had been largely abandoned. The American corporate elite had transformed itself, and in doing so had altered, perhaps forever, the environment within which it operated.

The American Corporate Elite in the Early 1970s

As we entered the 1970s, the moderate, pragmatic orientation of the American corporate elite remained strong. Barton's (1985) study of 130 leading corporate executives and owners, which, as we saw in Chapter 3, revealed broad support for Keynesian economic policies (including a government guarantee of employment) was conducted in 1971. The CED's statement on the social responsibilities of corporations appeared in the same year, and the organization published a comprehensive plan for a national health care system in 1973, one that was very similar to that later proposed by President Nixon. Although the construction unions' decision to exercise their muscle in the late 1960s led to the beginnings of a reaction from business, unions remained strong and highly legitimate in the eyes of the public

(Lipset and Schneider 1983). And the banks continued to provide a source of moderation, reining in recalcitrant individuals such as James Ling and Saul Steinberg, while serving as a meeting place and source of consensus for the leaders of the largest American firms. These forces were reflected in the major policy decisions by the Nixon administration, which not only continued to support the New Deal and Great Society programs instituted by Democratic presidents but added new ones as well.[1] So despite cracks in the system, the postwar moderate consensus remained solid as we entered the 1970s.

Things began to change as the decade unfolded, however. First, the economy began to experience difficulties that initially appeared to be cyclical but eventually proved to be structural. Inflation had remained low through the 1950s and the early 1960s, despite relatively high economic growth. From 1952 through 1965, inflation averaged 1.4 percent, yet real GDP growth averaged nearly 3.8 percent. In 1966, as the costs of President Johnson's Great Society programs rose simultaneously with the escalating costs of the Vietnam War, inflation began to slowly increase, moving to 4.3 percent in 1968, to nearly 6 percent in 1970 (despite an accompanying recession), and to even higher levels in the 1970s. From 1966 through 1979, inflation averaged 8.4 percent. The nation experienced virtually full employment during the late 1960s, averaging just 3.5 percent unemployment in 1968 and 1969, which undoubtedly contributed to the increased inflation and led to pressures for President Nixon to induce a slowdown in the economy (Economic Report of the President 1970, 6). Although Nixon had apparently not intended to induce a recession, the nation was already experiencing one in 1970 when he presented his State of the Union address. After a drop in interest rates in 1972, which spurred the economy in time for Nixon's reelection campaign (Abrams 2006), the economy experienced another recession in 1974 in the wake of the first of two major energy crises. From that point through the end of the decade, inflation continued to spiral, unemployment remained relatively high, and growth continued to stagnate. The economy of the 1970s began to violate a basic tenet of Keynesian economics: the inverse relation between unemployment and inflation. During this decade, the nation experienced simultaneously high levels of both. President Nixon took the step of adopting wage and price controls in 1971, but this only slowed the problem. Through Nixon's remaining years as president, and through the administrations of Gerald Ford and Jimmy

Carter, economic policy makers were unable to put a damper on inflation, even during recessions.

These economic difficulties were accompanied by (and perhaps to some degree caused by) the increased international competition faced by American manufacturers. As we saw in Chapter 4, the steel industry had already begun to experience this competition during the 1959 strikes. Operating in highly concentrated industries and therefore experiencing little competition, American manufacturers, especially in the core industries such as automobiles, chemicals, and steel, faced little pressure to innovate. As the economies of nations torn by World War II—especially Germany and Japan—began to recover, their firms were increasingly able to produce high-quality products at costs below those of their American counterparts. This was reflected in the decline of the U.S. balance of trade, which turned increasingly negative during the 1970s (Ferguson and Rogers 1986, 81; Vogel 1989, 228). The weakening American position in the international economy led President Nixon to abandon the Bretton Woods agreement—which had pegged national currencies to the U.S. dollar and guaranteed that dollars could be convertible to gold—in 1971 (Block 1977b). Although this decision initially led to feelings of relief among American investors (Sweezy and Magdoff 1972, 199–202), its longer term effect was more one of apprehension (Ferguson and Rogers 1986, 82).

Along with the economic problems that the nation confronted in the 1970s was an additional crisis, involving the legitimacy of American institutions. As we saw in Chapter 3, the turmoil of the 1960s had been accompanied by a decline in respect for government. This decline was exacerbated by the Watergate scandal. Although the scandal first broke in April 1972 after the break-in at the Democratic Party headquarters in Washington, it crested in the spring and summer of 1974, in the period leading up to President Nixon's resignation. By that time the economy was already in the midst of a severe recession. Public negativity toward government and business had begun to rise concurrently during the late 1960s. By 1974, nearly 60 percent of Americans expressed broadly negative attitudes toward business, compared with approximately 40 percent between 1958 and 1968 (Lipset and Schneider 1983, 32–34). In 1973, 74 percent of Americans surveyed by the Opinion Research Corporation believed that there was "too much power concentrated in the hands of a few large companies for the good of the nation," compared with about 50 percent during most of the 1960s (ibid., 30–31). The proportion of respondents who believed that "the profits of large companies help make things better for everyone" declined from approximately 65 percent in the mid-1960s to 41 percent by 1975 (ibid.). In the late 1960s, at the height of antiwar militancy, radical groups had expressed increasingly strident antibusiness rhetoric and engaged in several disruptive actions at corporate facilities, including in some cases bombings. Although these actions did not receive widespread support from the public, the survey data from the 1970s indicate that some level of antibusiness sentiment had diffused to the general population.

Finally, although large corporations had long accepted (and in some cases supported) a certain degree of government regulation, the new regulatory agencies—the EPA and OSHA—soon provoked fierce opposition. Neither of these institutions was originally opposed by the largest firms. Vogel (1989, 68) notes, for example, that the establishment of the EPA was "relatively uncontroversial." Although it was opposed by some members of the National Association of Manufacturers (NAM) and some agricultural interests (who wanted the supervision of pesticides to remain in the Department of Agriculture), the *National Journal* reported that "some corporate interests would welcome a centralization of environmental programs in the Federal government" (ibid.). The establishment of OSHA experienced greater resistance from business, most notably from the traditionally conservative NAM and Chamber of Commerce. Yet it too received support from some of the leading corporations, in line with the "general support among many corporate leaders for social reform" during the period (Noble 1986, 78; Vogel 1989, 84–85). Even the NAM and the Chamber eventually came to accept the inevitability that the bill would become law and worked to make it as palatable as possible (Vogel 1989, 86).

Not long after the bills establishing the EPA and OSHA were passed, however, business began to see the agencies as obstacles. This was especially the case with OSHA, whose regulations were increasingly seen by companies as arbitrary and unnecessarily costly. Although the majority of the complaints about excessive regulation came from small businesspeople, the heads of large corporations began to express opposition as well, with large firms more likely to focus their attention on the EPA than OSHA (Useem 1984, 160–165). In a 1977 speech to the Conference Board, a traditionally moderate business-funded study group, Robert H. B. Baldwin, president of

Morgan Stanley, described a case in which Dow Chemical had attempted to build a petrochemical plant on the Sacramento River: "After spending $6 million on land and $4 million on planning, Dow threw in the towel [in January 1975]. The reason? Environmental red tape—65 permits were necessary from 12 local, state, and federal agencies to get permission to begin construction" (*Vital Speeches of the Day*, April 15, 1977, 405–408; speech presented February 23, 1977).[2] Complaints about OSHA were even more graphic. One businessman compared the agency's treatment of employers to "harassment by mobsters," while another noted that the fines levied by the agency were worse than those leveled against "draft card burners, . . . vandals, and other gross disrespecters [*sic*] of property rights and government" (Kelman 1980, 260).

With the economy in serious trouble, with American companies facing increasingly severe foreign competition, with business legitimacy at an apparent all-time low, and with government and labor creating further constraints, it is not difficult to see why corporations began to see themselves as under siege. Through most of the 1960s, the elite members of the business community had preferred accommodation. Operating in organizations such as the CED, and working alongside presidents Kennedy and Johnson, the corporate elite maintained the moderate approach to which it had adhered throughout the postwar period. Officers of leading foundations associated with the great capitalists of the twentieth century—Carnegie, Ford, and Rockefeller in particular—dispersed their resources to an increasingly liberal set of causes, including civil rights organizations, the American Civil Liberties Union, and environmental and consumer groups (O'Connor 2008, 155–156). These gifts included support for controversial policies such as community control of schools in New York, an experiment that led to a confrontation between residents of minority communities and the heavily Jewish teachers union (Rieder 1985).

Although segments of the corporate elite remained moderate well into the 1970s, others began to believe that things had gone too far. We have already seen some of the reactions that the movements of the 1960s precipitated. The construction unions, experiencing an extremely flush job market in the late 1960s, were able to push their wages up significantly, creating a squeeze on corporate profits (Boddy and Crotty 1975).[3] The EPA and OSHA, even if they had been palatable to many corporate elites at the time of their formation, were increasingly seen as burdens, as enthusiastic agency staff members enforced a set of rules that companies viewed as arbitrary and unrealistic. What had begun as relatively benign criticism of business by members of the antiwar movement morphed into questions about the viability of capitalism as a system. Under these conditions, it is perhaps not surprising that corporations increasingly saw themselves, and their system, as under threat. In response to this perceived threat, businesspeople launched a counteroffensive that defined the politics of the 1970s and, some argue, redefined American politics in the decades that followed. A large number of scholars and journalists have written about this counteroffensive, and there is a high level of agreement on the general contours of the process, although certain authors attribute different levels of importance to particular individuals or events.[4]

The origins of the business backlash to this perceived threat were varied. Conservative businesspeople, of course, had never stopped advocating for rollbacks in government social spending and increased restrictions on organized labor. Their views, represented primarily by the National Association of Manufacturers and the Chamber of Commerce, were out of step with mainstream political discourse during most of the postwar period, however, and they had limited influence. When conservatives finally succeeded in nominating a compatible candidate for president, Barry Goldwater, in 1964, they were soundly trounced, and a sizeable proportion of large corporations threw their support to Lyndon Johnson (Vogel 1989, 24). By the late 1960s, however, some of the more moderate members of the business community had begun to resist the pressures that they faced from organized labor and the state.

One episode that has been cited as a turning point in the corporate shift away from moderation was an August 1971 memo written by Lewis F. Powell Jr., a lawyer from Richmond, Virginia, just weeks prior to his nomination to the Supreme Court by President Nixon. Powell had become increasingly troubled by what he perceived (with some justification, as we have seen) as a growing level of hostility toward business. After expressing his views to his neighbor, Eugene B. Sydnor Jr., an official with the Chamber of Commerce, Powell was encouraged by Sydnor to put his thoughts in writing (Judis 2001, 116; Phillips-Fein 2009, 156–158). The document, which was intended to be confidential, was eventually leaked to the journalist Jack Anderson about a year after its circulation. Anderson used the memo to raise questions about Powell's suitability for the Court, but the Chamber subsequently released the document to the public (Phillips-Fein 2009, 161–162).[5]

Powell began his screed by stating that "the American economic system is under broad attack." Although radical critics had always existed, he noted, the current "assault on the enterprise system is broadly based and consistently pursued," coming not only from leftists but from "perfectly respectable elements of society," including, most prominently, college campuses and the media. Business was partly to blame for this, Powell argued, because it had tolerated, and even participated in, its own destruction. He went on to point out that the institutions that criticize free enterprise are themselves recipients of tax dollars, contributions, and advertising revenue from the businesses that to a great extent fund them. Powell's strongest words, in fact, were reserved for businesses. "The painfully sad truth," he stated, is that business has often responded, "if at all—by appeasement, ineptitude, and ignoring the problem." It is true that they "have not been trained or equipped to conduct guerrilla warfare with those who propagandize against the system," but "they have shown little stomach for hard-nose [*sic*] contest with their critics, and little skill in effective intellectual and philosophical debate." Corporations must rectify this problem, Powell argued, by treating it as a "primary responsibility of management." Companies should appoint an executive vice president whose job is to counter attacks on the free enterprise system, and they should coordinate their activities with other firms.[6]

Powell then presented a list of tasks and the arenas in which the tasks should be carried out (the most important of which were college campuses, the media, and government). First, business should establish staffs of qualified scholars and speakers to present pro–free enterprise views, monitor textbooks, demand equal time on campus for probusiness voices, and urge colleges of the need for "balance" among the faculty. Similarly, the organized business community envisioned by Powell should monitor television, radio, and print media, and demand equal time to respond to programming perceived to be unfairly biased against it. It should also fund the publication of pro–free enterprise scholarship and devote 10 percent of its annual advertising funds to pro–free enterprise advocacy. Most important, according to Powell, was the need for business to organize politically, to influence both the legislative and executive branches as well as the courts. Business should be aggressive in pursuit of its interests, and show "no hesitation" in attacking those "who openly seek destruction of the system."

Organized labor and groups such as the American Civil Liberties Union were seen as role models in this regard, groups whose activities business should emulate.

It would be an exaggeration to suggest that Powell's memo actually triggered the business counteroffensive of the 1970s. Although Judis (2001, 116–119) and Phillips-Fein (2009, 156–165) treat it as a significant watershed, Vogel (1989, 57) devotes only a single sentence to it, and the other authors cited above do not mention it at all. Clearly, a number of other related activities were occurring at the same time, and some, as we have seen, had occurred earlier. Irving Kristol, a former Trotskyist who had become a conservative columnist for the *Wall Street Journal,* had been expressing sentiments similar to Powell's as early as 1970 (Judis 2001, 117), and other spokespersons seemed to echo similar thoughts, even if not directly influenced by Powell (Phillips-Fein 2009, 163). Moreover, Kristol and a number of other important figures were involved in the expansion or establishment of a series of organizations that were to play a significant role in the conservative turn in American politics.

In an article in *The American Prospect,* Mark Schmitt (2005) argues that Powell's memo was not actually a manifesto for a new conservatism but rather "a call for the mainstream establishment to defend itself against critics from the further left." This point may be accurate, given that Powell's focus was not on moving American political dialogue in a conservative direction per se but rather on offering a defense of the free enterprise system against its left-wing critics. Yet Powell's memo did have an impact, even if inadvertent, on the conservative movement. John M. Olin, the founder of the Olin Foundation, which became one of the leading conservative foundations in the 1970s, referred to it in a letter to William Baroody, the head of the American Enterprise Institute, citing Powell's memo in his proposal for a "well organized effort" to reestablish support for the free enterprise system. Joseph Coors, another important figure in the conservative movement in the 1970s, noted in an interview that he had been "stirred" by Powell's words (Judis 2001, 125–126). The right-wing Pacific Legal Foundation cited the memo in its literature, and executives of a number of companies made use of it as well (Phillips-Fein 2009, 162). Equally important, regardless of its direct impact, Powell's statement became a symbol of the movement, both as an articulate expression of a set of views that were becoming increasingly shared and for its list of recommendations that corresponded closely with a series of efforts that had already begun, and that picked up steam as the decade progressed.

Who Mobilized?

Like most social movements, the conservative mobilization involved a combination of many groups, some of which acting in concert but others either competing for the same audiences or operating at cross-purposes. Some of the actors consisted of traditional conservative organizations that grew and increased their presence. Others consisted of newly formed organizations. Ideologically, the groups ranged from conventional Goldwater conservatives to a relatively new group of former leftists and liberals who became known as neoconservatives.[7] Eventually, even organizations that had been traditionally moderate and nonideological took on an increasingly conservative slant.

Among the most important of the avowedly conservative groups were the American Enterprise Institute (AEI) and the Heritage Foundation. The American Enterprise Association (as it was originally called) was founded in 1943 by Lewis H. Brown, the president of the Johns Manville Corporation, and a group of similarly anti–New Deal businessmen (Peschek 1987, 28) whose goal was to promote free market economics. The group achieved little notoriety in its early years but began to grow after William J. Baroody assumed its presidency in 1962. Baroody changed the organization's name to the American Enterprise Institute to distinguish it from a trade association (Judis 2001, 123; Phillips-Fein 2009, 66). His goal, anticipating the views later expounded by Powell and Kristol, was to provide a forum and resources for the dissemination of conservative ideas, which he saw as a counterweight to the dominant liberal perspective of the period. Baroody initially ran into difficulty when he assembled a group of thinkers to provide support for the 1964 Goldwater campaign, which led to calls for the group to lose its tax-exempt status (Saloma 1984, 8–9). Baroody himself had taken a leave of absence from the organization to work in Goldwater's campaign, but his involvement raised questions about the group's commitment to nonpartisanship, and it was later revealed that he had remained on the AEI's payroll during his absence (Phillips-Fein 2009, 168). The organization grew significantly during the 1960s, however, even as conservatism in general had little impact on the political discourse of the period. Baroody was able to secure contributions from such major corporations as General Electric, General Motors, Mobil, and Procter and Gamble (ibid., 65), yet all four of these firms also had representatives who served as trustees of the CED, which was considerably more prominent at the time (Committee for Economic Development 1971).

Things started to change for the AEI in the 1970s. Helped by Bryce Harlow (a former speechwriter for presidents Eisenhower and Nixon and by the early 1970s a Washington lobbyist for Procter and Gamble) and Melvin Laird (Nixon's secretary of defense), the AEI began a major fundraising campaign that led the organization's budget to increase more than tenfold between 1970 and 1980 (Himmelstein 1990, 147). The AEI operated primarily by funding "fellows," whose charge was to write articles and books with a pro–free enterprise slant. Although the organization had engaged in some token sponsorship of liberal thinkers during the 1960s in order to maintain its tax exempt status, by the 1970s it had become unapologetically conservative. *The Public Interest,* a journal cofounded by Kristol and funded by the AEI, became a significant source of neoconservative thought, while another AEI journal, *Regulation,* edited by Murray Weidenbaum—a former Nixon administration official and a future chair of the Council of Economic Advisers under Ronald Reagan—became a source of criticism of government regulation of business (Ferguson and Rogers 1986, 86).[8] By 1980, the AEI had a budget larger than the venerable Brookings Institution. Brookings had been accused by Baroody and other conservative critics of having a liberal slant, although the organization was committed to nonideological social science and had been accused by radicals of being probusiness. The AEI was by then receiving funds from more than 600 corporations and included an eminent group of corporate leaders, including the heads of Citibank, Chase Manhattan, and Hewlett-Packard, as fundraisers (Peschek 1987, 28–29).

Despite its clear association with the political Right—as evidenced by Baroody's earlier involvement in the Goldwater campaign—some observers have suggested that by the 1970s the AEI had become associated with a relatively moderate form of conservatism. There is certainly evidence for this. The group had managed to secure a $300,000 grant from the relatively liberal Ford Foundation in 1972, as well as a $500,000 grant from the Lilly Endowment, an older organization viewed by many as a member of the "establishment" (Phillips-Fein 2009, 175). It hosted President Ford as a fellow after his presidency. As Peschek (1987, 30) put it, the organization was "drawn more to the Republicanism of George Bush and Gerald Ford than to that of Jesse Helms or Paul Laxalt."[9] On the other hand, the AEI supported the work of Jude Wanniski, an economic journalist who authored the best-selling book *The Way the World Works*, which popularized the emerging approach known as supply-side economics, a view associated with the right-wing of the Republican Party. It supported the work of such antiregulation conservatives as Arthur Burns, Robert Bork, and Antonin Scalia (Peschek 1987, 30), and more than thirty AEI fellows joined the administration of Ronald Reagan after his election as president (Judis 2001, 125). The characterization of the AEI as relatively moderate may reflect the extent to which the political discourse of the 1970s had moved rightward.

Yet for some conservatives the AEI was indeed seen as limited. Among the critics was Paul Weyrich, an aide to the Republican senator Gordon Allott. Weyrich believed that the AEI had become overly "respectable" and cautious, in part because of its earlier problems involving its tax-exempt status. He shared the view, expounded by Patrick Buchanan during his term in the Nixon administration, that conservatives needed to build a group that would be more partisan and aggressive than the AEI (Phillips-Fein 2009, 171). In collaboration with another congressional aide, Edwin Feulner, Weyrich secured a $250,000 grant from Joseph Coors and founded the Heritage Foundation, in 1973. Although Weyrich and Feulner's relationship with Coors subsequently soured, the two activists eventually secured support from Richard Mellon Scaife, who, after an initial gift of $900,000, contributed nearly $3 million over the next eight years (Saloma 1984, 14; Judis 2001, 126). Unlike the AEI, which attempted to maintain an aura of intellectual respectability and balance, the Heritage Foundation was militantly conservative. Instead of serious academic treatises, its staff members wrote brief synopses of contemporary political issues and then sent them to public officials and journalists. Whereas the AEI had produced detailed, often sedate analyses of pending legislation that sometimes did not even reach congressional legislators until after a vote was taken, the goal of the Heritage was explicitly to influence ideas and legislation (Saloma 1984, 18; Vogel 1989, 224). The Heritage Foundation also addressed a broader range of issues than the AEI, whose focus was almost exclusively on economic and foreign policy. Among its activities was the provision of support to a group of West Virginia parents who were boycotting local schools to protest the inclusion of material by African American writers in school textbooks. The group also issued critiques of "secular humanism," along with conservative economic polemics against labor unions and the minimum wage (Phillips-Fein 2009, 172). Although the Heritage Foundation may have had limited influence on the intellectual debates of the 1970s, the group's compilation of its position papers, *Mandate for Leadership*, which appeared at the start of Ronald Reagan's presidency, provided a detailed list of suggestions for each of the government agencies under the new administration's watch (Himmelstein 1990, 150; Weisberg 1998).

Although the Heritage Foundation and the AEI saw themselves as competitors, they attracted funding from many of the same backers. Among the companies that contributed to both groups were General Motors, General Electric, and the Chase Manhattan Bank (Judis 2001, 124–126). Conservative foundations, including the John M. Olin, Sarah Mellon Scaife, and Smith Richardson foundations, also contributed to both groups. The differences between the groups—the AEI as the voice of establishment conservatism and Heritage as the representative of a more militant, right-wing version—actually allowed both to maintain a separate niche and thus to operate in more of a complementary rather than oppositional manner (Phillips-Fein 2009, 173). Meanwhile, the family foundations themselves played a significant role in the 1970s conservative resurgence. The three largest and most prominent foundations at the turn of the 1970s were the Ford, Rockefeller, and Carnegie foundations. Although all three had their roots in the fortunes accumulated by the legendary businessmen who established them, all three had, by the early 1970s, become representatives of the moderate approach associated with the American corporate elite at the time. These organizations were favorite targets of the student radicals of the late 1960s and early 1970s, who viewed them as the ultimate embodiment of the establishment. Yet they were attacked, often savagely, by right-wing activists as well, who saw them as having gone out of their way to placate liberal and even radical groups. As Alice O'Connor put it (2008, 155):

> Liberal foundations could be found behind just about every cause, organization, and major study the postwar Right found objectionable—from Keynesian economic planning and U.N.-style internationalism to the American

Civil Liberties Union and the NAACP; from Gunnar Myrdal's *An American Dilemma* and Alfred Kinsey's "sex studies" in the 1940s and 1950s to public television's Children's Television Workshop in the late 1960s.

The officers of these foundations represented much of what the Far Right despised: moderate-to-liberal, Ivy League–educated Northeasterners. The prototypical example of this was McGeorge Bundy, a national security adviser in the Kennedy and Johnson administrations, who led the Ford Foundation from 1966 to 1979. Bundy was a moderate Republican, originally from Massachusetts, who presided over many of the foundation's most controversial programs. Like the CED and other moderate groups, the Ford and other traditional foundations chose a strategy of accommodation rather than confrontation toward the radical critics of the period (Judis 2001, 97). These actions raised the ire of conservatives and contributed to the sentiments expressed by Lewis Powell in his memo and Irving Kristol in his emerging neoconservative critique.

In the early 1970s, an alternative group of foundations with strongly conservative views began to raise its profile, the most prominent of which were the above-mentioned Olin, Scaife, and Smith Richardson foundations. All three of these foundations were headed by traditional conservatives, and the heads of two of them—Olin and Scaife—had been active in conservative causes prior to the 1970s. John M. Olin, the head of a St. Louis–based chemical firm, Olin Industries, that later, through an acquisition, became the Olin-Mathieson Corporation and relocated to New York, established the John M. Olin Foundation in 1953. From the start, the Olin Foundation focused its contributions on antilabor groups and conservative colleges, along with more traditional charities (O'Connor 2008, 163–165). After resigning from the board of trustees of his alma mater, Cornell, in 1970, in protest over what he felt was the university administration's capitulation to African American militants, Olin decided to focus on strengthening the cultural, economic, and political underpinnings of American capitalism. He was inspired in this effort by the Powell memorandum, which, as he put it in a letter to William Baroody of the AEI, provided "a reason for a well organized effort to re-establish the validity and importance of the American free enterprise system" (quoted in Phillips-Fein 2009, 162). During the 1970s, Olin made gifts to the AEI, the Heritage Foundation, and the Hoover Institution (a conservative-leaning research center at Stanford), and supported Chicago School economist Milton Friedman's television series *Free to Choose*. In 1977, Olin appointed William E. Simon—the treasury secretary in the Ford administration and a major figure in the 1970s conservative movement—as president of the foundation (*New York Times* [hereafter *NYT*], April 29, 1977, D3), noting that "his fundamental thinking and philosophy are almost identical with mine."

Scaife, an heir to the Mellon family fortune who gained control of his mother's foundation after her death, had been a Goldwater supporter and a benefactor of the AEI in the 1960s (Saloma 1984, 25–26; Judis 2001, 126). Once Scaife assumed control of the foundation, he used it to fund a variety of right-wing causes, including the Heritage Foundation (for which he was the leading backer), the AEI, journals such as Irving Kristol's *The Public Interest* and Murray Weidenbaum's *Regulation,* and organizations such as Accuracy in Media, whose goal was to challenge the presumed liberal bias in the media (Ferguson and Rogers 1986, 86). The Smith Richardson Foundation, formed in 1935, was not known for involvement in conservative causes prior to the 1970s, but this changed when Randolph Richardson, an heir to the family fortune, assumed control of the foundation in 1973 (Himmelstein 1990, 149). In addition to the foundation's support of *The Public Interest,* the organization became known for its sponsorship of several books that proved extremely influential in the late 1970s and early 1980s, including Jude Wanniski's *The Way the World Works,* George Gilder's *Wealth and Poverty,* and Michael Novak's *The Spirit of Democratic Capitalism* (Blumenthal 1986, 191–197).

These three foundations were small compared to the better-known Ford, Rockefeller, and Carnegie foundations. The Olin Foundation's budget was only $1 million per year as late as 1977, and Smith Richardson's was only $3 million, compared with the Ford Foundation's $160 million. The conservative foundations grew rapidly during the decade, however. The Olin endowment, for example, increased from $12 million in 1977 to $125 million in 1982 (Himmelstein 1990, 149; O'Connor 2008, 164–165). Moreover, the contributions from these foundations constituted only a portion of the funds that the conservative organizations received. When combined with the far larger amounts contributed by corporations as well as those given by wealthy individuals such as Joseph Coors, the impact was significantly greater, especially when considering that these contributions were directed almost exclusively toward conservative projects.

Conservatives thus launched a massive mobilization during the 1970s. This mobilization produced new (or greatly expanded) right-wing think tanks such as the AEI and the Heritage Foundation. The increased funding allowed for the proliferation of books and articles, all pushing various conservative perspectives. It included television and radio programming, op-ed pieces in newspapers, aggressive responses to what conservatives viewed as biased media, and support for conservative speakers and publications on college campuses. Yet the conservative movement by itself might not have been sufficient to turn the political tide in a rightward direction. After all, the Right had been organized since the 1950s. To be sure, they were better organized in the 1970s, and certainly better financed. They were also far more aggressive and confident in disseminating their views than they had been in earlier years. And the economic crisis of the period made policy makers and the public potentially more receptive to alternative ideas. The conservatives nevertheless continued to face significant obstacles. Public confidence in business was at a postwar low point. The Watergate scandal had brought a wave of Democrats to power in 1974, and the election of 1976 resulted in a new Democratic president and large Democratic majorities in both houses of Congress. The political environment remained largely liberal at least into the mid-1970s, as the consumer and environmental movements continued to make headway.

Conservative groups were certainly growing and making progress in having their voices heard, but they had not yet seized the offensive. What did occur, however, was a development that proved to be unique in postwar America: a shift in the orientation by the largest corporations. In the 1970s, the elite corporations began to retreat from their strategy of moderation and accommodation, withdrawing their reluctant but genuine acceptance of organized labor and an active and ameliorative state. The American corporate elite began to abandon its earlier commitment to a position of responsibility for the well-being of the larger society, focusing instead on its own, short-term interest. A key turning point in this shift was the establishment of a new organization of businesses.

The Business Roundtable

The business organizations that were politically active during the postwar period rarely acted in concert, and they often worked at cross-purposes.

While the National Association of Manufacturers (NAM) was advocating traditional conservative policies, the Committee for Economic Development (CED) was pursuing a more moderate approach. The Chamber of Commerce fluctuated, adopting a relatively moderate perspective during Eric Johnston's leadership in the 1940s but reverting to its more conventional conservatism after Johnston's resignation. Because the CED's approach was more in line with the dominant political perspective of the age, and perhaps because it tended to represent the views of the larger corporations, this group exercised considerably more influence than the NAM or the Chamber.

As the economy began to show signs of trouble in the late 1960s and early 1970s and the social turmoil of the period began to call into question the legitimacy of American business, the leaders of some of the largest corporations saw the need for a more concerted response. As we saw in Chapter 4, two business groups had formed in the 1960s to address labor issues. The Labor Law Study Group, a small group of executives from leading firms and trade associations, was formed in 1965 to uphold the "right-to-work" statute in the Taft-Hartley Act from attempts by union-supported Democrats to repeal it. The Construction Users Anti-Inflation Roundtable was established in 1969 by a group of executives in the construction and steel industries in response to the profit squeeze that their firms faced as a result of the tight labor market. The two groups cooperated during the early years of the Nixon administration in an unsuccessful effort to weaken the National Labor Relations Act, and they merged in 1972 (Levitan and Cooper 1984, 36).

Meanwhile, other executives were also beginning to act. Increasingly disturbed by what they viewed as the shrinking influence of business in the federal government, John Harper, the chairman of the Aluminum Company of America (Alcoa), and Fred Borch, the CEO of General Electric (and a member of the Anti-Inflation Roundtable), met in Washington with Treasury Secretary John Connally, Connally's deputy secretary, Charls [*sic*] Walker, and the chairman of the Federal Reserve, Arthur Burns (Judis 2001, 120–121; Phillips-Fein 2009, 192). After the meeting, Harper sent a letter to the CEOs of ten leading firms, including Ford, Gulf Oil, Procter and Gamble, and Westinghouse, asking if they would be willing to form an organization devoted to addressing the interests of American business (Phillips-Fein 2009, 192, 308).[10] Encouraged by Connally, Harper's group met in Washington in March 1972, after which it became known as the March Group (Levitan and Cooper 1984, 36). Harper's original goal was for the group to remain a small organization of elite executives, but a number of other firms wanted to participate, and Harper and Borch eventually decided to merge their group with the Construction Users Anti-Inflation Roundtable, of which Borch was also a member (Levitan and Cooper 1984, 36–37; Judis 2001, 120–121).

The new group, referred to as the Business Roundtable, was designed to be an elite organization of corporate leaders, distinct from the NAM and the Chamber of Commerce in its focus on big business and its rejection of their "knee jerk" conservatism (Levitan and Cooper 1984, 34). First, only CEOs of Fortune 500 firms were invited to join. By 1975, the group had 160 members, including 70 of the top 100 firms in the Fortune 500 (Himmelstein 1990, 140). Second, the organization adopted a unique political strategy. Instead of using lobbyists to influence legislation, the CEOs of major corporations were to lobby Congress directly. Legislators who might otherwise yawn at the sight of yet another corporate lobbyist requesting a meeting were far more attentive when called on by the chief executive of a major corporation (Vogel 1989, 198–199; Judis 2001, 121).

Perhaps most important, however, was the way in which the Roundtable differed from the CED, an organization whose membership was also dominated by the heads of leading corporations. As John Judis (2001, 121–122) has noted, the CED was a research organization that developed policies that its leaders viewed as representing the "national interest." Whether the group actually did this, as opposed to representing the class interests of its members, as critics such as G. William Domhoff (2006) have suggested, is certainly open to debate. The CED's position papers in the postwar period did indeed exhibit an underlying (and sometimes explicit) political position, which included support for the free enterprise system and the system of inequality that resulted, as well as an abhorrence of Soviet Communism, and these views were certainly consistent with the maintenance of their standing as privileged members of American society. It is undeniable, however, that the CED's leadership believed that it was acting in a balanced, nonideological manner, and that it valued the application of what it saw as disinterested, state-of-the-art scholarship. It is also clear that the positions that the CED typically adopted were not the traditional ones associated with the American business community. On virtually every major issue—

from the role of government in the economy, to the issues of employment and taxes, to the role of organized labor, to the social issues of the day—the CED took positions that deviated in significant ways from what both conservative and liberal forces would have preferred. Its members made a genuine effort, manifested in the group's actions, to stand above the ideological fray and to provide a responsible perspective that would result in the greatest good for the greatest number, even if it simply reflected the doctrine of "enlightened self-interest."

The Business Roundtable took a different approach. Unlike the CED, which viewed itself as a policy-planning organization whose suggestions were made in the national interest, the Roundtable was a lobbying group, explicitly devoted to advancing the interests of business. The group was formed by a combination of those who believed that business had insufficient power in Washington and those who were concerned about the growing influence of organized labor. It quickly became a part of the conservative resurgence, backing organizations such as the AEI (Peschek 1987, 29) and committing itself to the primary conservative goals of the period: reducing government regulation of business, limiting the power of unions, and reforming the corporate tax code. The group had a series of quick successes. In 1975, it led an organized lobbying effort that defeated an amendment to the antitrust laws that would have allowed state attorneys general to sue violators of antitrust law on behalf of their state's residents (*NYT*, November 16, 1975, 1). The *New York Times* described the event as a "carefully organized lobbying effort, chiefly directed by a little-known organization whose members are all giant corporations," and quoted Richard Bolling, a Missouri Democrat, who added, "The Business Roundtable, that's the name I keep hearing." The group was able to convince President Ford to publicly state that he would veto a bill establishing a Consumer Protection Agency before the bill was voted on by Congress, and it was credited with keeping a bill that would have provided an audit of the Federal Reserve Board bottled up in the House Rules Committee. Representative Wright Patman, the Texas Democrat known for his investigations of bank trust department stockholdings during the 1960s, stated in frustration, "I have been very curious about this organization—the Business Roundtable—which seems to sweep out of the night, kill public interest legislation, and then disappear. . . . Our curiosity has been piqued by its clout, its aim, and the size of the corporations it represents" (*NYT*, March 17, 1976, F3).

The Business Roundtable also played a significant role in the defeats experienced by organized labor in the late 1970s, as well as in efforts to roll back government regulatory efforts. After Jimmy Carter assumed the presidency in 1977 with large Democratic majorities in both the House and the Senate, liberals were optimistic that they could accomplish a number of goals on which they had been frustrated during eight years of a Republican presidency.[11] One of these goals involved labor law reform, an attempt to force the National Labor Relations Board to speed up the resolution of disputes over unfair labor practices and to increase the fines assessed to employers who failed to comply with the board's rulings. Although certain segments of organized labor, especially construction unions, had fared well in the late 1960s and early 1970s, the labor movement as a whole had experienced a long-term decline of membership, from more than one-third of the workforce in the mid-1950s to fewer than one-quarter by the mid-1970s. There were several possible reasons for this decline, including the difficulties of organizing in the South as well as an alleged lack of interest in organizing by the AFL-CIO's leadership.[12] One reason suggested by union officials was that employers had become increasingly aggressive in thwarting union drives, in part by harassing workers who participated. The number of complaints to the NLRB regarding unfair labor practices more than doubled between 1967 and 1977 (Vogel 1989, 153).[13]

Soon after Jimmy Carter assumed the presidency, the AFL-CIO began a major campaign to secure labor law reform. The group negotiated an agreement with President Carter, who sent a list of recommendations to Congress. The bill easily passed in the House, but business groups, seeing that the Senate was their only hope for stopping the legislation, began a massive lobbying effort. The effort was initially led by the NAM, the Chamber of Commerce, and the National Federation of Independent Business, all groups that consisted primarily of small businesses that had traditionally been strongly antiunion. The Business Roundtable, in contrast, hesitated to become involved (*Wall Street Journal* [hereafter *WSJ*], June 24, 1977, 8; August 15, 1977, 14). Many of the group's members were either firms with relatively low labor costs or ones that were already unionized, and these firms either saw no need to become involved or wanted to avoid unnecessarily antagonizing their unions. Firms in more labor-intensive industries (such as Sears Roebuck), as well as those that faced increasing foreign competition (such as Goodyear Tire and Bethlehem Steel), were more inclined to actively oppose the bill. After considerable pressure by the antiunion forces, the Roundtable's Policy Committee voted to join forces with the bill's opposition. Once the Roundtable agreed to participate, the lobbying effort became significantly more intense. Most of the actual in-person lobbying was done by small business, but the large corporations provided most of the funding. The big companies hired a public relations firm, placed canned editorials in newspapers, financed a study that suggested the likely inflationary consequences of the bill, and made their company jets available for a demonstration in Washington. By the time the bill reached the floor of the Senate, business had secured enough opposition to sustain a successful filibuster. After several failed attempts to invoke cloture, the Democrats in the Senate withdrew the bill. Business had stopped what had earlier seemed to be a certain victory for organized labor (Levitan and Cooper 1984, 130–134).

Because of its diverse membership, the Business Roundtable at its formation had chosen to select a relatively small number of issues of broad scope, on which it was possible to forge an agreement. Here was a case in which considerable disagreement existed. And yet once the organization had voted to oppose the labor law reform, even the firms that had been neutral became active in the opposition. This willingness to take a unified position once internal differences had been resolved was not new. In 1962, as we saw earlier, the Bay Area Council, a group of corporate executives in the San Francisco Bay Area, had reached a unified position in support of a new mass transit system—the Bay Area Rapid Transit—despite the initial objections of oil company executives (Whitt 1982). But the Roundtable's action in opposing labor law reform showed on a national stage the extent to which a unified approach could allow members of the business community to exercise power.

It is possible that the bill would have failed even had the Roundtable not become involved. The small-business mobilization was intense. Members of Congress received up to six million postcards expressing opposition to the bill. More than 500 chapters of various small-business organizations were involved in direct lobbying (Vogel 1989, 155–156). The financial support provided by large corporations—including those that appeared to have no direct interest in thwarting labor law reform—was crucial, however, and it may have even been decisive. And irrespective of its impact, this action by the corporate elite represented a major shift in strategy, away from accommodation with labor and toward confrontation. This shift quickly became apparent to members of organized labor. Shortly after the labor law reform bill was defeated, United Auto Workers President Douglas Fraser angrily resigned from President Carter's Labor-Management Group (an advisory committee of business and labor leaders), stating that the business community was waging a "one-sided class war" (*NYT,* July 20, 1978, B4). By their actions, according to Fraser, even the presumably enlightened business leaders on the committee had "broken and discarded the fragile, unwritten compact previously existing during a past period of growth and progress" (quoted in Brody 1980, 249). The corporate elite's participation in the defeat of labor law reform thus signaled the cracking of the postwar moderate consensus. No longer could unions be assured that the members of the American corporate elite would accept, even grudgingly, their ability to operate. Even when their interests were not directly at stake, the heads of the leading firms had put a stop to legislation that would have benefited organized labor.

The Attack on Government

In addition to its offensive against organized labor, the corporate elite began to turn against one of the other major sources of postwar constraint: the role of government in the economy. This included the proposed Consumer Protection Agency, which the Business Roundtable had successfully opposed during the Ford administration and helped to block during the Carter presidency as well. It included changes in the tax laws. It included the set of regulations promoted by the EPA, OSHA, and the Federal Trade Commission. And ultimately, it included a reorientation of thinking about the nature of government economic policy as a whole.

The fate of the Consumer Protection Agency followed closely along the lines of the defeat of labor law reform. Although President Ford had vetoed the establishment of this agency during his presidency, the bill had passed both houses of Congress. Once Carter assumed office, he promised to sign a bill, and proponents were optimistic that the bill would become law within Carter's first few months. As with the labor law bill, however, business interests, including the Business Roundtable, quickly mobilized. The Roundtable's efforts included hiring former Watergate prosecutor Leon Jaworski to lobby against the bill, as well as the distribution of canned editorials and cartoons. Although the idea of the agency was supported by a majority of the public (albeit a narrow majority), and although the bill's supporters were also well organized, the House defeated the bill by a substantial thirty-eight-vote margin in February 1978. An attempt by the Federal Trade Commission to strengthen the regulation of advertising directed toward children, a seemingly uncontroversial issue, experienced a similar fate around the same time (Vogel 1989, 160–168).

A second issue on which elite corporations affected a political outcome was tax reform, one of President Carter's early campaign pledges. The proportion of federal revenues that came from individual (as opposed to corporate) income taxes had increased steadily for more than two decades before Carter took office—from slightly more than 50 percent in the early 1950s to nearly 80 percent by the mid-1970s (Ferguson and Rogers 1986, 100–101). Moreover, because of inflation, individuals were being pushed into higher tax brackets as their wages increased, despite the fact that their real earnings were failing to keep pace. To restore what he hoped would be some balance in the system, Carter proposed a series of measures, including an increase in capital gains taxes and a decrease in the deductions allowed for business meals (Vogel 1989, 174; Judis 2001, 141). In response to the president's plan, business organizations again mounted a sustained lobbying effort, led by an organization called the American Council for Capital Formation. This group, which had been formed in the 1975 with a goal of reducing corporate taxes, was led by the aforementioned Charls Walker, a cofounder of the Business Roundtable who, as deputy treasury secretary in the Nixon administration, had been present at the original meeting in Washington at which the idea for the Roundtable was hatched. The American Council received a large early grant from the paper corporation Weyerhaeuser and subsequently received funds from a broad range of Fortune 500 companies, including the New York Times Company (Blumenthal 1986, 80; Ferguson and Rogers 1986, 102). With Walker and the American Council in the forefront, the lobbyists were not only able to defeat Carter's proposal, but they were actually able to secure reductions in both the capital gains tax and the corporate income tax (Vogel 1989, 175–176; Judis 2001, 141–142).

Perhaps the most significant effort of the business counteroffensive during the 1970s involved the response to the broad set of regulations promoted by the EPA and OSHA. It had long been argued by scholars at both ends of the political spectrum that regulatory agencies often came to serve rather than monitor the industries that were under their watch. Proponents of this so-called capture theory included the Nobel Prize–winning Chicago-School economist George Stigler (1971) as well as political sociologists who maintained a critical focus on corporate power, such as G. William Domhoff (1970) and Ralph Miliband (1969). As Stigler put it (1971, 3), "As a rule, regulation is acquired by the industry and is designed primarily for its benefit. There are regulations whose net effects upon the regulated industry are undeniably onerous. . . . These onerous regulations, however, are exceptional."

One prominent feature of the capture theory is a usually implicit assumption that government regulation is directed toward particular industries. Much, although not all, of the early history of business regulation did involve industry-specific oversight (as we saw in Chapter 3). The two primary new agencies in the 1970s—the EPA and OSHA—affected business more broadly, however. Economic theorists have distinguished between what is sometimes called traditional, or "old," regulation, and social, or "new," regulation (Herman 1981a, 173–174). The old regulation, the primary subject of capture theory, typically involved the enforcement of a set of rules regarding pricing and profit rates within an industry, in exchange for guarantees against free entry and destructive competition. It would be untrue to say that individual businesses within the regulated industries, or even the industries in general, always supported these arrangements in the past. On the other hand, to the extent that these regulations benefited the relevant industry, they often did so at the expense of other industries, as in the case of protective tariffs on imported steel (Prechel 1990). This meant that these regulations had the potential to—and often did—serve as sources of cross-industry political conflict (Bauer, Pool, and Dexter 1963).

The new regulation had at least three important differences. First, although, as we have seen, there was some support among large corporations for occupational safety and (especially) environmental measures, the terms of the Environmental Protection Act and the Occupational Safety and Health Act were to a great extent imposed on business, in part at the behest of the environmental and labor movements. Second, the nature of the regulation promulgated by the EPA and OSHA was considerably more intrusive than that of the older, industry-based type, involving at times specific directives regarding factors such as noise levels and emissions. As Herman put it (1981a, 174), "The recent surge of ground rules presents an immediate challenge to managerial prerogatives." It also led to a more adversarial relation between the agencies and the affected companies, a problem that was exacerbated by the agencies' broad jurisdiction, which prevented the development of the sometimes "cozy" relations that existed with the old regulation agencies. Third, and perhaps most significant, because the new regulation was system-wide as opposed to industry-specific, virtually the entire business community was affected. This meant that it was easier for businesses to forge a unified front in opposing the agencies, rendering the situation ripe for political organization.

Much of the conservative and business political mobilization that emerged in the 1970s was therefore directed against what was seen as excessive government regulation. This opposition was evident in the meetings of corporate executives that Silk and Vogel attended in 1974 (Silk and Vogel 1976), although these executives were also willing to acknowledge that some degree of regulation was necessary. It was evident in the interviews conducted by Useem with fifty-seven executives and board members of large American corporations. One executive, for example, expressed his resentment of the EPA's "unscrupulous methods" and accused the agency of being unbalanced. "Did you ever see an important official in EPA," he added, "who wasn't a rabid environmentalist?" (Useem 1984, 161). In summarizing the views of his respondents, Useem noted that most of them believed that the regulatory agencies were more concerned with their own political interests than with genuine industry abuses. In response, "executives of large corporations reported that the business community became aware that each was experiencing increasingly burdensome federal demands and that a joint counteroffensive was long overdue" (ibid., 162). And it was evident in the funding provided by the AEI for economist Murray Weidenbaum's journal *Regulation,* as well as Weidenbaum's own studies that showed the costs that American companies faced due to these regulations (see, for example, Weidenbaum 1979).

Meanwhile, leaders of large corporations engaged in a concerted effort to publicize their predicament. Concerns about regulation were a frequent topic in the CEOs' public speeches during the decade. Charles B. McCoy, the chairman and president of DuPont in the early 1970s, told the American Institute of Chemical Engineers that "Congress and the executive branch . . . could help by taking greater notice of the effect government

regulation can have on productivity in the private sector." "Regulatory activities," he continued, "not only add to industry's costs; they also can
change the direction, the pace, and the payout of research and development" (*Vital Speeches of the Day,* April 15, 1973; speech presented March
12, 1973). Z. D. Bonner, CEO of Gulf Oil, spoke to an audience at Town
Hall of California in Los Angeles about the "increasing stranglehold of
octopus-like government regulatory agencies, which are hamstringing the
efficiency of business, cutting down the productivity of industry, increasing
prices to the consumer, and fueling our current double-digit inflation" (*Vital Speeches of the Day,* January 15, 1975; speech presented November 19,
1974).[14] Several speakers were careful to acknowledge their support of the
overall concept of regulation, but they expressed concern that existing regulations had become excessive. Joseph P. Flannery, president of Uniroyal,
provided a good example of this view in a 1978 speech to the National
Postal Forum in Washington. "I have said that no responsible businessman
can oppose reasonable regulations and I do not," Flannery stated. "I am no
more opposed to governmental regulation than I am to police protection.
But I am as opposed to over-regulation as I am to the police state. And
over-regulation is just that—an economic police state" (*Vital Speeches of the
Day,* October 1, 1978; speech presented September 11, 1978). Similarly,
William T. Ylvisaker, chairman of Gould, Inc., in a 1978 speech to the
Public Relations Society of America in Washington, expressed his belief
that while "government has a legitimate regulatory responsibility," "government regulation of business has gone too far." "Today government programs are smothering creativity and innovation," he argued. "They are
discouraging risk. They are, in short, stifling progress" (*Vital Speeches of the
Day,* July 15, 1978; speech presented May 9, 1978).

The Attack on Keynesianism

The reaction of elite American corporations in the 1970s—against organized labor, the consumer and environmental movements, what they
viewed as overly high taxes, and what they saw as excessive regulation—
represented a significant shift from the orientation that had predominated
during the postwar period. At the root of these reactions was an economy
that no longer appeared to be working. Keynesianism had remained the
dominant economic approach in American policy making during the en-

tire postwar period. Even Richard Nixon had ultimately come to conclude that he was "now a Keynesian in economics."[15] As inflation continued its upward spiral during the 1970s, attempts to temper it were repeatedly unsuccessful. President Nixon's wage-price controls were ineffective, as were his attempts during his aborted second term. Gerald Ford became so frustrated at the persistence of inflation that he introduced his "WIN" buttons, for "whip inflation now," as if inflation were at root a problem of individual behavior that could be cured by exhorting citizens to "whip" it.[16] Even as the unemployment rate during the recession of 1973–1975 approached 9 percent in early 1975, inflation rose to more than 11 percent in 1974 and stayed above 9 percent the following year. Although inflation declined to 5 percent in 1976, it quickly rose again, reaching double digits by 1979. As the nation experienced another recession in 1980, inflation was running at more than 13 percent (see Figure 6.1).

Keynesian theory suggested, of course, that unemployment and inflation would be negatively correlated. The cure for unemployment was stimulus, which would put people back to work but ran the risk of inflation, as workers gained leverage due to the lack of a replacement work force (or what Marx called the "industrial reserve army"). The cure for inflation was an economic

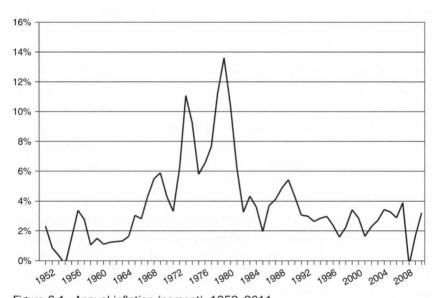

Figure 6.1. Annual inflation (percent), 1952–2011.
Source: http://www.inflationdata.com/inflation/inflation_rate/historicalinflation.aspx.

slowdown, including, if necessary, a recession. This thinking informed President Nixon's decision to "cool off" the economy after he took office during the tight labor market of the late 1960s. But the Keynesian approach simply stopped working in the 1970s. The problem could not necessarily be blamed on Keynesian policy per se. The two most important factors in the economic slowdown—the rapid spiking of oil prices (the "energy crisis") and the increasing weakness of American corporations in foreign competition—represented exogenous shocks that were almost certainly beyond the purview of policy makers, although American firms' failure to innovate, due in part to their presence in highly concentrated markets in which they had faced little pressure to do so, probably exacerbated the problem. The question was, what now could be done to address the declining performance of the American economy?

It was probably inevitable under these conditions that questions would begin to arise about the continuing relevance of Keynesian economics. One alternative that emerged during the 1970s presented a radically different diagnosis and set of recommendations. In Keynesian theory, a primary driver of economic activity is consumer demand. Insufficient demand can be both a cause and a consequence of recessions. Monetarists, the most eminent of whom was Milton Friedman, believed that adjusting the money supply by reducing interest rates was the best way to stimulate economic activity. For Keynes (as we saw in Chapter 3), a reduction in interest rates will stimulate economic activity only to the extent that companies see favorable investment opportunities. If these opportunities do not exist (or are thought not to exist), then even very low interest rates (such as those that prevailed after the 2008 recession) will not trigger investment. The alternative is to stimulate the economy through government spending, either through direct job creation, transfer payments, or tax cuts that provide consumers with greater disposable income. The problems associated with a stagnant economy are thus traced in this view to a lack of effective demand.

But what if the problem is not insufficient demand but insufficient supply? When goods are scarce, prices increase. One reason that goods might be scarce is a lack of productivity. Perhaps the increasing restrictions placed on firms by government regulation, as well as by overly powerful unions, placed a damper on productivity. Even radical economists had acknowledged that productivity gains among workers had begun to slow in the late

1960s (Weisskopf, Bowles, and Gordon 1983). If low productivity was the problem, and low productivity was caused by union rules and intrusive regulation, then it stood to reason that a weakening of unions and a relaxing of regulations might lead to improved productivity, greater supply, and thus lower inflation.[17]

The term "supply-side economics" came in the 1970s to signify a particular approach—associated with economist Arthur Laffer—that was either ignored or ridiculed by most American economists. The reason for this had to do with one aspect of Laffer's theory: the idea that a significant reduction in marginal tax rates would provide so powerful an economic stimulus that government tax revenue would actually increase as a result. This view, popularized by Jude Wanniski in *The Way the World Works*, was adopted by Representative Jack Kemp and later by Ronald Reagan, and it became one of the chief justifications for the Reagan tax cuts. But even if one rejected the idea that significant tax cuts would lead to increased government revenue, one could still accept the idea that insufficient supply, caused by insufficient productivity, was the primary cause of inflation and economic stagnation.[18] Certainly the corporate executives who spoke publicly about the issue believed that the lack of productivity was a problem, and that it was either caused or exacerbated by organized labor and, especially, excessive regulation. The fact that Keynesian economic policy no longer seemed effective as a means of managing the economy provided support for those who wanted to reduce taxes (especially corporate and capital gains taxes) and for those who supported a reduced role for government regulation. It also paved the way for a more serious critique of the role of government in the economy.

As we have seen, the idea that a market economy works most efficiently when the government plays a minimal role had been a staple of most businesspeople even during the Depression and the period of Keynesian dominance that followed. This view, associated primarily with groups such as the National Association of Manufacturers (NAM) and the Chamber of Commerce, had fallen out of favor for several decades once the New Deal was implemented, however. The business leaders who had embraced Keynesianism, which included a majority of the heads of the largest corporations, held views that were far more in line with the accepted political discourse of the period, and they therefore exercised far more influence in Washington than the small-business proponents of laissez-faire capitalism.

As Keynesian policy began to fail, however, even the heads of the largest corporations began to have second thoughts about the appropriate role of government intervention. Whether they had supported Keynesianism on philosophical grounds or—as is more likely—as a pragmatic response to the political environment they encountered, the American corporate elite had viewed it as an inevitable feature of the economic landscape. As the 1970s progressed, this inevitability began to crumble. The moderate elements of the American business community, along with policy makers themselves, began to reassess their positions.

Did the Actors *Change,* or Did the *Actors* Change?

The rightward move of big business that we have seen in this chapter raises a question: Did the members of the American corporate elite become more conservative during the 1970s, or did the composition of the elite change, with the more moderate corporate leaders of the postwar period being replaced by a group of more conservative newcomers? Some observers have suggested that what changed in the 1970s was not the orientation of the American corporate elite per se but rather the group's composition. In particular, some authors have argued that the older, moderate "establishment" centered primarily in the Northeastern United States began to give way to a newer, more conservative counterestablishment centered primarily in the newly developing regions of the South and West (Sale 1975; Silk and Silk 1980; Dye 1983; Blumenthal 1986). If true, this would suggest that the old corporate elite remained moderate but was replaced in positions of power by the insurgent Sunbelt upstarts.

There is certainly a wealth of anecdotal evidence consistent with this argument. All but one president since Lyndon Johnson has either had his origins in the Sunbelt or, as in the case of George H. W. Bush, has relocated there.[19] Republicans from Sunbelt states have tended to exhibit more conservative views than those from Northeastern and Midwestern locales. Examples of Sunbelt capitalists participating in right-wing causes, such as Joseph Coors, who provided startup funds for the Heritage Foundation, and Charles Koch, a major funder of the Libertarian Party and the Cato Institute, are plentiful.[20] And there is even some systematic evidence that Sunbelt capitalists tend to hold more conservative views. Barton's 1971 survey of leading corporate executives revealed that those born in the South or Southwest or in small towns were more conservative than those from other regions on virtually every dimension (Barton 1985, 67–70), although the effect of origins appeared to be mediated by whether one was Catholic or Jewish and whether one attended an elite college. On the other hand, in a systematic examination of contributions to "New Right" organizations, including the AEI and the Heritage Foundation, Jenkins and Shumate (1985) found that the vast majority of supporters were from Northeastern and Midwestern states. Although the Heritage Foundation was considered by some observers to be more conservative than the AEI, the geographic distribution of contributions was almost identical for both groups. Studies based on political contributions have yielded similar findings, indicating no differences in contribution patterns between Sunbelt-based and Rustbelt-based firms once other factors were taken into account (Clawson and Neustadtl 1989; Burris and Salt 1990; Mizruchi 1992, 139–141).[21]

How can one reconcile Barton's finding of greater Sunbelt conservatism with the findings of no difference presented by Jenkins and Shumate and the studies of campaign contributions? The answer may have to do with the timing of the studies. Barton's interviews were conducted in 1971, when moderation among the American corporate elite still dominated. The Jenkins-Shumate data—as well as those collected by Burris and Salt and Clawson and Neustadtl (as well as for my study)—came from years no earlier than 1978.[22] What these findings suggest is that the corporate elites from the Northeast were indeed relatively moderate in the postwar period, but that they shifted rightward during the 1970s. This would seem to run counter to the view that the rightward shift within the American corporate elite was merely a case of replacement by a new group of Sunbelt-based conservatives. It suggests instead that the older, Northeastern elite itself became more conservative during the 1970s. This is consistent with much of the evidence that I have already presented, and it is also consistent with the documented rightward turn of a number of key corporate elites during the period.

Consider four of the businessmen who signed the letter to Congress urging passage of President Johnson's Demonstration Cities Act (discussed in Chapter 3): Stephen D. Bechtel Jr., chairman of the Bechtel Corporation at the time of the letter, became the head of the foundation bearing his name. By the 1970s, the organization was among the most noted right-wing foundations (Vogel 1989, 223), contributing to, among others, the AEI, the

Heritage Foundation, the Pacific Legal Foundation, and Milton Friedman's television series, *Free to Choose* (Saloma 1984, 32–34). Fred Borch, the CEO of General Electric, was a vice chairman of the CED as late as 1973 and remained an honorary trustee as late as 1980, but he also became a member of the Construction Users Anti-Inflation Roundtable and, with John Harper, was a cofounder of the March Group, which eventually became the Business Roundtable.[23] Justin Dart, who at the time of the letter was the president of the Rexall Drug and Chemical Company, had been strongly conservative since at least the 1930s, when he actively opposed Franklin Roosevelt's presidency (Phillips-Fein 2009, 186–187), and he later became a leading figure in the attempts to move Congress in a more conservative direction (Handler and Mulkern 1982, 99–101; Clawson, Neustadtl, and Bearden 1986, 802). Yet Dart was sufficiently pragmatic during the 1960s to express support for a significant Great Society program.

Perhaps the most interesting of the four was Henry Ford II, who was known to have been moderate and pragmatic during the 1960s, including contributing to Lyndon Johnson's presidential campaign (Phillips-Fein 2009, 141). Although it would be inaccurate to suggest that Ford became strongly conservative in the 1970s, he did, in dramatic fashion, resign from the Board of Trustees of the Ford Foundation in 1977, frustrated at what he believed was the foundation's hostility to business. The event was likely triggered in part by the foundation's support of a 1974 report on energy conservation called *A Time to Choose*. According to Judis (2001, 161), the report's recommendations were "wise, prudent, and moderate—just the kind of thing one would expect from a dispassionate, but also cautious, application of social science." The report provoked a ferocious attack from conservatives, however, and McGeorge Bundy (the foundation's president) yielded to the pressure, publishing a critique by business opponents, who accused the report of containing "a pervasive, anti-market, pro-government bias." "The Foundation exists and thrives on the fruits of our economic system," Ford wrote in his letter of resignation. "The dividends of competitive enterprise make it all possible. A significant portion of the abundance created by U.S. business enables the Foundation and like institutions to carry on their work."

Ford was careful to maintain his commitment to the concept of philanthropy:

I'm not playing the role of the hard-headed tycoon who thinks all philanthropists are socialists and all university professors are communists. I'm just suggesting to the Trustees and the staff that the system that makes the Foundation possible very probably is worth preserving. Perhaps it is time for the Trustees and staff to examine the question of our obligations to our economic system and to consider how the Foundation . . . might act most wisely to strengthen and improve its progenitor. (quoted in Silk and Silk 1980, 147–148)[24]

Although not a signer of the Model Cities letter, Walter Wriston, the CEO of Citibank, had also been a supporter of President Johnson's candidacy. By the 1970s, Wriston had become a major fundraiser for the AEI and a fierce critic of government regulation (Silk and Silk 1980, 119, 124). The point here is not necessarily that these corporate leaders became more conservative in an ideological sense (Dart, and probably Bechtel, had been conservative long before their support for Lyndon Johnson). They nevertheless were sufficiently pragmatic during the 1960s to be willing to support a significant liberal social program that provided no clear immediate economic benefits. Their shift to an active conservatism far to the right of the political discourse that had prevailed during the postwar period may not have represented an ideological change, but it certainly represented a strategic one.

Whither the CED?

As we saw in Chapter 3, the moderate element of American business that was most significant during the postwar period was the group associated with the CED. Yet conspicuously missing from the current chapter thus far has been any extended discussion of the role that the CED played during the rightward turn of the 1970s. There is a copious amount of evidence indicating that the CED maintained its moderate perspective at least into the middle of the decade. Yet by 1976 there were also indications that the organization had lost power as the Business Roundtable increased in importance. The CED also began to experience increasing dissent during the decade, as proposals consistent with the organization's historically moderate perspective were challenged from a more conservative position (Domhoff 2011, chapter 8).

Examples of the CED's continuing moderation are numerous. In February 1972, the CED, along with the Business Council, expressed concern that President Nixon was "over-inflating" the economy in an attempt to improve his reelection prospects (*WSJ*, February 18, 1972, 2). In a 1972 speech in Paris, Ellmore C. Patterson, chairman of Morgan Guaranty Trust, praised the ability of large American corporations to deflect criticism by "co-opting" their critics and cited the CED report *Social Responsibilities of Business Corporations* (1971) as an example of this strategy of accommodation (*NYT*, May 3, 1972, 63). A CED report on law enforcement called for the legalization of gambling and marijuana and an outlawing of handguns (*NYT*, June 29, 1972, 20), although William F. Buckley Jr.'s conservative *National Review* and the American Bar Association took a similar position (*NYT*, December 3, 1972, E2).

In a 1973 report, the CED proposed a universal health care plan. The group outlined a program that would require that "a basic level of protection . . . be made available to all Americans regardless of their means, age, or other conditions." "This coverage should be continuous," the report continued, "without interruptions during a hiatus in employment or for any other cause; treatment should not be delayed for determinations of liability for payment, and care should not be foregone or deferred because of inability to pay" (Committee for Economic Development 1973, 22). The proposal recommended that all employers be required to provide a minimum level of insurance for all employees and their dependents, and that Medicare and federally sponsored "community trusteeships" cover anyone who was not employed at a particular time (ibid., 23–24). It also recommended that until the cost structure became fully known, the government should maintain control over at least some health care costs (ibid., 25). Planning of manpower needs, particularly those of physicians' assistants and other health care personnel, should be handled on the basis of "systematic central planning by a national health-manpower program located in the office of the Secretary of Health, Education and Welfare," the report stated (ibid., 26).

Although there is no evidence that the CED directly influenced the Nixon administration, less than a year after the release of the report President Nixon announced a plan for universal coverage that adhered closely to the organization's recommendations.[25] Meanwhile, although its proposals were not always politically moderate or liberal, the CED maintained its postwar orientation well into the 1970s. In 1974, for example, the group called for a tax on "inefficient" automotive vehicles, the labeling of appliances with energy use information, and increasing subsidies for mass transit, although the group also called for the relaxation of environmental standards to increase the use of coal (*WSJ*, December 9, 1974, 2). As late as 1975, the group was discussing a large tax cut for low- and middle-income workers and a stimulus package consisting of business tax cuts and government spending (*NYT*, January 10, 1975, 53).

Nevertheless, there is some indication that the CED was beginning to experience strains. From the organization's birth, CED reports had always contained space for individual members to comment on various aspects of the group's proposals. Discussions were often lively, and criticism was as likely to come from the left as from the right. During the late 1960s and 1970s, the level of dissent began to increase. This was evident in the 1971 report on corporate social responsibility—although perhaps not surprisingly, given the nature of the topic—but it was also evident in the statement on health care.[26] In the mid-1970s a significant split erupted within the group, prompted by a speech to the CED's Research and Policy Committee by the committee's chair, Philip M. Klutznick, a limited partner at Salomon Brothers. Klutznick called for a $20 billion tax reduction for low- and middle-income earners, a $5 billion fiscal stimulus, and "an explicit declaration" that the policy was being implemented "as part of a social compact among business, labor, and Government to restrain future inflation" (*NYT*, January 10, 1975, 53). Although these ideas were not unlike those proposed by President Ford in his "Whip Inflation Now" speech two months earlier, they triggered fierce reactions from several CED trustees, including John D. Harper, the CED vice chairman and Business Roundtable cofounder, R. Crosby Kemper, chairman of United Missouri Bank, and Marvin Bower, a director at the consulting firm McKinsey & Company, who suggested that the group consider replacing its Keynesian economic approach with that of the free market advocate Friedrich von Hayek (Domhoff 2011, Chapter 8). As the level of dissent within the CED continued to increase over the next two years, it dovetailed with another problem that became evident shortly after Jimmy Carter's election: the group was beginning to lose its influence.

Gauging the influence of any group is of course always a difficult task. One useful approach, developed by William G. Roy (1981), involves identifying the extent to which a group's views are taken into account by another group in the latter's decision-making process. Without access to internal government deliberations, it is not possible to measure this phenomenon directly. It is possible to measure it indirectly, however, by examining the extent to which an organization's views are given credence by respected national media. Figure 6.2 shows the number of mentions of the CED and the AEI in the *New York Times* between 1960 and 1980. As is evident from the figure, the frequency of attention given to the CED dropped sharply during the 1970s, after a brief uptick in the late 1960s. Mentions of the AEI, on the other hand, began to increase geometrically in the mid-1970s.[27]

Although its presence in the media appeared to be decreasing at a constant rate during the 1970s, the importance of the CED may have reached an inflection point after Carter's election. In a December 1976 article in the *Wall Street Journal,* entitled "Rehabilitation Project: Once-Mighty CED Panel of Executives Seeks a Revival, Offers Advice to Carter" (*WSJ,* December 17, 1976, 38), the reporter, Lindley H. Clark, cataloged the group's presumed decline, stating that the president-elect had turned to the Round-

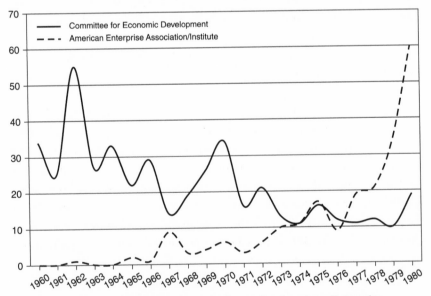

Figure 6.2. *New York Times* articles referring to the American Enterprise Institute and the Committee for Economic Development, 1960–1980.

table rather than the CED for advice. Examples of this decline were many: When Carter named W. Michael Blumenthal as his nominee for treasury secretary, the president-elect did not even mention Blumenthal's CED trusteeship. When Carter sought meetings with business leaders to discuss his policies, he turned to the chairman of the Business Roundtable, Irving S. Shapiro (the chairman of Du Pont), rather than the "old-line CED," as the article termed the group. "Such oversights wouldn't have happened in the CED's early days in the 1940s," the article continued. "In those days the organization was swaying public policies in economics, government, and education." Although the CED continued to list the chief executives of numerous major firms among its trustees, one academic economist stated that the organization had "lost its purpose." Herbert Stein, the long-time CED economist and subsequent chairman of the Council of Economic Advisers in the Nixon administration, argued that during the Kennedy-Johnson years, the CED "tried to influence the Democrats by joining them." The article also pointed to increasing dissent within the organization, stemming from the conservative trend among businesses. James Q. Riordan, senior vice president for finance at Mobil, noted that in earlier years, "the trustees were men who saw a need for some more government intervention." "Now," he continued, "some of the trustees believe the intervention has gone far enough." To examine the issue of internal dissent more systematically, I conducted an analysis of the number of dissents in twenty-seven CED documents from 1945 through 1973. The data revealed a strong trend toward greater dissent over time, with a correlation between year and average number of dissents per report of .83.[28]

Despite the difficulties that the CED was experiencing by mid-decade, the organization maintained its commitment to policies in what its members viewed as the national interest. As Franklin A. Lindsay, chairman of Itek Corporation and the chairman of the CED's Research and Policy Committee put it, the organization "should continue to put the broad public interest ahead of the narrow and short-term interests of business." "In the long run," he said, "I think this is what will serve business best" (*WSJ*, December 17, 1976, 38). The CED thus continued to issue its position papers, even if it lost influence compared to the Roundtable and the AEI. Its positions remained relatively moderate even into the Reagan administration, including reports that were directly critical of Reagan's policies toward the unemployed and the poor (*WSJ*, February 9, 1982, 30; *NYT*,

February 11, 1982, A28) as well as papers advocating expanded government support for university research (*NYT,* April 30, 1983, 31) and a national industrial policy (*NYT,* August 28, 1983, SM31)—the latter a highly controversial idea among American business leaders (Paretsky 2003). There is even speculation that the CED's influence was decisive in stopping an attempt by a group of conservative organizations to pass a constitutional amendment mandating a balanced budget during the first Reagan administration (Ferguson and Rogers 1986, 102).[29] Yet regardless of its impact in this particular case, the group's overall influence on policy in Washington had almost certainly declined by the late 1970s.

The Business Roundtable and the Continued Presence of Moderation

Although the American corporate elite did become increasingly conservative during the 1970s, this did not occur all at once. The Business Roundtable appeared to have overtaken the CED by the beginning of the Carter administration. Yet despite the fact that the Roundtable was a different kind of organization—a probusiness lobby, as opposed to a research group whose goal was to remain neutral and above the fray—the group did exhibit a relatively moderate and pragmatic orientation, at least when compared with the NAM and the Chamber of Commerce. The group also distinguished itself from the conservative groups of the period by trying to avoid divisive social issues such as abortion rights and feminism. Even in its work on taxes, its focus was primarily on corporate rather than individual or property taxes (Phillips-Fein 2009, 197).

The Roundtable's basic strategy was to identify a relatively small number of issues on which it could forge a consensus and then lobby aggressively in support of those issues. To do this, it was necessary for members to take a broad perspective that went beyond their immediate interests. George Shultz, a major figure in government over two decades as well as a leading business figure, discussed the need for business leaders to understand this approach if they were to work successfully with government officials. In their meetings with him during his early years in the Nixon administration, many business leaders, Shultz noted, offered "only general complaints and groans. . . . Increasingly, however, it seemed to me that businessmen were learning that homework pays off." This involved not only knowledge of the facts and an impartial view of them, Shultz argued, but also an ability to look "beyond the very narrow interests of the individual firm or industry and offering some connection between what you want and the broader public interest" (quoted in Singer 1980, 1367).[30] This broader perspective, which Useem (1984) has referred to as "classwide rationality," also made the Roundtable more willing to compromise than the more strident traditional business groups and New Right conservatives. This flexibility on policy as well as the stature of its members gave the Roundtable a level of influence within the Carter administration that was not available to the NAM or the Chamber of Commerce. The group's moderation—as well as its access to the administration—also created a level of friction between the group and other segments of the business community, a strain reminiscent of that between the CED and the NAM and Chamber in earlier years. In an article in *Fortune* critical of this style of "pragmatic politics," A. F. Ehrbar argued that "many large companies are pursuing a strategy that can be described only as one of accommodation and concession. They acquiesce to unwarranted demands by regulators and the White House, and they frequently take positions that are inimical to their long-term interests" (Ehrbar 1979, 77). "Such pragmatism is woefully misguided," the author asserted. "Not only does it yield few short-run benefits, it also . . . intensifies long-run threats to the free-enterprise system" (ibid., 79). The Roundtable also experienced criticism on the editorial page of the *Wall Street Journal* (see, for example, *WSJ*, October 6, 1976, 22), although not as frequently, or with as much derision, as the CED had received in its heyday.

Still, however moderate the group might have been compared with the traditional conservative business organizations as well as the New Right foundations and think tanks, the Business Roundtable did reflect a new, more conservative orientation among members of the American corporate elite. If the group did not completely abandon all concern about the larger public interest, it certainly paid considerably less attention to it than the CED had. The Roundtable's mission was to advance the interests of large corporations, and its strategy was focused less on accommodating the critics of business than on resisting them, as well as acting, sometimes aggressively, against them. The group's perceived need to take these actions had a basis in genuine changes that American companies had experienced. Certain segments of organized labor had taken advantage of tight labor markets in the late 1960s, although this became less of an issue during the

1970s, as unemployment increased. Government regulation had indeed expanded into areas that seemed to place limits on managers' ability to run their firms. Business did face increasing foreign competition and a seemingly out-of-control domestic economy. The reaction that the Roundtable took was nevertheless a departure from the approach that the American corporate elite had typically adopted during the postwar period.

Conclusion

The moderate consensus among business, government, and labor that had characterized the postwar United States broke down in the 1970s. The nation began to experience serious economic problems in the midst of increasingly intense social conflict, and the institutions that had sustained the postwar consensus began to lose their legitimacy with the larger public. The corporate elite began the decade at perhaps the height of its political moderation, with a general acceptance of a strong and ameliorative state and an accommodation, however fragile, with organized labor. As the economic crisis worsened and the attacks on business—and even the market system as a whole—intensified, the elite began to fight back. As traditional conservatives mobilized, especially those associated with the Far Right, large corporations began to slowly follow in their path. An important development in the rightward shift of the corporate elite was the formation of the Business Roundtable, in 1973. Although it was not until after Jimmy Carter's election that business began to experience success in turning back the reforms of the 1960s and in thwarting further ones, the narrative of American politics had by then turned against government regulation, taxes, and organized labor. By the end of the 1970s, the Business Roundtable had superseded the CED as the primary organization of the leaders of elite American corporations.[31]

Perhaps the key development among the American corporate elite was not simply that it became more conservative per se. Even the Business Roundtable remained relatively moderate compared with the Chamber of Commerce and the NAM, and—as we shall see—the group retained a level of statesmanship well into the 1980s. What changed was the elite's focus. Instead of attempting to accommodate the forces of the state and organized labor—to serve as a mediator between these groups and the most conservative elements of business—the corporate elite shifted its focus toward an effort to reduce the role of government and the power of labor. These efforts led to a weakening of these two forces, which increased the ability of corporations to act without the pressures of the state or their workers. Yet in significantly contributing to the demise of government and organized labor, the American corporate elite inadvertently began to dismantle two of the primary structures that had sustained its moderate postwar orientation, as well as its ability to act collectively to address its shared concerns. As a strongly probusiness administration prepared to assume office, the corporate elite had reason to feel on top of the world, or at least that its problems would finally be addressed in a sympathetic manner. The group was unaware that this very success would represent the beginning of its undoing.

7 ||| Winning the War but Losing the Battle
The Fragmentation of the American Corporate Elite

The undoing of the constraints on the American corporate elite had already been largely accomplished by the time that Ronald Reagan assumed the presidency in January 1981. Business and capital gains taxes had been significantly reduced. Redistributive policies by the federal government had been sharply curtailed. The labor movement had become increasingly weak. And the initiatives by the consumer and environmental movements, including those involving the regulation of corporate activities, had been thwarted. The demise of ameliorative government and organized labor accelerated after Reagan took over, however. This demise, along with two further developments—the decline of commercial banks and an acquisition wave of unprecedented proportions—created a tidal wave that ultimately resulted in the virtual dissolution of the American corporate elite that had reigned since the end of World War II. The corporate elite's victory over the forces that had constrained it had the paradoxical effect of leading to its undoing.

The Retreat from Ameliorative Government

Jimmy Carter had already made cuts in social spending, including during the year of his reelection campaign, in response to the continuing economic crisis (Ferguson and Rogers 1986, 111). Carter did this out of perceived necessity, however, and not as a result of an ideological aversion to government's role in the social safety net. Reagan, on the other hand, made his position on the proper role of government clear in his inaugural address. In an oft-quoted passage, the new president stated that "government is not the solution to our problem; government is the problem." Gone was the idea, born in Franklin Roosevelt's administration, that government should play a role in providing security for the poor and underprivileged. Also gone was the idea that government was a positive force for social good. Government was now seen as a behemoth, whose growing encroachment on individual decision making had shackled the economy, stifling productivity with its arbitrary and unnecessary rules. As president, Reagan wanted to remove these shackles and unleash the entrepreneurial spirit that in his view had once propelled America to greatness but was now being thwarted at every turn by stifling regulations.

Reagan quickly began to act on this philosophy by proposing a series of tax cuts for both individuals and businesses. He also planned to institute massive increases in defense spending in response to his view that the United States had become militarily weakened during the 1970s. As an adherent of the version of supply-side economics expounded by Arthur Laffer and Representative Jack Kemp, Reagan promoted the idea that the implementation of sharp tax cuts would create such a surge of economic activity that it would actually result in increased revenue. With the predicted explosion of economic activity that the tax cuts would release as well as the proposed reductions in social spending, there was presumably little to fear with regard to the ability to fund his massive military buildup. Still, although Kemp was not particularly hostile to social programs (Barone and Ujifusa 1983, 856) and believed that the revenue generated by the tax cuts could be used to fund them, Reagan was determined to reduce the programs. Several years later, evidence emerged, coming in part from his outgoing budget director David Stockman, that Reagan had known that his budget plans would generate large deficits and that he hoped to use the deficits as a rationale for a significant dismantling of government social programs (*New York Times* [hereafter *NYT*], July 11, 1985, A20; July 19, 1985, A27; Moynihan 1985). Reagan had made no secret of his disdain for these programs. In his campaigns dating back at least to 1976, he had used the example of a "welfare queen," who, through various schemes, had managed to secure a six-figure income and a Cadillac, as an example of the waste and futility of government social programs.[1]

The leaders of the nation's largest corporations were favorably inclined toward tax cuts, but their focus was primarily on business taxes rather than individual ones. Historically, small businesses have tended to support reductions in personal tax rates because the majority of small firm owners pay individual income taxes out of their companies' earnings. Although some leaders of large corporations, especially the highest paid, were also supportive of the cuts in personal taxes proposed by the Reagan administration given the substantial amounts involved (Ferguson and Rogers 1986, 120), most were more concerned with corporate tax rates, and many were skeptical of the individual cuts because of concerns about potential deficits. There was also a feeling, in part promulgated by members of Congress sympathetic to business tax reform, that a unified position from business would be necessary to produce reform. During the 1978 tax reform (discussed in the previous chapter), in which President Carter's attempt to shift the tax burden toward corporate and capital gains taxes was not only undermined but actually reversed by corporate lobbyists, some industries, especially capital-intensive ones, benefited less than others from resulting cuts in capital gains taxes. This time, Representatives Jim Jones, an Oklahoma Democrat, and Barber Conable, an upstate New York Republican, insisted to corporate leaders that they would support further reform only if business approached them with a unified perspective (Martin 1991, 117).

The primary idea supported by the largest corporations came out of discussions of an informal coalition known as the Carlton Group (so named because its original meetings had taken place at the Carlton Hotel in Washington). This group, led by Charls Walker, included representatives from the Business Roundtable, the Chamber of Commerce, and the National Federation of Independent Business, among others. The primary proposal that emerged from the group was a focus on expedited depreciation allowances, which became known as "10-5-3" for its goal of allowing businesses to depreciate buildings in ten years, automotive vehicles in three years, and all other equipment in five years (Vogel 1989, 242–243). Prior to that, depreciation on capital goods had to be taken over the entire assessed "useful life" of the asset, each of which was assigned separately. This led to considerable debate over what the appropriate useful life of an asset should be, as well as complaints that the time frame within which the cost of a capital good could be recouped was excessive (Martin 1991, 118). The idea behind 10-5-3 was to speed up the process by which the full value of an asset could be written off (from which its name, "accelerated cost recovery," was derived), and also to simplify the process by assigning all capital goods to three time frames.

The 10-5-3 proposal was more beneficial to some industries than to others. Capital-intensive firms stood to benefit the most, while industries such as banking and high technology, with fewer tangible assets, were poised to gain less. What followed, however, reflected the extent to which the Democrats as well as the Republicans had become beholden to business interests. A number of Democrats, especially those from the South, shared the concern of the large corporations that the personal tax cuts might trigger a large deficit. In order to appease Southern Democrats, whom he believed were sympathetic to his bill, President Reagan modified the bill to reduce not only the personal tax cuts but also the speed of the depreciation allowances. These allowances had limited support among Southerners: some of their most powerful constituents were oil drillers, who, because they were not likely to benefit significantly from the more generous depreciation allowances, were largely indifferent to 10-5-3. In contrast, businesses in other industries and regions had strongly supported the increased depreciation allowances, and President Reagan's proposed weakening of these expected benefits led to a flood of lobbying by corporate interests, who flew into Washington in June 1981 to press for the retention of the 10-5-3 plan, in what became known as "Lear Jet Weekend" (Ferguson and Rogers 1986, 121). Meanwhile, the Democrats in the House hoped to capitalize on the business discontent by offering an even more favorable alternative. This included a bill that would go far beyond 10-5-3 by offering full "expensing" of capital investment, in which the entire cost of the asset could be written off at the time of purchase (Vogel 1989, 244). The Democrats' proposal led to a bidding war, in which both sides continued to increase their offers. David Stockman, the administration's budget director, was famously quoted as saying, "The hogs were really feeding. The greed level, the level of opportunism, just got out of control" (quoted in Ferguson and Rogers 1986, 122). By the time the bill emerged from the joint House-Senate committee, it provided tax benefits for businesses that were beyond what the firms themselves had even proposed (Vogel 1989, 244–245).

This was behavior that American society had not seen from the federal government in many decades. Postwar critics of American capitalism had accused the state of serving the interests of business over those of the general public. Yet even many of these critics had acknowledged that the government had played a largely mediating role in the postwar period, compelled to by the forces that business interests faced. There was no mediation among competing societal interests by 1981. The only question was which corporate interests would be served in the event of a disagreement between various industries.

The Attack on Regulation

In addition to slashing individual and corporate taxes, the Reagan administration moved to weaken the enforcement of government regulations. A considerable amount of deregulation had already occurred prior to Reagan's assumption of the presidency. The airlines were deregulated under Jimmy Carter's administration, for example, as were trucking and railroads (Rajan and Zingales 2003, 268), and efforts were already under way to deregulate telecommunications and banking. These deregulation efforts involved traditional industry-based regulations, however, and in many cases were supported by liberals and consumer groups. Airline deregulation, for example, was supported by Ralph Nader, and it led to significantly lower airfare prices for the general population. Reagan's focus was less on these traditional forms of regulation than with the new "social" type of regulation that had emerged in the 1970s, in particular the statutes involving the environment and the workplace (Herman 1981a). Reagan was concerned primarily not with removing the legislation that existed but rather with enforcing this legislation in a manner that was less hostile to business. To do this, the president appointed avowed critics of regulation to head the major agencies. This included, most famously, James Watt as secretary of the interior and Anne Gorsuch (later Burford) as the head of the Environmental Protection Agency (EPA), as well as Thorne Auchter to head the Occupational Safety and Health Administration (OSHA). Among the president's other notable appointments were Murray Weidenbaum as chair of the Council of Economic Advisers and Raymond Donovan to head the Department of Labor.

There were limits to what these new agency heads could accomplish. The EPA and OSHA were staffed largely by career civil servants who believed in the goals of their organizations and made sincere attempts to enforce the law as they saw it, even if it meant antagonizing corporations in the process. The directors of the agencies had considerable power nevertheless, and they were able to institute significant changes in policy almost immediately after assuming their positions. This was most evident in the actions of Watt at the Department of the Interior, Gorsuch at the EPA, and Auchter at OSHA. Prior to his appointment as secretary of the interior, Watt had established the Mountain States Legal Foundation, a group that attempted to force the government to open up federal lands to mineral development. After assuming his position as secretary, Watt immediately acted to realize these goals, even against the opposition of Republicans in Congress who wanted to protect federal lands in their districts. He testified to the Senate Subcommittee on Commerce, Science, and Transportation that the Reagan administration wished to develop a policy to protect "the building blocks of an industrial economy" (Mosher 1981a, 2076). To further this, Watt expanded the use of federal lands for coal mining, leasing more than 150,000 acres with more than 2.4 billion tons of coal. He proposed a plan to lease the entire Outer Continental Shelf, more than one billion acres of submerged offshore land, for oil drilling (Mosher 1983, 2307). He removed more than one million acres of wilderness from federal protection. And he allowed private ranchers to manage water and wildlife on federal land, which the ranchers then used for grazing (*Chicago Tribune,* September 13, 1985).

At the EPA, Gorsuch, a former telephone company lawyer and member of the Colorado state legislature, instituted such radical changes in policy that she was under pressure from Democrats in Congress to resign within six months of her appointment. President Reagan had cut 12 percent from the EPA's budget in the first year and had asked for an additional 12 percent cut for 1983, but Gorsuch proposed to cut an additional 18 percent on top of that (Mosher 1981b, 1899). In her first year, the number of cases the agency sent to the Justice Department declined by 84 percent and the number of penalties the agency assessed declined by nearly 50 percent (Vogel 1989, 249). A former Carter administration agency official estimated that, taking inflation into account, the EPA's budget would be reduced by more than half. The official, William Drayton Jr., also learned (from an internal document leaked to him) that Gorsuch planned to fire more than 3,000 agency employees over the next two years, amounting to a reduction of one-third of the agency's staff during a period in which its workload was expected to double (Mosher 1981b, 1899–1900). Interviews with current and former EPA officials conducted by *National Journal* reporter Lawrence Mosher suggested that Gorsuch "did not trust the agency's career civil servants" but trusted members of industry "almost totally" (ibid., 1901). "On Capitol Hill," Mosher found, "there is suspicion that Gorsuch is prepared to gut her agency if necessary to please the White House" (ibid., 1902). As with Watt, Gorsuch managed to alienate even Republican members of Congress. She even raised concerns among some of the corporations she was attempting to placate. Peter B. Hutt, a Washington lawyer with a firm that represented the chemical industry, while admitting that the industry had disagreed with the way the agency administered the Toxic Substances Control Act, also stated that "the chemical industry certainly doesn't want to see EPA dismembered." Steven D. Jellinek, a former EPA officer working as a lobbyist during the time of Mosher's article, argued that "industry wants a reasonable EPA" but that many firms were now "becoming concerned about not being able to get decisions out of the agency" (ibid.). Both Watt and Gorsuch were eventually forced out of their positions, Watt because of some ill-timed, arguably racist comments and Gorsuch because of the continuing turmoil surrounding her management of the EPA. The industry-friendly policies that they initiated remained largely in place after their departures, however.

Not all of the Reagan administration's agency heads were as blatantly proindustry as Watt and Gorsuch. Thorne Auchter, who Reagan tapped to run OSHA, was viewed by one labor official as "sincere" and desirous of "a health and safety program that works" (Wines 1981, 1985). Auchter nevertheless received praise from the Chamber of Commerce and was sharply criticized by other labor leaders, and his policy measures at OSHA, although less extreme than those at the EPA, followed a similar pattern of reduced enforcement. Auchter had served as a manager of his family's construction firm in Florida, a firm that, like Labor Secretary Donovan's, had been cited multiple times by OSHA for safety violations. Auchter began his term by quickly relaxing the implementation of OSHA's inspection guidelines. He reduced the agency's staff by more than 20 percent (Wines 1981,

1985). He reduced inspections in response to complaints to a level 58 percent below what they had been in the last year of the Carter administration. The total number of penalties that the agency assessed declined by 78 percent, and the penalties that were rendered came to less than seven dollars on average (Ferguson and Rogers 1986, 134). "In the past, OSHA has always been in an adversarial position," Auchter explained. "The OSHA of today is a cooperative regulator" (Wines 1981, 1985). The same labor official who had described Auchter as "sincere" also stated that Auchter was "totally convinced that industry can do the job better than any federal program at all" (ibid.).

The reduced attention to regulation and the conciliatory attitude that the agencies exhibited toward the companies they were designed to regulate occurred in virtually every major federal agency, including the Federal Trade Commission, the Interstate Commerce Commission, and the Consumer Product Safety Commission. The Reagan administration's attempt to roll back regulation did have its limits, especially in the area of environmental legislation. Some of this was due to the overreaching of the EPA under Gorsuch—whose resignation led Thorne Auchter at OSHA to immediately act to tighten enforcement—and some of it was due to the continuing strength of the environmental movement (Vogel 1989, 266–268). Two places in which deregulation experienced continuing and lasting success, however, involved labor policy and antitrust policy. The administration's actions in these areas contributed to two of the most important developments of the decade: the almost complete decimation of organized labor, and the corporate takeover wave. Just as the government's abrogation of its role as moderator of the business cycle, source of the social safety net, and regulator of business removed one of the key forces behind the postwar moderation of the American corporate elite, the attack on organized labor removed another.

The Decline of Organized Labor

Organized labor in the United States had already lost considerable strength by the late 1970s, in the wake of the defeats over labor law reform and the Consumer Protection Agency, as well as the weakening of the Humphrey-Hawkins full employment bill. The proportion of nonagricultural employees in the American workforce belonging to unions had been in decline since the mid-1950s, dropping from a peak of 35 percent in 1954 to 27 percent in 1970 and 22 percent by 1980 (Mayer 2004).[2] Given the growth of public employee unions during this period, these figures mask the fact that the proportion of unionized workers in the private economy had experienced an even more precipitous decline.[3] And yet it was only in the 1980s that the labor movement received a near-death blow, facilitated not only by the companies that had fought against unions for decades but also by a government that had turned in a strongly antilabor direction. The pivotal episode in this process was President Reagan's decision in August 1981 to fire the striking members of the Professional Air Traffic Controllers Organization (PATCO). Air traffic control is an extremely high-pressure occupation, and the controllers had a series of grievances that had built up over several years. During the 1980 presidential campaign, PATCO received a promise from Reagan to be responsive to their concerns, and the union endorsed his candidacy. When the union struck in August, however, the president gave the controllers a 48-hour window to return to work. When they remained on strike, he fired the entire membership.[4]

The PATCO strike and its aftermath are often seen as the key precipitating events marking the decline of the American labor movement. Strikes by federal employees had been illegal since the 1950s, but thirty-nine such actions had occurred in the two decades leading up to the air traffic controllers' strike, and striking workers had returned to work in each case (McCartin 2011b).[5] Certainly the president's response to the strikers had a chilling effect on the willingness of other unions to strike, and it may have encouraged for-profit corporations to hire replacement workers during strikes, something that was relatively rare in earlier years. Although the number of strikes had declined sharply in 1980 and 1981, perhaps as a result of the recession, the drop became even more precipitous after 1981, as Figure 7.1 shows. The number of strikes involving 1,000 or more workers, which stood at 235 in 1979, dropped to 187 in 1980, 145 in 1981, and then to 96 in 1982. By the 1990s, the average number of large strikes had declined to fewer than thirty-five per year (despite a booming economy during most of the decade), and in the 2000s the figure dropped even further, to an average of barely twenty per year from 2000 through 2009. Moreover, after 1981, the historic negative correlation between strikes and unemployment (discussed in Chapter 4) began to disappear. The fact that strike activity actually declined during periods of low unemployment suggests that workers were unable to take advantage of whatever leverage these low rates might have provided.

The decline of organized labor was a result of more than the PATCO strike, however. The labor movement was already experiencing a period of long-run decline even before 1981, and the trend would likely have continued regardless of the strike. Increasing global competition and the increasing use of foreign workers by American firms reduced the leverage of the domestic labor force and created not only downward pressures on wages but also a credible threat that were workers to strike, they might not only fail to achieve their demands but might also lose their jobs altogether. Even if a firm's jobs were not shipped overseas, the increasing use of replacement workers during the 1980s—also an apparent consequence of the PATCO strike—further reduced the workers' leverage. Two labor economists, Peter Cramton and Joseph Tracy (1998), found that the probability of a strike declined as the risk of the use of replacement workers increased.

Yet whatever leverage the workers had lost by the 1980s, the policies of the Reagan administration exacerbated the situation. In addition to his

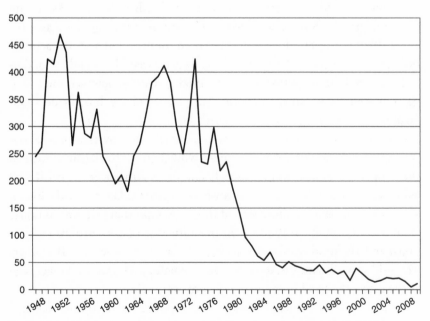

Figure 7.1. Strikes involving at least 1,000 workers, by year, 1948–2010.
Source: Bureau of Labor Statistics.

appointments of arguably antilabor officials such as Raymond Donovan and Thorne Auchter to head the Department of Labor and OSHA, respectively, Reagan also appointed antilabor officials to the National Labor Relations Board (NLRB), most notably Donald L. Dotson as chairman. The NLRB consists of five members who serve staggered five-year terms. Historically, although the board's rulings had tended to shift toward business or labor depending on whether a Republican or a Democrat was in the White House, the differences were relatively modest. In 1975, for example, a Republican-appointed board ruled that an individual worker who complained about safety law violations could be viewed as acting on behalf of his or her fellow workers and was thus immune from firing, a ruling that, according to *Business Week,* angered conservatives (*Business Week,* June 11, 1984, 122). When Reagan became president the NLRB was composed of two Democrats, one Republican, and one Independent. It took until December 1982 for Reagan's appointees to gain control of the board, but once they did, the board's policies shifted drastically. The NLRB immediately began reversing the decisions of previous boards, including the 1975 decision that protected individual workers who complained about safety law violations. According to estimates by the AFL-CIO, the NLRB's rulings had been probusiness in 46 percent of its union representation cases between 1979 and 1980 (during the Carter administration) and had actually been probusiness only 35 percent of the time between 1975 and 1976, during the Ford administration. Between 1983 and 1984, however, once Reagan's appointees became a majority, 72 percent of the board's decisions favored business (Ferguson and Rogers 1986, 136).

The combination of a weak economy, the threat of overseas job relocation, the increasing use of replacement workers for jobs that remained in the United States, and an increasingly antiunion attitude at the NLRB all led to a significant decline in the power of organized labor. The decline in strike activity was a manifestation of this, as was the sharp decline in union membership during the 1980s, their inability to win new certification elections, and the decline of real wages that workers experienced. If workers were still viewed with suspicion by management, they were no longer seen as the threat they had been during the postwar period.

By the mid-1980s, then, two of the most powerful constraints that had compelled the American corporate elite to behave in a relatively moderate, pragmatic fashion in the postwar period—an active, ameliorative state and the forces of organized labor—had been largely quieted. The government under Ronald Reagan appeared more interested in serving the business community than in regulating it, and more interested in taking the side of the companies rather than serving as a mediator between corporations and workers. For decades, Marxist political theorists argued that the role of the government in a capitalist society was to uphold the interests of the owners of capital. This formulation is nonfalsifiable, in that by definition any action that the state takes—whether violently suppressing an industrial strike or establishing Social Security and Medicare—is ultimately seen as serving the interests of the capitalist class.[6] Even if this formulation were true, however, the capitalist class whose interests the state was placating became considerably different in the 1980s from what it had been in the postwar period. As we shall see, the enlightened self-interest hailed by the Committee for Economic Development (CED) began to give way to a form of naked self-interest, unencumbered by the pragmatic application of Keynesian economic principles or an accommodation with organized labor. Yet despite the decline of the ameliorative state and the unions, one source of constraint remained: the banks. But the banks too shifted their focus during the 1980s. And along with this shift came a wave of acquisitions and hostile takeovers that drastically altered the role of corporate management.

The Money Center Could No Longer Hold

We saw in Chapter 5 that the large commercial banks played an important role in the postwar United States. Although they no longer exercised control over large nonfinancial corporations as they had in the early years of the twentieth century, the banks contributed to the maintenance of the moderate, pragmatic perspective that characterized the American corporate elite at the time. Because of their possession of the universal corporate resource—investment capital—virtually every large firm had dealings with the banks, and in some cases, especially as capital became scarce in the late 1960s, these relations became ones of dependence. At the same time, the banks' boards of directors became the meeting place for the leaders of the corporate community, a desired destination for numerous officers of Fortune 500 firms. From as far back as the 1870s, there had been one constant in the structure of the corporate interlock network in the United States: the disproportionate centrality of financial institutions, especially commercial banks (Mizruchi 1982; Bunting 1983). In 1912, seventeen of the twenty-five most central firms among a network of 167 companies were financial institutions (Mizruchi 1982, 126). In 1962, thirteen of the twenty most central corporations among a network of 1,131 firms were financial institutions (Mintz and Schwartz 1985, 157). And in 1982, nine of the eleven most interlocked firms and six of the ten most central firms in a network of 648 companies were financial institutions (Davis and Mizruchi 1999, 229). Remarkably, five of the six commercial banks that were among the ten most central firms in 1962—Morgan Guaranty Trust, Chase Manhattan, Chemical, First National City Bank, and Manufacturers Hanover—were still among the ten most central in 1982. The sixth—Mellon National Bank—was among the ten most interlocked firms in the latter year.[7] In 1982, the chief executives of fourteen Fortune 500 corporations sat on the board of the Chase Manhattan Bank. Among the 648 largest American firms in that year, directors of 43 percent of them either sat on the board of Chase or served with Chase directors on other boards, and Chase was not even the most central bank in the network (Davis and Mizruchi 1999, 218). It is unlikely that the centrality of banks in the 1960s and 1970s was a function of bank control over nonfinancial corporations, as it had been in the early part of the twentieth century. But this centrality, and the behavioral consequences associated with it, suggests that the banks played an important role in integrating the corporate community.

As we moved into the 1980s, the role of the banks began to change. First, alternative sources of capital became increasingly available. Technological advances, including increased worldwide access to low-cost information about borrowers, led to a reduction in the informational advantages on which the banks' strength had been based. One consequence of this was an increase in the use of commercial paper, in which nonfinancial corporations raise capital by selling promissory notes, either directly to other firms or through a mediator, usually an investment bank (Berger, Kashyap, and Scalise 1995, 64–65). Although commercial paper could be used only by financially strong firms borrowing large sums, the rates paid by the issuers tended to be lower than those paid to commercial banks (Stearns and Mizruchi 1993, 290). American companies also relied increasingly on bonds placed by banks outside the United States (known as Eurobonds, because of their origins in Europe). Not only did nonfinancial corporations thus depend less on American banks for their financing, but as purchasers of commercial paper, they became increasingly involved in lending themselves. By the mid-1990s, the largest American commercial lender was GE Capital, an arm of General Electric (Davis and Mizruchi 1999, 220). Between 1950 and 1970, the proportion of nonfinancial firm profits that came from financial activity (including lending to consumers as well as businesses) hovered at around 10 percent. By the early 1980s, this figure had reached as high as 40 percent, and it reached 50 percent in 2000 (Krippner 2011, 35–36). Whatever leverage the banks had experienced over nonfinancial corporations in the past was in significant decline by the 1980s.

A second problem that the banks experienced in the 1980s was the proliferation of alternative sources of investment for bank depositors. As late as the early 1970s, individual savers of modest means had few alternatives to passbook savings accounts. Moreover, the interest rates that banks could pay on these accounts were regulated by the federal government and were capped at values that during the 1970s were below the rate of inflation. In response to this, individuals began to increasingly invest in a range of newly formed or expanded instruments that were offering higher rates of return. Meanwhile, under pressure from consumer activists, President Carter and Congress deregulated bank interest rates in 1980. This allowed consumers to receive higher interest rates in passbook savings accounts, but the increasing competition that the banks faced, as well as the need to pay higher rates, placed significant pressure on their profit margins (Berger, Kashyap, and Scalise 1995, 78–81).

The banks were now being squeezed from both sides. On the lending front, they were losing out as nonfinancial corporations relied increasingly on commercial paper and on bonds placed outside the United States.[8] On the deposit front, they were losing out as savers relied increasingly on alternative forms of investment. The banks responded to the loss of their lending business by pursuing a series of high-risk activities, most notoriously in real estate speculation and in loans to unstable Latin American countries, both of which led to significant write-offs. Between the lack of income from lending and the increasingly difficult environment for acquiring deposits, the banks experienced a period of decline between the early 1980s and the early 1990s. The share of total credit market debt held by commercial banks stood at 26 percent in 1979, but it began a slow and steady decline to 17 percent by 1994, a drop of more than one-third (Berger,

Kashyap, and Scalise 1995, 75). The share of lending to nonfarm, nonfinancial corporations held by commercial banks declined from 20.5 percent in 1980 to 14.5 percent in 1994, a decline of nearly 30 percent (James and Houston 1996, 11). In 1948, commercial banks held approximately 56 percent of the assets of financial institutions in the United States. By 1980, this figure had dropped below 35 percent and by 1993 to only 25 percent (ibid., 10).[9] The number of bank failures, which had been fewer than 10 per year from 1979 through 1981, increased to nearly 50 in 1982 and to approximately 200 per year by 1987, before declining in the 1990s (Berger, Kashyap, and Scalise 1995, 82). Overall, the number of commercial banks declined by 36 percent—from 12,463 to 7,926—between 1979 and 1994 (ibid., 67).

By the early 1990s, several of the largest commercial banks were in serious trouble. Representative John Dingell (D-Michigan), chairman of the House Committee on Energy and Commerce, argued that Citicorp, the nation's largest bank at the time, was "technically insolvent" (quoted in Barth, Brumbaugh, and Litan 1992, 54). Dick Kovacevich, the CEO of Norwest, stated more broadly, "The banking industry is dead, and we ought to just bury it" (James and Houston 1996, 8; see also Davis and Mizruchi 1999, 221). Yet the banks recovered, and the way they did so had its roots in a strategic shift that began in the 1980s. This reorientation, which represented a fundamental change in the industry, had unanticipated consequences for the American corporate elite.

The source of the banks' recovery was their willingness to expand their business away from lending and toward fee-for-service activities. These services included currency swaps, derivatives, capital market services, securities underwriting, and general financial advice; in other words, activities that more closely resembled investment banks than commercial banks. Of course, commercial and investment banking had been legally separated by the Banking Act of 1933, the Depression-era statute known as Glass-Steagall. American commercial bankers had increasingly complained during the 1980s that their foreign competitors were not subjected to similar restrictions, which placed the American banks at a competitive disadvantage (Calomiris 1997). As new financial instruments grew in prominence during the 1980s, interpretation of Glass-Steagall became increasingly ambiguous, and American commercial banks continued to push their way into these new activities. By the time that Linda Stearns and I studied the corporate banking unit of a leading money market bank beginning in 1997, the bank was engaging in lending primarily as a means to generate more lucrative fee-based business from its corporate customers. Of the 230 deals on which we collected at least partial information, only 27.3 percent involved lending as their primary component (Mizruchi and Stearns 2001, 654). In April 1998, Citibank and Travelers Insurance (one of whose subsidiaries was the investment firm Smith Barney) announced that they planned to merge to create a new financial institution, Citigroup. In November 1999, Congress passed the Graham-Leach-Bliley Act, which repealed the mandated separation of commercial and investment banking from Glass-Steagall (Funk and Hirschman 2011).

As commercial banks became increasingly involved in investment bank–like activities, an interesting development occurred: their centrality in the interfirm network began to decline. As Davis and I found (Davis and Mizruchi 1999, 228), the mean board size among the fifty largest American banks declined from twenty-two in 1982 to seventeen in 1994. The mean number of bank interlocks with other firms in the network dropped from 16.4 in 1982 to 10.3 in 1994, a decline of more than 37 percent. The associated decline for nonbanks was from 8.5 to 7.5, a decline of only 11.7 percent. Eight of the eleven most interlocked firms in our 1982 network were commercial banks, and a ninth was a diversified financial corporation. By 1994, only four of the thirteen most interlocked firms were commercial banks.[10] The median number of nonfinancial firm executives on the boards of banks declined from 4.0 in 1982 to 2.1 in 1994. Although banks remained more central on average than nonfinancial firms, at least in terms of statistical significance, for the first time ever, after more than a century of continuity, they lost their dominant position in the network.

The results of the Davis-Mizruchi study indicate that the commercial banks' reduced role in the allocation of capital was reflected in their reduced centrality in the social network among large firms. This decline in bank dominance also rendered the network as a whole significantly less dense than it had been, suggesting a growing fragmentation of the American corporate elite. The primary reasons for the decline in bank centrality were twofold and interrelated: bank boards became smaller, decreasing in size by more than 20 percent; and the presence of nonfinancial executives on bank boards declined sharply, to barely one-half of its former frequency. There are two possible explanations for this latter decline. Either Fortune

500 CEOs began to decline invitations to join bank boards, or the banks decided to reduce the number of invitations to Fortune 500 executives. This is a difficult question to answer without direct access to the motives of both the bank and nonfinancial directors. There is evidence that the latter is the more likely explanation, however. If nonfinancial executives were increasingly less willing to serve on bank boards, then we would expect the relative prestige of those who did agree to serve to decline over time. We found, however, that the status of the nonfinancial executives who accepted bank board appointments—in terms of their number of other board positions and whether they were CEOs of other firms in the network—stayed roughly constant over the twelve-year period of the study (Davis and Mizruchi 1999, 232). Not only does the evidence suggest that nonfinancial executives were not becoming more likely to reject offers to join bank boards, but there is evidence to suggest that the decline of Fortune 500 executives on bank boards was a result of a deliberate choice by the banks. If the decline in bank board size and centrality were the result of a strategic shift away from traditional lending activity, then the banks that reduced their commercial and industrial lending should have been disproportionately likely to experience reduced board size and declining centrality. This was exactly what we found (ibid., 232–234). Although we had data on only twenty-five banks for this analysis, we found that a decline in commercial and industrial lending between 1986 and 1994 was associated with declines in board size, appointments of nonfinancial executives, and interlocks.[11]

What, then, does the declining centrality of banks say about the role of banks as a moderating force in the corporate community? Faced with an increasingly competitive environment, the leading American commercial banks shifted their focus, away from their traditional role in the allocation of capital and toward a role as a financial service provider. In making this shift, the banks changed the nature of their boards of directors, extending fewer invitations to the executives of leading nonfinancial corporations. The banks thus became less central in the network of large firms. The inadvertent outcome of this declining bank centrality was the fragmentation of the network. No group of firms replaced the banks as the glue that held the system together. Instead, a vacuum emerged.[12] In becoming more like investment banks, the commercial banks abdicated their role as the arbiters of the corporate community, the actors that helped forge a consensus among the nation's leading firms.

An example of how the money center can no longer hold—to paraphrase the title of the Davis-Mizruchi paper—is illustrated by the declining effect of network ties on firm behavior. In a study of the effects of director interlocks on nonfinancial corporations' use of debt financing, Linda Stearns, Christopher Marquis, and I found that in the 1970s, firm financial strategies were affected by the strategies of the firms with which they shared directors. Over time, however, the effect of these network ties disappeared. By the 1990s, firms' financial strategies were no longer affected by the firms with which they were interlocked (Mizruchi, Stearns, and Marquis 2006). We argue, and show, that a series of broad, institutional changes occurred during the period of our study that contributed to the decline of the network effect, including the acquisition wave of the 1980s that I will discuss in the following section. What the findings also suggest, however, is that between the early 1970s and the mid-1990s, the American corporate elite gradually lost its ability to generate either a consensus of ideas or a similarity of behavior.

By the end of the 1980s, then, the three forces that had contributed to the moderation of the postwar corporate elite—the state, organized labor, and the financial community—were no longer playing this role. The state had abandoned its commitment to economic regulation and social amelioration. Labor was in disarray, a shrunken and weakened movement fighting for its life and increasingly irrelevant. And the banks, by shifting their focus away from the allocation of capital, inadvertently abdicated their role in forging cohesion within the corporate community. The absence of these forces, along with the victories the group had achieved, led to the fragmentation of the corporate elite. With this fragmentation came a renewed commitment to solitary, self-interested action coupled with a retreat from the moderation that had prevailed in the postwar period, a retreat that—as we saw in the previous chapter—began in the 1970s. The corporate elite, constrained in its actions for so long by forces that it had only grudgingly accepted, had, by throwing off the reins of government and labor, seemingly won the war. And yet this victory, virtually complete as it was, had an unintended consequence. Success led to fragmentation, which ultimately led to the undoing of the elite itself. When collective action became necessary in subsequent years, the ability to act, which had propelled the elite to great accomplishments in the years following World War II, was nowhere to be found.

Success and Fragmentation

The American business community as a whole was not unified in the post-war period. A major disjuncture existed between the interests of large and small companies, and even among the larger firms differences existed over issues such as trade and, to a lesser extent, labor policy. Yet there was a relatively small group at the top of the corporate world that managed to achieve a basic unity around a moderate, pragmatic approach to politics. As the American economy, and the social order underlying it, experienced a severe set of exogenous shocks during the 1970s, American business developed a perhaps unprecedented degree of political unity. Corporations both small and large, both capital and labor intensive, and both globally and domestically focused, came together in an effort to redirect the efforts of the government and to reduce the power of organized labor. Even then differences remained, especially on questions of international trade, but the overall unity of American business far exceeded the divisions, a point agreed upon by both pluralist political scientists and their critics.

This high level of business unity corresponded with a period of great political success. By the late 1970s, business had significantly turned the tide of state action, stopping labor reform, quelling the consumer movement, and reducing both the statutes and, especially, the enforcement associated with government regulation. As Ronald Reagan consolidated his presidency, the victory of business became even more complete. Corporations saw significant declines in their tax burden. The administration severely curtailed the nation's regulatory apparatus. The president increased defense spending to a level that, according to his budget director David Stockman, led to "squealing with delight throughout the military-industrial complex" (Stockman 1986, 109). And through the Federal Reserve's tight money policy, the administration's cuts in the social safety net, the increasingly promanagement NLRB, and the president's response to the air traffic controllers' strike, the business community was now facing a significantly weakened labor movement. Business had won the war begun in the 1970s. With the shift in government priorities, the retreat of organized labor, and the corresponding decline of commercial banks, the corporate community, even its most enlightened elements, was no longer constrained to act in a moderate and accommodating fashion toward its adversaries.

Yet an interesting consequence resulted from this victory. Having won the war, there was nothing left over which to fight. As a result, the corporate community began to fragment. This fragmentation involved not only a return to the old divisions between large and small business and between foreign-oriented and domestically oriented firms. It also occurred even at the top. Although vestiges of the old, moderate corporate elite remained well into the 1980s, the group of enlightened, pragmatic corporate leaders began to dissolve. Increasingly, the decade saw each firm go its own way, pursuing its individual interests without the group of leaders at the top to forge a broader, longer-term consensus. Just as Michael Useem was publishing his book about the "inner circle" in 1984, the inner circle was starting to disappear. The group's death knell came as a result of the acquisition wave that engulfed corporate America later in the decade. But even prior to that assault on management, the corporate elite was already in significant decline as an organized entity.

One of the first sources of fragmentation occurred in 1982. We saw earlier that the bidding war between the Reagan administration and congressional Democrats led to a tax bill that was probusiness beyond what even the companies themselves had proposed. Once the tax bill was enacted, the deficit immediately zoomed to record levels. The tax cuts for businesses were designed to spur investment, but capital expenditures actually declined after the passage of the bill. Business fixed investment declined by 8.4 percent in the year after the bill was passed, and orders for new plants and equipment declined by 12 percent (Martin 1991, 137). Along with the deficit came double-digit unemployment, for the first time since the Great Depression.[13]

Business leaders were concerned about the deficit that had emerged following the 1981 tax cuts, and President Reagan agreed that something had to be done. Although both the business community and the administration supported the idea of cuts in social spending, both groups acknowledged that some kind of tax increase would be necessary. Unlike the period leading up to the passage of the bill, however, this time business was unable to maintain a unified position. The largest corporations had always been cool to the idea of tax cuts for individuals (as opposed to businesses). The president, on the other hand, was partial to the individual tax cuts, which he viewed as a crucial component of his economic recovery plan (Vogel 1989, 252). He instead proposed a set of tax increases that fell almost exclusively on businesses.[14] Not surprisingly, this plan triggered a series of strong reactions by corporations, but it also led to a fraying of the unity that business had achieved prior to the passage of the 1981 bill. The financial, housing, and high-technology sectors, the groups most concerned about the deficit, supported an increase in both personal and corporate taxes. Manufacturers, who were less concerned about the deficit, publicly opposed all of the tax increases, but they were especially concerned about those involving the 10-5-3 depreciation allowances and less concerned about the individual rates. Small businesses were split. Some, led by the National Federation of Independent Business, were opposed to any tax increases, while others, led by the National Small Business Association, shared the financial and housing sectors' concerns about high interest rates, which they saw as having a particularly devastating effect on themselves (Martin 1991, 138–141).[15] The divisions among small businesses—based apparently on ideology—were interesting, but those between small and large firms were more expected. They were merely a reprise of the big business–small business splits that had persisted throughout the postwar period. More relevant for our purposes was the division among the largest firms.

Disagreements among large corporations were not unprecedented, of course. Deficits, because they are often associated with government efforts to stimulate the economy, have typically been of less concern to nonfinancial corporations than to financials. On the other hand, nonfinancial firms do care about interest rates; they need capital for investment. To the extent that large deficits are associated with high rates (as they had historically been up to that point), they would seem to be a concern for all firms. The issue in this case was not the deficit per se but what the president proposed to do about it. Banks and home builders did not benefit from generous depreciation allowances, but those in capital-intensive industries did. All business sectors at the time supported cuts in spending (although not in defense spending), but the large firms understood that spending cuts would not be sufficient to eliminate the deficit. The question of who was going to pay the increased taxes that were therefore necessary is what created the conflict. And in this case, big business might have pushed too far.

The difficulty that large corporations experienced reached a head in a meeting of the Business Roundtable's forty-two-member policy committee in March 1982. The meeting was described by A. F. Ehrbar, a reporter for *Fortune,* as "one of the group's stormiest ever" (Ehrbar 1982, 62). According to Ehrbar's account, the CEOs of five major companies—Walter Wriston of Citibank, George Shultz of Bechtel, Roger Smith of General Motors, J. Paul Sticht of R. J. Reynolds, and Philip Caldwell of Ford—"all objected loudly" to the recommendations that came out of the meeting, especially the suggestion to delay the president's personal income tax cut.[16] The proposal that ultimately emerged from the committee included reductions in Social Security but also in defense spending, as well as taxes on natural gas (whose price had recently been decontrolled) and gasoline. The committee did not recommend any adjustments in the tax cuts that businesses had received, however. When a six-person group from the committee brought its proposal to the White House, Treasury Secretary Donald T. Regan blasted the plan. In response to the Roundtable's proposal to pull back on tax cuts for individuals while leaving business tax cuts in place, Regan stated, "It's somewhat ironic to hear $200,000 executives saying, 'Don't give a tax cut to $20,000 workers'" (quoted in Ehrbar 1982, 58). Like Richard Nixon before him, President Reagan was evidently not afraid to take a stand against at least some elements of the business community to protect programs that were popular with the larger public. Reagan did ultimately work hard to secure corporate support for his plan, and he was able to convince even most members of the Roundtable to go along. The plan that passed reduced by approximately one-half the capital investment incentives from the 1981 bill, but it did not include the minimum corporate tax that the administration had originally pursued (Vogel 1989, 253–254).

The disunity among the corporate elite that the 1982 tax bill exposed was a case in which business saw its interests as threatened, with each group scrambling to protect what it had won in the previous bill. Interestingly, however, unlike the 1970s, when business mobilized in a largely unified fashion in response to adversity, the response this time led to conflict rather than cohesion. The fact that even large businesses responded with multiple voices rather than a single one may have been precisely because they were no longer under the kind of threat that they had faced in the previous decade. Even if big business experienced a setback in the 1982 tax increase, what led to the decline in corporate unity over the next several years was not that business was facing defeats, but rather that it had so thoroughly won. Not only had the threats from government regulation and labor unions been almost completely extinguished and the tax rate reduced, but the general cultural environment toward business had swung in a much more favorable direction as well.

Although considerable antipathy toward business remained even during the Reagan era, it was focused on specific sectors, while attitudes became far more positive in other areas. The proportion of Americans who expressed a "highly favorable" view toward large corporations stood at 18 percent in 1981, dropped to 12 percent in late 1982 (during the height of the recession), rebounded to a still-low 21 percent in the spring of 1984, and remained at this level into 1986 (Lipset and Schneider 1987, 11). On the other hand, in 1984 a *Washington Post* survey found that a number of industries, including computers, food, airlines, and even automobiles, received highly favorable ratings from a majority of respondents (Vogel 1989, 275), and surveys by the Roper Organization showed that between 1978 and 1985 business improved its reputation in areas such as prices, product quality, and safety (Lipset and Schneider 1987, 12). Perhaps because of a reduced set of opportunities due to the weakened economy, the number of college students majoring in business had already begun to increase during the 1970s. By 1983, the proportion of undergraduates majoring in business had nearly doubled from ten years earlier, and the number of master's degrees in business nearly doubled between 1975 and 1985 (Vogel 1989, 274). The antipathy toward business that remained was directed not against the idea of business in general or against the newer, more dynamic industries but rather against companies' unwillingness to reduce pollution or to pay their fair share of taxes. It was also increasingly focused on the faceless managers of the old-line bureaucratic companies, those that were losing out to Japan and others in global competition (Lipset and Schneider 1987, 12–14).

As the social and political environment became increasingly hospitable for American business, the corporate elite was becoming less politically cohesive and less willing to maintain a broad, moderate approach toward the larger society. Each firm could now pursue its own interests, without the need to organize to turn back the groundswell of antibusiness sentiment (and especially, activism) that business had faced in the late 1960s and early 1970s. Meanwhile, the organizations that had facilitated business collective action began to decline as well. The Committee for Economic Development (CED) had already seen itself rendered virtually irrelevant by the late 1970s. The organization continued to issue its reports in the 1980s, and it occasionally received attention for them from the news media. The frequency of this attention continued to decline, however, and it was nowhere near what it had been in earlier years.[17] Even the Business Roundtable began to experience difficulties. The group, as we saw, had fractured during the 1982 tax increase debate, but rallied to play a major role in the 1983 tax increase on individuals.[18] The Roundtable was unable to stave off the business tax increases that were included in the 1986 tax reform bill, however, in part because its members failed to achieve a unified position. As Richard Darman, a Reagan administration official, noted in reacting to business's lobbying effort on that bill, "They were brought down by the narrowness of their vision. Precisely because they defined themselves as representatives of single special interests, they failed to notice their collective power" (quoted in Vogel 1989, 282). As Martin (1991, 174) described it, in the context of fleshing out the myriad of business positions on the bill, "the Business Roundtable was unable to reach consensus on the 1986 tax reform act" (see also Judis 2001, 181).

By the 1990s, articles were appearing reporting a decline in the organization's influence (see, for example, *Fortune* 1997). As for the moderation that had characterized the American corporate elite in earlier years, this too was becoming a thing of the past. The Roundtable did support a personal income tax increase in both 1982 and 1983, and leading chief executives also urged President George H. W. Bush to institute a tax increase in 1989 (*Fortune*, January 16, 1989). Some business leaders supported the idea of a national industrial policy in response to the success of Japan and other East Asian nations—a position much like that advocated by the CED in the immediate postwar period (Paretsky 2003). This issue received some traction, not only from traditionally moderate figures such as investment banker Felix Rohatyn, but also from John Young, the CEO of Hewlett Packard and a long-time Republican. President Reagan actually established a commission to address the issue and appointed Young as its chair. Young's group issued a report after the 1984 election suggesting that the government invest in job training, education, and nonmilitary research and development. These recommendations were strongly opposed by conservatives, however, and the administration failed to act on them or even to publicize them (Judis 2001, 183–185).[19]

By the mid-1980s, then, the three primary forces—the state, organized labor, and the banks—that had constrained the American corporate elite in the postwar era were no longer providing an effective form of countervailing power. The unity that the corporate elite had achieved in the late 1970s had largely disappeared as a consequence, and the moderation that had characterized the group into the early 1970s was largely gone as well. And yet despite the corporate elite's apparent victory over these forces, another movement was emerging during this period, a near-revolution that began to dwarf everything that the elite had achieved: corporate management was finding itself under siege.

The Revolt of the Owners

Most large corporations of the postwar period were dominated by management. Although managers had important stakeholders with which they had to deal—among them government, labor, consumers, and financial institutions—they had a relatively high degree of autonomy in the day-to-day direction of their firms. As early as the 1930s, as we saw in Chapter 5, Adolf A. Berle Jr. and Gardiner C. Means (1968 [1932]) had raised concerns about this system, fearing that managers would lack accountability to the firm's owners as well as to the larger society. Few complaints about this arrangement were heard during the postwar period, as the American economy experienced an era of sustained growth. On the contrary, many observers saw the management-controlled firm of the time as an institution, an ongoing enterprise whose policies, even if implicitly, exhibited concern for the larger community (Mizruchi and Hirschman 2010). As we have seen, compared to the period that preceded the managerial revolution, there may have been some truth to this view. But scholars were slowly beginning to question the role of management. Some of these accounts came from left-wing critics, who viewed profit-seeking corporations as the root of many societal problems, but others came from the mainstream of economics and law, and this latter group had a very different set of concerns.

If Berle and Means had feared management's lack of responsiveness to both the larger community and the firm's owners, the law and economics movement (as it came to be known as) was concerned exclusively with the latter. Among the first such works was a 1965 paper by a legal scholar, Henry G. Manne. According to Manne (1965, 112), "The control of corporations may constitute a valuable asset . . . that exists independent of any interest in either economies of scale or monopoly profits." A fundamental premise underlying this market, Manne stated, is "the existence of a high positive correlation between corporate managerial efficiency and the market price of shares of that company" (ibid.). In other words, a company's stock price provides a window into the efficiency of its management. To the extent that a firm's share price pales in comparison with its industry peers, the firm can be viewed as "poorly managed." This proposition had one particularly significant implication. If a firm's stock is lower than it "should" be, Manne reasoned, then the firm becomes a legitimate target for a takeover: "The lower the stock price," he contended, "relative to what it could be with more efficient management, the more attractive the take-over becomes to those who believe that they can manage the company more efficiently" (ibid., 113).

Manne's thesis was extended in the 1970s by Michael Jensen and William Meckling (1976). Jensen and Meckling conceptualized the problem raised by Berle and Means as one of "agency," in which a "principal . . . engage[s] another person to perform some service on their behalf which involves delegating some decision making authority to the agent" (Jensen and Meckling 1976, 308). Applied to the theory of the firm, the stockholder is the principal and management is the agent. The problem, according to Jensen and Meckling, is that the interests of the principal and the agent do not necessarily coincide. Stockholders may prefer higher dividends, for example, while managers might prefer to pay themselves higher salaries. The solution to this problem is to align the incentives so that those of ownership and management are the same (ibid., 308). One way to do this is to ensure that managers have a significant ownership stake in the company. The use of executive stock options began to emerge on a significant scale during the 1980s, representing 19 percent of total CEO compensation in the 1980s, more than 30 percent by 1996, and nearly 50 percent by 2000, before dropping back to 25 percent in 2006, perhaps in response to the bursting of the dot-com bubble.[20] Payments in stock grants increased sharply during the 2000s as stock option levels declined, however, growing to 32 percent of compensation by 2008. By 1998, less than half of CEO compensation was coming from the combination of salary and bonus (Frydman and Jenter 2010, 80–81).

Beyond the idea of alignment of incentives in Jensen and Meckling's work was a perhaps even more significant idea. In a 1937 article that later won him the Nobel Prize in economics, Ronald Coase raised the question, if markets were always the most efficient means of organizing transactions, then why do firms exist? After all, taken to its logical conclusion, neoclassical economic theory implied that every transaction could be most efficiently handled by self-interested buyers and sellers contacting one another, coming to an agreement on quantity and price, and drawing up a contract. In practice, of course, such a system is absurd. It would mean that every time a customer wanted a gallon of milk or a pair of sneakers, he or she would have to identify an individual seller able to provide the most favorable combination of quality and price. Each seller would have to establish a contractual relationship with every potential buyer. Such a system would quickly become unworkable due to the enormous friction involved, or what later became known as transaction costs. Firms were established to reduce these transaction costs, Coase argued. It was more efficient to have a single producer specialize in a product (or a set of related products) than to have to rely on the market for every transaction. For Coase, what defined the firm was its system of authority. That is, the firm was an organization with an established and regularized system of roles, including those involving the direction of the enterprise. This conception of the firm has been shared by virtually the entire field of organizational and management science since the time of Max Weber.

Jensen and Meckling took issue with this view. The boundaries of the firm were in fact illusory, they argued. Most organizations "are simply legal fictions, which serve as a nexus for a set of contracting relationships among individuals" (1976, 310). What occurred inside the firm was no different from what occurred outside of it. In both cases, relations are simply a series of contracts between individuals, not only between the firms' employees, but also between individuals within the firm and suppliers, customers, or creditors. Rather than trying to distinguish things that are inside the firm from those that are outside of it, there is, the authors state, "only a multitude of complex relationships . . . between the legal fiction (the firm) and the owners of labor, material and capital inputs and the consumers of output."[21]

This view of firms as simply a nexus of contracts had serious implications for the role of management. As Zajac and Westphal (2004, 435–437) describe it, the prevalent view of the firm during the managerial era (which corresponds roughly to our postwar period, but persisting into the early 1980s) was of an institution, an organization persisting over a long period of time, whose existence was taken for granted and whose totality was greater than the individuals who worked within it. The managers who ran the firm were viewed as professionals with a highly developed set of specialized knowledge who were uniquely capable of efficiently administering its operation. In the agency perspective, by contrast, the firm was not an institution but rather a constellation of contractual relations that were at least potentially episodic. The idea of the firm as institution was a myth, or a legal fiction. Managers in this view were not uniquely qualified professionals but rather mere agents of shareholders, "hired hands," in Rakesh Khurana's (2007) apt term, who had no specific claim to their status beyond what ownership had decided, however temporarily, to grant them. As Zajac and Westphal put it (2004, 436), "If managers are merely fungible agents with no particular strategic expertise, and if firms are merely [nexi] of contracts without unique core competencies, then resources can be allocated by investors in capital markets rather than by executives in corporations." Moreover, the primary raison d'etre for managers was no longer the maximization of profits per se but rather the maximization of the firm's stock price, or what came to be known as "shareholder value" (Useem 1993, 11).

It would be a stretch to suggest that agency theory was the *cause* of the shareholder value logic that engulfed the corporate world beginning in the 1980s, nor was it the cause of the 1980s merger wave. The theory did emerge prior to the practices that conformed to it, however, and it certainly played a role in the ex post justifications of those practices. Still, the correspondence between theory and practice took some time to develop. Manne's article preceded the 1960s merger wave, and that wave, dominated by managers seeking to diversify their firms into what were often unrelated industries, was, if anything, a Jensen and Meckling nightmare, a management power play to increase the CEOs' reach over broad swaths of the business world. It was not until the 1980s that the movement that paid homage to Jensen and Meckling—even if inadvertently—developed, as agency logic replaced managerial logic as a rationale for firm actions. In the area of executive compensation, for example, justifications used by companies that implemented long-term incentive plans for their CEOs changed from an emphasis on the need to attract scarce managerial talent in a competitive market for skilled labor to one based on the need to maximize shareholder wealth by aligning the incentives of managers and owners (Zajac and Westphal 1995). The "firm-as-portfolio" model, an outgrowth of management's quest for conglomeration in the 1960s, was delegitimized by the business press in the late 1980s. *The Economist* described it as a "colossal mistake, made by the managers, for the managers" (Davis, Diekmann, and Tinsley 1994, 563). The arena in which agency logic had its greatest triumph, however, was the takeover wave itself.

The takeover wave of the 1980s had its roots in the stock market decline of 1973–1974 and the general economic malaise of the 1970s. The price of stocks remained relatively low in the early 1980s, and the economy continued to struggle even with the Reagan administration's attempts to reduce government regulation. One reason that stocks remained undervalued, some observers believed, was the prevalence of conglomerates—firms that were highly diversified, often in industries that had virtually no relation to one another. Conglomerates had emerged in the 1950s in part as a reaction to the Celler-Kefauver Act of 1950, which placed significant limits on vertical mergers (Fligstein 1990). With restrictions on their ability to acquire suppliers or distributors—units that operated in the same general industry—firms responded by acquiring firms in unrelated areas. Conveniently, managers could also justify diversification as a means of protecting the firm from market fluctuations that might exert disproportionate harm on particular units. The problem was that conglomerates did not perform particularly well, and their stock price lagged in addition. One fascinating explanation for the undervaluing of diversified firms was provided by Ezra Zuckerman (1999), who argued that securities analysts tended to refrain from rating firms that they found difficult to classify. Yet the firms' lack of value might have also resulted from a simple lack of competence. Beatrice Foods, known as the producer of Dannon Yogurt and La Choy Foods, by 1980 was also involved with plumbing equipment, stereo components, luggage, and car rentals. The median Fortune 500 firm by 1980 operated in three separate industry categories, and these firms were typically undervalued on the stock market (Davis 2009, 84). Given their relatively weak performance, it was perhaps inevitable that these companies would be vulnerable.

This vulnerability became manifest with the onset of the Reagan administration, which filled units such as the Justice Department's Antitrust Division and the Securities and Exchange Commission with staffers who were sympathetic with the Manne-Jensen-Meckling view about the efficiency gains available through takeovers. In 1982, the Antitrust Division issued a new set of guidelines that significantly reduced the restrictions against horizontal and vertical mergers. Similarly, the Federal Trade Commission reduced both its size and its willingness to intervene in antitrust cases (Stearns and Allan 1996, 705). Also important during this period was a 1982 Supreme Court decision *(Edgar v. MITE)* that an Illinois law regulating tender offers was unconstitutional. This decision was used to invalidate similar laws in other states, all of which further improved the environment for acquisitions (Davis 2009, 84). The combination of bloated, poorly performing conglomerates and a legal environment no longer hostile to economic concentration set the stage for the takeover wave that was about to occur. All that was necessary at this point was for the capital necessary to fuel the boom to become available.

As Stearns and Allan note (1996, 703–705), this capital emerged from three sources: the increasing flow of foreign capital into the United States, the deregulation of savings and loan institutions, and the rise of mutual funds. As we saw earlier in the chapter, these forces contributed to the decline in the role of the leading commercial banks. One consequence of this decline was that large sums of capital became available to a wider group of actors. Among those who took advantage of this situation was a group of relatively peripheral actors known as corporate raiders, who brought the concept of a hostile takeover to new heights. Stearns and Allan found that these raiders—who included people such as T. Boone Pickens, Carl Icahn, and Saul Steinberg (of the 1968 Chemical Bank case fame)—shared an interesting set of characteristics. All of them had come from relatively privileged economic origins, but none was a hereditary member of the "WASP" upper class. They tended to be the sons or grandsons of immigrants, and they were often either of Eastern European Jewish extraction, Southern, or both. And although several of them had graduated from elite universities, none had worked for a Fortune 500 firm (Stearns and Allan 1996, 706).[22]

Several things occurred during the takeover wave, which lasted through most of the 1980s but peaked from 1984 through 1989. First, given the degree of diversification among companies and the downward effect that this appeared to have on stock prices, raiders discovered that they could buy up conglomerate firms, divide them into parts, and sell off the parts for more than the prior value of the entire firm. In other words, the sum of the parts was greater than the whole (Davis, Diekmann, and Tinsley 1994,

548). Between 1980 and 1990, 28 percent of Fortune 500 companies received tender offers from outsiders—more than two-thirds of which were hostile—and by the end of the decade, one-third of the Fortune 500 from 1980 had disappeared as independent entities (Davis 2009, 85).[23] The two strongest predictors of the likelihood of receiving both a bid in general and a successful bid were the firm's degree of diversification (the more diversified, the greater the likelihood of a bid) and its market-to-book ratio (the lower the ratio, the greater the likelihood of a bid) (Davis et al. 1994, 557). The level of unrelated diversification among these firms declined by more than 40 percent over the decade, and the number of firms that operated in four or more different broad (two-digit) industries declined by more than 50 percent (ibid., 562).

Second, a relatively new form of acquisition, the leveraged buyout (LBO), gained prominence. An LBO occurs when a firm's management, often in conjunction with an investment banker, purchases the firm's stock using enormous levels of debt, typically raised by leveraging the firm's assets (Burrough and Helyar 2005, 5). Because the firm's management now owns the stock, the firm has in effect been "taken private." Given the high levels of debt involved in LBOs, the firm often meets its obligations either by selling off pieces of the company (in a manner similar to the deconglomeration process described by Davis) or by making massive cuts to company operations. In some cases, management subsequently issues the firm's stock to the public, at a price considerably higher than the group originally paid, yielding an enormous return for its owners.

The LBO was first used in 1965 by the head of the corporate finance department at Bear Stearns (a second-tier Wall Street investment bank), Jerome Kohlberg. As with many innovations, the LBO was initially viewed with suspicion. When Kohlberg and his associates, Henry Kravis and George Roberts, were repeatedly unable to gain the support of Bear Stearns's CEO Salim (Cy) Lewis, they eventually left in 1976 to form their own firm, Kohlberg, Kravis, and Roberts, which became known as KKR (Burrough and Helyar 2005, 133–138). The LBO, of which KKR became the largest and best-known proponent, started slowly in the late 1970s, amounting to $11 billion of activity between 1977 and 1983. During the peak years of the takeover wave (1984 through 1989), however, LBO activity amounted to $233 billion (Stearns and Allan 1996, 706–707). The proportion of the total dollar value of acquisitions involving LBOs increased from

4.1 percent in 1981 to 20.7 percent in 1985, and to 39 percent in 1988 before dropping sharply in 1989 and 1990, as the takeover wave came to an end (Useem 1993, 256).[24]

Much of the LBO activity as well as the takeovers in general were funded by another innovation: a form of low-grade debt that became known as "junk bonds."[25] Junk bonds are a form of debt that is rated below "investment grade," meaning that the rating agencies have significant doubt as to whether it will be repaid. Because of the high level of risk involved, low-grade bonds typically pay a high rate of interest; hence they are often referred to as high-yield bonds. Like LBOs, low-grade debt had been in existence well before the 1980s. In most cases, however, high-yield bonds consisted almost exclusively of bonds that were initially rated as investment grade but whose ratings had been subsequently lowered. The first bonds that were rated below investment grade from their origin were issued in 1977, interestingly, by a high-status investment bank, Lehman Brothers. Lehman pulled back, however, apparently due to concern over what the association with such a product would do to its reputation, and a second-tier bank, Drexel Burnham Lambert, became the leading issuer of junk bonds. The force behind Drexel Burnham's ascent was one of the best-known (and most notorious) figures from the 1980s, Michael Milken. Milken was so successful in establishing the market for junk bonds that Drexel Burnham increased its revenue from $150 million in 1977 to $2.5 billion in 1985. Given the staggering amounts of money involved, even the high-status investment banks, which had initially resisted them, began to participate in both LBOs and the issuing of junk bonds (Stearns and Allan 1996, 709–711).[26]

The 1980s takeover wave eventually came to an end. The excessive use of junk bonds, along with a range of illegal activities that accompanied it, led to the downfall of many of the leading figures of the period, including Milken. But this wave, unlike the much smaller movement of the 1960s, significantly altered the environment in which corporate CEOs operated. Although some sitting managers were themselves involved in the acquisition wave, many more were targets of it, and many of these ended up as casualties. Michael Useem has termed this wave the "revolt of the owners." Passive, far removed from management for most of the postwar period, and—as the 1970s wore on—increasingly unsuccessful in realizing returns on their investment, the forces of ownership began to direct their ire toward management. These forces were not the firms' original family owners, however, but rather the corporate raiders, as well as the growing (and increasingly active) cadre of institutional investors (Useem 1993, 21–22).[27] The CEOs of the largest companies were no longer able to run their firms, insulated from their owners (or from the capital market in general), confident in the knowledge that they were secure in their positions. In the 1980s, no one was safe. From the turn of the twentieth century, the identity of the leading American corporations had remained remarkably stable (see Chandler 1977, 503–513). In the 1980s, as we have seen, nearly one-third of the Fortune 500 disappeared, in most cases through hostile takeovers. Even in cases in which management was able to hang on, it did so only under significantly different conditions. Lockheed, for example, was able to stave off several takeover bids by Harold Simmons in the late 1980s. By the time the dust had settled, however, the company had laid off 10 percent of its workforce, added four outside directors, and shifted its orientation in a much more shareholder-friendly direction. Polaroid, in its successful resistance of a takeover threat, engaged in similar changes (Useem 1993, 27, 54).

Management did not accept this turn of events without a fight. In the early 1980s, many large firms proposed what became known as "shark repellents," amendments to corporate charters that raised barriers to takeovers (Davis 1991, 586; Useem 1993, 48–51). Among the devices used in these efforts were the staggering of board elections (so that only a subset of directors stood for election in a given year); the "supermajority" provision, which raised the proportion of shareholder votes necessary to approve a merger; and anti-"greenmail" proposals, which prevented significant blocks of stock from being sold at an above-market price. Perhaps the most widespread antitakeover device was what became known as a "poison pill." The most common such pill allowed existing shareholders to purchase additional shares in the firm at a significantly below-market rate should a takeover attempt occur without the approval of the board. These devices also often included a provision in which the firm's current shareholders continued to have a right to purchase discounted shares even after a takeover occurred, thus placing the burden of this sale on those making the acquisition. Although the pills were rarely activated, they did pose a threat to potential raiders. The first such pill among Fortune 500 companies was adopted by Crown Zellerbach in 1984. By the end of 1989, more than 60 percent of the Fortune 500 had adopted a poison pill (Davis 1991, 586–587; Useem 1993, 49–51).

It was one thing for corporate managers to institute firm-level policies designed to ward off takeovers. More interesting, perhaps, was the way in which corporations suddenly turned to the government for protection. As Useem put it (1993, 170), "Long opposed to state intervention in the marketplace, large companies faced with a loss of control were not to be inhibited by this concern. The antiregulatory principle seemed to pale by comparison with the higher principles of sheer survival." A prominent attorney, Michael Lipton, speaking in reference to the institutional investors whose support was behind many of the takeovers, argued that these investors "show no restraint and no regard for the public good. They must be policed" (quoted in ibid.). Not surprisingly, the raiders themselves objected to these pleas, sometimes with barely concealed ridicule. T. Boone Pickens, one of the most renowned raiders, stated in a 1987 speech that "most Business Roundtable CEOs . . . barricade themselves from stockholders" and "take the stockholders' money and use it to lobby against the stockholders' interests" (quoted in ibid.). The attempts for relief at the federal level, pushed for by the Business Roundtable, proved ineffective (Khurana 2002, 55). Reagan administration officials, with their antiregulatory mentality as well as their adherence to the Manne-Jensen-Meckling view of corporate takeovers, were unsympathetic to managers seeking protection, viewing such requests as counter to the dictates of the free market. The Roundtable, meanwhile, had lost much of its clout by the late 1980s, in part as a result of the divisions caused by the 1986 tax reform (*Wall Street Journal* [hereafter *WSJ*], March 25, 1987).

Management groups were more successful in gaining protection at the state level. Although only five states had passed antitakeover legislation as of 1987, by 1991 forty-one states had passed such laws (Useem 1993, 171). The passage of these laws coincided with the end of the takeover wave (Khurana 2002, 55–56), although it is difficult to know how much of an effect it had. The firms' own antitakeover policies probably had an effect, as did the exhaustion of the junk bond market.[28] Even with the wave of takeovers at an end, however, the environment that corporate chief executives faced bore little resemblance to that experienced by their predecessors.

The New Chief Executive Officer

The takeover wave of the 1980s left the CEOs of large American corporations in a paradoxical position. CEO compensation had begun to increase earlier in the decade, and by 1990 it was rising sharply. Yet corporate leaders were operating in a far more constrained environment, with considerably less autonomy and far more pressure. The CEOs no longer faced the powerful resistance of organized labor. The state, although still viewed as a nuisance, was far more compliant than its counterpart in the postwar period had been. The CEO faced a new kind of pressure, however: from the investment community, more formally known as the capital market. These pressures had always been present, of course, but they were of far greater magnitude by the late 1980s than anything CEOs had experienced from the 1940s through the 1970s.

One of the most important forces behind the increasing power of the capital market was the rise of institutional stockholders. As recently as the 1960s, the vast majority of corporate stock in the United States was held by individuals. Over the ensuing decades, however, increasing amounts of stock began to be purchased by institutional investors, including bank trust departments, insurance companies, mutual funds, and pension funds. In 1965, only 16 percent of the stock of American publicly traded companies was held by these institutions. The remainder was held by individuals. By 1990, the proportion held by institutions had grown to 46 percent. Among the 1,000 largest publicly traded companies, 50 percent of the stock was held by institutions in 1990, and 57 percent by 1994 (Useem 1996, 25).

The managerial era had been characterized by a large number of individuals who owned small amounts of stock and played virtually no role in managing the company. There were exceptions even during this period, of course. Firms such as Ford and DuPont, for example, continued to be owned and controlled by their founding families. Yet despite some skepticism (Zeitlin 1974), it is now widely agreed that most American firms were controlled primarily by their leading officers (Cheffins and Bank 2009).[29] As institutional investors gained a larger share of the pie, however, they gradually became more active, both in takeovers and by intervening in the affairs of the firm. One reason that institutional stockholders may become active is the sheer size of their investments. Historically, the most common way for stockholders to express their dissatisfaction with management was to sell their shares, the so-called Wall Street Rule (Herman and Safanda 1973, 102–103). As the size of one's stockholding increases beyond a certain point, however, it becomes difficult to sell without incurring a significant loss. Under such circumstances, it occasionally is more prudent to exercise "voice" rather than "exit" (Hirschman 1970).[30]

Useem (1996) provides numerous examples of institutional stockholders exercising influence on internal company decisions, including the 1992 ouster of Robert Stempel as CEO of General Motors, an act that the business press found shocking (*WSJ*, October 23, 1992, A1, A4). Not all institutional investors are likely to intervene, and, as we saw in Chapter 5, most have historically tended to vote with management (Herman and Safanda 1973; Davis and Kim 2007). The threat of stockholder intervention has grown, however, and it is now far more necessary for managers to take their owners into account when making decisions than it had been in earlier decades. This is reflected in the rise of investor relations departments and the increasing amounts of time that top executives spend dealing with their owners (Useem 1993, 131–136).

Another indicator of the increasing volatility of the environment that CEOs confronted during the 1980s is the decline in CEO tenure. Among sitting chief executives of Fortune 500 firms, the mean number of years in office stood at approximately 9.4 years in 1980, increased to nearly 9.7 years in 1982, and then began a steady decline through the remainder of the decade. This decline, which is displayed graphically in Figure 7.2, continued through 2002—at which point the mean stood at 6.8 years, or nearly 30 percent below its 1982 peak—before rising slightly in 2004.[31] The fact that CEO turnover continued to increase even after the end of the 1980s takeover wave is an indication that the greater volatility that CEOs faced had become a permanent feature of the corporate environment.

Perhaps as a consequence of this newly experienced turbulence, the prototype of the chief executive began to change as well. In the postwar period, the heads of giant corporations, including those involved in the CED and in the formation of the Business Roundtable, were largely unknown to the general public. They were also overwhelmingly white, male, and Protestant (Baltzell 1964), and they were disproportionately from elite backgrounds. There is evidence that the heads of the largest American corporations have become more diverse over time, in terms of race and gender as well as socioeconomic background (Zweigenhaft and Domhoff 2006), although most of the change in socioeconomic origins involves an increase in those from professional and managerial backgrounds as opposed to the traditional upper class. One correlate to the increased diversity of the elite, although not necessarily a consequence of it, is that the cohesiveness of the elite—at least as measured by the network of director interlocks among firms—declined during the 1980s. The network that Davis and I studied revealed a decline in mean bank interlocks from 16.4 in 1982 to 10.3 in 1994, and a decline in mean industrial firm interlocks from 8.4 to 7.2 during the same period (Davis and Mizruchi 1999, 228). Barnes and Ritter (2001, 204), in a study of 250 Fortune 800 firms, found that the density of the network declined by more than 20 percent between 1983 and 1995. The density of the American interlock network continued to decline beyond that point as well. Between 2000 and 2010, the frequency of interlocking among the Standard & Poor's 1500 firms declined by more than 30 percent, from an average of 7.14 ties in 2000 to an average of 4.98 in 2010. The mean number of steps between any pair of firms in the network increased from 3.21 in 1997 to 4.23 in 2010 (Chu and Davis 2011).

More than simply the decline in cohesiveness, however, was a change in the nature of the corporate leaders themselves. The image of the postwar corporate executive was that of an almost "faceless" bureaucrat, yet one who exhibited a calm, statesmanlike demeanor, presiding over an organiza-

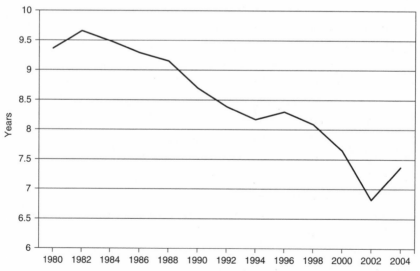

Figure 7.2. Mean CEO tenure by year, 1980–2004 (in two-year intervals).

tion that understood its responsibility to the larger community. The new corporate leader who emerged in the 1980s was a brash, swashbuckling celebrity, far more colorful than his predecessors, yet often viewed as lacking responsibility to anyone but himself, and perhaps his shareholders. A prototypical example of this generational change can be seen by comparing Reginald H. Jones, the CEO of General Electric (GE) during the 1970s, with his successor, John F. (Jack) Welch Jr.

Jones, according to Thomas J. Leuck of the *New York Times* was "a polished, disciplined, and eminently formal man who rose through G.E.'s accounting and finance departments" (*NYT,* May 5, 1985, F8). According to a leading figure in the corporate world who was familiar with both men and spoke with me about them, Mr. Jones was "almost patrician," as if he were "born with a tie on."[32] Jones was also heavily involved in forging relations between business and government. He was a founding member of the Business Roundtable (and cochair of the organization from 1974 to 1980), led the Business Council, and, according to the *Times,* "became a familiar figure in Washington, and was called on repeatedly by the Carter Administration for his advice on economic policy" (*NYT,* May 5, 1985, F8). As my source described it, Jones was "very engrossed in the politics of the day," and "one of the last great business statesmen."

Welch, who took over GE in 1981 after being selected for the position by Jones (Vancil 1987), was the polar opposite of Jones in many ways. The grandson of Irish immigrants and the son of working-class parents who did not complete high school, Welch earned a doctorate in chemical engineering from the University of Illinois and went to work at GE in 1960.[33] Welch's management style was marked by a strong distaste for what he saw as the "formal and massive bureaucracy" that had characterized the company prior to his appointment (Welch 2001, 92). He saw himself as having been someone who was "180 degrees from what was then the 'model GE executive'" (ibid., 87), conceding that he was "too young and too brash," with "little respect for the company's rituals and traditions" (ibid., 77). Although Jones had more than doubled the firm's revenues and nearly tripled its earnings during his nine-year tenure, GE was "not in good shape when Jack took over," according to my informant. As the *Times* noted, "While Mr. Welch and most veteran G.E. watchers praise Mr. Jones's management concepts as right for the 1960s and 1970s, Mr. Welch is rebuilding the company in a manner more attuned to . . . the hotly competitive environment of the 1980s" (*NYT,* May 5, 1985, F1). Welch's changes included

reducing the firm's planning department from thirty to eight people, elimi-
nating several layers of management, and shedding multiple businesses.
Perhaps most notable (or notorious), however, was his policy of laying off the
lowest 10 percent of performers each year, a policy that led *Newsweek* to dub
him "Neutron Jack," for removing people while leaving the buildings standing (Welch 2001, 125, 158). In his first five years, Welch removed 118,000
employees (25 percent of the firm's workforce), either through firing or selling subsidiaries (ibid., 121). "Any organization that thinks it can guarantee
job security is going down a dead end," Welch stated. "Only satisfied customers can give people job security, not companies" (ibid., 128).

In fairness to Welch, he did praise the idea of corporate social responsibility, serving as a corporate chairman for the United Way in his early years
with GE (Welch 2001, 126). Moreover, he was not only willing to praise
the firm's unions, but in one case he even refrained from moving a plant to
Mexico out of regard for the union's efforts to make the firm more competitive (ibid., 179). What most endeared Welch to the business and investment community, however, was the trajectory of GE's stock price during
his reign. GE was valued at $13 billion when Welch took office in 1981. By
the time he stepped down in 2001, the company was valued at "several
hundred billion," according to the company's website. This spectacular rise
in the firm's equity made Welch a hero, a celebrity symbolic of the new
preoccupation with shareholder value.

Welch's lack of political involvement also distinguished him from
Jones. Welch was (and has been) involved in philanthropy, but there is no
evidence of him playing a leadership role in the Business Roundtable, although he did serve a two-year term as chairman of the Business Council, from 1991 through 1992. Welch's relative lack of engagement in
business-wide political activity appears to have also been more typical of
the newer breed of corporate leaders. According to the business leader I
interviewed:

> Leaders in American business in the 1970s and before viewed themselves as
> a part of the political process in a way that later ones were not. Each succes-
> sive generation has become less interested in being part of the process than
> they were in the 1970s. . . . They don't know each other as well. They don't
> socialize the way they used to . . . [and] tenure is shorter. (phone interview,
> July 28, 2010)

Managerial Autonomy and Corporate Philanthropy

The increased external pressure on CEOs to maximize shareholder value may have even affected a venerable area of business activity: philanthropic contributions. Long an object of managerial discretion, corporate philanthropy has been used as a form of public relations similar to advertising, an attempt to invest strategically in areas that will benefit the firm (such as schools), a response to social pressures within the business community, and even a reflection of the company's values. To the extent that the rise of the shareholder value orientation led to a reduction of managerial autonomy, was it possible that it led to a reduction in philanthropic contributions as well? On one hand, the raw value of corporate philanthropic contributions continued to increase from the early 1980s into the twenty-first century. On the other hand, there is evidence that philanthropic contributions as a proportion of revenue actually declined over time.

Christopher Marquis and Matthew Lee, both of the Harvard Business School, have assembled a comprehensive data set that includes between 1,017 and 1,600 firms in two-year intervals from 1980 through 2004 (Marquis and Lee 2012). Using these data (which I describe in more detail in the appendix to this chapter), I examined, quantitatively, the extent to which managerial autonomy affected the firms' philanthropic contributions as a proportion of firm revenue. Because I have argued that CEOs began to experience increased scrutiny and pressure from the investment community over time, I considered two indicators of managerial autonomy: the year, with the expectation that the level of philanthropy would decline over time; and the average aggregate CEO tenure among Fortune 500 firms in a given year, with the expectation that as CEO tenure declines (meaning that individual executives face a more turbulent environment), philanthropic contributions would decline as well. The year and average CEO tenure are almost perfectly negatively correlated, at $-.955$, meaning that average CEO tenure declined over time. Because it is not feasible to examine both indicators simultaneously due to their high correlation with one another, I used each variable as a predictor in separate models.

Table 7.1 provides a truncated version of two random effects generalized least squares regression equations, with philanthropic contributions as a proportion of total revenue as the dependent variable, and year and average CEO tenure respectively as independent variables. The equations from which the table is drawn also include control variables for firm size, income, profitability, age, advertising expenditures, and industry. The coefficients for these variables are not shown here, but they are presented in the appendix, along with further details and explanation about the nature of the analysis.

As is evident from the two equations, both year and CEO tenure have the predicted effects on philanthropic contributions, even when we control for several other possible explanations. The coefficient for year in equation 1 is negative, as predicted, indicating that contributions were relatively high in the earlier years and became increasingly lower as the years progressed. The coefficient for CEO tenure in equation 2 is positive, also as predicted, indicating that contributions were relatively high when average CEO tenure was high, and relatively low when average CEO tenure was low (as it was in the later years). Both coefficients were strongly statistically significant.[34]

These findings have implications beyond academic debates about the sources of corporate philanthropy. The American corporate elite has increasingly rejected a significant role for government as a solution to societal problems—a development that, as we have seen, began in the 1970s and has continued unabated since then. In response to this, the resulting breach in the delivery of social services was supposed to be filled by private contributions. To the extent that the private sector is reducing its responsibility in this area, at least relatively, it is unclear from where these services will emanate. Corporate philanthropy is about more than delivering services to the

Table 7.1   Random Effects Models Predicting Standardized Philanthropic Contributions (Hypothesized Variables Only)

	(1)	(2)
Constant	61.255	−2.215
	(5.35)	(−4.09)
Year	−0.031***	
	(−5.43)	
Mean CEO tenure		0.128**
		(3.05)
Wald χ^2	618.37***	596.51***

$N = 8,293$ in both equations. **$p = 0.001$ ***$p < 0.001$.
All probabilities are one-tailed.
Z statistics are in parentheses. See chapter appendix for details.

poor, of course. It includes support for the arts, as well as museums, zoos, and other institutions that benefit the general public. As government support for these institutions declines and private support shrinks as well, the future provision of these public goods may be increasingly in peril.

Conclusion

By the beginning of the 1980s, the American corporate elite had become more politically conservative and had become increasingly aggressive in opposing government regulation, taxes, and labor unions. As the Reagan administration pursued its probusiness policies, the forces of ameliorative government and organized labor—two of the key elements of the postwar moderate consensus—receded into the woodwork, no longer representing a significant constraint on large firms. The waning of these forces had the paradoxical effect of reducing the level of elite political unity. The decline in the importance of commercial banks and their shift toward fee-for-service activities led them to the abdication of their role as arbiters of inter-firm conflict. And finally, the takeover wave that crested later in the decade created a major threat to the autonomy that corporate managers had enjoyed in the postwar period. The result was a new era, in which the moderate, pragmatic, and well-organized elite that had been present at the top of the corporate world since at least the 1940s began to disappear. The CED became a shadow of its former self, almost invisible in the nation's political life. The Business Roundtable, hurt by the conflicts over the 1986 tax reform, experienced its own retreat into the background. The American corporate elite, a group that had played such a significant role in providing solutions to national problems in the postwar period, was breaking apart at the seams, entering a period in which its increasing irrelevance would render it incapable of providing solutions to a growing array of problems faced by its members. By the early 1990s, we were witnessing the decline of the American corporate elite. This decline would have serious consequences not only for the larger society but for the business community itself.

Appendix

In this appendix I provide further details on the analyses of corporate philanthropic contributions. Corporations typically make their philanthropic contributions through their foundations, which are legally distinct from the firm but operate as an arm of it. Marquis and Lee (2012) assembled a comprehensive panel data set on philanthropic foundations covering twenty-one individual years dating back to 1954 and including every other year beginning in 1980. The data include between 795 and 870 firms for seven different years between 1954 and 1976, and between 1,017 and 1,600 firms in the years from 1980 through 2006. Because several of the variables in the dataset are available only from more recent years, and because my concern here is primarily with the changes that have occurred since 1980, I use only the data from 1980 in this analysis. Data from 2006 were incomplete, so I ended the analysis in 2004.[35]

Marquis and Lee collected their data on corporate philanthropy from the *National Directory of Corporate Giving*. We measured the firm's total philanthropic contributions by summing the firm's total dollar amount of grants through its foundation and from the firm directly. Because a firm's level of corporate giving is meaningful only as a function of its size, we standardized this variable by the firm's sales. Because the resulting measure was still highly skewed, we transformed the value to logarithms, after adding 1 to each value to ensure that cases in which no contributions were made would not be omitted from the analysis.

Our primary independent variable, as described in the chapter text, is the degree to which a firm's top management experiences autonomy from the firm's external environment. As noted in the text, we accounted for this environmental pressure in two ways: using the year, with the prediction that contributions would be expected to decline over time, and using the mean aggregate tenure of Fortune 500 CEOs, with the prediction that contributions would be expected to decline as CEO tenure declined. Because the correlation between year and mean CEO tenure was −.955, we examined each measure separately.[36]

We also considered a number of control variables. The first, which we have used as a substantive predictor in another study, is a firm's expenditures on advertising. We used this variable as a proxy for the firm's orientation toward the general public. There is evidence from other studies that firms that deal directly with the public have a greater incentive to engage in philanthropic contributions than do firms that sell directly to other producers (Burt 1983).

Although we scaled our dependent variable to take firm size into account, a firm's size could independently affect the proportion of its revenue that it disburses for philanthropic contributions. Other things being equal, large firms will have greater amounts of slack than smaller firms. This means that large firms will have more opportunity to engage in discretionary spending. We included three variables to control for firm size: sales, assets, and income, the last of which is also in part a measure of performance. Although these variables are correlated with one another in the .4 to .5 range (the correlation between size and assets, the largest of the three, is .52), the correlations are low enough to suggest that we should consider all three. We took the logarithms of sales and assets to account for their high levels of right-skewness.

In addition to size, corporate philanthropy may also depend on firm performance. Presumably, firms that perform well will have more disposable cash with which to make contributions than will firms that have performed poorly. We used return on assets as our measure of performance, measured here as income divided by assets. This is the most commonly used indicator of performance in the organizational literature.

Although we included a control for a firm's advertising expenditures, which is in part driven by the industries in which it operates, we also included dummy variables for the broad sectors within which the firms were situated. The Census Bureau's Standard Industrial Classification Index uses a total of ten major industry groups, each of which contains a range of industries classified at the two-digit level, which are further subdivided into more detailed categories. We chose as dummy variables four broad sectors: manufacturing, retail, service, and financial. These four sectors accounted for more than 78 percent of our observations. The remaining observations, which range across the remaining sectors, served as the reference category.

Finally, Marquis and Lee (2012) suggested that to the extent that corporate philanthropy is affected by firms' embeddedness in interfirm networks, older firms would be more likely to make high levels of contributions than would younger firms, a conjecture that was supported in their findings. For this reason, we controlled for a firm's age, which is its number of years since founding.

The data are in pooled cross-sectional time-series format with an unbalanced design. Some firms that appeared in the first year of data, 1954, exited the data set before the final year, 2006. Other firms entered the data set at various points. The standard way to handle data of this type, given a quantitative dependent variable with a relatively symmetric distribution, is with either a fixed or random effects generalized least squares estimator.

Following Marquis and Lee, we used a random effects model because some of our variables, most notably the industry dummies, are time-invariant within firms. Unlike Marquis and Lee, we did not include year fixed effects, because two of the key variables, year and firm age, do not vary within years. The variable firm age was removed by Stata in all equations that include year fixed effects. We did run our model using a fixed effects design. This model yielded conclusions consistent with those presented in the primary equations.

The full set of coefficients and z-statistics (in parentheses) for the variables in the model from which equation 1 of Table 7.1 was drawn are as follows, where in both equations * designates $p < .10$, + is $p = .001$, and ** is $p < .001$: constant, 61.255** (5.35); log of sales, $-.282$** (-4.29); log of assets, .652** (11.72); income, 6.55×10^{-6} (0.43); return on assets, .261 (1.22); firm age, .044** (11.73); year, $-.031$** (-5.43); retail, $-.104$ (-0.56); service, $-.154$ (-0.84); manufacturing, .714** (5.71); and advertising as a proportion of sales, .031* (1.67).

The full set of coefficients and z-statistics (in parentheses) for the variables in the model from which equation 2 of Table 7.1 was drawn are as follows: constant, -2.216** (-4.09); log of sales, $-.311$** (-4.73); log of assets, .635** (11.40); income, 3.62×10^{-6} (0.24); return on assets, .281 (1.31); firm age, .041** (10.97); mean aggregate CEO tenure, .128+ (3.05); retail, $-.129$ (-0.70); service, $-.207$ (-0.70); manufacturing, .733** (5.86); and advertising as a proportion of sales, .035* (1.89).

Finally, in an equation not reported here, we controlled for each foundation's (as opposed to firm's) log of total assets to account for the fact that all foundations are legally required to spend a certain proportion of their endowments. Inclusion of this variable had little impact on the size, and no impact on the statistical significance, of our two primary predictors.

8 ||| The Aftermath

So what were the consequences of the decline of the American corporate elite for the group's ability to act collectively? To address this question, it is useful to return to Robert Dahl's classic 1958 article on the sources of group power. Dahl, as we saw in Chapter 1, argued that for a group to be powerful, two things are necessary: a high level of resources and a high level of unity. If this formulation is correct, then if large corporations, with their impressive resources, are able to achieve a high degree of political unity, they pose a considerable threat to American democracy. I have suggested that precisely the opposite occurred, however: American democracy actually thrived during a period in which the corporate elite—those at the very top—experienced a broad level of unity. It is perhaps equally ironic, therefore, that as this unity frayed in the 1980s and then disappeared in the 1990s, American democracy found itself imperiled. The fragmentation of the corporate elite created a vacuum of leadership that led to political stagnation, a system "stuck in neutral," to use Cathie Jo Martin's fitting phrase (2000). The triumph of big business over the constraints of government and organized labor had removed the need for a united front. The decline of the banks had weakened a key source of consensus formation. The takeover wave had decimated corporate management, leaving in its wake a collection of highly paid, high-profile figures who, under a level of external pressure virtually unknown a generation earlier, exhibited an increasingly "slash and burn" mentality. The result of these developments was an elite that had become a fragmented, ineffectual group incapable of acting collectively to address not only the concerns of the larger society—as its predecessors had done—but even the concerns of its own members. The corporate elite had won the war, but it no longer had the ability to do battle.

This decline was evident at the level of the individual firm as well as the collectivity. On an individual level, the newly precarious position of management led to a series of changes in firm behavior. Some of these innovations—if they can be called that—were the result of a simple increase in the level of market competition, much of it global. But some of the changes also reflected the changing culture of corporate life and the changing expectations that accompanied it. The emphasis on shareholder value at the expense of every alternative meant that firms began to withdraw from their commitment to the larger community. The Business Roundtable, in its 1981 statement on corporate social responsibility, took note of the expectations of the time, stating that "more than ever, managers of corporations are expected to serve the public interest as well as private profit." Ten years later, in contrast, concern with corporate social responsibility was no longer even mentioned as a task for the board of directors (Whitman 1999, 96). Layoffs became an epidemic, even for firms that were otherwise successful (McKinley, Sanchez, and Schick 1995; Budros 2002), and despite unclear evidence that they improved a firm's performance or stock price (Datta et al. 2010, 321, 335). The focus on shareholder value had consequences for corporate philanthropic contributions as well. As we saw in the previous chapter, corporate philanthropic contributions as a proportion of firms' revenue declined over time, as CEO tenure became more precarious.

At the collective level, meanwhile, the corporate elite proved incapable of addressing the kinds of issues that it had routinely tackled in the postwar period. One of these failures was the group's unwillingness, or inability, to address the enormous post-2001 deficit by doing what the corporate elite had typically done in similar previous situations: call for a tax increase. Another example of ineptitude was the striking inability of the corporate elite to come up with a coherent plan for health care reform—in both the Clinton and Obama administrations—despite the increased urgency for some kind of action to avoid a potential economic catastrophe. A third issue was the elite's unwillingness to accept—or inability to develop a plan for—reform of the financial system, despite the fact that the 2008 financial crisis and the continued inability to address it has threatened to destroy the entire system. In each of these cases, the inability of the corporate elite to organize for effective action, even when individual firms support such action, has led to a stalemate that has placed the entire American polity—not to mention the larger global economy—in an increasingly precarious position.

In this chapter I discuss the consequences of the developments of the 1980s on the subsequent behavior of the American corporate elite. I examine—using tax policy and health care—the ways in which the elite that once gave us the Marshall Plan and a tenfold increase in federal spending for scientific research was, by the 1990s, no longer able to address the most salient economic, political, and social issues of our age.

The Retreat from Taxation

The American corporate elite, along with small business, political leaders, and significant segments of the general public, have long supported the idea of a balanced federal budget. The need to avoid deficit spending was relaxed during World War II, of course, and the idea that deficit spending could stimulate the economy finally triumphed at the federal level with President Kennedy's 1963 tax cut (Stein 1969). For most of the postwar period, however, there was overwhelming support for, if not a fully balanced budget, then at least a relatively small deficit. When deficits became large—during the late 1960s and especially the early 1980s—business leaders, among others, sounded an alarm, and major efforts were undertaken to reduce them.

One way to reduce a deficit is to curtail spending, and business groups, including the Committee for Economic Development (CED) and the Business Roundtable as well as the Chamber of Commerce and the National Association of Manufacturers (NAM), were perfectly willing to suggest cuts in spending, especially to non-defense-related programs, in order to achieve this goal. On the other hand, the general consensus among the corporate elite, repeatedly demonstrated over several decades, was that spending cuts alone were not sufficient to balance the budget. Tax increases were necessary to address at least part of the problem.

There were numerous occasions in the postwar period in which the corporate elite proposed tax increases to balance the budget. In the fall of

1950, in order to pay for the Korean War (which the United States had recently entered), President Truman proposed a tax on the excess profits that corporations were receiving as a result of the increased defense spending. In congressional testimony, Treasury Secretary John W. Snyder proposed a 75 percent tax rate on these profits, which would be computed in a manner similar to what had been done during World War II (*New York Times* [hereafter *NYT*], November 16, 1950, 1). Perhaps not surprisingly, the CED and the Chamber both spoke against this tax in hearings the following week (*Wall Street Journal* [hereafter *WSJ*], November 22, 1950, 4). J. Cameron Thomson, president of Northwest Bancorporation and chairman of the CED's monetary and fiscal policy committee, argued that this kind of tax would "weaken the drive for more productivity" and "penalize the enterprising firm." Yet both groups, as well as the NAM, acknowledged the need for a tax increase. The Chamber proposed $6 billion worth of cuts in nondefense spending, but it was willing to support along with this a 50 percent corporate income tax—which would raise $2 billion—as well as a tax on all manufacturers and a series of excise taxes that would raise an additional $5 billion. The CED suggested a tax on all corporations, which would raise about $6 billion per year—$3 billion of which would come from a defense profits tax set at an equal rate for all corporations—plus a temporary increase in personal income taxes. The president and the business groups continued to argue over the size of the proposed tax increase. In March 1951, President Truman proposed a $16.5 billion tax increase, while the CED proposed a tax increase of $10 billion plus $6 billion in spending cuts (*NYT*, March 30, 1951, 1). By July, the CED was suggesting a 5 percent tax hike on disposable personal income as well as a retail excise tax and a dividend tax (*WSJ*, July 11, 1951, 3). What was not at issue was that some kind of tax increase was necessary. The Senate ended up passing a bill that closely approximated the CED's proposal (*NYT*, August 22, 1951, 1).

The CED was not protax by any means. The group frequently called for tax cuts during this period, including a 1955 proposal for a personal tax cut, especially on high earners (*NYT*, May 8, 1955, 74). Yet even when the CED recommended tax cuts, the group often suggested that the cuts be balanced with reductions in military spending. As the temporary taxes on excess profits, individual income, and corporate income reached their expiration date in 1953, the CED did recommend $6.6 billion in spending cuts, but most of these proposed cuts came from defense (*NYT*, April 8,

1953, 23). Two months later, Marion Folsom, the former Eastman Kodak treasurer and early CED official who had become treasury undersecretary under President Eisenhower, noted that with spending remaining high, taxes could not be cut, even with a truce in the Korean War (*WSJ*, June 6, 1953, 2). When President Eisenhower sought a six-month extension of the excess profits tax, the CED reluctantly supported the idea, despite opposition from the NAM and the Chamber of Commerce (*NYT*, June 6, 1953, 1). In accepting this tax extension, the CED received praise from the editorial page of the *New York Times* for taking a "broader view" (*NYT*, June 10, 1953, 28). The CED's willingness to raise or maintain taxes continued throughout the decade. In 1956, the group called for an increase in fuel taxes to fund the building of highways (*WSJ*, January 16, 1956, 4), and in April 1959 it endorsed the president's balanced budget, saying that "spending increases should be matched by higher taxes" (*NYT*, April 8, 1959, 28).

As we saw in Chapter 3, the CED was not only a strong proponent of President Kennedy's 1963 tax cut but also played an important role in convincing Congress and the president to enact it, despite the fact that it at least temporarily increased the deficit. By the late 1960s, however, with deficits mounting due to the Vietnam War and Lyndon Johnson's Great Society programs, the CED was again in the forefront of a proposed tax increase. The organization's president, Alfred C. Neal, supported the idea of increasing taxes to fight inflation, although he preferred a value-added tax to increases in personal income taxes (*NYT*, March 19, 1966, 12).[1] There was also support (albeit minority support) among many firms for suspending the 7 percent tax credit for capital investment. In December 1966, the CED called for a tax increase sufficient to achieve a $3 billion surplus as a means of reducing inflation (*NYT*, December 2, 1966, 24; *WSJ*, December 8, 1966, 10). Congress eventually enacted a temporary 10 percent income tax surcharge in 1968.[2]

Business groups again played a role in recommending tax increases in the early 1980s, after President Reagan's tax cuts led to record deficits. By this point, the Business Roundtable had become the primary voice for the corporate elite, although the CED occasionally weighed in with an opinion. As we saw in the previous chapter, the Business Roundtable was supportive of tax cuts for business but was skeptical about Reagan's plan to reduce individual income taxes. By March 1982, as the deficit skyrocketed, the group argued that the president's tax cuts for individuals be delayed. The president, on the other hand, preferred to raise taxes on business while maintaining the individual-level cuts.[3] On March 12, five officials from the Roundtable, led by Clifton Garvin, the CEO of Exxon, and including the CEOs of TRW, Morgan Stanley, and Connecticut General Life Insurance, met with the president and told him that he might have to reduce defense spending, raise excise taxes (on alcohol and tobacco), and delay the 1983 portion of the income tax cut in order to reduce the deficit (*NYT,* March 13, 1982, 31, 38).[4]

There were, of course, significant divisions within the business community on this issue, as we saw in Chapter 7. The NAM and the National Federation of Independent Business (NFIB), an organization of small businesspeople, opposed the Roundtable on the delay of the tax cuts. There were disputes within various organizations as well (*NYT,* June 21, 1982, D1, D4). Paul Thayer of LTV Corporation, chairman of the Chamber of Commerce, supported the president's proposed tax increase bill while Richard L. Lesher, the Chamber's president, opposed it. Even Charls Walker decided not to publicly take a position on the plan. Ultimately, the Roundtable called for a compromise, in which the accelerated depreciation rule (which benefited large, capital intensive firms) would be reduced for three years in exchange for a more generous policy subsequent to that. As Useem notes (1984, 109), this position by the Business Roundtable reflected the center of gravity of overall business opinion on the tax increase. It also reflected the acknowledgement by the representatives of the largest firms that a tax increase was necessary.[5] The Roundtable called for tax increases at least two additional times before the end of the decade. In 1985, the group advocated a $35 billion increase over a three-year period to reduce the deficit (*WSJ,* August 1, 1985, 23).

The above examples, dating from 1950 into the mid-1980s, indicate that the corporate elite was willing on several occasions to encourage the federal government to enact a tax increase. As the elite continued to dissolve in the late 1980s, large corporations engaged in one final effort to lobby for higher taxes. George H. W. Bush had run his 1988 presidential campaign with the promise, "Read my lips, no new taxes." Yet within weeks of Bush's election, business leaders were calling on him to raise taxes to reduce the deficit. An article in *Fortune,* just days before the inauguration, was titled "CEOs to Bush: Raise Taxes Now" (*Fortune,* January 16, 1989). "The latest Fortune

500/CNN Moneyline CEO poll finds that a majority of corporate chiefs think taxes should be raised—and will be," the reporter, David Kirkpatrick, noted. Sixty-eight percent of the respondents, who consisted of 225 Fortune 500 and Service 500 CEOs (the latter the 500 largest service firms), believed that taxes or user fees should be raised to reduce the deficit. Not surprisingly, they also advocated cuts in spending along with the tax increases, but they were willing to make cuts even in areas in which their firms were directly affected. "When a defense contractor wants to cut defense spending and a maker of auto products advocates a higher gas tax— and they do—that's no-fooling determination to bring the deficit down," Kirkpatrick continued. Lawrence O. Kitchen, the CEO of Lockheed, for example, stated that there was a need for "a combination of reduced defense expenditures, reduced or streamlined entitlements, and increased taxes" (ibid., 96).

By 1990, as debates over the budget continued, both the Business Roundtable and the NAM encouraged President Bush to raise taxes if necessary to balance the budget. "The Roundtable has long held that the budget deficit is the number one economic issue that the nation faces," the group stated, in endorsing the plan proposed by House Ways and Means Chairman Dan Rostenkowski (D-Illinois) that included a fifteen cent per gallon increase in the gasoline tax (Darman 1996, 245). The Chamber of Commerce and the NFIB opposed any tax increase, but given the deficit, the position of Democrats in the House, and the efforts of the Roundtable and the NAM, President Bush signed a bill that included $140 billion in tax increases over the next five years, including an increase in the top individual rate from 28 percent to 31.5 percent (Greene 2000, 87; Judis 2001, 191).

As late as 1990, then, even after the corporate elite had become weakened by the takeover wave it had faced during the 1980s, corporate leaders were still calling for tax increases when they believed that the deficit had become uncomfortably large. The fact that the Business Roundtable and the NAM supported a tax increase was not necessarily the decisive force that led President Bush to eventually break his "no new taxes" pledge. The Democrats in Congress were unwilling to consider budget cuts without a tax increase, and the president was himself concerned about the deficit. Still, Richard Darman, director of the administration's Office of Management and Budget, alluded in his memoirs not only to the Roundtable's support of Rostenkowski's plan that included a tax increase but also to the group's praise for the president's willingness to sign the eventual bill passed by the Democratic Congress (Darman 1996, 264).[6]

After agreeing to support a tax increase, thereby breaking his "no new taxes" pledge, President Bush was excoriated by conservative Republicans and mocked by Democrats. Although his approval ratings skyrocketed after the invasion of Kuwait and the successful effort against Saddam Hussein, the president remained vulnerable on the taxation issue. Given this decision, as well as a recession that began around the same time as the budget negotiations, Bush was subsequently defeated in his bid for reelection. Although Bill Clinton managed to enact another tax increase in his first year in office, including an increase in the top individual rate from 31.5 percent to 39.6 percent, he did this with a Democratic Congress. Once the Republicans won both houses of Congress in 1994, the party's leadership came increasingly to support the goal of a lobbyist, Grover P. Norquist, who in 1986 unveiled a "taxpayer protection pledge," which asked elected officials to oppose "any and all tax increases." As of 2011, 238 of the 244 Republican members of the House of Representatives and 40 of the 47 Republican members of the Senate had signed the pledge. This unwillingness of Republican legislators to consider any possible tax increase played a major role in the "gridlock" that permeated the government after Barack Obama assumed the presidency in 2009.

The Bush II Tax Cuts

The corporate elite's response to taxation during the presidency of George W. Bush provides an illustration of the extent to which the group was unwilling to take a potentially unpopular position.[7] President Bush's approach to taxation was almost identical to that taken by Ronald Reagan two decades earlier. Although the economy that Bush faced was not as weak as the one that Reagan had inherited, both were experiencing downturns, and both presidents advocated significant tax cuts as a means of stimulating the economy. In 2001, President Bush's first year in office, he enacted, with the support of the Republican-controlled Congress, an across-the-board reduction in marginal tax rates for individuals. This tax cut reduced the top marginal tax rate from 39.6 percent to 35 percent over a five-year period, with similar reductions for the lower brackets, as well as a reduction of the lowest rate—which had been 15 percent—to 10 percent. Although these rates remained higher than those during the latter part of the Reagan era and early Bush I era, when the tax cuts were combined with the onset of the wars in Afghanistan and Iraq and continued high levels of domestic spending, the deficit quickly reached record levels. Yet unlike the period following the Reagan tax cut, when the deficit also increased precipitously, there was a puzzling silence from the corporate elite on the need for a tax increase.

Why was there was no call for a tax increase following the Bush II tax cuts? Several possible reasons present themselves. First, unlike President Reagan, who quickly saw the growing deficit as a problem and acknowledged the need for a tax increase to address it, President Bush had no such reaction. Perhaps, given what had happened to his father after he reluctantly agreed to a tax increase, the president was simply unwilling to repeat what he saw as a near-suicidal decision.[8] Another possible reason for this silence was that policy makers' views about the nature of deficits had changed. In 2002, when Treasury Secretary Paul O'Neill raised objections toward Vice President Dick Cheney's plan for further tax cuts, fearing its effect on the deficit, Cheney reportedly told him that "Reagan proved deficits don't matter." O'Neill left his post soon afterward.

There were in fact a number of conservative economists who by the early 2000s had come to accept the view that deficits were not a serious concern (Weisman 2004), and the issue remains extremely controversial. The American economy experienced an expansion during the Reagan years despite a high deficit, yet a number of economists attributed the recession of the Bush I years to the high interest rates triggered by the deficits of the late 1980s.[9] It is also true that many conservative commentators who expressed little concern about the deficit during the Bush years experienced an about-face once Barack Obama took office. And despite Dick Cheney's claim and the temporarily revised views of conservative economists, there is evidence that business leaders maintained their suspicion of deficits through the entire period. A survey of top CEOs by the Business Council in 2003 revealed that more than 60 percent viewed the predicted federal deficit "as a problem that could lead to higher interest rates" (*WSJ*, October 9, 2003, A13). Only about one-quarter of the respondents believed that the economic benefits of the deficit (in terms of its ability to stimulate the economy) would outweigh the costs.

The continued concern about the deficit, along with the mysterious silence regarding taxes, was evident in a speech given by John J. Castellani, the president of the Roundtable, at a speech at the Detroit Economic Club in April 2004.[10] Although the topic of the speech was outsourcing, Castellani, departing from his prepared text, spoke for several minutes about the dangers of the deficit. Because he was speaking in his capacity as president of the Roundtable, it is reasonable to assume that Castellani was representing the views of the majority of the organization's members. Yet in his discussion of the deficit, Castellani made no mention of either the Bush tax cuts as a possible cause or of the possibility that a tax increase might be necessary to address the problem. This was in stark contrast to the group's position during the Reagan and Bush I years. In fact, barely two weeks before Castellani's speech, the *Wall Street Journal* criticized the Roundtable for its lack of attention to the deficit. The Roundtable had expressed concern about the deficit in 1988 when it was 3.1 percent of the nation's GDP, in 1995 when it was 2.2 percent of GDP, and even in 1997 when the deficit was just 0.3 percent of GDP. Yet when the deficit hit 3.5 percent of GDP in March 2003, the Roundtable was silent, according to the *Journal* (*WSJ*, April 8, 2004, A2). The article's author, David Wessel, quoted Castellani's testimony before Congress a year earlier, in which Castellani had argued that "the primary cause of the current deficit situation is declining revenues due to the 2001 recession and the anemic growth coming out of the recession." But "that logic isn't . . . sound," Wessel argued. "Bigger factors this year and in years ahead are tax cuts and spending increases that Mr. Bush has blessed," he suggested.

Why, then, was the Business Roundtable unwilling to recommend a tax increase during the Bush II years, despite having done so in earlier decades? There is a third possible reason: the group might have been acting out of loyalty to the president. As described by Michael J. Graetz and Ian Shapiro (2005, 156–166) in a detailed account of the Bush II tax cuts, the president was insistent in the early weeks of his term that his tax cuts focus primarily on individual and estate taxes (which were concerns of small-business owners) rather than business taxes. He made it clear to the representatives of large corporations—including the Roundtable—that reductions in business taxes were off the table, at least initially. The president's strategy was to try to get big business to support the cuts in personal and estate taxes, with the idea that if they agreed to support him on this, he would encourage reductions in corporate taxes at a later point. President Bush's leader in this effort, Dirk Van Dongen, the head of the National Association of Wholesale Distributors, managed to gain the cooperation not only of the Chamber of Commerce, whose support was expected because of its dominance by small business, but also the NAM, whose membership, although predominantly small firms, included a number of large corporations as well. Five days after the NAM's announcement of its support, in February 2001, the Roundtable also agreed to support the president's plan. As Graetz and Shapiro put it (2005, 162), "Ultimately, the large corporations' patience would pay off, and they would obtain tax cuts from George Bush." Although the passage of corporate tax cuts was delayed because of the September 11th attacks, three separate bills, in 2002, 2003, and 2004, all benefited business. In 2003, for example, President Bush signed into law a bill that further cut individual rates and the estate tax but also cut rates on capital gains and dividends, and increased the rate by which equipment could be depreciated.

This scenario suggests that President Bush had an agenda that he wanted to achieve and that he was able to gain the support of large corporations by promising them that he would support them in the future. When the future arrived, he responded by keeping his word, rewarding big business with a series of cuts in response to the support they had given him in the initial round of tax reform. Having seen the president keep his promise, it is not difficult to see why the Business Roundtable was reluctant to criticize him even after the deficit rose to record levels.

Yet this account is insufficient to explain big business's failure to recommend a tax increase. First, the Business Roundtable had initially supported (or at least not opposed) President Reagan's tax cuts as well, yet the group quickly moved toward opposition when the deficit skyrocketed after the first round of cuts. The Roundtable had never been enthusiastic about President Reagan's tax cuts for individuals, and Reagan himself was willing to risk antagonizing the group by insisting that the tax increases be limited to corporate taxes. Is it possible that George W. Bush was more skillful in handling the large corporations than Reagan had been? This seems unlikely. Few would argue that Bush was a craftier politician than Reagan. Perhaps Reagan was simply less interested in placating large corporations than Bush was. The fact is, however, that the Business Roundtable was prepared to recommend a tax increase in response to the deficit in the early 1980s (as well as the late 1980s, during the Bush I presidency), but it was not willing to do the same during the Bush II years, despite far higher deficits.[11] Second, the Roundtable's unwillingness to recommend a tax increase continued beyond the Bush II years into the Obama administration. Whereas big business experienced warm relations with the Bush administration, the group had a considerably more adversarial relation with President Obama. Yet this did not lead the Roundtable to recommend any kind of tax increase, even on individuals, during the Obama administration, despite the administration's clear willingness to support such an increase, at least on the highest income earners. The group could not even bring itself to do this during the debate over raising the debt ceiling in August 2011. Responding to the stalemate, which threatened to send the nation into default, the Roundtable, led at that point by former Michigan governor John Engler, issued only a brief, vague letter imploring President Obama and Congress to reach a resolution. The group called on the president and Congress to "enact legislation now that raises the debt limit and puts the United States on an immediate and real path toward fiscal responsibility" (July 29, 2011), without offering a single suggestion for how such an agreement might be reached.[12] As David Leonhardt of the *New York Times* suggested in a column from July 6, 2011, although Roundtable officials described the deficit in "sober, common-sense language that can make them sound more reasonable than either political party," the group "is actually part of the problem." (p. B1). He went on to note that the Roundtable "defends corporate tax loopholes and even argues for new ones," "pushes for a lower corporate tax rate," "favors permanent extension of the Bush tax cuts," and "opposes a reduction in the tax subsidy for health insurance." The group's support of low taxes for corporations is consistent with the positions it has held since its formation in the 1970s. Its insistence on maintaining, and even making permanent, the personal tax cuts enacted under George W. Bush was not consistent with the group's earlier positions, however. In the debate over the national debt ceiling, the Business Roundtable, an organization that from its inception was in the forefront of national policy making, was either unwilling or unable to provide any guidance to the federal government in a period of grave crisis.[13]

The Twilight of Responsibility

No one wants to pay more taxes. Yet for more than four decades, corporate leaders, Republican presidents, and Democrats alike were willing to raise taxes when necessary. The willingness of a nation's leaders, including corporate leaders, to recommend a tax increase, especially when such an increase falls on them personally, is therefore appropriately viewed as an exercise of responsibility. It is true that corporations have often attempted to divert tax increases away from business, preferring instead to shift the burden to individuals. Yet the business leaders who have proposed these ideas are themselves among the highest paid individuals in the world. Under any system of progressive taxation, especially given the rates prevalent in the postwar period (including a top marginal rate of 90 percent in the 1950s), those with high incomes will tend to pay more with any tax increase. Although these individuals were unlikely to suffer any significant financial hardship from such an increase, they would nevertheless bear a disproportionate burden. The fact that business leaders were willing to accept tax increases on individual income thus suggests at least a modicum of concern for the greater national good. The Business Roundtable in 1982 was willing to forego, or at least delay, the personal income tax cuts in Ronald Reagan's plan, despite the fact that the group's leaders would individually be required to pay thousands of dollars in additional taxes. One can argue, with some justification, that the Roundtable's members were still acting in their self-interest when they insisted on continuing the earlier reductions in corporate tax rates. Yet to reiterate, they were doing this with the full knowledge that they were simultaneously rejecting a reduction in their own personal taxes.

There is certainly a range of opinions on the relative seriousness of deficits and who stands to suffer most from them. A number of economists believe that deficits create more harm for the wealthy than they do for wage workers, which may explain why the wealthy express greater concern for deficits than they do for the overall state of the economy (Page, Cook, and Moskowitz 2011).[14] It is nevertheless true that few corporate leaders, even those who have expressed concern over the deficit since the turn of the twenty-first century, have been willing to call for a tax increase. And no major organization, including the Business Roundtable, has been willing to go on record as supporting an increase either, despite the organization's history of doing so. The one exception to this is the venerable Committee for Economic Development (CED), which twice during the Bush II years, in 2003 and 2005, issued calls for a tax increase to reduce the deficit (*NYT,* March 6, 2003, C2; *WSJ,* October 13, 2005, A2). Yet these announcements received little publicity and appear to have been ignored by the administration. The Roundtable, meanwhile, went on record in September 2004 not only in support of the Bush tax cuts but also in support of the idea that the cuts be made permanent (*WSJ,* September 2, 2004, A2). The Roundtable continued to describe itself as favoring fiscal conservatism, but continued to support the Bush tax cuts "to maintain the long-term health and prosperity of the economy" (*WSJ,* September 22, 2005, A6).[15]

Perhaps the political environment of the 2000s is the primary cause of the Business Roundtable's unwillingness to exercise the kind of responsibility that the group demonstrated in earlier years. As we saw earlier, the vast majority of Republicans in the House and Senate had by 2011 signed Grover Norquist's pledge to refuse to raise taxes under any circumstances. Perhaps the Roundtable's leadership believes that it is unable to confront those in Congress who refuse to consider a tax increase. Yet in 1989, the Roundtable faced a president who had emphatically stated that there would be "no new taxes," and still the group was willing to urge that president to raise them nevertheless. The Roundtable's retreat from responsibility on the issue of taxes is emblematic of the decline of the American corporate elite.[16]

Health Care

Health care is an issue to which the American corporate elite paid relatively little attention prior to the 1970s. There were private efforts to include health coverage during the period of welfare capitalism—by the mid-1920s, more than 400 large companies provided on-site medical care for their employees (Martin 2000, 72). There were several attempts by presidents and members of Congress to enact a national health care plan. Franklin Roosevelt declined to include health care as part of the Social Security Act in 1935, fearful that it would endanger the entire bill. He did attempt to pass a health care bill in 1938, only to be rebuffed by a more conservative Congress, and he tried again during World War II, an effort that was cut short by his death. Senators Robert Wagner and James Murray and Representative John Dingell Sr. also introduced a bill during World War II, and Harry Truman made a serious effort to pass a comprehensive national health care plan as well. In all of these cases, the primary opposition came not from business but from the medical profession, in particular the American Medical Association (AMA) (Starr 2011, 35–41). The physicians within the AMA saw government-administered health insurance as a threat because they feared that it would impose price controls on them, thus reducing their revenue.

Although the attempt to enact national health insurance would have faced difficulty under any circumstances, one reason that it stalled after President Truman's efforts may have been due to a development within the private sector: the adoption of employer-sponsored health care. American labor unions had exhibited ambivalence toward government health insurance dating back to the early days of the American Federation of Labor (AFL). The AFL under Samuel Gompers initially opposed attempts to enact health care legislation in the pre–World War I period, concerned that it might cut into unions' own efforts (Starr 2011, 32). Even at this time, some AFL locals did support a national health care policy, and by the 1930s the AFL's national office had come to support the policy as well. The United Auto Workers (UAW) also supported the idea of national health insurance during the 1940s. Two important developments occurred during this decade, however. First, in response to the government-instituted wage freeze during World War II, a number of companies began to offer fringe benefits, including health insurance, as a means of raising compensation without violating the wage freeze. Second, the failure of President Truman's effort to enact national health care, an outcome almost ensured by the election of a Republican Congress in 1946, led the UAW to reassess its strategy. As we saw in Chapter 4, faced with the prospect of having no health coverage at all, Walter Reuther, the UAW's president, decided to press for health care as part of the union's epic 1950 agreement with General Motors. Reuther was confident that once the management of heavy-industry firms became aware of the enormous costs associated with their benefits plans, they would eventually see the value of supporting government-funded programs. This, of course, did not occur, at least at the time, because the companies did not experience these costs as a strain. As Lichtenstein put it (1995, 297), "Given their well-insulated market and GM's leak-proof price umbrella, most larger firms proved quite willing to fold pension, health insurance, and SUB [supplementary unemployment benefit] costs into their product prices."[17] Once the UAW realized that the companies were not going to support a federal policy, the union made a pragmatic decision to "go it alone."

One reason that the corporate elite was relatively inactive with regard to national health care issues may have been precisely because in the postwar period cost was not a major concern. Health care expenditures as a percentage of GDP were relatively low during this period and were not appreciably different from those of other developed countries, including those with national health care systems. Health care spending as a proportion of GDP stood at approximately 5 percent in 1950 and remained at that level for the next decade. These relative expenditures gradually began to rise during the 1960s, reaching 6.2 percent in 1967 and 7.2 percent in 1970. As Figure 8.1 illustrates, the problem became far more severe in subsequent years, as health expenditures rose to 10.3 percent of GDP in 1982, 13.5 percent in 1992, and 17.9 percent by 2010. In the absence of some kind of intervention, health care costs are, at this writing, projected by the Congressional

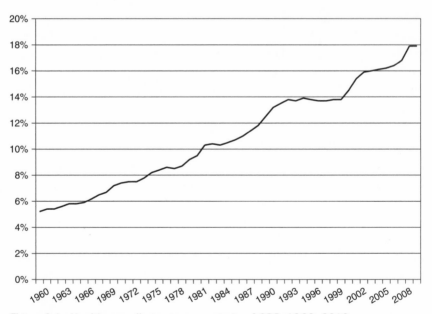

Figure 8.1. Health spending as a percentage of GDP, 1960–2010.
Source: Center for Medicare and Medicaid Services, National Health Expenditure Accounts, www.cms.gov/National-HealthExpendData/.

Budget Office to rise to 25 percent of GDP by 2025, and 37 percent by
2050.[18] Because most health insurance costs in the United States have been
borne by private employers, these costs have become a major national issue,
one with potentially catastrophic consequences.

The period leading up to the 1970s is precisely when the cost of health
care began to appear on the national political agenda. On July 10, 1969,
less than six months after taking office, President Nixon addressed the
growing crisis in health care spending. "The problem is much greater than
I had realized," the president stated. "We face a massive crisis in this area;
and unless action is taken . . . to meet that crisis within the next 2 to 3
years, we will have a breakdown in our medical care system which could
have consequences affecting millions of people throughout this country."[19]
Around the same time, Senator Edward Kennedy proposed the idea of a
comprehensive, single-payer program administered by the federal government that would replace the private health insurance system (Starr 2011,
53). In response to Kennedy's proposal, Nixon offered his own, in 1971.
Although Nixon's plan retained the private insurance system, it included a
mandate that all employers provide health insurance for their employees
and pay at least three-quarters of the cost, as well as a government-run system for everyone not covered by employer-based insurance. Moreover, the
proposal included a plan to reduce costs by relying on what it called "health
maintenance organizations" (HMOs). These organizations were already in
existence in some parts of the country, including the president's home state
of California, where the Kaiser plan had existed since the 1940s. They relied on a single general payment for complete medical coverage, as opposed
to the traditional fee-for-service model. This was believed to reduce costs
because it removed the economic incentive for unnecessary tests and procedures.[20] The president later exempted employers with fewer than ten employees from the insurance mandate in response to protests by Republicans
in Congress, but he strongly defended the general concept of an employer
mandate, comparing it to the requirement that employers contribute to disability and Social Security (ibid., 54).

The proposal by President Nixon was considerably more radical and
more inclusive than either the plan presented by Bill Clinton two decades
later or the plan ultimately adopted during Barack Obama's first term in
2010. The president and Congress were unable to reach an agreement
prior to the 1972 presidential election. After winning reelection, however,

President Nixon introduced a new plan that went even further than his earlier one. In 1973, between the first and second Nixon plans, the Committee for Economic Development (CED), still an influential force at the time, introduced a plan of its own. As we saw in Chapter 6, the CED plan called for an employer mandate as well as government planning of manpower needs and control over some health care costs (Committee for Economic Development 1973, 22–25). The second Nixon plan, outlined in a speech to Congress in February 1974, closely mirrored the CED proposal.[21] Like his previous plan, the 1974 proposal—the Comprehensive Health Insurance Plan—included an employer mandate and a publicly funded system for everyone not covered by the employer-based one. Included in the president's plan were treatment for mental health, alcohol and drug addiction, dental care up to age 13, and a limit of $1,500 per year in cost to any family, regardless of the total cost of care.[22] The plan, unfortunately, never made it to a vote, and exactly why it failed is a matter of some disagreement. Although it did not go nearly as far as Senator Kennedy's earlier proposal, Kennedy had shown a willingness to compromise, and he entered negotiations with the president, as well as with Representative Wilbur Mills, the chairman of the House Ways and Means Committee. There was opposition on both sides, however. The labor unions preferred a stronger plan, with no deductibles; some union officials even referred to Senator Kennedy as a "sellout" for being willing to compromise. Many Republicans in Congress remained hostile to the employer mandate and had reservations about the entire plan (Starr 2011, 56–57). Moreover, the discussion took place in the final days of the Nixon presidency, when the Watergate scandal was occupying most of the government's attention. The importance of President Nixon's support for health care reform became evident after his resignation. Although President Ford appeared supportive of health care reform, the resistance in Congress led Mills to abandon the fight, and the bill died.

The liberals who had withheld their support for the Nixon bill did so in part because they hoped that with a Democrat in the White House, they would be able to pass a stronger plan. By the time Jimmy Carter assumed the presidency, however, the weakening economy and the growing conservative reaction and rightward turn by the corporate elite put an end to hopes for reform. Although Senator Kennedy reintroduced a comprehensive plan in 1978, President Carter refused to support it. Carter's own plan, which focused almost exclusively on catastrophic insurance, received little support and died in the House in 1979 (Starr 2011, 60–62). With the nation's economic problems worsening and Ronald Reagan's election on the horizon, this spelled the end of health care reform for more than a decade.

Business Gets Involved

As health care became an important national issue in the 1970s, one group for the most part remained conspicuously absent: business. It is true that small-business interests, as represented by the Republicans in Congress, had played a role in modifying the Nixon proposals. It is also the case that the CED was ahead of the curve in seeing health care as a growing problem for large corporations down the road. Yet in terms of its overall activity, business, especially the corporate elite, remained strangely invisible during the debates of the 1970s. The Business Roundtable in 1974 formed a spinoff group, the Washington Business Group on Health (WBGH), whose task was to give large companies—though primarily purchasers rather than providers of health care—a voice in health care policy (Bergthold 1990, 41–47; Mintz 1995, 413; Martin 2000, 118–119). This group played little role in the public debates of the 1970s, however, nor was the Roundtable itself or individual large corporations actively involved. In a study of organizations involved in national health policy from 1977 through 1980, Laumann and Knoke (1987, 409) found only six business corporations among the 135 organizations identified as players in the field, only three of which were Fortune 500 firms. All three—Merck, Pfizer, and Upjohn—were pharmaceutical companies, and only Upjohn was rated by representatives from other organizations as even "average" in terms of its total influence. The WBGH was also rated as "middle of the pack" in influence. In contrast, 66 of the 198 organizations in the energy policy area were corporations, and most of them were either in the Fortune 500 or were among the fifty largest utilities (ibid., 404–406). Not a single reference to the WBGH appeared in the *New York Times* from the date of its formation in 1974 through the end of 1979, and there was only a single reference to the group in the *Wall Street Journal* (May 10, 1978, 1).

Things began to change in the 1980s. The escalating costs that companies paid for their employees' health care were becoming an increasing burden. Moreover, business leaders were becoming increasingly aware that the growing number of uninsured Americans—more than thirty million by the mid-1980s—was contributing to these costs. In a 1987 article in the *Wall Street Journal,* for example, William S. Woodside, chairman of the executive committee of Primerica Corporation and head of a health care subcommittee at the CED, lamented this situation and recommended a comprehensive health care plan for the poor, suggesting that this would not only be the morally right thing to do but would be a good investment as well (*WSJ,* May 29, 1987, 26). Two years later, a *New York Times* article (May 30, 1989, D1) further underscored this point: "Many business leaders, worried that in the long run they may be hit with the cost of health care for millions of uninsured people, are beginning to advocate a greater role for the Federal Government in extending coverage to all Americans," the article stated. Willis B. Goldbeck, the president of the Washington Business Group on Health, which had become significantly more active in the 1980s, noted that "there is grudging recognition among a hefty majority of our members that health care has moved to being a right."[23] The cost of health care had become so burdensome that some corporate officials were even willing to relax their ideological opposition to government intervention, in much the same way that the corporate elite of the postwar period had done. Robert E. Mercer, the recently retired chairman of Goodyear, for example, noted, "I never thought I would be in favor of a Government health policy, but there are things that Government must do." Even the National Association of Manufacturers (NAM) was concerned about the problem. The group's chairman, Richard E. Heckert, stated that "no matter how the system is designed, we're all going to pay for it." Heckert even questioned the decades-old American tradition of having employers maintain responsibility for their employees' health care: "Running these costs through industry and business is one of the dumbest things we can do if we want to be internationally competitive." Representatives from Caterpillar and Chrysler raised similar concerns, suggesting, as a subsequent *Times* article noted, that "national health insurance might be a less expensive and more efficient alternative" to the employer-based system (*NYT,* May 1, 1991, A1). Perhaps the most emphatic among this group were the representatives of two of the automobile industry's "Big Three," Ford and Chrysler. Chrysler Chairman Lee Iacocca began to raise the issue of national health insurance after Chrysler's health care costs increased from $432 million in 1985 to $702 million in 1988 (*NYT,* May 8, 1989, D1). "When you look around the world, there appears to be a common denominator," noted Chrysler's director of employee benefits, Walter B. Maher. That standard, Maher stated, was "a process that gets all the players involved in a political decision as to how much of their money as a nation will be set aside for health care."

That these quotes were not simply anecdotal is illustrated by the results of a survey of Fortune 1000 CEOs conducted by Cantor et al. (1991). Among the 387 CEOs who responded, 91 percent believed that either "fundamental changes are needed" or "we need to completely rebuild" the American health care system. Only 8.7 percent believed that the system "works pretty well" and that "only minor changes" were needed. More than half of the CEOs surveyed by Cantor et al. believed that costs could not be controlled without some form of government intervention (Cantor et al. 1991, 100). Fifty-three percent were willing to consider employer mandates, either immediately or in the future, and 32 percent were even willing to support replacing the existing system with a "public health insurance system" (ibid., 101). Among the CEOs who believed that government help was needed to bring their costs under control, 50 percent supported a public insurance system.

The question of whether health care should be tied to one's employment was a controversial one, to which we shall return shortly. What was important at this point is that the health care crisis was sufficiently serious that officers of some of the country's leading corporations were beginning to consider even radical solutions. One issue that resurfaced in discussions among corporate officials was an idea raised during the Nixon administration: employer mandates. Senator Kennedy and Representative Henry Waxman of California had proposed a bill that included a requirement that employers offer health coverage for their employees, or pay a tax if they did not. The administration of George H. W. Bush was vehemently opposed to the idea. In contrast, a number of large corporations actually favored such a system. In the Cantor et al. survey, 29 percent believed that such mandates should be adopted immediately, while another 24 percent believed that they should be considered for the future (Cantor et al. 1991, 101).

The reason for this support was the desire for a balanced playing field. The vast majority of major American firms were already offering health insurance, and they were concerned that the companies—even small ones— that did not offer this benefit were experiencing an unfair advantage.

Vernon R. Loucks Jr., chairman of Baxter International, a diversified health care firm in Deerfield, Illinois, expressed this logic in explaining his support for Senator Kennedy's plan: "The argument is that the little guys can't afford that kind of cost. . . . But if they are selling products against me, I'm at an acute disadvantage." Anne H. McNamara, a senior vice president at American Airlines, was also supportive, citing Continental, which after its Chapter 11 bankruptcy cancelled its union contracts, giving the airline a cost advantage (*NYT,* May 30, 1989, D11). A representative from the National Federation of Independent Business (NFIB) acknowledged that health care costs were a growing concern for small business as well, although the group's members, in her view, were "overwhelmingly opposed" to a mandated benefit. Yet this spokesperson's view might not have been representative of the entire small-business community. According to a Dun & Bradstreet survey, there was a virtual tie among small companies in the extent to which they favored "national health insurance," with 38 percent saying yes, 39 percent saying no, and 23 percent responding "don't know." There was controversy among large corporations as well. While Chrysler and Ford were considering the possibility of a national health care system, General Motors, whose costs were even greater, remained skeptical. Tom J. Morr, the head of GM's benefits department stated, "We are not going to fold our tents and wait for the Government to solve this problem. . . . We are not ready to give up on the free enterprise system." On the other hand, the health care management director at Alcoa, Dick Wardrop, argued that government programs must be expanded, and funded with taxes (ibid.).

This was the environment that existed when Bill Clinton campaigned for the presidency with a promise to enact health care reform. The members of the corporate elite faced an enormous and growing problem that, through their own private efforts, they had been unable to solve. Significant elements within this group seemed willing to consider, out of desperation, an expanded role for government. Even the NAM, an organization that had never accepted the Keynesian compromise even at the height of liberalism in the postwar era, now seemed poised to support major reform. In the early 1970s, when President Nixon introduced his proposals for national health care, the problem was emerging, but it had not yet approached crisis proportions. Less than two decades later, the crisis was upon us, and the corporate elite, even if fractured by the events of the 1980s, had an opportunity to address the problem.

Health care presented an enormous difficulty, however. Most corporations were consumers of health care through their benefit plans for their employees. Many corporations were providers of health care, either through insurance, medical care itself, or drugs. Although the former firms were hurt by rising health care costs and had an interest in reining them in, the latter firms benefited as health care costs increased and therefore had little incentive to change the system. Complicating the issue was the fact that an increasing number of nonmedical firms now owned subsidiaries that were on the provider side, even as the firm's primary activity was on the consumer side. An examination of Fortune 500 firms in 1994 that Todd Schifeling and I conducted indicated that 42 of the 480 firms whose primary industry we could identify (approximately 8.7 percent) were in the health care sector. Another 36 firms (7.5 percent) whose primary industry was not health care had other operating units in the health care sector. And an increasing number of large non-health-care firms had operations in industries—including hotels and restaurants—that did not provide employee health insurance, even as these firms provided insurance for most of their other employees (Mintz 1998, 215).

Business has never been completely unified, of course. Even in the postwar period there were conflicts between domestic steel companies and those that benefited from inexpensive imported steel, including the automotive industry. Large and small business often had conflicting interests over international trade, taxation, and regulatory policy. In the postwar period, however, there were mechanisms that allowed companies to successfully resolve these conflicts, most notably a strong and highly legitimate state, but also the financial community and organizations such as the CED, whose goal was to provide solutions that transcended the sectarian interests of individual industries. The health care crisis of the early 1990s was certainly a difficult one, and the business community faced a series of extremely difficult decisions. Yet the conditions under which the Marshall Plan, the educational expansion of the 1960s, the Civil Rights Act, and Medicare were established were no less daunting. If ever there were an occasion for the American corporate elite to show its mettle, addressing a problem that was not only a concern for the larger society but of immediate and growing importance for the elite itself, this was it. It would be unfair to say that the corporate elite did not try to find a solution to the health care crisis of the early 1990s. It might not be unfair to accuse the group of ineptitude, however. The corporate elite proved at this point, and years later, with the Obama plan, that it was incapable of solving not only societal problems but even its own.

The fate of the Clinton health care plan in 1993–1994 provides a good example of the inability of the American corporate elite after its decline in the 1980s to constructively address a major problem. The Clinton plan, based on the concept of "managed competition," was extremely complex, and some segments of the business community as well as members of Congress felt excluded from the decision-making process (Skocpol 1996, 49–55; Starr 2011, 92–95). Yet the plan was not only moderate—representing a significant compromise between a single-payer system favored by many liberals and a fully market-based system favored by Republicans—but it also contained a number of elements favored by large corporations. The plan called for virtually universal coverage, primarily through the establishment of regional "health alliances." These alliances would offer a series of options, including traditional fee-for-service coverage as well as HMOs, from which subscribers could choose. Employers would be required to contribute 80 percent of the cost of premiums, but the plan included a limit on total employer contributions. In cases in which the cap on employer costs left employees with insufficient coverage, the government would cover the difference. Premiums for those not covered by employers (including the poor and the unemployed) would be subsidized by the government (Starr 2011, 95–99). The large scale of the regional alliances, as well as the choice in plans offered to consumers, were both expected to contribute to a reduction in costs.

One indication of how serious the health care crisis was to large corporations is the fact that in the early stages of debate over the Clinton plan, even the Chamber of Commerce and the NAM were positively disposed toward the bill. A 1991 task force report suggested that more than $11 billion in health care costs had been shifted onto NAM members due to a lack of universal coverage. In the summer of 1993, a survey of NAM members revealed majority support for employer mandates. The organization's president, Jerry Jasinowski, entered negotiations with administration officials and appeared willing to support the Clinton plan subject to changes in a series of issues considered important by large firms (Martin 2000, 176). The Chamber was even more supportive. Robert E. Patricelli, chairman of the Chamber's Health and Benefits Committee, convened a group of representatives of purchaser companies, while excluding insurance and pharmaceutical representatives. Not only did this group express its support for an employer mandate as well—as long as the government was willing to subsidize low-wage workers and their employers—but Patricelli even testified in support of this idea before the Senate Labor and Human Resources Committee (Clymer 1993, 1; Judis 1995; Martin 2000, 177). Ironically, the Business Roundtable, historically the most moderate of the three groups, may have had the most difficult time reaching a consensus. The problem in the Roundtable's case was that the group's health care task force was controlled by providers, in particular the insurance companies (Martin 2000, 177); more than half of the firms represented on this committee were either in the health care industry or had employees who were not covered by health insurance (Judis 1995). Although the insurance companies and pharmaceuticals generally shared the manufacturers' support of employer mandates—since it meant more business for them—they were strongly opposed to price controls on care, which they feared would accompany the mandates—since such controls might cut into their profits. Other companies appeared to oppose the Clinton plan on ideological grounds, even when it appeared that they would benefit economically from it.

Although President Clinton's September 1993 speech outlining his plan was well-received by the public, by early 1994 the business community's support for the bill had wavered. In addition to their own inability to reach a consensus in support of the plan, two other factors appear to have played a role in the corporate retreat. First, small businesses, especially those associated with the National Federation of Independent Business (NFIB), were not only vehemently opposed to the plan but were highly unified, organized, and active in their opposition. The NFIB mounted an intense lobbying campaign, targeting key legislators such as Senator Max Baucus, a Montana Democrat who would later be a major player in the debate over the Obama health plan (Starr 2011, 115–116). Second, Republicans in Congress were becoming increasingly irritated with business groups for their willingness to work with the administration. In one case, House Republicans threatened to "punish" Ameritech with further regulations if the company failed to cancel a planned speech by President Clinton. House Republican leader Newt Gingrich told members of the Roundtable that they should be "principled" rather than "going for short-term deals" (Martin 2000, 187). And the Conservative Opportunity Society, a group of seventy-five House Republicans chaired by Representative John Boehner, encouraged local chambers of commerce to protest against the national Chamber's conciliatory approach toward the administration. As Boehner told the heads of the Chamber, it was the group's "duty to categorically oppose everything that Clinton was in favor of" (quoted in Judis 1995).[24] Given the increasing disaffection of the Chamber's rank-and-file, the NFIB began to raid the group for new members. The competition with the NFIB ultimately led the Chamber to drop its support for reform.

The combination of divisions among large corporations and opposition among smaller firms reached a head by early February of 1994. On February 2, the Business Roundtable announced, despite an intense last-minute plea by both Bill and Hillary Clinton, that it was supporting a rival plan developed by Representative Jim Cooper (D-Tennessee), a plan that contained managed competition but without an employer mandate. The head of the Roundtable's task force on health, welfare, and retirement income was Robert C. Winters, the CEO of Prudential Insurance, and John Ong, the Roundtable's chairman, felt that it was necessary to deny that Winters had a conflict of interest. "We try to ignore as much as we can the interests of our companies," Ong told the *New York Times*. "I don't think there is any merit in supposing that Mr. Winters or anybody else had any bias or prejudice" (*NYT,* February 3, 1994, A1). Senator John D. Rockefeller IV, a West Virginia Democrat, took issue with this view, noting that the task force was dominated by members of the insurance and pharmaceutical industries. "They don't want the people to get insurance at a better price," he said. Speaking of the corporations that served as consumers rather than providers of health care, Rockefeller stated, "I think business did themselves a disservice in this. I think they let their peers in the insurance industry snooker them" (ibid.).

The following day, Robert Patricelli of the Chamber, who in October had testified in front of the Senate in support of employer mandates, was scheduled to testify before the House Ways and Means Committee. In a preappearance written version of his testimony, Patricelli had stated that the Chamber was open to employer mandates if the employer share, set at 80 percent in the president's plan, could be reduced to 50 percent. When Patricelli testified in person, however, he did not mention this support but instead stated that the group "[could not] support the president's Health Security Act." "If employer mandates become the vehicle for those who favor the trappings of a government-dominated system," he added, "we will not accept those mandates" (*WSJ*, February 4, 1994, A3).

This about-face by the Chamber and the Roundtable led to angry reactions not only from labor and consumer groups, but especially from Senator Rockefeller. "Shame on big business," the Senator said. Referring to the Roundtable, he said that the group's members had "walked away from their workers," and that there was a "special place in hell" for Robert Winters, the Prudential CEO who headed the Roundtable's health care task force (*WSJ*, February 4, 1994, A3). The reason for the abrupt shift in the Chamber's position appeared to be an intense campaign by House Republicans, who were able to pressure the Chamber's president, Richard Lesher, to change Patricelli's testimony (Judis 1995; Skocpol 1996, 158–161).[25] Meanwhile, the NAM, which, like the Chamber, had originally been predisposed to support reform, switched its position in February 1994 as well. A group of NAM staff members noted that they had gone into the group's February board meeting having "good things to say about the Clinton bill" but then watched the board do a "180-degree turn," an apparent result of a letter opposing the bill circulated prior to the meeting by board members representing health care providers and fast-food managers (Martin 2000, 176). From this point on the Clinton plan, although still debated in Congress, was effectively dead.[26]

Several explanations have been offered for the failure of the Clinton plan, and all of them probably contain at least some truth. Small businesses never fully accepted the idea of employer mandates, and even some large firms, especially those with units that did not provide health care, were dubious. Health providers, including insurance companies, dominated the decision-making body of the Business Roundtable. The plan was extremely complex and created a considerable amount of uncertainty regarding its ultimate cost and the degree of government control. The American public, although originally supportive of the bill, became skittish as the debates in Congress wore on. Moreover, many Americans were satisfied with their health care and were reluctant to support a plan that might require changes, including possible reductions in service, to accomplish universal coverage. Even those that stood to gain the most—large manufacturing firms with enormous and rapidly increasing health care costs—had their doubts. It is often less risky for political actors to stick with a known evil than to support an unknown, even if the latter has an opportunity to reduce costs.

Faced with a "put up or shut up" decision, many businesses simply contracted a case of "cold feet," the *New York Times* suggested (*NYT,* May 15, 1994, E1). And ideology appeared to play a role as well. For some corporate officials, the thought of greater government involvement in health care, even if it were to save their firms millions of dollars, was just too difficult to accept.[27]

Ultimately, however, what prevented constructive reform from occurring was the ineffectuality of the corporate elite. While small business was organized, unified, active, and effective, big business was disorganized and unable to reach a consensus. The task for small business—simple opposition—was an easier one to accomplish. Small firms, at least those associated with the NFIB, were unified by a single issue: their steadfast opposition to the requirement that they offer health insurance to their employees. Although there may have been an ideological rather than economic basis for this opposition as well—the Clinton plan contained a number of subsidies for small employers—it was certainly easier to maintain a blanket opposition to the bill than to deal with its nuances and complexities. Yet despite the organizational advantages that small business possessed, if the corporate elite had been capable of exercising responsibility in the way that its counterparts did in the postwar period, health care reform—whether with the Clinton plan or a universal-coverage alternative—could have been accomplished. The problem was that the American corporate elite no longer had this capability. No longer faced with significant pressure from its workers—the labor movement's weakness was fully apparent during the debates over the Clinton plan—or from a state that now lacked legitimacy in the eyes of the public; lacking a mechanism to forge a group-wide consensus, as the politically neutral financial community had done in the past; and disorganized and fragmented from the tumultuous events of the 1980s, the American corporate elite was no longer able to exercise leadership in what was now not only a society-wide problem but also a crisis for the corporate community itself. As Judis (1995, 72) noted in his assessment of the failure of the Clinton health care plan:

> American business . . . lacks today the kind of farseeing leaders who have the intelligence, objectivity, and authority to unite it around its long-term interests. In the Business Roundtable, Chamber of Commerce, and NAM, business leaders deferred in the end to CEOs who were acting primarily in

their narrow, immediate self-interest without regard to the larger effects that health care reform could have on American industry.[28]

As we have seen in earlier chapters, it is questionable whether the Chamber of Commerce or the NAM ever demonstrated an ability to unite the American business community around its long-term interests. The Business Roundtable, on the other hand, was at least able to do this in its earlier years. This group may not have had the balanced, above-the-fray character that the CED exhibited in its golden postwar years, but it did demonstrate some degree of responsibility through the 1980s, especially on taxation. The Roundtable failed to rise to the occasion on health care, however. Instead, the group was hijacked by an aggressive minority that profited greatly from the health care crisis and was unwilling to compromise. Judis again captured this failure (2001, 215):

> In the past, elites within the business community had intervened to prevent the most venal interests from dominating Congress. In 1946, the Committee on [sic] Economic Development, acting not as another business group but as an elite organization committed to the national interest, rescued the Employment Act. There were, however, no comparable organizations and no comparable leadership that could have rescued health care reform from oblivion.

The CED was still in existence during this period, as it is today, but it had become all but invisible in major policy circles and was no longer a player in national debates. An example that illustrates the CED's lost influence occurred in a speech on the Senate floor in October 1997 by Senator Russ Feingold (D-Wisconsin). This episode represents one of the CED's finest hours in recent years, yet it ironically also demonstrates the organization's relative weakness compared with its golden age in the postwar era. The CED had published what Senator Feingold referred to as a "strongly worded" report on campaign finance in March 1997, suggesting that "no reform is more urgently needed than a ban on national party 'soft money' financing." During the debate over the McCain-Feingold bill, which proposed to ban such soft money, Senator Mitch McConnell (R-Kentucky), who would later become the Senate Republican leader, referred disparagingly to the CED as a "little known business group," one that "until a few months ago no one had ever heard of."

"Let me tell the Chair and my colleagues a little about the CED, this 'little-known' group," Senator Feingold continued. The Senator went on to discuss the CED's founding in 1942, its early influence on the Bretton Woods Agreement, the Marshall Plan, the Council of Economic Advisers, and the Joint Economic Committee. After describing the CED's role in the Truman administration and its influence on the Marshall Plan, Senator Feingold entered into the *Congressional Record* letters praising the CED from presidents Eisenhower, Johnson, Carter, Reagan, and Bush I. He then described Senator McConnell's efforts to persuade more than a dozen corporate executives to resign from the CED (U.S. Congress 1999, 26954–26955). What is remarkable about this case is that rather than demonstrating the CED's significance, as Senator Feingold had intended to do, it actually showed just how far the organization had fallen by the late 1990s. Every one of the CED contributions that Feingold described occurred in the 1940s, a half-century earlier. Under such circumstances, Senator McConnell could perhaps be forgiven for thinking that the CED represented a "little-known" group that virtually "no one had ever heard of." It is inconceivable that a senator would have made such a claim in the 1950s or 1960s.[29]

As for the Business Roundtable, it too had continued to lose influence by the late 1990s. A 1997 article in *Fortune,* titled "The Fallen Giant," described the Roundtable's apparent demise. Back in the 1970s, the article suggests, the Roundtable was the "biggest and baddest lobbying group in Washington." Now, however, the group is "an also-ran in the rapidly changing world of Washington persuasion." In a poll of approximately 2,200 "Washington insiders" taken by the magazine, the Roundtable was ranked a lowly thirty-third among the most influential lobbying groups in Washington, "outranked by the likes of the American Trucking Association and the National Retail Federation." The NFIB, meanwhile, was ranked fourth while the NAM was ranked thirteenth and the Chamber of Commerce fifteenth.

One possible reason suggested by the article for the Roundtable's low ranking was the dominance of the Republican Party in Congress at the time. The other business groups were all more closely aligned with the Republicans (*Fortune,* December 8, 1997). In fact, earlier that year, Republicans in Congress had criticized the Roundtable for its alleged willingness to cooperate with Democrats. "Annoyed that big business has been hedging its bets by giving lots of money to the Democrats as well as the Republicans," the *Wall Street Journal* (January 9, 1997, 14) reported, "the GOP says the Business Roundtable . . . is about to receive an ultimatum: Stop donating so much to the Democrats and become more involved in partisan politics, or be denied access to Republicans in Congress." Less than two weeks later, *Roll Call* reported that the GOP was "turning up the heat on one of its key allies: the Business Roundtable. Still angry that big business failed to adequately bankroll their campaigns . . . last fall, the Republicans want the BRT to purge Democrats from its staff of nine directors" (Keller 1997). Congressional Republicans not only urged individual company CEOs to fire their Democratic lobbyists and replace them with Republicans, but they also exhorted the Roundtable to fire its executive director, Sam Maury, whom they accused of being a "Democratic operative." The Roundtable did offer some resistance. The organization, according to a spokeswoman, Johanna Schneider, was founded by CEOs "committed to improving public policy," and that—not funding political campaigns—was the group's appropriate role, she noted. The group also resisted the call to fire Maury, who remained in his position through April 2001.

The aggressiveness and hostility with which congressional Republicans attacked the Roundtable suggested a degree of vulnerability that the group did not experience in its earlier years. It is true that a delegation from the Roundtable had been attacked by Treasury Secretary Donald Regan during the debates over taxes in Ronald Reagan's first term, but criticism over a single idea—in this case whether to increase taxes on individuals or corporations—is a far cry from questioning a group's basic orientation, the core of its being. The attack by Republican politicians on the Business Roundtable recalled their earlier successful effort to bully the Chamber of Commerce into opposing the Clinton health care plan. Few observers of the Roundtable during its halcyon first decade would have expected the group to have ever had to endure such insolence by members of Congress, at least Republican ones. This weakened state may explain in part why the Roundtable was unwilling to confront the second President Bush over the deficit in 2004.

The Obama Health Care Plan

The failure of the Clinton health care plan kept the issue of broad reform off the political agenda for most of the following decade. The issue resurfaced in 2002, however, for the same reasons it had arisen in the late 1980s. In the four years after 1994, spending on health care had stabilized at slightly less than 14 percent of GDP, but between 2000 and 2002, this figure had jumped to 16 percent (see Figure 8.1). In the thirteen-month period up to February 2002, more than two million Americans lost their health insurance. Just as in the earlier period, this development raised concerns that the cost of caring for the uninsured would be shifted onto those who paid for health insurance, most notably companies. The explosion in health care costs had become so severe that a broad coalition formed that included such varied actors as the AFL-CIO and the Service Employees International Union (SEIU) on one hand, and the Chamber of Commerce, Business Roundtable, and Health Insurance Association of America (HIAA) on the other, as well as the American Medical Association (AMA) (*NYT,* February 9, 2002, A12).[30] The Bush administration did offer a plan that would provide tax credits for the uninsured to purchase insurance. The credit in the plan was viewed by critics as far too small to be helpful to low-income families, however, and the plan went nowhere.

If President Bush's plan for the uninsured disappeared into the background, the issue of health care did not. Discussions within the business community and between business and labor groups continued in the period leading up to the 2008 election. A full-page advertisement sponsored by the Roundtable, the SEIU, and the American Association of Retired Persons (AARP) appeared in the *New York Times* in January 2007. "If the nation's largest membership organization [the AARP] and leaders from the business and labor sectors can unite to call for meaningful action for America's future," the ad stated, then "surely our elected officials should be able to do the same" (*NYT,* January 17, 2007, A12). A *Times* article the following week described an "emerging consensus" about how to address the fact that forty-seven million Americans now lacked health insurance. Helen Darling, president of the National Business Group on Health (a descendant of the WBGH), noted that "there is more frustration and less acceptance of the current system among employers than we have ever seen in my 30 years in this field." John Castellani, the Roundtable's president, added that health care costs were "the single largest cost pressure that employers face—far exceeding energy, labor, material, even litigation." Safeway, for example, spent $1 billion on employee health care in 2006, more than its net income (*NYT,* January 25, 2007, C1). Three months later, an article in the *New York Times Magazine* described a news conference on Capitol Hill featuring Senator Ron Wyden (D-Oregon), Andy Stern (president of the SEIU), and Steve Burd (the CEO of Safeway). Two years earlier, Burd had mounted an attack on Safeway's unionized workforce, wringing significant concessions on health care costs and being vilified for it, even by local clergy. At the press conference, however, Burd described health care as "a crisis that demands immediate attention." "Working together, business, labor, government, consumer groups, and health-care providers can collectively solve this problem," he said (Cohn 2007). Perhaps this time, health care reform would actually be accomplished.

The likelihood of health care reform seemed even greater after Barack Obama was elected president in November 2008. At a meeting the following month, representatives from the Roundtable, America's Health Insurance Plans (an industry lobbying group known primarily by its acronym, AHIP), the NFIB, the AARP, and the major pharmaceutical firm Pfizer maintained that the possibility of change was far greater at this point than during the Clinton administration. "This is not 1994," John Castellani of the Roundtable pointed out (quoted in Broder 2008, B7). Sensing that reform was inevitable, both the insurance and pharmaceutical companies were open to compromise. As the *Times* put it in February 2009, "Many insurance executives say they are willing to accept stricter regulation, including a requirement to offer coverage to people with pre-existing medical conditions, if the federal government requires everyone to have coverage" (*NYT,* February 20, 2009, A16). The drug companies, represented by the Pharmaceutical Research and Manufacturers of America (PhRMA), negotiated a deal with the administration to provide $80 billion in cost savings on drugs in exchange for a promise to refrain from bargaining over Medicare drug prices and from importing inexpensive drugs from abroad (Starr 2011, 205).

Despite these compromises, achieving reform did not turn out to be easy. Congressional Republicans refused to participate in the discussion, and business groups, large and small, chipped away at various components of the plan. Among the most notable of these was the attempt by Congress to include the so-called public option, a government-run program that would serve as a health plan of last resort for individuals not covered by employer insurance. Large corporations, including the Roundtable, opposed this feature because in the initial plan the payments to physicians and hospitals would be capped. Big consumers of health insurance (most large corporations) feared that these price caps would lead health providers to pass the costs onto them. As Antonio Perez, the CEO of Eastman Kodak and chairman of the Roundtable, asserted, "That cost is going to come back to you one way or another" (*WSJ*, October 29, 2009, A4). Small firms, which seemingly stood to benefit from the program, opposed it on ideological grounds. The Roundtable did ultimately offer its qualified support to the Obama plan, but the insurance companies, despite their initial support, ultimately came to oppose it, as did the Chamber of Commerce and the NFIB. The AHIP had initially agreed to accept the idea of providing plans to those with preexisting conditions, as long as the government required universal coverage. When the Chamber of Commerce decided to oppose the plan, however, the five leading for-profit insurance companies sent a check for $86 million to the Chamber to run advertisements critical of the measure (Starr 2011, 218–220).

The Obama health care plan did eventually pass, of course (in March 2010), although only through a complicated reconciliation procedure that allowed Senate Democrats to pass the final bill without having to face a filibuster from Republicans. Although the business community—large and small, provider and consumer—was involved at all stages of the process, its role was far less central than it had been during the debate over the Clinton plan. Sociologist Paul Starr, who was involved in both plans, suggested that big business stayed "relatively aloof" and was "not a decisive force" during the debate over the Obama plan, perhaps diverted by its concern with the financial crisis (Starr 2011, 219–220). In one of the most crucial debates of our time, on an issue that was not only of great concern to its members but almost certainly of greater concern than it had been even a decade earlier, the corporate elite essentially sat on the sidelines. In a situation that cried out for leadership, this group was barely visible.

In June 2012, the Supreme Court upheld the constitutionality of the requirement that all Americans purchase health insurance or pay a penalty. This element of the plan was deemed necessary by the plan's proponents to ensure that individuals did not free ride on the new guarantee that applicants cannot be denied coverage due to a preexisting condition.[31] Although the plan that passed promised to greatly reduce the number of uninsured, its effects on costs in general, and its costs for business, remain unclear. On one hand, the creation of virtually universal coverage would be expected to greatly increase the level of preventive care as well as reduce the use of emergency rooms, both of which are likely to reduce costs. On the other hand, the plan does not place a cap on hospitalization costs nor does it change the basic fee-for-service model, in which there is no incentive for health providers to reduce unnecessary procedures. Whereas the insurance companies and other medical providers can thus be expected to remain highly profitable (if not more so), the major consumers of health care, the large corporations, may continue to face sharply increasing costs. This raises a question: Why have the large, health care consuming corporations been unwilling to consider further reform? Why, for example, have they refused to consider a single-payer system along the lines of the Canadian model, or at least a decoupling of health insurance from employment, along the lines of a proposal offered by Senator Ron Wyden?

Why No Single Payer?

One question has been lost in much of the discussion of both the Obama and Clinton health plans: Why did American business—at least those segments of business not involved in the insurance industry—not support a single-payer system? In 2009, according to an estimate I computed, Fortune 500 firms alone spent approximately $375 billion on health care for their employees, or an average of $750 million per firm. It is not surprising, given these costs, that many large corporations have been willing to support health care reform. The reforms that have dominated conventional political discussion in the United States have all involved the maintenance of the employer-sponsored system as the primary means of health insurance. Yet this still leaves employers responsible for insuring their employees, and it ensures that as health care costs rise, employers will continue to shoulder the bulk of the increase. In 1971, Canada established a national health insurance program in which all citizens are automatically covered by the government, which provides reimbursement to private care providers and sets rates in negotiation with them. At the time, health care costs relative to GDP were equal in the United States and Canada—approximately 7 percent in both countries. By 2008, the United States spent 16 percent of its GDP on health care, compared with 10.4 percent in Canada. Total health expenditures per person were 85 percent higher in the United States than Canada in 2008, despite the fact that more than forty million Americans had no coverage (compared to zero without coverage in Canada). Health outcomes are also superior in Canada. Infant mortality is lower than in the United States, and longevity is higher.[32]

One can have a legitimate discussion regarding the pros and cons of the two systems, and it is not my intention here to take a position on which one is superior. My concern is with why, given the far lower cost of health care in Canada and the fact that private employers there are relieved from the responsibility of providing health care for their employees, have American companies not considered a single-payer system as at least a potential alternative? Employer costs for health care are not zero even in a single-payer system, of course. First, employers in Canada often offer supplemental health insurance that provides benefits that go beyond those provided by the government program. Second, in any system, single payer or not, the cost of health care still has to be paid. Businesses would surely have to pay in higher taxes at least a portion of what they would no longer pay in compensation. On the other hand, these costs would be spread across the entire population of individuals and businesses. Moreover, the enormous decrease in administrative costs that would ensue with the shift to one source of insurance would virtually guarantee that the costs for business would be far lower in a single-payer system than in the current one.

One answer to the question of why American companies have not supported or even considered a single-payer system may be that some of them actually have, at least privately. Maria Farkas and I have begun a study in which we are interviewing corporate CEOs and human resources (HR) officers on health care. We have conducted only a small number of interviews at this point—two CEOs and three HR officials, all at Fortune 500 companies, all of whose CEOs were members of the Business Roundtable—but we have already observed an interesting pattern: the CEOs were more willing than the HR officials to consider alternatives to the American health care system. One CEO actually admitted to supporting a "European-style" system, while the second was neutral on the issue, providing a sensitive, reasoned discussion of the pros and cons of the two systems. The first CEO, in response to a question about what outcome from the health care debates he would like to have seen, told us:

I wanted a European style system. I wanted healthcare to be separated from an employer. . . . In most countries . . . there's a payroll, just like our Social Security system, deduction off of the employee's wages. There's an employer match. It provides access to two or three programs that the employee can choose which one and then citizens who [are unemployed] in these countries have access to government mandated or run, depending on the country. The Kennedy bill back in the mid-90s was fine. Hillary's proposals . . . would have been fine. We settled for a plan that was passable. It only provides coverage to about half of those who don't have coverage. It's going to be messy, as we are now working on the rules as to how it provides access to healthcare for the free agent population. It is not a pretty bill. It is an advance in many areas, but we're going to have to revisit this debate yet again in another decade.

As to why more of his colleagues did not appear to share his perspective, this CEO, who had not expressed his support for a European-style system in public, suggested two possible reasons. The first was that it was a function of simple ideology:

One [view] inside the business community is a belief that anything the government touches is bad. There is a strong libertarian component, and I share some of that, within the business community. . . . So there are many who, regardless of any pragmatic benefit to their company, are opposed in any way to government run programs, government mandated programs. It just doesn't sit well with their philosophy.

On the other hand, opposition to a government-run system was not entirely ideological, at least for some companies, he suggested:

I am not certain, by the way, that they are not often right. In this particular case, the quantitative data would argue that that's a wrong conclusion about healthcare [that the current American system is in fact less efficient than a European-style one], although the ability of the U.S. government to be exceptionally bad I don't dismiss, so I understand that. I understand it and I sympathize with it. Some of the really large companies who are really good and who have a highly centralized workforce can make an argument and in fact have pretty good quantitative data that they can do it more cheaply than what the average cost would be. . . . If you're a company where you have 80 to 90 percent of your employees parked in five or six locations, beyond any shadow of a doubt, you can, with a direct provision of health care . . . perform significantly better than average. There's . . . a big pocket of them that want nothing to do with a government program because the fact is they can do it cheaper.

It may be, then, that for some corporate consumers of health care, it might be more efficient to operate their own benefits programs than to abandon the practice and rely on a government-administered system. Yet this CEO believed that a state-run system would have been more efficient for his firm, and he suggested that the scale efficiencies of employer-administered plans, to the extent that they existed, were most likely to have been applicable to a small number of firms. My point here is not that one or the other position is correct. Rather, it is that the single-payer alternative was never a significant component of the public discussion over health care reform during either the Clinton or the Obama presidencies, despite the fact that such an approach might have made sense from an economic perspective. The corporate elite seemed to be so hamstrung by its own anti-government ideology that its members were unable to even consider an alternative that might have collectively saved them hundreds of billions of dollars.

Although these two CEOs were either supportive, or at least willing to acknowledge the possible advantages, of a government-administered system, all of the HR officers with whom we spoke were strongly opposed to such a system. One possible reason for the difference might be that the HR officers have a particular stake in the existing employer-based system. Indeed, Martin, in her study of the Clinton health plan, found that HR officers were especially concerned about what a government-administered system might imply for their livelihoods. Speaking about the position of business in the period prior to the debate over the Clinton plan, Martin (2000, 173) noted, "Company benefits managers, consultants, and insurance administrators were drawn to system rationalization, but not at the expense of their own livelihood." As one HR officer told her, "If someone said, 'Turn the management of the benefits system over to us,' I would have more of a willingness to say, 'Be my guest.' . . . But I'd also want to see what kind of job opportunities there are out there before phasing out the employer-based system" (ibid.).

The vested interests of company HR officers may provide one explanation for why two ideas proposed by Senator Ron Wyden gained little traction, even though both preserved the private health insurance industry. Wyden in 2006 had introduced a plan in which individuals and families, rather than receiving health insurance through their employers, would instead purchase insurance from state-regulated exchanges that would provide choices in the private insurance market. Wyden received support for his plan from a strikingly diverse group that included Andy Stern of the Service Employees International Union, Steve Burd of Safeway, and Utah Republican Senator Bob Bennett, who agreed to cosponsor the bill along with six other Republicans (Starr 2011, 178–180). The issue was still under discussion as late as 2009, but it never came close to gaining significant support, despite its bipartisan character (Murray 2009).[33] In October 2009, Senator Wyden proposed an amendment to the Baucus bill in the Senate that would have required employers to issue health care vouchers to their employees with which they could purchase private insurance if their companies failed to offer a sufficient number of plan choices. In a *Wall Street Journal* opinion piece in which he praised Wyden's idea, management consultant Matt Miller (2009) chided the Roundtable, the Chamber, and the NAM for "making sure that big business remains at the heart of the welfare state." "Big business thinks that giving employees this choice would be a calamity," Miller continued, "to which one can only ask: Have these business lobbies lost their minds?" In answer to the question of why big business had worked so hard to maintain its responsibility for employee health care when far less expensive alternatives were possible, Miller suggested an answer: "human resources executives threatened by change."[34]

Although it is certainly understandable why company HR officers might have a stake in maintaining the employer-based health care system, this does not mean that those at the top—the companies' CEOs—have the same interest. Yet the CEOs of large corporations, having made thousands of layoffs over the years, often benefiting as a consequence (at least in the short run), were either unwilling or unable to challenge their own subordinates on an issue that threatened to bankrupt their companies, not to mention the larger society. This suggests that what prevented a full consideration of the role of employer-based insurance and the possible value of a single-payer system was not the intransigence of human resource officers but rather the ineffectuality of the corporate elite itself.

Health care has been an especially intractable problem in American political life, and perhaps it is too much to ask of any group to have been able to solve this vexing issue. On the other hand, would the American corporate elite of the postwar period have allowed such an irrational, and potentially destructive, system to persist? There is no way to know the answer to this question, of course. Based on the evidence we have seen about the role of the postwar elite, however, I believe that the answer is no. The corporate elite of those years was far from perfect. American corporations certainly engaged in a plethora of actions that were destructive to both consumers and the environment, and the business and political elite of the time presided over a series of foreign policy excursions of which many Americans, both then and now, are not proud. The issue of health care, however, was not as critical prior to 1970 as it became in the 1980s and beyond. Had the sense of urgency been present in the postwar years, I believe that the American corporate elite, working with the moderate, pragmatic elements that—in part because of the elite—dominated the political process at the time, would have helped make a solution possible.

Conclusion

The American corporate elite, since the early 1990s, has become fragmented, without an organized group of pragmatic leaders capable of addressing the major issues with which the group has been confronted. No organized group has stepped forward to insist that Congress raise taxes on the wealthy—something that the corporate elite in earlier years was willing to do, and that occurred within a distribution of income and wealth that was far more equitable than what exists in the twenty-first century. No organized group has stepped forward to provide a positive plan for dealing with a health care crisis that threatens to bankrupt the nation. Organized business lobbies have been able to prevent reform from occurring, but an organized corporate elite has been unable to accomplish reform. Taxes and health care are not the only issues on which the corporate elite has been negligent. Despite three significant financial crises since the late 1980s— following a half-century of remarkable stability—members of the financial community have continued to thwart attempts to regulate the system, even when such regulations might prevent the collapse of their own firms. In the debate over the debt ceiling in the summer of 2011, the best the Business Roundtable could come up with was a bland statement imploring Congress and the president to fix the problem without providing a single specific recommendation for how to do so.

The corporate elite has lost its ability to restrain the most insidious elements of American political life, contributing to an extremism in politics that the country has not seen in nearly a century, if not longer. Rather than helping to provide a moderating counterweight to these elements of what Richard Hofstadter (1965) famously called the "paranoid style in American politics," the corporate elite has allowed itself to be bullied and cowed by them, unable to stand up against a group that it had helped to marginalize in earlier years. This is an elite that, rather than leading, has retreated into narrow self-interest, its individual elements increasingly able to get what they want in the form of favors from the state but unable collectively to address any of the problems whose solution is necessary for their own survival.

9 ||| The Ineffectual Elite

The goal of corporations is to generate profits, and returns to shareholders. But corporations, as they grew large in the late nineteenth century, became more than just profit-making machines. Given their size, they became a presence in their local communities as well as on the national scene. Although the corporation was the source of great wealth, this wealth was sometimes achieved at the expense of the firm's workers and customers, and it also created costs that were borne by the larger society, including despoliation of the natural environment within which it operated. The costs that the firm created—externalities, in the term used by economists—led to resistance. Employees in particular objected to their low wages and difficult working conditions. In response to this, they attempted to organize to secure better conditions for themselves. In some cases, they began to question the viability of the wage-labor system itself. Concerned that the private enterprise system might be in peril, a group of farsighted financiers and industrialists organized the National Civic Federation in 1900. In subsequent decades, corporations instituted a system of workplace benefits, including medical and disability protection. In the 1930s, although most business leaders opposed an active role for the state, others believed that it was necessary for government to address the shortcomings of the market economy. During World War II, as the positive role of the state became increasingly evident to American business leaders, another farsighted group formed the Committee for Economic Development (CED).

The corporate leaders who led the CED believed in the market system, and they were concerned, just as the Civic Federation had been, about the potential power of organized labor. The CED also believed, however, that the days of untrammeled free market capitalism were gone, and that both private and government-led economic management would be necessary for the market economy to survive. In order to maintain the system from which their privileges derived, they believed that it would be necessary to attend to the well-being of the broader population. This meant a high level of employment, the alleviation of poverty, the amelioration of racial disadvantage, and the provision of sufficient purchasing power in the population to consume the goods that American business was so proficient at producing. The individuals who presided over this system were a minority within the larger business community, but they had a disproportionate level of power. They had ready access to government policy makers and often served as cabinet members and advisers in both Democratic and Republican administrations. They were not altruists. They were pragmatists, who understood that a moderate approach to politics would provide the best chance of strengthening and preserving the society, and their positions within it. They also had a sense of responsibility, gained perhaps from their experiences during the Depression and World War II, an understanding that they had at least some obligation to the larger community as well as to their firms.

The system over which these elites presided worked smoothly for nearly three decades following the end of the war. There were problems to be sure. The United States was not only involved in a dangerous arms race with the Soviet Union, but it continued to back a series of brutal dictatorships in all parts of the world. In the 1960s—a period of unprecedented prosperity—the nation became bogged down in a war that contributed not only to grave internal conflict but also to the subsequent economic malaise of the 1970s. In addition to its foreign policy debacles, the nation was torn by poverty, racism, and a repressive social environment at home, all of which contributed to the turmoil of the decade. As we acknowledge the often positive role that the American corporate elite played in the postwar period, it is worthwhile to remember that the United States of that era was not a utopia, and there is no need to be nostalgic about it.

In terms of both economics and politics, however, the system was considerably more effective than what succeeded it. Economically, not only was the country becoming increasingly affluent, but the majority of the population was experiencing the benefits of this affluence. Median real family income nearly doubled between 1947 and 1970 (Mishel, Bernstein, and Allegretto 2007), and the poverty rate declined from 23 to 12 percent in the decade between 1959 and 1969.[1] Inequality was also relatively low. From 1946 through 1979, the top decile of the American income distribution earned between 31 and 32 percent of national income annually, after averaging in the 40 to 45 percent range between 1917 and 1940 (and before returning to those earlier rates by the late 1990s). The income share of the top 1 percent of earners also dropped sharply during the postwar period, before rising again after 1980 (Piketty and Saez 2003, 9–10).

Politically, the American system also worked relatively effectively. Certainly there were problems: a seniority system that allowed long-tenured Southern legislators to stymie civil rights reform for many years, and a nominating system in which party bosses in smoke-filled rooms rather than the voting public largely determined who would stand for election as president are two examples. Yet even with these problems, the executive and legislative branches were able to produce a series of accomplishments. Democrats and Republicans opposed one another, at times as fiercely as in the conflicts of the twenty-first century. Compromise on both sides of the aisle was the rule, however, and members of Congress found it necessary to achieve genuine gains for their voters, even with the relatively low number of competitive congressional districts. Extremist elements existed in the United States, just as they do today, but the ideas of the Far Right were marginalized, seen as part of the political fringe.[2] When this fringe movement managed to nominate one of its own as the Republican presidential candidate in 1964, he was defeated in a near-historic landslide by a liberal Democrat. Behind this well-functioning, moderate political system was a corporate elite that was both constrained by the countervailing forces of organized labor and the state, and that helped keep things in check by pragmatically agreeing to work with these forces.

Perhaps this system could not have lasted forever. The willingness of American corporations to accept the moderate political environment was certainly made easier by the nation's global economic power. When that power began to recede, as it almost inevitably did as the rest of the world began to recover from World War II, it became increasingly necessary for Americans to fight over the spoils of a shrinking pie. Yet the turn that the American corporate elite took in response to this predicament—its successful attack on organized labor and government regulation—ironically proved to be the beginning of its own undoing. The elite, by aligning itself with what had been formerly considered a group of extremists, sowed the seeds of its own destruction. It took several years for this to become evident, but by the early 1990s the transformation had largely occurred. From a group with a moderate, pragmatic orientation, the corporate elite was now reduced to a collection of firms, powerful in their ability to gain specific benefits for themselves but no longer able or willing to address issues of concern to the larger business community or the larger society. This development, already evident by the 1990s, reached a crescendo in the twenty-first century, reflected in the gridlock that came to characterize American politics at both the national and local level.

Fragmentation, Conservatism, or Both?

But why has the American corporate elite become so unable to act collectively to address issues of business-wide or society-wide concern? Is it the result of increased fragmentation, or has the group simply become more conservative? The answer is both. The American corporate elite became more conservative in the 1970s, leading to its assault on government regulation and organized labor. Its success in this assault led to the group's subsequent dissolution.

The American business community has always had significant divisions, but in the postwar era there was a relatively high level of unity among the largest firms (Useem 1984). By the 1990s, even the elite corporations had become less cohesive (Barnes and Ritter 2001). This is reflected in the declining density in the network of board of director overlaps—a development that accelerated in the first decade of the twenty-first century (Chu and Davis 2011)—as well as the declining prominence of the old, New York–based commercial banks (Davis and Mizruchi 1999). It is reflected most importantly, however, in the inability of the contemporary corporate elite, unlike its predecessors, to effectively engage in collective action to advance its interests.

American corporations have also become more conservative. Much, although not all, of this shift occurred in the 1970s, when large firms began to aggressively attack both government regulation and organized labor. It is difficult in the 2000s to imagine a majority of large-firm CEOs expressing a belief that the government should provide jobs to alleviate unemployment, as this group did in the early 1970s (Barton 1985). As recently as the early 1990s, the largest American firms, represented by the Business Roundtable, continued to maintain a moderate stance in certain areas, including their willingness to support tax increases and to consider a national health care program. Whatever pragmatism and moderation that remained was thwarted by the inability of these firms to mount a sustained effort to address these issues, however. The Roundtable signed on to the Bush tax cuts, despite their effect on the deficit, and the group proved unable to provide significant input into the debate over President Obama's health care plan or the debt ceiling crisis of 2011.

Private Goods, Collective Bads

The fact that the American corporate elite is no longer able to engage in effective collective action does not mean that its members have lost power. On the contrary, American corporations, including the financial institutions, have become extremely proficient at gaining favors for themselves. They have gained unparalleled access to legislators. They have enormous resources. They have developed historically high levels of political skill. And they have enjoyed the support of a sympathetic judiciary. That American corporations make campaign contributions and engage in lobbying is not new, nor is the fact that they hire former government officials and/or see their own officers appointed to government positions. Corporate efforts to influence the national government have grown enormously, however. In 1980, corporate political action committees contributed a total of $31 million to congressional campaigns. By 2006, corporate PACs contributed $278 million to congressional campaigns (Burris 2009). The number of lobbyists representing S&P 500 companies increased from 1,475 in 1981 to 2,765 in 2005. Although this rate of increase does not seem overwhelming, it dwarfs that of the lobbyists representing labor unions, which increased only 9 percent between 1981 and 2005 (compared to 87 percent among corporate lobbyists) to a total of 403 (Drutman 2010).

Unlike lobbying, which is typically devoted toward influencing specific legislative outcomes, campaign contributions appear to have been motivated in the past primarily by a quest for access to legislators (Clawson, Neustadtl, and Scott 1992). In part because of this, it has been extremely difficult to demonstrate that campaign contributions actually affect the legislators' behavior (Mizruchi 1992, chapter 5). More recent evidence, however, suggests that campaign contributions, as well as lobbying activity, do positively affect a firm's profitability (Hillman 2005; Rabern 2009). The 2010 Citizens United decision by the United States Supreme Court, which allows corporations and labor unions to make unlimited contributions to groups attempting to influence elections, may in the future shed further light on whether corporate contributions lead to measurable electoral outcomes. For now, a strong case can be made that when it comes to getting what they want for themselves, American corporations have rarely, if ever, been more powerful.

When it comes to accomplishing broader goals, however, the largest corporations in the United States are less effective. As Drutman found in his interviews with corporate lobbyists, these individuals believe that given the nature of what they can receive from government—in terms of earmarks, contracts, revisions to the tax code, and other relatively narrow concerns—the companies they represent are most effective when they work individually rather than through trade associations or larger business associations. Although the benefits of individual action may have been evident even in earlier decades, the lobbyists themselves believe that these benefits have increased since the 1980s, in concert with the changes in the corporate world that we observed in Chapter 7. One indication of the growing emphasis on firm-specific activities is that lobbying efforts on appropriations issues, in which funds are often directed toward the benefit of individual firms, increased nearly fourfold between 1998 and 2008, suggesting further attempts by firms to gain individually tailored advantages (Drutman 2010, 77).

That this increase in narrowly focused lobbying corresponds with a decline in the ability of corporations to act collectively to address larger issues is not an accident. It is consistent with what we have seen with regard to tax policy and health care, and it affects other significant issues as well, including financial reform. The American corporate elite, although increasingly adept at lobbying for specific favors, is increasingly incapable of solving problems that concern not only the larger society from which its privileges derive but even its own collective interests. American corporations have power without efficacy.

One could argue that the gridlock that now characterizes the American political system is a direct outcome of the inability of corporations to exercise collective—as opposed to individual—influence. There has long been an element of extremism in American politics, especially on the right. With the exception of the Goldwater nomination in 1964, however, this group of right-wing extremists was, during the postwar period, at the margins of American politics, outside the realm of legitimate political discourse. Despite its association with certain elements of American business, it was thoroughly rejected by the postwar corporate elite. In fact, one could argue that the relative moderation exhibited by the leaders of large American corporations played a significant role in keeping these elements in check.

When the corporate elite began to move rightward in the 1970s, however, it slowly, if inadvertently, found itself aligned with these extremist elements. In its early stages, this alliance worked well for the elite. Its members were able to accomplish their goals of weakening government regulation and organized labor, without having to face the consequences that might have occurred—such as attempts to return to the gold standard—had the extremist elements achieved prominence. As the Far Right elements grew stronger, however, the elites found themselves increasingly unable to control them. By the early 1990s, these extremists had begun to wrest control of the Republican Party, evident both in the response to George H. W. Bush's tax increase and then, especially, in the reaction to Bill Clinton's health care plan. As we saw in the previous chapter, Republicans in Congress actually intimidated some members of the corporate elite into dropping their support for Clinton's reform effort. During President Obama's own health care reform efforts, the corporate elite stood by as members of the Tea Party denounced the plan, often with fabricated claims, despite the fact that many large corporations had supported it. Seemingly cowed by conservatives in the Republican Party, satisfied with their ability to gain specific political favors for themselves, and mired in a state of disarray that rendered collective action virtually impossible, the leading American corporations sat passively by as the nation's political life lurched from stagnation and gridlock on one hand, to aggressive efforts at reactionary change on the other.

Did Globalization Cause the Decline?

I have argued that the reason for the American corporate elite's apparent lack of concern for American society is a result of its lack of organization as well as a shift in ideology. I have suggested that this resulted from a decline in the constraints on the group's ability to pursue its members' narrow self-interests, brought on by the decline of organized labor, the weakening of the ameliorative state, the abdication by the banks of their role as purveyors of interfirm consensus, and the growing vulnerability of management after the takeover wave of the 1980s. But is it possible that the entire process can be explained by the onset of globalization? After all, the most recent explosion of international economic activity occurred in the 1970s, just as the elite began its turn to the right. Perhaps, as a number of commentators have suggested (see, for example, Whitman 1999), it is simply the increasing international competition in which American firms found themselves that accounts for their retreat into narrow, short-term concerns. Instead of an unchallenged domination of highly concentrated markets, American corporations were, by the 1970s, faced with a level of competition that placed not only their profitability but even their survival at stake. This threat was seen as forcing corporations to rethink everything about their operations, including their commitment to their employees and their communities. When competition was low and profits were flowing, the argument suggests, it was relatively easy for firms to virtually guarantee their employees secure employment and opportunities for advancement, and it was possible for firms to concern themselves with their local communities as well. The emergence of a more competitive international arena called everything into question. Faced with declining profit margins and no prospect of a return to the period of unquestioned American dominance, no previous accommodation was off-limits. In addition to layoffs of blue-collar workers, even management was now subject to the consequences of downsizing. Concerns about the community were a luxury that corporations could no longer afford. And with companies now moving their workforces offshore and threatening to hasten the process, the state lost whatever power it had to mitigate the damage. With the economy now fully globalized, proponents of this view suggest, American workers—as well as the state—lost whatever leverage they might otherwise have had.

This argument has much to recommend it. International trade did grow rapidly in the 1970s after being relatively dormant for several decades, in part as a consequence of the two world wars and in part a consequence of the relatively high level of protectionism that characterized the earlier period. As Fligstein (2001, 196–197) shows, international trade as a percentage of American GDP grew from about 9 percent in 1969 to 16 percent by 1981, before leveling off. For the United States, imports as a percentage of GDP nearly doubled between 1970 and 1980, from 5.4 to 10.6 percent, and continued to increase thereafter, reaching nearly 15 percent in 2000.[3] One could argue that with the proliferation of outsourcing, it became less necessary to care about the fate of, say, the American educational system or the general welfare of the nation. After all, if American high school graduates cannot read, certainly those in China can.

There is reason to question the tenability of these claims, however. First, despite its increase in the 1970s, international trade was far from new historically. In 1913, on the eve of World War I, international trade had reached approximately 14 percent of world GDP, nearly as high as in the post-1980 period (Bairoch and Kozul-Wright 1996, 6; Fligstein 2001, 196). Second, and more importantly, Western European countries have been far more involved in international trade than has the United States, yet the governments of these nations have been far more active than the American government in providing a social safety net for their citizens. In 1995, for example, imports as a percentage of GDP in Germany, France, and Britain ranged from 21.5 to 28.4 percent, while that for the United States was only 12.3 percent. Ten years later, the corresponding figures for the three European countries ranged from 27.0 to 36.1 percent, while that for the United States was 16.1 percent.[4] Studies by Garrett (1995) and Rodrik (1998) suggest that Western European nations actually compensated for their heavy involvement in world trade by increasing their social spending. These findings call into question the claim that the rightward turn in American politics was a necessary consequence of globalization. On the contrary, they suggest that there is no automatic means by which governments respond to an increase in foreign trade. Instead, the manner in which a government reacts to economic globalization appears to depend on the nature of a country's domestic politics.

There is evidence, however, that the recent retrenchment of welfare policies among Western European nations has corresponded with a fragmentation of the corporate elites in their societies. Evidence of declining network density exists for Germany (Beyer and Hoppner 2003; Höpner and Krempel 2003), the Netherlands (Heemskerk 2007), and Switzerland (David, Ginalski, Rebmann, and Schnyder 2009), and Heemskerk has documented a decline in class consciousness among Dutch elites as well. Correlation does not prove causation, of course, and I am not suggesting that a decline in elite cohesion is the single or even the largest cause of the retrenchment of European welfare states. It does represent one possible factor, however, and it is consistent with my argument for what has occurred in the United States. Regardless of the role of elite fragmentation, the preceding discussion suggests that whether a state increases or decreases its social safety net depends primarily on the internal politics of the nation, and not on the globalization of production.

Finally, there is little compelling evidence to suggest that globalization played a major role in either the decline in American manufacturing employment or the sharp rise in economic inequality that has concurrently ensued. In a review of several studies, Richard Cooper (1995) noted that the rise in imports accounted for only five to six percent of the decline in American manufacturing employment during the 1980s, and only 10 percent of the relative decline in wages among unskilled workers.[5] It is true that the increased overseas production activities of American firms as well as the growing dependence on imports might have contributed to the free trade policies that gained support in the 1990s from both Democrats and Republicans. It is less clear that these policies had an effect on domestic government policies in the United States. As we saw in the case of European countries, the government could have increased the social safety net to address the deleterious consequences of free trade had there been sufficient pressure to do so. The political behavior of the American corporate elite was undoubtedly affected by the growing international competition that American firms began to experience in the 1970s. This competition is in part what led the elite to mount its attacks on government regulation and organized labor in the first place. It does not follow, however, that international competition was the source of the elite's subsequent lack of effectiveness in addressing its own collective domestic concerns. This outcome must be explained by factors other than globalization.

There is one other issue related to globalization that might have affected the behavior of American corporations. Perhaps the decline of the American corporate elite is a consequence of the rise of an alternative: an increasingly cohesive, transnational "capitalist class." A number of scholars (Sklair 2001; Kentor and Jang 2004; Staples 2006) and popular writers (Rothkopf 2008) have argued that such a class exists. As with the arguments about globalization in general, this claim has some support. From the time that David Rockefeller helped organize the Trilateral Commission in the 1970s, there have been efforts by elites in various nations to address global issues. Certainly the World Trade Organization, and even the Organization for Economic Cooperation and Development, are based in part on this model. The annual meeting of the World Economic Forum at Davos, Switzerland, attended by business and government elites from dozens of nations, certainly has the trappings of a worldwide version of the kinds of "ruling class" gettogethers that appear in the writings of C. Wright Mills and G. William Domhoff. There is also evidence that the decline in the cohesion of interfirm networks in European nations such as Switzerland is in part due to the expansion of ties cross-nationally (David, Ginalski, Rebmann, and Schnyder 2009). A careful examination of the evidence leads to a different, or at least more tempered, conclusion, however. In the most comprehensive study to date of cross-national connections among firms, William K. Carroll (2010; see also Carroll and Fennema 2004) shows that although the number of cross-national ties among Western European nations, as well as between Western European and North American firms, has grown over time, there is little evidence to suggest that an international economic elite has superseded the various national ones. There is even less evidence to suggest that the international ties of firms from the United States come close to exceeding their domestic ones, even as the latter have declined over time. Again, international ties exist, but they are too few and far between to suggest that membership in a worldwide corporate elite has become a newly salient identity for American corporate leaders.

The Decline of the American Empire?

More serious than the consequences of globalization is the possibility that the corporate elite's lack of leadership may be contributing to the overall weakening of American society. In a study remarkable for its breadth and historical sweep, Richard Lachmann (2009, 2011) has examined the rise and fall of several European empires, including Rome, Habsburg Spain, the Netherlands, czarist Russia, and Britain. There are a number of widely held views for why these empires declined, but Lachmann advances a unique and compelling argument. All of them, with the exception of the British, eventually fell because their elites began to hoard resources for themselves, thus depriving their governments of the funds necessary to maintain their societies' infrastructures. The British Empire was successful for a longer period than the others because its parliamentary system became a setting in which the landed gentry and large merchants competed for control. This competition forced these parties into coalitions that transcended the interests of particular groups, leading the elites to contribute sufficient tax revenue to keep the state on a strong footing. As Lachmann put it (2011, 46), "British elites forged agreements that controlled policy and operated the state's fiscal levers in their collective self-interest." In seventeenth-century Spain, in contrast, when the Habsburgs attempted to tax the Spanish nobility to pay for the empire's war efforts, they were rebuffed. This forced the state to scale back its military operations, which led to the decline of Spain's position in European power politics (Lachmann 2009, 59–60).

It is important to exercise caution in drawing conclusions from such a comparison, but there do appear to be parallels between Lachmann's description of the later stages of the Roman, Spanish, Dutch, and Russian empires and the contemporary United States. Although those proclaiming the death knell for American society have been proven wrong in the past—note, for example, the widespread belief in the 1980s that the United States would be surpassed by Japan—there are a series of troubling long-term problems that even after the American economy fully rebounds from the 2008 financial crisis (as it almost certainly will at some point) are not likely to disappear. China may or may not prove to be another Japan—a society apparently on the verge of world economic domination only to sink back into the fold—but the Chinese have certainly taken steps that may allow their country to surpass the United States. Whereas China has spent an enormous effort building up its infrastructure and funding scientific research and education, the United States has continued to lag in these areas. Federal spending on general science, space, and technology declined from 4 percent of the budget in 1967—at the peak of the nation's postwar dominance—to 0.9 percent in 2009 (Lachmann 2011, 47). While China spends billions on state-of-the-art rail systems and other forms of green energy, travel by road and air have become increasingly congested in the

United States, while passenger train service is deemed prohibitively expensive and barely survives in a single region of the country. One 2011 report suggested that nearly 12 percent of the bridges in the United States were in need of replacement.[6]

Other aspects of American society are also experiencing severe strains, in particular the educational system. According to a report distributed by the U.S. Army in 2010, nearly one-fourth of American high school students who took the army's entrance exam failed. Even more disturbing, the group that took the test was already a relatively elite subset of the young adult population: 75 percent of those in the 17-to-24 age group failed to qualify to even take the test, due to either a lack of physical fitness, failure to graduate from high school, or the presence of a criminal record.[7] Thirty percent of high school–age Americans fail to graduate, including more than half of African American males, and nearly half of those who do graduate have reading skills insufficient for a first-year college course.[8] Even the relatively privileged Americans who manage to attend college appear to be lagging in the skills necessary to handle professional-level occupations (Arum and Roksa 2011). Meanwhile, infant mortality in the United States is at Third World levels, and the poverty rate reached 15.1 percent in 2010, a figure exceeded only once—nearly three decades earlier in 1983—since the 1960s.[9] Childhood obesity has become a national epidemic, more than tripling between 1980 and 2008, a combination of poor diet and inactivity.[10]

One must be careful to avoid an overly alarmist tone in discussing these subjects. To take the example of education, there has probably never been a time in which a majority of Americans have left high school with a thorough complement of academic skills (although this was undoubtedly less of a problem in earlier years because it was possible for individuals with little or no education to earn a decent living in the manufacturing sector, an opportunity that has all but vanished in recent decades). Nor is the corporate elite necessarily to blame for these problems. The causes of the deficiencies in education, health, and infrastructure in general are many, and in some cases are the result of global forces that are beyond the control of any one group.

The issue here is not whether the corporate elite is to blame for the problems of American society but what, if anything, the group has done to address them. Unfortunately, like the elites in the declining Dutch and Spanish empires, today's American elites appear to be focused on accumulating resources for themselves while showing little regard for the precarious state of the national treasury. The budget deficit is indeed large and threatens to become a significant drag on the nation's economy in the coming years. A major (albeit not the only) reason for the size of the deficit is the extremely low tax rates currently paid by the wealthiest Americans. At a time when inequality is at its highest level since the 1920s, the top marginal tax rate is barely one-third of what it was in the 1950s and barely one-half of what it was during the Reagan presidency, and capital gains taxes are at their lowest rate since the 1920s. At a point at which the very wealthy are perhaps better able to contribute than at any time in history, the rates that they pay are in many cases—given the low taxes on capital gains—lower than the rates paid by those at the middle of the income scale.

Some authors have suggested that the wealthy will resist redistribution with all necessary means. In a striking study, Jeffrey Winters (2011, chapter 5) describes the rise of what he calls the "income defense industry," a group of accountants, lawyers, bankers, and investment advisers whose job is to protect the assets of the most prosperous Americans. This group of very wealthy individuals—a fraction of the top 1 percent of earners—constitutes an oligarchy, Winters argues, a group that has both the goal and the means to ensure that the government allows it to accumulate wealth without limit. To provide a sense of the extent of this group's wealth, in 2007, the top one-hundredth of 1 percent of American earners (approximately 15,000 individuals) received more income than the bottom ninety-six million (Winters 2011, 216). Given the enormous increases in the compensation of corporate chief executives in recent years, many of these individuals have now moved from the "ordinary rich" into a level that places them in this top category. This may be another reason for the corporate elite's unwillingness to support tax increases to address the deficit, as well as for its unwillingness to accept responsibility for more general social problems.

On the other hand, as compelling as Winters's study is, the view that wealthy Americans are unwilling to increase their contributions to the treasury may be open to question. After billionaire Warren Buffett suggested that his tax rate, which is lower than that of his secretary, be increased, a *Wall Street Journal* blog reported the results of a survey in which 61 percent of respondents with net worth of $5 million or more expressed support for a tax increase on those with incomes of greater than $1 million.[11] This suggests that wealthy individuals might be willing to support a higher tax rate for themselves. Yet despite this willingness, not a single significant organization of corporate leaders has endorsed such a suggestion.[12] This stands in contrast to the corporate elite of previous decades. As we saw in Chapter 8, the Business Roundtable in the early 1980s called for an increase in individual tax rates to address the deficit at the time. The budget deficit of the twenty-first century, both prior to and after the crisis of 2008, has provided an opportunity for the corporate elite to take a stand in the national interest, one that, if enacted, would have little if any tangible effect on their own standard of living.[13] As of this writing, neither the Roundtable nor any other major business organization has been willing to come forward. This failure of responsibility is reminiscent of the elites of the declining empires described by Lachmann.

There are reasons for even the wealthiest Americans to be concerned about the level of inequality. The decade leading up to the Great Depression saw rising levels of inequality (Piketty and Saez 2003, 8). The lack of societal-level purchasing power was a concern even among corporate executives in the 1920s (as we saw in Chapter 3), and if Keynesian theory is correct, it was likely a precipitating cause of the Depression. Keynesian theory appeared to stop working in the 1970s, as traditional policy measures failed to put a dent in the simultaneously high levels of unemployment and inflation.[14] Suggestions that the problem of the American economy was now insufficient supply due to a lack of productivity rather than insufficient demand began to fall on receptive ears. If a high level of inequality led to a shortage of purchasing power, then it is certainly possible that the relatively low level of inequality in the postwar period—accompanied by nearly three decades of significant wage increases—may have created upward pressure on prices. If so, one could argue that the inflation of the 1970s represented a mirror image of the situation that preceded the Great Depression.

Since that time, however, nearly three decades of sharply increasing inequality appear to have brought us full circle. As inequality increased during this period, so did productivity. From 1980 to 2005, productivity among nonfarm American workers increased at an average yearly rate more than five times greater than wages (Harrison 2009, 2). As productivity increased and incomes failed to keep pace, we entered a period that resembled the 1920s. The causes of the financial collapse of 2008 are many, but a lack of collective purchasing power, as the population found itself unable to keep pace with its rising debt levels, could very possibly be one of them. Perhaps one reason that a majority of the wealthy in the United States now appear willing to pay more taxes is that they realize that it is in their long-term interest to prevent another similar collapse.

Yet regardless of the extent to which wealthy individuals are concerned about preventing another financial crisis, the organizations at the center of the financial community have been fighting virtually every attempt to regulate their industry, with every resource at their disposal. These institutions have done this despite the fact that requirements such as minimum reserve levels could prevent their own firms from imploding should another crisis occur. As with other aspects of national policy, the twenty-first-century corporate elite appears to be more interested in accumulating further wealth in the short run, without concern for its own interest in the long run. By standing idly by during the depletion of the national treasury and the starving of the nation's infrastructure and by failing to step forward to recommend a tax increase, the American corporate elite of the twenty-first century is following in the footsteps of the declining European empires dating back to the Romans. In doing so, it has begun to resemble, in Lachmann's words, a collection of "first class passengers on a sinking ship" (2011, 49).

A Light in the Wilderness?

There have, of course, been numerous efforts by individual business leaders and particular companies to address the problems not only of American society but of global concern as well. Bill Gates has given billions of dollars to address worldwide health problems. In addition to his advocacy of tax increases, Warren Buffett has contributed billions to Gates's foundation. Dozens of large corporations have signed on to the Pew Foundation's project to work toward the reduction of greenhouse gas emissions. Others have engaged in a range of socially responsible activities, from Merck & Company's efforts to fight river blindness in Africa to the efforts of major firms in Cleveland and Columbus to address housing and children's issues, respectively, even when there are no clear economic benefits to doing so (Margolis and Walsh 2003; Marquis, Glynn, and Davis 2007). Even Wal-Mart, for all the criticism it has received for its labor policies, has earned praise for its steps to emphasize waste reduction and renewable energy.

Starbucks CEO Howard Schultz has made a conscious effort to adopt socially responsible practices with respect to the firms' employees, suppliers, and customers.[15] Clearly, there is no shortage of corporations making efforts to do good. Yet important as these efforts have been, they have lacked two features that characterized those of the postwar corporate elite. First, they are piecemeal, pursued by individuals or firms, unilaterally or in small groups, but they are not part of a larger, organized, corporate-wide effort. Second, they are entirely private. Nowhere is there an acknowledgement of the CED's dictum in its 1971 statement about the need for a business-government partnership, based on the realization that private efforts, no matter how useful, are not a substitute for a sustained government-directed approach.[16]

But to what extent could the corporate elite address societal problems in a systematic way even if it wanted to? As I have noted, some of the difficulties that afflict the United States are the fault of no one in particular but are simply the outcome of global forces over which no single entity has control. American corporations were not going to be able to dominate the world economy forever. The rising standard of living within the United States created pressures on resources that led to distributional conflicts that were probably unavoidable.

Other problems have been created or exacerbated by groups that have little to do with the business community. Although many critics blame the problems of the American political system on the intransigence of both major parties, the evidence is quite clear that the Republican Party has moved sharply to the right while the Democrats have remained relatively moderate. This can be seen in Figure 9.1, constructed by political scientist Keith T. Poole, which shows the mean levels of conservatism among all Republicans, all Democrats, Southern Democrats, and Northern Democrats in the House of Representatives from 1879 through 2011.[17]

Northern Democrats have maintained virtually identical ideological positions since the early 1960s, positions that are relatively moderate compared to the Democratic positions during the earlier part of the twentieth century. Republicans, on the other hand, have become continuously and sharply more conservative since the early 1980s. Virtually the entire increase in the gap between Democrats and Republicans over the past three decades can be accounted for by the Republicans' increasing conservatism. Still, even if the rightward turn of the Republican Party bears a disproportionate level of responsibility for the inability of legislators in Washington to achieve compromise, it is clear that something is broken in Washington for which political officials of both parties will have to find solutions.

Nor can we Americans escape blame for the failures of our political system. The level of apathy among the public has long been a concern in American politics, but the issue has more serious consequences when members of Congress and the White House face the kinds of pressures from special interests that today's public officials experience. The fickle nature of public opinion (in which Wall Street is blamed for the financial crisis one month and the government is blamed for trying to fix it the next, in which the government is accused of meddling in the economy and then blamed when oil prices increase due to the movements of global market forces), the simplistic response to complex issues (unemployment has increased, so it must be the fault of the incumbent president), the rejection of science, including the willful ignorance about global warming and evolution—all of these are problems that place what are sometimes intractable constraints on

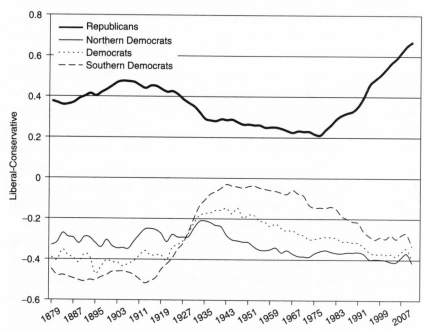

Figure 9.1. Party means on Liberal-Conservative dimension, House, 1879–2011.

Source: http://voteview.com/political_polarization.asp.

elected officials, even those who genuinely want to do the right thing. Certainly the role of money in politics may dwarf these other factors, and the public's own views are in part a function of disinformation campaigns mounted by opportunistic politicians, campaigns that appear to have grown even more severe in the wake of the Citizens United decision.[18] Still, we Americans must place part of the blame on ourselves.

Ultimately, however, one has to raise the question of whether the problems of political gridlock, as well as apathy, fickleness, and ignorance are themselves symptoms of a lack of leadership. Would Congress be able to wallow in dysfunction if it had a strong group of responsible leaders to hold it accountable? Would extremist politicians be able to contribute to the rejection of the science underlying global warming if they were not encouraged to do so by self-serving elements in the energy industry? Would other nations be moving ahead of the United States in stem-cell research if the corporate elite were not willing to tolerate the mentality that underlies the opposition to it? Would school boards be able to even consider the teaching of creationism in the schools if the business community were to put a stop to it, on the ground of national security? Surely we do not want to trust our entire future to a group of corporate officers who are bound to have concerns other than the general public interest in mind. On the other hand, at one time the United States had a corporate elite that, although admittedly self-serving—note the CED's mantra of "enlightened self-interest"—had at least a modicum of concern for the well-being of the larger society, an understanding that one does not kill the goose that lays the golden eggs. Enlightened self-interest may be self-interest, but it is very different from narrow, parochial self-interest. Given the choice, our society would be much better off with the former.

But what about the limits of corporate power, even for good? Could the corporate elite engender positive changes even if it wanted to? The perilous state of American politics certainly gives one pause. Large corporations were unable to secure health care reform in the 1990s, and they were left standing on the sidelines during the debate over the Obama health care plan. The efforts that companies have made, including those described above, have made barely a dent in confronting the daunting problems with which we are faced. Yet we may have no choice but to rely on the corporate elite. In a 2005 column, *New York Times* writer Thomas Friedman bemoaned the seeming inability of American business leaders to address the problems of the society:

> As a nation, we have a mounting education deficit, energy deficit, budget deficit, health care deficit and ambition deficit. The administration is in denial on this, and Congress is off on Mars. And yet, when I look around for the group that has both the power and interest in seeing America remain globally focused and competitive—America's business leaders—they seem to be missing in action. (Friedman 2005, A25)

The American corporate elite has been a model of ineffectuality since at least the 1980s. Yet it would seem to be in the group's interest to support the revitalization of the nation, and its members at least potentially have the power to effect constructive change, if they are able to generate the kind of collective action in the larger interest that their predecessors in an earlier era were able to accomplish.

The Responsibility of Privilege

E. Digby Baltzell, the great sociologist who was himself a hereditary member of the Philadelphia upper class, authored a well-known book on the divergent historical trajectories of Philadelphia and Boston (1979). Boston had experienced greater success as a city than Philadelphia, Baltzell argued, because the Puritan-influenced Brahmins who dominated the former accepted their mission as elites and were comfortable in their positions. The Quakers in Philadelphia, on the other hand, were overly preoccupied with equality, Baltzell argued, which led to an excessive level of democracy and a vacuum of leadership. The Quakers, Baltzell reasoned, were too egalitarian to exercise the kind of leadership necessary to propel their community to greatness.

Baltzell was an elitist, and he made no apologies for it. One need not accept his views, which could be interpreted as patronizing at best and antidemocratic at worst. Yet he did raise a point that is worth taking seriously. Every society has an elite, Baltzell argued. The extent to which that elite is willing to act responsibly, with concern for the general welfare, is an indicator of the strength and vitality of the society, he suggested. The American elite, based in our largest corporations, has abdicated the responsibility that it exercised in the postwar era. Perhaps this sense of responsibility represented a peculiar historical moment, the ascendance of the so-called "greatest generation," those who had experienced the Great Depression and World War II and who saw themselves as carrying a special burden. Yet traces of this approach were evident at the turn of the twentieth century, and they are present even in the twenty-first. The current American corporate elite seems to be leading us toward the fate of the earlier Roman, Dutch, and Habsburg Spanish empires, starving the treasury and accumulating vast resources for itself. There are individuals who seem able to transcend this approach, however. Such individuals existed in these long-gone empires as well, but their warnings were not heeded. Will the people who need to hear them listen this time? Although the window is closing, sufficient time remains for the American corporate community to assume a position of leadership and responsibility. A resurgence of mass social movements, including organized labor, might compel the return of a more forward-thinking elite, one that resembles, and perhaps even moves beyond, the group of corporate leaders in the postwar era. Based on the analysis I have presented here, this seems to be the most likely means of ensuring the kind of change necessary to save the best elements of American civilization.

We may not have time to wait for these movements, however. No elected official is going to be in a position to tell the American public what it needs to hear about the imminent crisis brought on by global warming. Such a tack would amount to political suicide. But a group of corporate officials, speaking with one voice, able to bring together politicians from both major parties as well as respected scientists, might be able to persuade our political leaders that they have no choice but to create a unified front to do what is necessary to save the world as we know it. Some will claim that this plea is as utopian as Emile Durkheim's dream of an orderly society or Karl Marx's yearning for a communist nirvana. But the American corporate elite has provided leadership in the past. It is long past time for its members to exercise some enlightened self-interest in the present.

Notes

References

Index

Notes

1. Introduction

1. For a discussion of the role of the Committee for Economic Development (CED) in facilitating education reform, see Schriftgiesser (1960, 190–191, 218). For the CED's report on education, see Committee for Economic Development (1959). The organization's annual report from 1957 includes the following quote from the group's president, Alfred C. Neal: "Behind weapons there is technology. Behind technology there is science. And behind science there must be education. . . . Our future depends importantly on our ability to attract our most capable people into government, into science, and into education. A higher value must be placed on these occupations and professions; beginning with how much we pay them and continuing into the more intangible realm of the respect and freedom we extend them" (Committee for Economic Development 1957, 11). For the Rockefeller Brothers Fund study, see Special Studies Project (1958).

2. Some authors, most notably Johnson and Kwak (2010), have suggested that the twenty-first-century United States is dominated by a highly unified Wall Street financial oligarchy. An "old-boy" network certainly exists within the financial sector. I argue that the financial community no longer provides a forum for the creation and maintenance of corporate-wide unity, as it did in earlier decades, however. In that sense, the community of Wall Street financial companies is merely one of many groups, albeit a highly powerful one, that exhibit a narrow self-interest.

3. In an earlier work (Mizruchi 1992, chapter 3), I distinguished unity, which I defined as the similarity of behavior among members of a group, from cohesion, which I defined as the density of relations within a group. Neither of these definitions required a level of awareness among the group's members. It was therefore possible for a group to achieve either unity or cohesion without its members necessarily sharing sentiments or even goals. In this book, I define unity as the extent to which a group is able to act collectively to advance its interests. To accomplish this, the group's members must share the same goals and consciously attempt to accomplish them through joint action. Most researchers, as I noted in my earlier work, have used the terms unity, cohesion, and solidarity interchangeably. For two exceptions, see Markovsky and Lawler (1994) and Moody and White (2003). For the purposes of this book, I shall primarily use the term *unity* to describe the varying character of the American corporate elite's ability to act collectively over time. I will occasionally use the term *cohesion*, either in describing the density of the network (consistent with my earlier definition) or as a rough synonym for unity.

2. The Rise of the American Corporate Elite

1. See Bullock (1903), Pratt (1904), Youngman (1907a, 1907b), and Keys (1910) for indications that the Morgan and Rockefeller interests constituted rival groups.

2. The account that follows draws on Allen (1935, 49–66), but the story has been recounted by other histories of the period as well (see, for example, Corey 1930; Cochran and Miller 1942; Sobel 1965; Carosso 1970).

3. Northern Securities, the holding company consisting of the combination of the Great Northern and Northern Pacific, which Morgan and Hill had established as part of the resolution of the Northern Pacific proxy fight, was dissolved in 1904 under the Sherman Antitrust Act (Allen 1935, 73–74).

4. Harriman and Rockefeller were not bankers, but because of the wealth they controlled, both were sometimes referred to as "finance capitalists."

5. This account draws primarily on Corey (1930) and Allen (1935). See also Cochran and Miller (1942), Sobel (1965), and Carosso (1970).

6. The topic of corporate liberalism was the theme of the entire August 1978 issue of the *Business History Review.*

7. G. William Domhoff (1990, 37), who was long associated with the term corporate liberalism, later rejected the term in favor of corporate moderation. Jensen, in a dissertation about the Federation, referred to its ideology as "business progressivism," in part to emphasize the Federation's connections to the Progressive Movement (1956, iii).

8. References to articles in the *New York Times,* the *Wall Street Journal, Fortune,* and *Vital Speeches of the Day* are listed at the end of the References section in the backmatter, ordered by the date of the article. The one exception to this rule is with articles that are cited in the text by the author's name (such as Friedman 2005). These articles are cited alphabetically within the primary list of references.

9. Unfortunately, the authors of the article describing the survey were extremely vague regarding the nature of their respondents. Readers were told only that the data were derived from "personal interviews with hand-picked samples of businessmen" (*Fortune* 1939).

10. In addition to the works that I cite dealing with the Committee for Economic Development in this and the following chapters, my discussion draws on material from more than 2,700 pages of original documents made available by the organization at its library in Washington. I thank Manuel Trujillo of the CED for his generous support in the securing of these data, and Todd Schifeling for his yeoman work in collecting and assembling them.

11. Schriftgiesser (1960, 25–26) provides a list in his narrative of the individuals nominated by Hoffman and Benton (including those rejected by Jones) and those nominated by Jones. This combined list, which contains seventeen people, does not completely match the list presented in the book's appendix. Among those listed in the text but missing from the appendix are Beardsley Ruml (although he was listed as a member of the organization's research committee), Owen D. Young (the chairman of General Electric), John Stewart Bryan (president of the College of William and Mary), and James M. Kemper (a Kansas City merchant and banker).

12. Collins (1981, 238) notes that two of the original eighteen trustees were replaced in December 1942, meaning that a total of twenty individuals served on the board during that year.

13. The chamber was led during this period by an unusually moderate chair, Eric A. Johnston, who was also a charter trustee of the CED. Although Johnston worked hard to move the Chamber in a more moderate direction during his three-year term, which ended in 1945, he faced continual resistance from the organization's far more conservative rank and file. Johnston was also a Republican and had run in the primary for U.S. Senate in the state of Washington. After leaving the Chamber, Johnston became president of the Motion Picture Association of America, where he played a role in developing the "blacklist" against members of the film industry who had alleged ties to the Communist Party.

14. McQuaid (1978, 365) also uses this quote from Folsom, although his transposition is slightly different from Jacoby's.

3. The State and the Economy

1. See www.usgovernmentspending.com.

2. It is important to emphasize that this relative acceptance of government and labor (the latter of which I take up in the following chapter) was driven to a great extent by perceived necessity rather than ideology. As Krooss put it (1970, 211), "Unlike the 1920s, when government could be and was regarded as a force whose importance could be minimized, business leaders at the end of the Second War went all the way in the opposite direction and became obsessed with the importance of government." This was necessary, Krooss argued, because business now saw government as "an immensely influential force" (ibid., 210).

3. The classic account of the Employment Act remains the work by Bailey (1950).

4. Interestingly, although the standard conservative position at the time focused on balanced budgets, the Chamber, in 1947, adopted a position closer to that of twenty-first century conservatives. The group supported a tax cut, in opposition to President Truman (whose goal was to balance the budget). Ironically, the Chamber used Keynesian rhetoric about deficit spending and hailed the benefits of the increased purchasing power that a tax cut would provide for low-income Americans. According to Collins (1981, 125–127), the group was actually motivated by a desire to reduce the size of government, a use of tax cuts in a manner many years ahead of its time.

5. Consider a 1946 editorial in opposition to a CED report in support of the idea of full employment. The editors began by praising the organization's behavior in its "early days," for having made "several contributions to the then lively discussion of post-war planning which were commended in these columns." "We regret to express the opinion," the editors continued, "that some of the more recent pronouncements with which the name of the CED has been connected have failed to meet the same standard." The editorial went on to state that "the less said of the report itself the better," referring to its "dreary discussion," which is "as contrary to American political and social tradition as some of the proposals which come from the extreme left" (*Wall Street Journal*, March 1, 1946, 6). In a later editorial, the *Journal* accused the CED of being "communistic," which forced the group to subsequently reaffirm its faith in free enterprise (*New York Times* [hereafter *NYT*], January 22, 1947, 15).

6. This reluctance to disband was consistent with one of the major approaches in organizational sociology, typically now referred to as the "old" institutional theory (to distinguish it from a related but alternative approach known as the "new" institutional theory). In the traditional model—expressed in prototypical form in Philip Selznick's classic *TVA and the Grass Roots* (1949)—organizations'

primary goal is survival, even if they have accomplished the goals for which they were originally formed. In fact, institutional theorists argued, many organizations may seek to delay (or even undermine) the realization of their stated goals in order to maintain the justification for their existence. Some organizations are able to survive after goal attainment by redefining their mission, as the March of Dimes (Sills 1957) and the YMCA (Zald 1970) did. The dilemma faced by the CED was thus one that many organizations experience. For a classic discussion of the old institutional theory, see Perrow (1986, chapter 5).

7. Although it was probably far from the only reason for it, Johnston himself resigned soon after this episode.

8. Business support for increased Social Security payments was evident as far back as 1949. In a speech to the American Bottlers of Carbonated Beverages, Charles E. Wilson, president of General Motors, stated, "If the present social security pensions were approximately adequate when the law was passed, they are certainly inadequate now. They do not reflect the change in the purchasing power of the dollar. Social security pensions were not increased as wages and collections were increased. It would seem reasonable with the minimum wages increased from forty to seventy-five cents per hour to increase minimum pensions in about the same proportion" (Wilson 1949).

9. Eisenhower's own moderation was evident in a 1954 letter to his brother Edgar, which was apparently written in response to Edgar's criticism that the president had made an insufficient break with previous Democratic administrations. The president began by acknowledging his distaste for the "centralization of governmental functions." His concern was tempered, however, by a sense of responsibility to carry out the will of the public. "To attain any success," he wrote, "it is quite clear that the Federal government cannot avoid or escape responsibilities which the mass of the people firmly *believe* should be undertaken by it. The political processes of our country are such that if a *rule of reason* is not applied in this effort, we will lose everything—even to a possible and drastic change in the Constitution. This is what I mean by my constant insistence upon 'moderation' in government. Should any political party attempt to abolish social security, unemployment insurance, and eliminate labor laws and farm programs, you would not hear of that party again in our political history. There is a tiny splinter group, of course, that believes you can do these things. Among them are H. L. Hunt (you possibly know his background), a few other Texas oil millionaires, and an occasional politician or business man from other areas. Their number is negligible and they are stupid. To say, therefore, that in some instances the policies of this Administration have not been radically changed from those of the last is perfectly true. Both Administrations levied taxes, both maintained military establishments, customs officials, and so on. But in all governmental

fields of action a combination of purpose, procedure and objectives must be considered if you are to get a true evaluation of the relative merits." (The Presidential Papers of Dwight David Eisenhower, Document #1147, November 8, 1954, http://www.eisenhowermemorial.org/presidential-papers/first-term /documents/1147.cfm; emphasis in the original).

10. In his testimony at the Pujo Hearings, J. P. Morgan was asked by Samuel Untermyer, "Your idea is that when a man has got a vast power, such as you have—you admit you have, do you not?" Morgan responded, "I do not know it, sir." Untermyer: "You admit you have, do you not?" Morgan: "I do not think I have." Untermyer: "You do not feel it at all?" Morgan: "No, I do not feel it at all" (U.S. Congress 1913, part 15, 1052). In his 1980 PBS documentary *The World of David Rockefeller,* Bill Moyers asked his subject if he believed that he was part of a "ruling class." Rockefeller responded that he did not.

11. In the 1964 election, Johnson received approximately one-third of the votes of business executives, an unheard of level of support for a Democratic candidate at the time (Bazelon 1965, 41). According to *New York Times* reporter Eileen Shanahan, nearly all were associated with large companies, while the vast majority of small businessmen supported Goldwater. Johnson's corporate support came primarily from large cities, Easterners, and those who had been involved in public affairs (*NYT,* September 16, 1964, 13).

12. "Statement of a Group of Leading Businessmen Urging Passage of Demonstration Cities Act," October 10, 1966, Edgar F. Kaiser papers, Bancroft Library, University of California, Berkeley.

13. There is some indication that Johnson himself encouraged the production of this letter (Martin 1994, 63). The fact that these corporate leaders agreed to speak out in support of the president's program is important, however, regardless of the origin of the idea. Kaiser later formulated the ideas behind Johnson's Housing and Urban Development Act of 1968 and helped generate support among business leaders for the bill (ibid., 63–64). At least one person among the signers, Stephen Bechtel, might have had a direct economic interest in supporting the program, given his company's role in building construction. There is no evidence that the Bechtel Corporation benefited directly from this program, however. In fact, most of Bechtel's well-known projects over the years have involved the construction of power plants and other energy-related projects (including the Hoover Dam), airport and rail terminals, and smelting facilities. None of the major projects listed on the company's website have involved housing construction.

14. As this book went to press in the fall of 2012, an organization of business leaders and former public officials called Fix the Debt began to mention the possibility of "raising revenue" to address the fiscal crisis. The group's proposal

was extremely vague in explaining how the revenue was to be raised, however, and did not specifically mention a tax increase. See Chapter 8 for a further discussion of this issue.

15. A *New York Times* opinion piece by Kurt Andersen (2011) provides a revealing discussion of President Nixon's many domestic accomplishments.

16. As noted earlier, the "Fortune 500" historically referred to *Fortune's* list of the 500 largest American manufacturing companies. Along with this list, which was first published in 1955, *Fortune* also provided lists of the fifty largest firms in six other sectors—retail, transportation, utilities, commercial banking, insurance, and diversified financial firms. For this reason, some observers referred to the Fortune 800 as well as the 500. In 1995, *Fortune* dispensed with the breakdowns by sector, and instead published a list of the 1,000 largest corporations regardless of sector. This list is now known as the Fortune 1000.

17. These percentage figures do not add up to 100 because 11 percent of Barton's executive respondents were classified into two other categories: 9 percent were "anti-Keynesian moderates," who supported federal antipoverty programs but did not support either Keynesian deficit spending or redistributive reform. Two percent were "anti-Keynesian liberals," who supported federal antipoverty programs and redistribution of income and/or wealth but did not support Keynesian deficit spending. In all, 68 percent of the ninety-five executives supported federal antipoverty programs, and 90 percent were either Keynesians or non-Keynesian moderates or liberals.

4. Labor as Uneasy Partner

1. The question of which companies were more willing to accommodate unions is a surprisingly difficult one to answer, and the issue has been the subject of considerable debate. In an attempt to address this question by studying an earlier stage, Howard Kimeldorf (2011) has examined the determinants of unionization across industries as of 1910. He argues that the primary factor underlying high unionization rates was the difficulty with which workers could be replaced. This in turn was a function of three primary conditions: the degree to which the labor required high levels of skill, the degree to which production was geographically remote, and the degree to which tasks were completed under severe time pressure. Kimeldorf also suggests, contrary to the assumptions of many labor scholars, that unionization was more difficult in large firms because these firms' managements had the resources to withstand long work stoppages. This last point is counterintuitive, because historically, the largest firms in core manufacturing industries, such as automobiles, steel, and chemicals, have been among the most highly unionized in the United States, presumably because these

firms face relatively low market competition and are thus able to grant wage increases and then pass the increased costs on to their customers. It may be that both views are correct: large firms may initially be relatively difficult to unionize, but once unionized, they may be better able than smaller firms to absorb the associated labor costs.

2. A recognition strike, as its name implies, is an event in which workers walk off their jobs as a means of compelling management to recognize their proposed union.

3. Benton authored this article with "extensive input" from the CED's Research Committee, suggesting that it reflected the views of the organization's leadership.

4. One aspect of the wildcat strikes that proliferated during the war is frequently unmentioned (or deemphasized) in labor histories of the period: the extent to which such strikes were driven by racism. In an overview of labor relations during the war years, Joshua Freeman (1978, 585–587) provides several examples of wildcat strikes driven by overt racism, among them a 1943 strike by 25,000 white Packard workers in Detroit who refused to work alongside black workers who had been upgraded due to the war-induced labor shortage, a succession of strikes at a Bethlehem shipyard in Maryland, and a 1944 strike of Philadelphia transit workers in response to the upgrading of eight African American workers. The CIO leadership was vehemently opposed to these actions but was powerless to stop them. Freeman notes the fact that many of the new union members in the North were migrants from the rural South, who not only brought with them the racial attitudes of that region but also lacked the experiences of those who had been involved in the formation of their unions. Understood in this context, Freeman suggests that the frequent wildcat strikes during the war may have represented not so much the actions of a highly conscious working class vanguard but rather a "more primitive form of activity" (ibid., 588).

5. Harris referred to Johnston as a "corporate liberal."

6. Judis (2001, 69–70) argues that the decision to maintain industry-wide bargaining was made under pressure from "corporate executives in the CED and in the American Management Association," who preferred to bargain on an industry-wide basis rather than having to reach potentially hundreds of separate contracts with local unions. Although this suggestion is plausible and is compatible with Lichtenstein's account cited above, Judis provides no documentation for the CED's role in this process. Lichtenstein, meanwhile, notes that despite the views of most historians, who see Senator Taft's decision as a reflection of the power of large corporations in concentrated industries, virtually all American businessmen opposed industry-wide bargaining, at least based on their rhetoric

(1997–1998, 786). Charles E. Wilson of General Motors, for example, feared that industry-wide bargaining would lead to employer-based cartels, leading to state control of both labor and industry, a situation that, he argued, followed a "Nazi-Fascist-Communist pattern" (ibid., 787). If virtually all companies opposed industry-wide bargaining, however, it is not clear why Senator Taft decided not to oppose it as well. It is difficult to argue that Taft was responding to pressure from organized labor. It may have been because he believed, as most observers at the time did, that President Truman was prepared to sign the bill and that the provision banning industry-wide bargaining might precipitate a veto. In private correspondence, Lichtenstein (June 4, 2011) explained that the steel industry "actually liked the system [of industry-wide bargaining] since it protected US Steel's de facto price leadership; and in various service and transport industries, management more or less wanted industry bargaining as a way to keep out rivals and avoid price wars. So there was probably some division in management ranks at that time. That is why Taft thought of it as a killer amendment." Tomlins (1985, 303) suggests that most of the opposition to industry-wide bargaining came not from firms in competitive industries but from relatively peripheral firms in the more concentrated industries.

7. Even after it was over, the UAW seemed perplexed by Chrysler's willingness to engage in such a long strike. In a 1950 interview with Guy Nunn, a UAW radio news commentator, Nat Weinberg, of the union's Research Department, noted both the enormous profits that Chrysler had recently made and the bonuses paid to its officers, the latter of which, Weinberg estimated, amounted to more than one-half of the UAW's pension and medical care demands of approximately $18 million. According to Weinberg, the strike, which had lasted nearly seventy days at the time of the interview, was costing the company more than $500,000 per day after taxes, or almost $35 million at that point, nearly twice the total amount of the union's demands. In trying to understand Chrysler's motive for the strike, Weinberg speculated that the company might have been acting at the behest of major financial interests—the company had director interlocks with Chase National Bank and Central Hanover Bank—that wanted to use the Chrysler case as an example to discourage further union militancy. This account seems less plausible when one considers the very different behavior of General Motors, however, as well as Harris's point that Chrysler's obstinacy had by then rendered it a relative deviant among the largest firms. Nat Weinberg, interviewed by Guy Nunn, April 2, 1950, Series III, Box 87, folder: Negotiations; misc. correspondence, UAW Chrysler Department Collection, UAW Archives, Walter P. Reuther Library, Wayne State University. I thank J. Adam Cobb for locating and sharing this document.

8. It is probably not an accident that Herbert Simon's theory of profit "satisficing" (as opposed to maximizing) appeared during this period, along with other alternatives to the profit maximization model (Baumol 1959; Simon 1959).

9. All three of these people had extensive experience outside the university. Aaron had served as a mediator for the federal government in the 1940s and continued to mediate labor disputes for several decades after assuming his position at UCLA in 1946. Bell had been a labor reporter for *Fortune* prior to joining the sociology department at Columbia in 1959, where he taught until moving to Harvard a decade later. Solow, who spent his entire academic career at MIT and later won the Nobel Prize in economics, served on the Council of Economic Advisers in the early 1960s.

10. As we saw in Chapter 3, a majority of the leading American CEOs surveyed by Barton (1985) in 1971 expressed support for the idea that if the private economy was incapable of providing jobs for everyone willing to work, then the government should step in to fill the gap.

11. After the 1964 Democratic sweep, union officials had hoped to overturn (or at least weaken) the Taft-Hartley Act. Aware of this likelihood, a group of corporations and trade associations formed the Labor Law Study Group as a means of countering the expected labor offensive. Members of this group included the heads of AT&T, Ford, General Dynamics, and Minnesota Mining and Manufacturing (3M) as well as the NAM and the Chamber of Commerce. The bill to repeal section 14-b of Taft-Hartley—which allowed workers in union shops in certain states to refrain from joining the union—was filibustered in the Senate by Illinois Republican Everett Dirksen (Levitan and Cooper 1984, 35–36; Ferguson and Rogers 1986, 62; *Time* 1965).

12. I would like to thank Parker A. Harvey, an economist at the Chicago office of the Bureau of Labor Statistics, for his assistance in locating these data.

13. Because the strike and unemployment data represent a time series, it is necessary to account for the level of autocorrelation in order to ensure that the observed statistical association in the simple correlation is not overestimated (or, more specifically, that the standard error of the regression coefficient for unemployment is not underestimated). A generalized least squares (GLS) model using the Prais-Winsten estimation technique yielded a coefficient for unemployment of −29.54, with a T-statistic of −2.49 (with 24 d.f., two-tailed $p = .02$). The correlation between strikes and unemployment from 1948 through 2010 was −.43, and the GLS regression coefficient was −17.55, with a T-statistic of −2.95 (with 61 d.f., two-tailed $p = .004$). Interestingly, the correlation between strikes and unemployment was −.63 from 1948 through 1980 but was actually positive, .39, from 1981 through 2010. A GLS model using an interaction effect between unemployment and a dummy variable for post-1980 revealed an interaction effect

of 38.22, with a T-statistic of 3.79 (with 59 d.f., $p < .001$). This means that the effect of unemployment on strikes became significantly less negative (or more positive) after 1980. The main effect of unemployment (which represents the 1948–1980 period) was -33.75, with a T-statistic of -4.65 (with 59 d.f., $p < .001$). The effect of unemployment in the 1981–2010 period was 4.47, computed as $-33.75 + 38.22$. A recomputation of the equation to test the main effect of the 1981–2010 coefficient revealed a nonsignificant T-statistic of 0.62 (two-tailed $p = .54$). This means that the effect of unemployment on strikes was negative from 1948 through 1980 but null after 1981. I will have more to say in Chapter 7 about the disappearance of the effect of unemployment on strike activity in the post-1980 period.

14. An excellent example of this concern is evident in an October 1969 speech by R. Heath Larry, vice chairman of the board of directors of U.S. Steel, presented at Canisius College in Buffalo as part of the Federal Mediation and Conciliation Service Seminar on Collective Bargaining. The speech, entitled "An Inflationary Binge: The Morning After," contained strong—perhaps even angry—criticisms against unions in general and George Meany, the head of the AFL-CIO, in particular. Union officials, according to Larry—referring to the economic slowdown that had begun in recent months and that we discussed in the previous chapter—"accuse the Administration of pursuing a course specifically designed to raise the level of unemployment and thus put the burden of cooling off the inflation mainly upon the workers who, it would seem, according to union orthodoxy, *never* share any responsibility for inflation." "Clearly," Larry concluded three pages later, "something has to change—either in the structure of collective bargaining—or in the structure of union power—or in the structure of employers' resistance to that power—if we are to have any hope for man's longstanding dream of maintaining both a full-employment economy—and an economy not plagued with inflation" (*Vital Speeches of the Day*, December 1, 1969, 1, 4; emphasis in the original).

15. In 1957, 76 percent of Americans expressed approval of labor unions, and as late as 1965 more than 70 percent of Americans expressed approval. This figure declined from the late 1960s through the 1970s, dropping to 55 percent by 1979. The percentage expressing disapproval increased from 14 percent in 1957 to 33 percent in 1979 (Lipset and Schneider 1983, 203).

16. One interesting case that reveals a shift from progressivism to active opposition, followed by an apparent retreat toward moderation, involves the actions of General Electric. Led in the 1930s and early 1940s by pro–New Dealers Gerard Swope and Owen D. Young, GE had been in the forefront of business progressivism. After a 1946 strike by the United Electrical Workers that devastated the company, GE, now led by Charles E. Wilson (a different person

from the Charles E. Wilson of General Motors) and Ralph J. Cordiner, turned to a sales manager, Lemuel R. Boulware, to deal with the union (Phillips-Fein 2009, 90–101). Boulware, who became notorious among unions but a hero to businesspeople, was, in keeping with his sales background, a persuasive spokesperson for management as well as a tough negotiator. In 1954, during Boulware's tenure, GE hired a former New Dealer and union president turned conservative, Ronald Reagan, to host its Sunday evening television show, *GE Theater,* and to tour its factories giving pep talks to workers (ibid., 111–114). Boulware and Reagan became lifelong friends and political allies, both personifications of the new conservative ideology promulgated by GE. Yet GE's rightward shift during this period stood in contrast to the dominant trend toward accommodation exhibited by such giants as U.S. Steel, General Motors, and Ford. And even GE may have been less conservative than appearances suggested. According to Cannon (1982, 96–97), in 1962, when Reagan's contract was up for renewal, he received a call from a GE executive whom he did not know, mandating that he limit his speeches to the selling of the company's products rather than the political ideas he had been espousing. Cannon suggests that with John F. Kennedy as president, Reagan's political orientation had become too "controversial" for the company. Reagan was reportedly incensed by this decision and refused to comply, which ended his association with the company (Phillips-Fein 2009, 296).

5. The Banks as Mediators

1. After years of lobbying by bankers, the Glass-Steagall Act was repealed in 1999 with the passage of the Graham-Leach-Bliley Act. See Funk and Hirschman (2011) for a discussion of the history of Glass-Steagall.

2. See Mizruchi (2004) and Mizruchi and Hirschman (2010) for more detailed discussions of Berle and Means's book, including its Jeffersonian concerns about the concentration of power.

3. Gordon did note that the banks had increased their power by serving as representatives of large estates and trust accounts, and he also claimed that insurance companies had increased their power (1945, 215–216). He did not suggest that the insurance companies were able to use this power to control or influence nonfinancial corporations, however, and the overall thrust of his discussion suggests that bank power in general had declined.

4. One of the more controversial claims made by Fitch and Oppenheimer involved their treatment of depreciation allowances. As they showed (1970a, 74), the majority of the internal funding came from depreciation allowances, which the Federal Reserve viewed as a component of available funds. Fitch and Oppen-

heimer argued that depreciation is actually a cost of operating, not a source of revenue (ibid., 69). In a critique of their article, Sweezy (1972, 124–125) sided with the Federal Reserve. That depreciation represents a cost rather than a gain is "all perfectly true in elementary accounting theory," Sweezy argued. In corporate finance, however, "matters stand very differently" (ibid., 124). Sweezy went on to explain that corporations use depreciation allowances to reduce the level of profits on which they are taxed. This actually increases their available cash, which in turn reduces their dependence on banks. As we shall see in Chapter 7, the correctness of Sweezy's argument became evident in the late 1970s and early 1980s, when large corporations lobbied for a more rapid depreciation schedule, which they viewed as tantamount to a significant tax cut.

5. See also Kotz (1981); Herman (1981b).

6. In fairness to Kotz, his definition of control—"the power to determine the broad policies guiding a firm" (1978, 1)—was similar to Herman's concept of constraint, and Kotz's concept of "managing"—"the activities of directing and administering a business" (ibid., 16)—was similar to Herman's definition of control. Once we take these distinctions into account, Kotz's finding that 34 percent of his firms were subject to bank control is not greatly different from Herman's finding that 20 percent of his firms were subject to bank constraint. The idea that control can be viewed as a largely latent process is akin to what Perrow (1986, 128–131), drawing on March and Simon (1958), called "unobtrusive control." For a discussion of this issue involving the role of corporate boards of directors, see Mizruchi (1983).

7. This measure was based on an approach developed by Phillip Bonacich (1972). The Bonacich measure takes into account the number of other firms to which a firm is tied, the strength of the tie (in this case, the proportion of overlap between the two firms' boards), and the centrality of the firms with which a firm is tied (a firm tied to highly central firms will have higher centrality than a firm with the same number of ties to less central firms). The modification we used, which was originally developed by Michael Schwartz and his students, gave disproportionate weight to "sending" as opposed to "receiving" interlocks. In other words, when an officer of a bank sat on the board of a nonfinancial corporation, the bank received a greater weight for its tie than the nonfinancial did for its tie, and vice versa. Mathematically, the Bonacich index is computed by the matrix equation $\lambda C = RC$, where C is an $N \times 1$ vector of centrality scores, R is an $N \times N$ matrix representing the ties between the firms, and λ is the eigenvalue of the first principal component of R. We computed the entries in R as $d_{ij} / \sqrt{(d_i * d_j)}$, where d_{ij} is the number of directors in common between firms i and j, and d_i and d_j are the number of board members of firms i and j, respectively. Because it was not possible to compute the C vector unless when $ij > 0$, ji was also > 0, we

assigned a weight of .9 to each sending tie and a weight of .1 to each receiving tie. See Mizruchi and Bunting (1981) for details.

8. These percentages were based only on what are called "primary" or "strong-tie" interlocks, which involve a director whose principal affiliation is with either the financial or nonfinancial firm in question.

9. For reasons that remain unclear, commercial banks had relatively few sending interlocks in 1904—only 57, or 46.3 percent of their primary ties. This number rose sharply to 103 (58.2 percent) by 1912, and it remained at that level through 1935, before dropping in 1964.

10. Given the proprietary nature of board meetings, there is little direct evidence, beyond a series of anecdotes, on what actually gets discussed at them. Since the 1980s, however, a sizeable body of research has found that director interlocks are associated with a broad range of firm behaviors, suggesting that at least some valuable information is being exchanged. I provide examples from this literature in the following two sections. For a more detailed overview, see Mizruchi (1996).

11. The five banks were Bankers Trust, Chase Manhattan, Citibank, Manufacturers Hanover, and Morgan Guaranty Trust.

12. After the episode, Steinberg observed, "I always knew there was an establishment. I just thought I was a part of it" (*Business Week* 1970, 54).

13. A banker who was familiar with the Steinberg case at the time it occurred (and whose identity I have chosen to protect) told me in an interview (February 17, 2012) that despite Chemical's success in fending off Steinberg's bid, the episode was a "traumatic" one for the bank. The reaction of the bank at the time was one of bewilderment: "How could someone have the gall to upset the system like this?" According to my informant, Chemical's chairman, William S. Renchard, "had to go out and ask for support from the system." "The bank came out of it victorious but bloody," he told me. In fact, although Steinberg's takeover attempt failed, this banker suggested to me that the bid was a portent of things to come. "It was clear that the ground rules were being rewritten."

14. Useem conducted most of his interviews in 1979 and 1980, after the American business community had already begun to shift toward a more conservative stance. Two points, I believe, render his comments relevant to the postwar period (which I define as having ended in the early 1970s). First, virtually all of the American executives whom Useem interviewed were based in New York or Boston, the home of the traditional "Eastern Establishment," whose views we would expect to be relatively moderate in relation to the rest of the American business community. Second, as I shall argue in Chapter 7, vestiges of the moderate, pragmatic corporate elite remained at least into the early 1980s.

15. In a similar study conducted around the same time but using data from 1982, Burris (1987) found, consistent with Clawson and Neustadtl, a positive effect of interlocks on contributions to incumbents and negative effects on contributions to Republicans and candidates supported by "New Right" groups, but Burris's coefficients were not statistically significant in the presence of controls. Clawson and Neustadtl (1989, 760–761) pointed to several possible reasons for this discrepancy, including the fact that Burris's data were from 1982, at which point the Congress had become considerably more conservative (and the Senate had been taken over by the Republicans). This shift may have given contributions to incumbents a very different meaning.

6. The Breakdown of the Postwar Consensus

1. The list of Nixon's accomplishments in domestic policy is striking, not only when considered by twenty-first-century standards, but even by the standards of the time. Government social spending increased from 28 percent of the federal budget when Nixon took office in 1969 (after Lyndon Johnson's presidency) to 40 percent at his resignation in 1974. Nixon oversaw significant increases in funding for Johnson's Model Cities program, he proposed automatic cost-of-living increases for Social Security, and he increased federal spending on the arts by 400 percent. In addition, Nixon enacted affirmative action programs and signed into law the establishment of the Environmental Protection Agency, the Occupational Health and Safety Administration, and the Consumer Product Safety Board (Hayward 2001, 230). Reflecting on his years as a member of Nixon's administration, Daniel Patrick Moynihan, the future liberal Democratic Senator from New York, noted, "We may well have been the most progressive administration on domestic issues that has ever been formed" (quoted in ibid., 232).

2. One could argue that, given the risks associated with petrochemical plants, a high level of caution is necessary and that the required permits may in fact have been justified by the potential dangers that the proposed plant might have created. My point here is that Dow, and other companies, often viewed these requirements as excessive. In this example, Dow found the permit process sufficiently burdensome that the company was led to abandon the project.

3. Based on data from the Council of Economic Advisers, the net profit rate (before taxes) for U.S. nonfinancial corporations averaged 17.3 percent from 1947 through 1967, including 16 percent in the five years from 1963 through 1967. From 1968 through 1972 the net profit rate averaged 11.6 percent, and from 1970 through 1972 only 10.2 percent. For the twenty years prior to 1968, the lowest yearly profit rate was 14.2 percent, in 1958, during a recession. See Boddy

and Crotty (1975, 5). Corporate profits as a percentage of GDP declined from more than 8 percent in 1966 to approximately 4.4 percent in 1971 (Bureau of Economic Analysis data, http://seekingdelta.files.wordpress.com/2010/11/11-19_chart1_corp-profit-to-gdp2.png). This figure fluctuated over the next four decades, reaching low points of 3.8 percent in 1975 and 3.9 percent in 1980, but it began a general upward path around 1990, reaching a level of 9.5 percent in 2006.

4. For a sampling of these works, see Edsall (1984), Saloma (1984), Jenkins and Shumate (1985), Blumenthal (1986), Ferguson and Rogers (1986), Clawson and Clawson (1987), Peschek (1987), Vogel (1989), Domhoff (1990), Himmelstein (1990), Judis (2001), O'Connor (2008), and Phillips-Fein (2009). The historical narrative that follows relies heavily on these writings.

5. The statement is available at multiple sites online. I used the version at http://reclaimdemocracy.org/corporate_accountability/powell_memo_lewis.html, the first hit on my Google.com search. The text of Powell's memo on this site is preceded by an introduction by the sponsor of the Web page, ReclaimDemocracy.org. Although the slant of the introduction reflects the group's liberal political leanings, it contains an interesting, albeit not fully documented, discussion of the statement's impact.

6. Powell suggested that this coordination be conducted through the Chamber of Commerce—not surprising given that his memo was addressed to that group—but he was careful to add the phrase "or other groups" so as not to limit his recommendations to the Chamber alone. As it turned out, although the Chamber did gain membership in the years following Powell's memo (Vogel 1989, 199), it is generally not treated as one of the most important organizations in the works on the 1970s business counteroffensive cited above.

7. These two groups sometimes experienced friction. The former were primarily interested in free markets, while the latter were more concerned with social issues (and were usually willing to support at least some aspects of the welfare state). Conflict between these groups has continued to divide the Republican Party in the twenty-first century. In the 1970s, however, both groups were united in their opposition to what they saw as the excesses of the 1960s.

8. Kristol's cofounder of *The Public Interest* was Daniel Bell. Although the two remained friends, Bell left the publication during the 1970s because he believed that it was becoming too conservative. See, among other articles, Bell's obituary in the *New York Times* [hereafter *NYT*], January 26, 2011.

9. Laxalt was a very conservative senator from Nevada from 1975 to 1989. Writing in the 1980s, Peschek was referring to George H. W. Bush, the more moderate of the two Bush presidents.

10. The other firms were DuPont, General Electric, Libbey-Owens-Ford, Reynolds Metal, Standard Oil of New Jersey (Exxon), and U.S. Steel (Phillips-Fein 2009, 191–192, 308). It is not clear why Harper sent the letter to Borch at GE, but it was probably for purely informational purposes.

11. The following account relies heavily on Levitan and Cooper (1984, 122–135) and Vogel (1989, 153–163). Vogel himself draws liberally from Levitan and Cooper's detailed discussion.

12. When asked in 1972 why his organization appeared to be uninterested in organizing new members, George Meany, the head of the AFL-CIO, replied, "I don't know, I don't care. . . . Why should we worry about organizing groups of people who do not appear to want to be organized? . . . I used to worry about . . . the size of the membership. . . . I stopped worrying because to me it doesn't make any difference. . . . The organized fellow is the fellow that counts" (quoted in Freeman 2008, 77).

13. One of the difficulties that organized labor experienced in the 1970s could be traced to the section of the Taft-Hartley Act that prohibited supervisors from unionizing. The consultants hired by companies during the 1970s were often able to coerce foremen into reporting on the union activities of rank-and-file workers. According to Lichtenstein (1997–1998, 781–782), in the 1950s supervisors were typically protected by NLRB officials from having to engage in this kind of reporting. As the judiciary became more sympathetic toward management in the 1970s, foremen no longer received this protection. This allowed companies to threaten to fire supervisors who refused to cooperate.

14. Town Hall of California is (or was) a Los Angeles–based organization devoted to bringing "top speakers of the world to discuss and debate vital issues" (Loper 1987). There is some indication that the organization may now be defunct, since it does not appear to have an active website.

15. The quote usually attributed to Nixon is, "We are all Keynesians now." In fact, that statement was made by the militantly pro–free market economist Milton Friedman (Krugman 2009). Friedman's full quote, as he explained in a letter to *Time* magazine (February 4, 1966), in which he claimed he had been quoted out of context in an earlier interview, conveyed a very different meaning: "In one sense, we are all Keynesians now," Friedman said he had stated. "In another, nobody is any longer a Keynesian." See Friedman (1966).

16. In fairness to President Ford, his "Whip Inflation Now" speech of October 8, 1974, just two months after he became president, did include a number of serious measures to address the problem. Moreover, he simultaneously introduced several proposals to address the 1974 recession. These measures, like those of his Republican predecessors Nixon and Eisenhower, demonstrate not only Ford's moderation but also how far the American political environment has

shifted in the twenty-first century. In the speech, Ford noted that he had released funds to provide public service employment for 170,000 Americans, as well as supplemental unemployment benefits for those who had either exhausted their benefits or were not covered by regular unemployment insurance. He also proposed a $1.6 billion tax cut, exclusively for low- and middle-income Americans, to be paid for by a new windfall profits tax on oil producers. The speech can be found at http://millercenter.org/president/speeches/detail/3283.

17. Weisskopf, Bowles, and Gordon (1983) acknowledged that shop-floor conflict between labor and management was likely to have contributed to the productivity decline that they observed. They also argued that a lack of innovation by management was an equally significant factor.

18. See Evans (1980) for an excellent presentation of this position. See Feldstein (1994) for a more extensive discussion. Although Feldstein's memoir deals primarily with economic policy in the 1980s, there are numerous references to events in the 1970s. For his critique of the idea that large tax cuts would result in increased government revenues, see Feldstein (1994, 24–25).

19. Gerald Ford is the one exception. Barack Obama could also be viewed as an exception. Although Obama is originally from Hawaii, technically a Sunbelt state, his Ivy League education and his adult residence in Chicago do not fit the typical profile of a "cowboy."

20. The Koch family is from Wichita, Kansas, which is technically in the Midwest. Both geographically and culturally, however, one could make a case that Wichita has more in common with Oklahoma and Texas than with Illinois and Michigan.

21. Burris (1987) found, based on political contribution data from 1982, that corporations with headquarters in the South were disproportionately likely to contribute to conservative candidates. This may have been due to the fact that the candidates in geographic proximity to these firms were themselves disproportionately conservative (Clawson and Neustadtl 1989, 760–761). Burris and Salt (1990, 352) found that Frostbelt firms were less likely to contribute to Democrats than were Sunbelt firms between 1978 and 1982, but this may have been due to the fact that the Southern congressional delegation was predominantly Democratic at the time. Burris and Salt also found that in 1980, Frostbelt firms were actually less likely to contribute to liberals than were Sunbelt firms (1990, 353). This finding raises further questions about the Yankee-Cowboy thesis.

22. The one exception involved two years of data presented by Burris and Salt, from 1956 and 1972 (1990, 352). In both cases the authors found a positive association between Frostbelt location and contributions to Democrats, although neither coefficient was statistically significant. Three issues suggest that these

findings should not be taken as running counter to Barton's. First, the effects of Frostbelt location on contributions to Democrats turned significantly negative beginning in 1978, suggesting, if anything, a trend away from moderation among Northeastern and Midwestern firms. Second, it is well known that political contributions do not necessarily reflect ideological predilections, so it is difficult to compare the results of these studies with Barton's, which directly asked respondents for their ideological positions. Third, as noted earlier, given the prevalence of conservative Southern Democrats well into the 1980s, it is difficult to identify the meaning of Burris and Salt's variable measuring contributions to Democrats.

23. Harper was also a vice chairman of the CED and remained an active trustee in 1980.

24. Bundy, in an interview with Leonard and Mark Silk, responded to Ford's letter by insisting that rather than failing to appreciate the free enterprise system, the foundation's actions could be viewed as "making the world safe for capitalism." The organization accomplished this, in Silk and Silk's paraphrase of Bundy (1980, 148), by "reducing social tensions by helping to comfort the afflicted, provide safety valves for the angry, and improve the functioning of government." This statement provides an eloquent defense and a lucid portrayal of the American elite's moderation during the postwar period, even as that moderation was beginning to fray.

25. See http://www.kaiserhealthnews.org/Stories/2009/September/03/nixon -proposal.aspx for the full text of Nixon's speech. Senator Edward Kennedy had been negotiating with Nixon on health care reform, but he eventually withdrew from the negotiations, believing that he could get a stronger bill under a Democratic president. As the economic crisis of the 1970s worsened, the prospects for health care reform became increasingly remote. Although presidents Ford and Carter had both hoped to pass health care legislation, neither made progress, and the issue did not resurface until the 1990s. Years later, Senator Kennedy acknowledged that he regretted his decision to reject the Nixon proposal. For a discussion, see http://www.thedailybeast.com/newsweek/blogs/the-gaggle/2009/08 /26/echoes-of-kennedy-s-battle-with-nixon-in-health-care-debate.html. I further discuss the issue of health care reform in Chapter 8.

26. In the case of the health care document, most of the dissent came from one member, Donald Searle, the recently appointed CEO of his family's Searle Drug Company. Perhaps surprisingly, given the nature of the subject, there was little dissent from the other trustees.

27. Mentions of the Business Roundtable also increased sharply during the period that references to the CED were declining, although the group's number of mentions peaked at seventeen in 1977.

28. Given the time-series nature of the data, I also computed a regression of number of dissents on year using a Prais-Winsten generalized least squares (GLS) model to correct for possible autocorrelation. The coefficient for year had a *T*-statistic of 6.12, $p < .001$. Although caution is recommended due to the small number of observations—only twenty-three individual years—the likelihood that this association was due to chance is extremely remote. Even in the GLS model, nearly two-thirds of the variation in the number of dissents is accounted for by the year. I thank Todd Schifeling for providing these data.

29. Leonard Silk, in his *New York Times* column "Economic Scene," indicated that the CED opposed the amendment as "unworkable" and "likely to do more harm than good" (*NYT,* July 1, 1983, D2).

30. Shultz served as both secretary of the treasury and secretary of labor in the Nixon administration and served as secretary of state under Ronald Reagan. In between, he served as president of the Bechtel Corporation.

31. Fletcher Byrom, chairman of the CED in the late 1970s, was also the chairman of the Pittsburgh-based Koppers Company and a member of the Business Roundtable. In a 1979 interview with Leonard and Mark Silk, Byrom argued that the CED and the Roundtable were complementary rather than antagonistic. "I don't find the two contradictory, and I don't find this position [his comembership] contradictory," Byrom stated. "The Roundtable is taking a very pragmatic, short-term approach to specific legislation at the present time. The CED, through the trustees and its Research Advisory Board, is trying to understand the external issues that are going to impact on society" (quoted in Silk and Silk 1980, 259). Despite the presumed compatibility between the two groups, by the time of the interview the CED had already become a far less important player in national politics. The organization, although not completely invisible, received far less attention from established print media than it had in earlier years.

7. Winning the War but Losing the Battle

1. An examination of several entries under the Google searches "Reagan" and "welfare queen" suggests that Reagan's example was probably drawn from an actual case of welfare fraud, but that he greatly exaggerated the amount of funds involved, inflating the figure by a factor of nearly twenty. See Prasad (2006, 86–87) for a useful discussion of this issue.

2. This proportion fell precipitously during the 1980s and 1990s and had declined to under 12 percent by 2010, its lowest level in more than seventy years (*New York Times* [hereafter *NYT*], January 21, 2011).

3. Private sector unionization percentages closely matched the proportions for all nonagricultural workers through the early 1980s but have since declined at a higher level, to 6.9 percent in 2011, see http://www.bls.gov/news.release/union2 .nr0.htm; *NYT,* January 21, 2011).

4. McCartin (2011a) provides a detailed history of the forces leading up to the strike, as well as the strike's consequences over the following three decades.

5. See also http://www.npr.org/templates/story/story.php?storyId=5604656.

6. There are several versions of Marxist state theory, and by the 1970s these formulations had become increasingly sophisticated and complex and had spawned a series of intense debates. What all of these approaches shared, however, was the view that the state in a capitalist society functioned first and foremost to uphold the interests of the business community. For an excellent overview of these debates written at the peak of their popularity, see Carnoy (1984).

7. By 1982, Morgan Guaranty Trust had changed its name to J. P. Morgan & Company, and First National City Bank had changed its name to Citicorp. In all three of the data sets described here, financial institutions made up a minority of the firms in the sample, ranging from a high of 25.1 percent in the Mizruchi 1912 data to a low of 15 percent in the Davis-Mizruchi data for 1982.

8. American banks had increased their offshore lending beginning in the 1960s, when numerous major institutions established branches overseas. Ironically, most of these banks began closing these overseas branches in the 1980s (Mizruchi and Davis 2004). Although they continued to lend to non-American corporations during this period, they faced severe international competition for this business, and whatever gains they achieved in this arena were insufficient to compensate for the losses they were experiencing at home.

9. The largest increases corresponding to this decline were in pension funds and mutual funds (James and Houston 1996, 11).

10. The interlock comparison between the two years involved different numbers of firms in the denominator, because some firms had equal numbers of interlocks. Based on the Bonacich (1972) centrality index (see Chapter 5), six of the ten most central firms in 1982 were commercial banks, while three of the ten most central firms in 1994 were commercial banks. Unlike Mizruchi (1982) and Mintz and Schwartz (1985), Davis and I did not include insurance companies in our sample.

11. Our data on commercial and industrial lending by banks were generously provided to us by Dr. Philip Strahan of the Federal Reserve Bank of New York. Although the Fed collects these data, they are not normally provided to the public.

12. Using the measure developed by Freeman (1979), the centralization of the network declined by nearly 36 percent between 1982 and 1994.

13. In an effort to tame the inflation that had skyrocketed in the late 1970s and early 1980s, the Federal Reserve raised interest rates to record levels, which helped precipitate the severe recession of 1981 and 1982. This move was ultimately successful in reducing inflation. The high rates also encouraged foreign investors to purchase U.S. Treasury securities, which helped spur the recovery that began in 1983. See Krippner (2011, especially chapter 4) for a discussion of this history.

14. Reagan's preference for maintaining individual tax cuts at the expense of business tax cuts may have stemmed from his traditional base of support among small businesses. A majority of these firms are owned by individuals whose profits are reported as personal income and are thus taxed at individual rather than corporate rates.

15. The negative impact of high interest rates on small companies (which typically pay significantly above the prime rate for business loans) raises the question of why any small-business interests would oppose a set of tax increases that would primarily have affected large companies. According to Martin (1991, 141), the explanation was ideological: "NFIB [National Federation of Independent Business] agreed that, although their members hated the deficits and suffered from the high interest rates, the best way to lower interest rates was to cut spending, not increase taxes." This willingness of the NFIB membership to support policies on the basis of ideology, even against their own apparent economic interests, would resurface in debates over health care policy during the Obama administration, a topic I address in the following chapter.

16. It is perhaps understandable why the heads of General Motors, Ford, and R. J. Reynolds would be concerned about the personal income tax cuts. All three companies depended heavily on consumer spending. It is less clear why the CEOs of Citibank and Bechtel were also so invested in these cuts. It might have had to do with the significant tax savings that these high-income CEOs were poised to receive under Reagan's policy. This does not explain why most of the other also highly paid CEOs were willing to dispense with the individual tax cut, however.

17. The CED was mentioned in the *New York Times* an average of 31.6 times per year in the 1950s and 1960s. By the 1980s, the group was mentioned only 12.9 times per year. A similar decline occurred in the number of times the organization was mentioned in the *Wall Street Journal* (hereafter *WSJ*), from 8.7 in the 1950s and 1960s to 3.7 in the 1980s. For a case in which the CED received attention for its criticism of President Reagan's cuts in social programs, see *NYT* (February 11, 1982, A28) and *WSJ* (February 9, 1982, 30).

18. I take up this issue in Chapter 8.

19. Young continued to pursue his ideas during the first Bush administration. At one point he, John Scully of Apple (another Republican), and John Akers of IBM approached White House Chief of Staff John Sununu. When they failed to receive support for their ideas, Young, Scully, and twenty-nine other Silicon Valley executives decided to support Bill Clinton, whom they found more receptive (Judis 2001, 185).

20. Stock options are agreements that allow managers to purchase the company's stock at a time of their choice for the price at which the stock was selling at the time the option was granted. Because the executive's compensation is based on the extent to which the firm's stock has increased since the granting of the option, the executive has an incentive to increase the firm's stock price. In the 1990s, the average value of options to CEOs increased tenfold (Davis 2009, 87).

21. There is an interesting parallel between this conception of the firm and the conception of organizations among social network theorists. For network theorists, the important "stuff" of social life is in the interactions among social actors, many (if not most) of which span formal organizational boundaries. In this view, conceptions of entities such as "the state" as a unitary actor are misleading, because they mask the more micro-level social interactions that occur both across subunits of the larger organization as well as between those inside and those outside the organization. A succinct early statement of this position was presented by White, Boorman, and Breiger (1976, especially 730–736). This view does have one important difference from Jensen and Meckling's perspective: the social relations conceptualized by network theorists do not necessarily reflect contractual exchange relations between self-interested actors but may instead represent affective relations based on personal ties.

22. Jewish Americans had experienced some degree of prominence in investment banking (although not commercial banking) dating back to the late nineteenth century, but this group was primarily descended from German Jews who had arrived in the United States in the mid-1800s. Members of this group were believed by some observers to have "looked down on" the descendants of Jews from Russia and Poland who had immigrated to the United States at the turn of the twentieth century. See Baltzell (1964, 53–70) for a fascinating discussion of this issue. For a classic novel that describes the experiences of a Jewish immigrant from Russia, see Abraham Cahan, *The Rise of David Levinsky* (1917). For a discussion of Cahan's novel in the context of the literature on business in the early twentieth-century United States, see S. Mizruchi 2008, chapter 7, especially 218–224.

23. The two-thirds figure comes from my calculation from data generously provided by Gerald Davis. To reach this figure, I computed the proportion of

bids by outsiders (that is, those not involving management buyouts) that Davis coded as "hostile."

24. Perhaps the best-known leveraged buyout, one chronicled in riveting fashion by two *Wall Street Journal* reporters, Bryan Burrough and John Helyar (2005), was the attempt by F. Ross Johnson, the CEO of RJR Nabisco, to take the company private. Johnson, who was in a relatively strong and secure position as CEO, was nevertheless frustrated by what he saw as the inadequacy of the firm's stock price. Johnson ended up in a three-way battle with LBO specialist Theodore R. Forstmann and KKR for control of the firm. KKR eventually won, and Johnson was ousted as CEO.

25. The account in this paragraph draws on Stearns and Allan (1996, 707–709).

26. A quote by the late Theodore (Ted) Forstmann, extracted by Stearns and Allan from Burrough and Helyar's book, so beautifully captures the basis for the high-status investment banks' adoption of a low-status product that it is worth repeating here in full: "'Imagine ten debutantes sitting in a ballroom,' Forstmann told a gathering of Securities and Exchange commissioners. 'They're the heads of Merrill Lynch, Shearson Lehman, and all the other big [and high-status] brokerages. In walks a hooker. It's Milken. The debutantes wouldn't have anything to do with a woman who sells her body for a hundred dollars a night. But this hooker is different. She makes a million dollars a night. Pretty soon, what have you got? Eleven hookers'" (Burrough and Helyar 2005, 239–240).

27. A classic, and well-known, dramatization of this process occurs in a scene from the movie *Wall Street,* in which a corporate raider, Gordon Gekko (played by Michael Douglas), grabs the microphone at a stockholders meeting and, chastising the firm's managers, opines that "greed is good." The scene nicely captures the Manne-Jensen-Meckling model of the efficiency-generating role of corporate takeovers. All the elements are there: the bumbling, out-of-touch managers, the charismatic corporate raider, the spellbound stockholders, and the clear implication that the raider will be able to do a far better job of increasing shareholder value than the inept sitting management had done.

28. It is extremely difficult to identify the effect of antitakeover policies such as poison pills on a firm's likelihood of being a target. The problem is that the institution of a poison pill might itself have been a consequence of an earlier takeover threat, either real or perceived.

29. See LaPorta, Lopez-de-Silanes, and Shleifer (1999) for a cross-national analysis that shows the extent to which high levels of stock dispersal are associated primarily with the United States and Great Britain.

30. In describing the situation faced by large public pension funds such as the California Public Employees Retirement System (known as Calpers), Steve Lohr,

a *New York Times* reporter, noted that "because their investment in corporate America is so extensive, the big funds are being forced to act more like long-term owners. 'We can't bail out easily,' said DeWitt Bowman, the chief investment officer of Calpers. 'So the only way we can improve our performance is to prod corporate America into better performance'" (*NYT*, April 12, 1992, 5).

31. These data were generously provided by Jiwook Jung, a graduate student in sociology at Harvard University. Kaplan and Minton (2008) found that CEO turnover (among Fortune and Standard & Poor's 500 firms) not involving acquisitions was 24.2 percent higher from 1998 through 2005 than from 1992 through 1997. Total turnover, including that involving acquisitions (but not that involving the death of an incumbent CEO), was 33.1 percent higher from 1998 through 2005 than from 1992 through 1997. My own data, drawn from Fortune 500 firms, suggest a decline in mean CEO tenure from approximately 7.5 years in the early 1980s to approximately 5.7 years in the early 2000s, a decline of 24 percent. The reason for the differences in mean tenure between Jung's data and mine is unclear and may be the result of different firm populations. The trends in all three data sets are roughly the same, however. All three indicate that CEO tenure declined during the 1980s and that it continued to decline well after that decade.

32. This quote came from a phone interview (July 28, 2010) with a source whose identity I have chosen to protect. Interestingly, in at least one respect, Jones did not fit the stereotypical view of the postwar corporate elite: although he may have carried himself in a patrician manner and although he was a graduate of Wharton, Jones was in fact, according to the Harvard Business School Leadership database, the son of a skilled laborer. See http://www.hbs.edu/leadership/database/leaders/reginald_h_jones.html.

33. The fact that Welch spent virtually his entire career at GE, as Jones did, also defies stereotype. One of the most notable characteristics of the new breed of CEOs that emerged in the 1980s was their tendency to be hired from outside the organization (Khurana 2002).

34. Given the nature of the model and the variables, it is difficult to provide a straightforward interpretation of the coefficients for year and CEO tenure. Literally, the year coefficient indicates that for every subsequent year, the logarithm of the level of philanthropic contributions as a proportion of sales is predicted to decline by a value of .031. The CEO tenure coefficient indicates that for every one year increase in the average CEO tenure, the logarithm of the ratio of philanthropic contributions to sales is predicted to increase by .128. The mean of the logarithm of the ratio of contributions to sales is 2.825 (this mean is greater than zero because we measured sales in thousands and contributions in raw numbers, meaning that our ratios of contributions to sales were often greater

than 1). This indicates that for each year, the measure of contributions is predicted to decline by a value approximately 1.1 percent of the mean, and for each one-year increase in average CEO tenure, the measure of contributions is predicted to increase by a value approximately 4.5 percent of the mean.

35. Christopher Marquis contributed to the work from which these analyses were drawn. I thank Chris for making the data available to me and for his help with every aspect of these analyses. From this point on, I use the pronoun "we" in this discussion to underscore Chris's contribution.

36. In an analysis not shown here, we examined the effects of both variables simultaneously. Remarkably, the effect of year remained significantly negative, even controlling for mean CEO tenure. The coefficient for CEO tenure turned from positive to negative, however—the opposite of what we predicted— although the coefficient was not statistically significant. Given its extremely high correlation with year, this nonsignificance was almost certainly a result of collinearity.

8. The Aftermath

1. The value-added tax is paid by each business along the production-distribution stream as a proportion of the product's increased value at each step.

2. The Chamber of Commerce broke ranks with the more moderate CED during the early debate over the necessity of a tax increase. In testimony before the Joint Economic Committee of Congress on March 18, 1966, the Chamber's chief economist, Carl H. Madden, argued that government spending should be cut when inflation increases and taxes should be cut during recessions. At the time, Madden's view was unusual. As the *New York Times* (hereafter *NYT*) put it, Madden was "the first witness before the joint committee to contest the fundamental concept that tax increases are a proper action when an inflationary boom appears likely" (*NYT*, March 19, 1966, 1). Ten other spokespersons, including Neal of the CED, endorsed the value of tax increases as a means of fighting inflation.

3. As this was occurring, Treasury Secretary Donald Regan chastised Wall Street bond traders, stating that they should stop "spooking" Congress about the dangers of tax cuts. Regan also wanted to send "a message to the heads of American business that by criticizing high deficits, 'You have the Congress spooked'" (*NYT*, March 12, 1982, D3).

4. TRW, Inc. was a major diversified corporation that was regularly among the 100 largest American manufacturing firms in the second half of the twentieth century. The company was acquired by Northrop Grumman in 2002. See http://en.wikipedia.org/wiki/TRW for an overview.

5. President Reagan was quick to note publicly that both the Roundtable and the NAM supported his proposed tax increase (*Wall Street Journal* [hereafter *WSJ*], August 18, 1982, 4).

6. The group titled its press release "Roundtable Applauds President Bush's Budget Statement" (Darman 1996, 264). Darman's detailed discussion of the negotiations between the administration and congressional leaders in 1990 illustrates a level of collegiality and willingness to compromise that stand in stark contrast to the contentious political environment that emerged in the mid-1990s and worsened in subsequent years. I shall argue below that the corporate elite's retreat from responsibility played a significant role in the deterioration of American politics.

7. Because I discuss both George H. W. Bush and his son, George W. Bush, in this chapter, it might occasionally be unclear regarding to which of the two I am referring. Although I hope that the subject will be self-evident in most cases, when in doubt I shall refer to the senior Bush as "Bush I" and the junior Bush as "Bush II."

8. On the other hand, the younger President Bush had not gone out on a limb during his campaign by saying, "Read my lips, no new taxes," as his father had.

9. One account of the Reagan recovery suggests that it was fueled by foreign investors buying up U.S. Treasury bills in response to the high interest rates of the early 1980s (Krippner 2011). This resulted in the United States moving from the world's largest creditor to the world's largest debtor. The increased foreign holdings of U.S. government debt became a concern even for conservative economists who were otherwise indifferent to the increased deficits of the Bush years (Weisman 2004).

10. I was in attendance at this speech on April 26, 2004.

11. My efforts to reach John Castellani, as of this writing the president and CEO of the Pharmaceutical Research and Manufacturers of America (PhRMA), were unsuccessful. I was able to speak with a current officer of the Business Roundtable, who was extremely cordial and asked me to send him my question via email so that he could direct it to someone who might be able to answer it. Although I promised in my email message that I would maintain the anonymity of the person who responded to me by stating only that it was someone "familiar with the Roundtable's deliberations at the time," I did not receive a response, either to my first message or to a follow-up that I sent sixteen days later. The text of my question was as follows: "My question involves the BRT's [the Business Roundtable's] position on taxes and the deficit. In 1983, after the deficit rose to a very high level during President Reagan's first term, the BRT recommended a tax increase on individuals (along with spending cuts) to help balance the budget.

After George H. W. Bush was elected President in 1988, the BRT also recommended that he raise taxes in order to close the high deficit at the time, even though Mr. Bush had promised during his campaign to not raise taxes. In 2004, during George W. Bush's first term, a large tax cut had been followed by a record deficit. In his speech at the Detroit Economic Club in April 2004, Mr. Castellani spoke with great concern about the deficit. He did not say anything about the possible benefit (or disadvantage) of raising taxes, however. In my research on that period, I found that the BRT expressed support for the Bush tax cuts- and even supported the idea of making them permanent. The BRT, as far as I know, has not supported a tax increase during the Obama presidency either, despite the increasingly large deficit. This seems to indicate a change in the BRT's position from the early and late 1980s. The question I had was, why has the BRT, which had supported tax increases (at least on individuals) in earlier years to reduce the deficit, not supported an increase in more recent years? I would appreciate any insights that you (or one of your colleagues) might be able to provide on this."

12. As of this writing, the letter appeared on the Roundtable's website, at http://businessroundtable.org/news-center/P215.

13. In an editorial on August 20, 2011, the *New York Times* opined, "When the federal government was on the brink of default and the economy hung in the balance, the nation's business leaders had a chance to step forward and push for a long-term solution. They could have supported a grand bargain that cut spending and raised tax revenue. They could have warned House Republicans that it was far too risky to use the debt ceiling for political leverage. Instead, the United States Chamber of Commerce, the Financial Services Forum, and other important players wrote a series of weak letters to the White House and Congress saying, in essence, 'just don't default'" (*NYT*, August 20, 2011, SR10). The *Times'* ire at the Chamber of Commerce was misplaced. The Chamber, with the exception of the brief period in the 1940s when it was led by Eric Johnston, has virtually never been willing to take a position beyond its members' immediate interests. The Business Roundtable, on the other hand, has taken such positions in the past. The fact that the *Times* did not mention the Roundtable is a telling reminder of the group's reduced influence in recent years. Yet the Roundtable could have recaptured some of its earlier stature had it been willing to exercise a position of responsibility on this issue.

14. This does not explain why Dick Cheney and other conservatives temporarily suspended their concern over deficits during George W. Bush's administration, however.

15. The group also expressed support for President Bush's proposal to privatize Social Security (*NYT*, February 21, 2005).

16. One group of wealthy Americans did call for a tax increase during the 2010–2011 debates over the deficit. The group, Patriotic Millionaires for Fiscal Stability, consists of approximately 140 individuals, but few of them play significant roles in running large corporations. In fact, as of 2010, not a single one of these individuals was a chief executive of a Fortune 1000 firm. The list did include a onetime CEO of AT&T Broadband, a vice president at Goldman Sachs, a retired chief operating officer of Prudential Financial, and a managing director of Black Rock (number 282 on the Fortune list in 2010). Most members of the group were partisan Democrats, however, including convention delegates. Some wealthy individuals who are not members of this group—most notably Warren Buffett—have also called for a tax increase on high income Americans. None of these calls represent those of the organized business community, however. The latter group has, as of this writing, continued to remain silent on the issue of taxation.

In fall 2012, in anticipation of the impending expiration of George W. Bush's tax cuts and the significant budget cuts that were mandated to ensue if President Obama and Congress failed to reach an agreement, a new group, Fix the Debt, offered a proposal to solve the nation's long-term debt problems. This organization, founded by former Republican senator Alan Simpson and former Clinton administration official Erskine Bowles, included a number of former public officials as well as the CEOs of twenty-two major corporations. Although newspaper reports (*NYT*, October 26, 2012, A25; *NYT*, November 12, 2012, B1) indicate that the group was willing to call for a tax increase, the organization's position statement offered only an oblique (and potentially contradictory) reference to this possibility. According to the statement on its website, the group advocates "comprehensive and pro-growth tax reform, which broadens the base, lowers rates, raises revenues, and reduces the deficit" (http://www.fixthedebt.org /core-principles). Although the phrase "raises revenues" has become a euphemism for a tax increase, it is difficult to reconcile this with the group's recommendation, in the same sentence, for lowering tax rates. The Business Roundtable also weighed in on the deficit crisis in November 2012, but as it did during the debt ceiling crisis of 2011, the Roundtable merely exhorted the president and Congress to reach an agreement. See *NYT*, November 12, 2012, B1.

17. Lichtenstein goes on to argue that "managers recognized that company-specific benefits built employee loyalty, and at some level they understood that a low social wage was advantageous to their class interest, even if their own firm had to bear additional costs as a consequence" (1995, 297). This latter point would be extremely difficult to verify under any circumstances, since it imputes motives to managers that are virtually impossible to decipher. It does raise two interesting questions: First, to what extent were managers willing to forsake their

economic interests in an effort to exercise control over their workers? Second, to what extent was the managers' antigovernment ideology sufficiently strong to override these interests? This latter question would subsequently become a central issue in debates over health care policy.

18. See http://www.cbo.gov/ftpdocs/87xx/doc8758/MainText.3.1.shtml.

19. Richard Nixon, "Remarks at a Briefing on the Nation's Health System," The American Presidency Project, University of California, Santa Barbara, Paper 261, http://www.presidency.ucsb.edu/ws/index.php?pid=2121#axzz1jqIqZGVG.

20. Although the HMO model did a good job of removing the incentive to provide unnecessary services, it also created a potential incentive to not provide services or tests that might be necessary, or at least helpful. The value of this approach to health care continues to be a source of debate.

21. It is unclear whether the CED report influenced the Nixon proposal or vice versa. A *Wall Street Journal* news brief in April 1973 referred to a "secret government analysis" of the CED plan suggesting that it " 'reflects quite closely the administration's bill' in the last Congress" (*WSJ*, April 12, 1973, 1). It is not unreasonable to think that there was some communication between CED and Nixon administration officials, but the similarity in the plans could also simply indicate that one group was aware of the other's.

22. The speech can be found at http://www.kaiserhealthnews.org/Stories /2009/September/03/nixon-proposal.aspx.

23. After receiving no mentions in the *New York Times* from 1974 through 1979, the WBGH was mentioned in thirty-nine articles during the 1980s. The group was mentioned in thirteen *Wall Street Journal* articles during the 1980s, after being mentioned only once from 1974 through 1979.

24. In saying this, Boehner (almost certainly inadvertently) was paraphrasing a quote from the classic tract of Chinese Communism, the "Little Red Book" of Chairman Mao Tse-tung. Mao's original quote (1967, 9) was, "We should support whatever the enemy opposes and oppose whatever the enemy supports." This attitude, already in evidence in the early Clinton years, was not unlike that adopted by congressional Republicans during Barack Obama's first term as president.

25. A few weeks after this episode, the *Wall Street Journal* reported that the Chamber had dismissed William Archey, the Chamber's senior vice president of policy and congressional affairs, blaming him for the group's earlier support of employer mandates and its conciliatory attitude toward the Clinton plan. Representative Dick Armey (R-Texas) accused Archey of seeking acceptance in Washington rather than advancing "pro-growth economic policies" (*WSJ*, April 6, 1994, B9). Later that month, Robert Patricelli also resigned (*WSJ*, April 27, 1994, B2).

26. Representative John Dingell (D-Michigan), chairman of the House Energy and Commerce Committee, whose father had been a coauthor of the Wagner-Murray-Dingell health care bill during World War II, told the *Washington Post* in October 1994 that "when the president failed to get the [Business Roundtable], there was a big shift in sentiment inside the committee. That was a defining event" (Priest and Weisskopf, 1994; see also Mintz 1998, 216–217).

27. As the *Times* put it in an editorial four days after the Roundtable had come out for the Cooper plan (and not the Clinton plan): "It might seem odd that the Business Roundtable . . . voted in favor of Representative Cooper's bill over Mr. Clinton's. Mr. Cooper's bill would raise taxes on these corporations because they provide workers with expensive coverage, whereas Mr. Clinton's bill offers them a bribe by promising to absorb their huge costs of insuring early retirees" (*NYT,* February 7, 1994, A16). Another account of why big business eventually dropped its support for health care reform is that increases in health care costs do not actually affect profits (Starr 2011, 118). This argument has been made by a number of health economists, who argue that when health care costs rise, employers compensate by reducing wage gains (see, for example, the chart in Ezra Klein's *Washington Post* blog, http://voices.washingtonpost.com/ezra-klein /2009/10/will_lower_health-care_costs_m.html). This claim has generally been used when discussing whether American firms are at a competitive disadvantage relative to firms in countries with national health care systems. Even those who have made this argument concede that a reduction in compensation costs would be likely to provide cost savings (and therefore profit advantages) in the short run (see http://www.cbo.gov/ftpdocs/99xx/doc9924/12-18-KeyIssues.pdf for a Congressional Budget Office discussion of this issue). Moreover, there is copious evidence to suggest that American corporations that consume health care are very concerned about health care costs, and little if any evidence to suggest that they are not.

28. Theda Skocpol (1996) has argued that the nature of the American government, with its many veto points, renders any large-scale reform exceedingly difficult to accomplish, and that this structure was a primary cause of the failure of the Clinton health care bill. It is certainly true—as also became evident in the debate over the Obama health care bill—that the American state creates a number of obstacles that raise the bar for achieving reform. On the other hand, the reforms of the New Deal and the Great Society, however aberrant they might have been, demonstrate that it is possible to accomplish major change within the American system if there is sufficient will for it.

29. The CED also called for deficit reduction through a tax increase during the Bush II presidency in the early 2000s. The group's report received little attention, however, and had no influence on congressional Republicans.

30. The Health Insurance Association of America (HIAA), an organization consisting primarily of smaller health insurance companies, had played an important role in defeating the Clinton health plan. The group is perhaps best remembered for its sponsorship of the "Harry and Louise" commercials that raised fears about the plan's viability. See Skocpol (1996, 134–139) for a discussion of this group.

31. Without this feature, anyone could avoid signing up for health insurance until he or she got sick. No insurance system can operate under this principle.

32. These figures come from the Kaiser Family Foundation's website feature Snapshots, from an article called "Health Care Spending in the United States and Selected OECD Countries," April 2011 (http://www.kff.org/insurance /snapshot/OECD042111.cfm). The data on health care spending as a proportion of GDP presented here—assembled by the Organization for Economic Cooperation and Development (OECD)—are slightly different from those presented in Figure 8.1—which came from the Congressional Budget Office. See Lasser, Himmelstein, and Woolhandler (2006) for further comparisons between Canadian and American health outcomes.

33. Unfortunately for Senator Bennett, his willingness to work with Democrats contributed in part to his ouster by Tea Party–inspired Utah Republicans, who at the state party convention in May 2010 voted him out of office (after three terms), denying him even an opportunity to run in the party's primary election (*Christian Science Monitor,* May 8, 2010, http://www.csmonitor.com /USA/Politics/2010/0508/Tea-party-movement-ousts-Sen.-Bob-Bennett-in-Utah).

34. In addition to an ideological aversion to government, economies of scale, and the vested interests of HR officers, others have suggested a fourth possible reason for American corporations' insistence on continuing the employer-based health care system: power. In an article on the website of the group Physicians for a National Health Program, a labor organizer argued, "Corporations like having healthcare linked to employment. They like having people held captive in jobs they hate for fear they'll lose their health coverage. They like it that, when you go on strike, you generally lose your health insurance" (Dudzik 2011). As we saw earlier, Nelson Lichtenstein (1995, 297) had made a similar point in explaining why General Motors, to the surprise of Walter Reuther, did not support the United Auto Workers in the group's quest for national health insurance. This is a position that few corporate executives would be likely to acknowledge, even if it were true. Yet regardless of whether there is some truth to this view, it seems insufficient to provide more than a partial explanation for corporations' curious support for employer-based insurance. The prospect of losing one's job remains a major basis of employer leverage over workers, even without the threat of losing one's health insurance.

9. The Ineffectual Elite

1. For historical data on American poverty rates, see http://www.stateofwork ingamerica.org/files//poverty_actual_and_simulated_with_gdp_all-years.png.

2. As we saw in Chapter 3, President Eisenhower, in a letter to his brother, referred to the members of this group as "stupid."

3. World Bank and Organization for Economic Cooperation and Development national accounts data files.

4. Ibid.

5. Cooper's article was a comment on a piece by Paul Krugman (1995). Krugman developed a model, simulated with estimates drawn from other empirical studies, suggesting that the observed level of international trade led to a wage reduction of 1.7 percent among unskilled workers.

6. The report was prepared by Transportation for America, a coalition of groups that include the National Association of Realtors, the National Association of City Transportation Officials, the Natural Resources Defense Council (NRDC), and the American Public Health Association (APHA). Because some of these groups may have a vested interest in infrastructure spending, it is possible that the report may have identified a higher number of structurally deficient bridges than a study by a more neutral entity would have. On the other hand, the APHA and the NRDC consist of highly respected scientists. Even if the 12 percent figure, which represents nearly 70,000 bridges, represents a slight exaggeration, it is difficult to deny the significant magnitude of the problem. The report is available at http://t4america.org/docs/bridgereport/bridgereport-national.pdf.

7. These figures, based on data released by the U.S. Army, were reported in the *Huffington Post* in December 2010. The article is available at http://www .huffingtonpost.com/2010/12/21/high-school-grads-fail-military-exam_n _799767.html.

8. For the graduation rates, see Intercollegiate Studies Institute American Civic Literacy Program, "The Shaping of the American Mind (Summary)," 2010, http://www.americancivicliteracy.org/2010/summary_summary.html. For college readiness, see Alliance for Excellent Education Fact Sheet, "Adolescent Literacy," 2011, http://www.all4ed.org/files/AdolescentLiteracyFactSheet.pdf.

9. See http://www.census.gov/hhes/www/poverty/data/historical/people.html, table 5.

10. See http://www.cdc.gov/healthyyouth/obesity/facts.htm. According to the Centers for Disease Control and Prevention website, more than one-third of American children and adolescents were overweight or obese in 2008.

11. See http://blogs.wsj.com/wealth/2011/10/27/most-millionaires-support -warren-buffetts-tax-on-the-rich/.

12. This includes the group Fix the Debt, which, as we saw in Chapter 8, has not, as of this writing, explicitly called for an increase in the income or capital gains tax rates paid by those at the upper end of the distribution. In addition to Warren Buffett, some prominent businesspeople began to call for an increase in tax rates after the 2012 election. See, for example, op-ed pieces by former treasury secretary and Citigroup officer Robert E. Rubin (*New York Times* [hereafter *NYT*], November 13, 2012, A27) and financier Steven Rattner (*NYT*, November 25, 2012, SR12). Although all three of these businessmen appear regularly on various news outlets, they appear as individuals rather than as representatives of an organization of business leaders.

13. As we saw in Chapter 7, in 1982 Ronald Reagan's treasury secretary, Donald T. Regan, admonished a group of Business Roundtable leaders who were recommending the rescinding of a portion of President Reagan's individual tax cut. As Regan put it, "It's somewhat ironic to hear $200,000 executives saying, 'Don't give a tax cut to $20,000 workers'" (quoted in Ehrbar 1982, 58). According to the Bureau of Labor Statistics CPI Calculator, an income of $200,000 in 1982 was equivalent to approximately $466,000 in 2011. A study by the Associated Press indicated that the average CEO compensation at publicly traded American companies in 2011 was approximately $9.6 million. If Regan was willing to accuse executives of being greedy when their real incomes were less than one-twentieth the size of today's average for all publicly traded firms (most of which are not in the Fortune 500), then one can assume that an increase of 4.6 percent in their marginal tax rate would not lead to a significant decline in the CEOs' standard of living.

14. In fairness to Keynesian theory, the economic problems of the 1970s were certainly exacerbated, and perhaps even caused, by the exogenous shocks created by the energy crises of 1973–1974 and 1979 and the increasing global competition faced by American firms.

15. On Merck, see http://www.unicefusa.org/news/news-from-the-field/merck-pia.html. On Wal-Mart, see http://www.smartplanet.com/blog/business-brains/walmarts-sustainability-hits-and-misses/15204. On Starbucks, see *NYT*, October 17, 2011, A27, and *NYT*, March 17, 2012, A21.

16. For a sensible proposal for corporate collective action to address unemployment, see Useem (2011). One promising group that has been willing to propose government involvement in addressing global warming is the U.S. Climate Action Partnership (USCAP), an organization of major corporations and environmental groups that has come together "to call on the federal government to quickly enact strong national legislation to require significant reductions of greenhouse gas emissions" (http://www.us-cap.org/). The group's members include such distinguished firms as Alcoa, Chrysler, Dow Chemical, Duke

Energy, DuPont, General Electric, Honeywell, Johnson & Johnson, PepsiCo, PG&E, Shell, Siemens, and Weyerhaeuser, as well as the Environmental Defense Fund and the Natural Resources Defense Council.

17. This page was reproduced from Professor Poole's website, Voteview.com, on a page entitled "The Polarization of the Congressional Parties," dated March 6, 2012. It is available at http://voteview.com/political_polarization.asp. The Wikipedia entry for "Nominate (scaling method)," available at http://en.wikipedia .org/wiki/NOMINATE_(scaling_method), contains a discussion of the method used by Poole and his colleague, Howard Rosenthal, to compute the scores on the conservatism-liberalism dimension from which the data in Figure 9.1 were drawn. See also Poole and Rosenthal (1997). I thank Clem Brooks at Indiana University for directing me to this site, and Keith T. Poole for permission to reprint the figure.

18. The decline of labor unions, which promoted a widely disseminated alternative to business and conservative-dominated views, may have also contributed to the confusion of at least some segments of the public.

References

Abrams, Burton A. 2006. "How Richard Nixon Pressured Arthur Burns: Evidence from the Nixon Tapes." *Journal of Economic Perspectives* 20:177–188.

Allen, Frederick Lewis. 1935. *The Lords of Creation*. New York: Harper and Brothers.

Andersen, Kurt. 2011. "The Madman Theory." *New York Times,* August 6, A17.

Ansell, Christopher. 2001. *Schism and Solidarity in Social Movements: The Politics of Labor in the French Third Republic*. New York: Cambridge University Press.

Arnold, Thurman W. 1937. *The Folklore of Capitalism*. New Haven: Yale University Press.

Arum, Richard and Josipa Roksa. 2011. *Academically Adrift: Limited Learning on College Campuses*. Chicago: University of Chicago Press.

Averitt, Robert T. 1968. *The Dual Economy: The Dynamics of American Industry Structure*. New York: W. W. Norton.

Bailey, Stephen Kemp. 1950. *Congress Makes a Law: The Story behind the Employment Act of 1946*. New York: Columbia University Press.

Bairoch, Paul and Richard Kozul-Wright. 1996. "Globalization Myths: Some Historical Reflections on Integration, Industrialization, and Growth in the World Economy." United Nations Conference on Trade and Development, discussion paper 113.

Baltzell, E. Digby. 1964. *The Protestant Establishment: Aristocracy and Caste in America.* New York: Random House.

————. 1979. *Puritan Boston and Quaker Philadelphia: Two Protestant Ethics and the Spirit of Class Authority and Leadership.* New York: Free Press.

Baran, Paul A. and Paul M. Sweezy. 1966. *Monopoly Capital: An Essay on the American Economic and Social Order.* New York: Monthly Review Press.

Barnard, John. 2004. *American Vanguard: The United Auto Workers during the Reuther Years, 1935–1970.* Detroit: Wayne State University Press.

Barnes, Roy C. and Emily R. Ritter. 2001. "Networks of Corporate Interlocking: 1962–1995." *Critical Sociology* 27:192–220.

Barone, Michael and Grant Ujifusa. 1983. *The Almanac of American Politics: 1984.* Washington, DC: National Journal.

Barth, James R., R. Dan Brumbaugh Jr., and Robert E. Litan. 1992. *The Future of American Banking.* Armonk, NY: M. E. Sharpe.

Barton, Allen H. 1985. "Determinants of Economic Attitudes in the American Business Elite." *American Journal of Sociology* 91:54–87.

Bauer, Raymond A., Ithiel de Sola Pool, and Lewis Anthony Dexter. 1963. *American Business and Public Policy: The Politics of Foreign Trade.* New York: Atherton Press.

Baumol, William J. 1959. *Business Behavior, Value, and Growth.* New York: Macmillan.

Bazelon, David T. 1965. "Big Business and the Democrats." *Commentary* 39(5):39–46.

Bearden, James. 1987. "Financial Hegemony, Social Capital, and Bank Boards of Directors." Pp. 48–59 in Michael Schwartz (ed.), *The Structure of Power in America.* New York: Holmes and Meier.

Bell, Daniel. 1950. "The Treaty of Detroit." *Fortune* (July):53–55.

————. 1960. "The Subversion of Collective Bargaining." *Commentary* 29:185–197.

————. 1973. *The Coming of Post-Industrial Society: A Venture in Social Forecasting.* New York: Basic Books.

Bendix, Reinhard. 1963. *Work and Authority in Industry: Ideologies of Management in the Course of Industrialization.* New York: Harper and Row.

Benton, William. 1944. "The Economics of a Free Society." *Fortune* (October):162–165.

Berger, Allen N., Anil K Kashyap, and Joseph M. Scalise. 1995. "The Transformation of the U.S. Banking Industry: What a Long, Strange Trip It's Been." *Brookings Papers on Economic Activity* 1995(2):55–201.

Bergthold, Linda A. 1990. *Purchasing Power in Health: Business, the State, and Health Care Politics.* New Brunswick, NJ: Rutgers University Press.

Berle, Adolf A., Jr. 1954. *The Twentieth Century Capitalist Revolution.* New York: Harcourt, Brace, and World.

———. 1959. *Power without Property.* New York: Harcourt, Brace and World.

———. 1966 [1959]. "Foreword." Pp. ix–xv in Edward S. Mason (ed.), *The Corporation in Modern Society.* New York: Atheneum.

Berle, Adolf A., Jr. and Gardiner C. Means. 1968 [1932]. *The Modern Corporation and Private Property.* Revised ed. New York: Harcourt, Brace and World.

Bernstein, Irving. 1947. "Recent Legislative Developments Affecting Mediation and Arbitration." *Industrial and Labor Relations Review* 1:406–420.

Beyer, Jürgen and Martin Hoppner. 2003. "The Disintegration of Organised Capitalism: German Corporate Governance in the 1990s." *West European Politics* 26:179–198.

Block, Fred L. 1977a. "The Ruling Class Does Not Rule: Notes on the Marxist Theory of the State." *Socialist Revolution* 7(3):6–28.

———. 1977b. *The Origins of International Economic Disorder: A Study of United States International Monetary Policy from World War II to the Present.* Berkeley: University of California Press.

Blumenthal, Sidney. 1986. *The Rise of the Counter-Establishment: From Conservative Ideology to Political Power.* New York: Times Books.

Boddy, Raford and James Crotty. 1975. "Class Conflict and Macro-Policy: The Political Business Cycle." *Review of Radical Political Economics* 7:1–19.

Bonacich, Phillip. 1972. "Technique for Analyzing Overlapping Memberships." *Sociological Methodology* 2:176–185.

Bowles, Samuel, David M. Gordon, and Thomas E. Weisskopf. 1983. *Beyond the Wasteland: A Democratic Alternative to Economic Decline.* Garden City, NY: Anchor Doubleday.

Bowman, John R. 1989. *Capitalist Collective Action: Competition, Cooperation, and Conflict in the Coal Industry.* Cambridge: Cambridge University Press.

Boyer, Robert. 1990. *The Regulation School: A Critical Introduction.* New York: Columbia University Press.

Braverman, Harry. 1974. *Labor and Monopoly Capital: The Degradation of Work in the Twentieth Century.* New York: Monthly Review Press.

Broder, David S. 2008. "Health Reform's Moment." *Washington Post,* December 14, B7.

Brody, David. 1980. *Workers in Industrial America: Essays on the Twentieth Century Struggle.* New York: Oxford University Press.

Budros, Art. 2002. "The Mean and Lean Firm and Downsizing: Causes of Involuntary and Voluntary Downsizing Strategies." *Sociological Forum* 17:307–342.

Bullock, Charles J. 1903. "The Concentration of Banking Interests in the United States." *Atlantic Monthly* 92:182–192.

Bunting, David. 1983. "Origins of the American Corporate Network." *Social Science History* 7(2):129–142.

Burch, Philip H., Jr. 1972. *The Managerial Revolution Reassessed: Family Control in America's Large Corporations.* Lexington, MA: Lexington Books.

Bureau of Labor Statistics. 1945. *Strikes and Lockouts in 1944.* United States Department of Labor, Bulletin 833. Washington, DC: U.S. Government Printing Office.

———. 1982. *Analysis of Work Stoppages, 1980.* United States Department of Labor, Bulletin 2120. Washington, DC: U.S. Government Printing Office.

———. 2011. "Table 1. Work Stoppages Involving 1,000 or More Workers, 1947–2010." Economic News Release, May 26. http://www.bls.gov/news.release/wkstp.t01.htm.

Burris, Val. 1987. "The Political Partisanship of American Business: A Study of Corporate Political Action Committees." *American Sociological Review* 52:732–744.

———. 2009. "Corporations, Capitalists, and Campaign Finance." Pp. 247–262 in Kevin T. Leicht and J. Craig Jenkins (eds.), *Handbook of Politics: State and Civil Society in Global Perspective.* New York: Springer Publishing.

Burris, Val and James Salt. 1990. "The Politics of Capitalist Class Segments: A Test of Corporate Liberalism Theory." *Social Problems* 37:341–359.

Burrough, Bryan and John Helyar. 2005 [1990]. *Barbarians at the Gate: The Fall of RJR Nabisco.* New York: HarperCollins.

Burt, Ronald S. 1983. *Corporate Profits and Cooptation: Networks of Market Constraints and Directorate Ties in the American Economy.* New York: Academic Press.

Business Week. 1970. "Why the Big Traders Worry Industry." July 25, 53–61.

——— 1984. "NLRB Rulings That Are Inflaming Labor Relations." June 11.

Cahan, Abraham. 1917. *The Rise of David Levinsky.* New York: Harper and Brothers.

Calomiris, Charles W. 1997. "Prepared Testimony of Mr. Charles W. Calomiris," Senate Banking, Housing, and Urban Affairs Committee, March 20. http://banking.senate.gov/97_03hrg/032097/witness/calomeri.htm.

Cannon, Lou. 1982. *Reagan.* New York: G. P. Putnam's Sons.

Cantor, Joel C., Nancy L. Barrand, Randolph A. Desonia, Alan B. Cohen, and Jeffrey C. Merrill. 1991. "Business Leaders' Views on American Health Care." *Health Affairs* 10(1):98–105.

Carnoy, Martin. 1984. *The State and Political Theory.* Princeton: Princeton University Press.

Carosso, Vincent P. 1970. *Investment Banking in America: A History*. Cambridge, MA: Harvard University Press.

Carroll, William K. 2010. *The Making of a Transnational Capitalist Class: Corporate Power in the Twenty-first Century*. London: Zed Books.

Carroll, William K. and Meindert Fennema. 2004. "Problems in the Study of the Transnational Business Community: A Reply to Kentor and Jang." *International Sociology* 19:369–378.

Carver, Charles S. 2003. "Pleasure as a Sign You Can Attend to Something Else: Placing Positive Feelings within a General Model of Affect." *Cognition and Emotion* 17:241–261.

Chandler, Alfred D., Jr. 1977. *The Visible Hand: The Managerial Revolution in American Business*. Cambridge, MA: Harvard University Press.

Cheffins, Brian and Steven Bank. 2009. "Is Berle and Means Really a Myth?" *Business History Review* 83:443–474.

Chicago Tribune. 1985. "James Watt's Fleeting Legacy." September 13, 18.

Chu, Johan S. G. and Gerald F. Davis. 2011. "Who Killed the Inner Circle? The Breakdown of the American Corporate Elite Network, 1999–2009." Paper presented at the Fourth Annual Political Networks Conference, University of Michigan, June.

Clawson, Dan and Mary Ann Clawson. 1987. "Reagan or Business? Foundations of the New Conservatism." Pp. 201–217 in Michael Schwartz (ed.), *The Structure of Power in America*. New York: Holmes and Meier.

Clawson, Dan and Alan Neustadtl. 1989. "Interlocks, PACs, and Corporate Conservatism." *American Journal of Sociology* 94:749–773.

Clawson, Dan, Alan Neustadtl, and James Bearden. 1986. "The Logic of Business Unity: Corporate Contributions to the 1980 Congressional Elections." *American Sociological Review* 51:797–811.

Clawson, Dan, Alan Neustadtl, and Denise Scott. 1992. *Money Talks: Corporate PACs and Political Influence*. New York: Basic Books.

Coase, R. H. 1937. "The Nature of the Firm." *Economica* 4:386–405.

Cobb, J. Adam. 2011. *From the "Treaty of Detroit" to the 401(k): The Development, Evolution, and Consequences of Privatized Retirement in the United States*. Unpublished PhD diss., Ross School of Business, University of Michigan.

Cochran, Thomas C. and William Miller. 1942. *The Age of Enterprise: A Social History of Industrial America*. New York: Macmillan.

Cohn, Jonathan. 2007. "What's the One Thing Big Business and the Left Have in Common?" *New York Times Magazine*, April 1, E44.

Collins, Robert M. 1978. "Positive Business Responses to the New Deal: The Roots of the Committee for Economic Development, 1933–1942." *Business History Review* 52:369–391.

————. 1981. *The Business Response to Keynes, 1929–1964*. New York: Columbia University Press.

Committee for Economic Development. 1944. *A Postwar Federal Tax Plan for High Employment*. New York: Committee for Economic Development.

————. 1945a. *American Industry Looks Ahead: A Business Estimate of Postwar Markets for Manufactured Goods*. New York: Committee for Economic Development.

————. 1945b. *Toward More Production, More Jobs, and More Freedom*. New York: Committee for Economic Development.

————. 1946. *Fiscal Policy to Fight Inflation: The Field Development Division*. New York: Committee for Economic Development.

————. 1947. *Collective Bargaining: How to Make It More Effective*. New York: Committee for Economic Development.

————. 1957. *Annual Report*. New York: Committee for Economic Development.

————. 1959. *Paying for Better Public Schools*. New York: Committee for Economic Development.

————. 1971. *Social Responsibilities of Business Corporations*. New York: Committee for Economic Development.

————. 1973. *Building a National Health-Care System*. New York: Committee for Economic Development.

Cooper, Richard N. 1995. "Comments and Discussion." *Brookings Papers on Economic Activity* 1995(1):363–368, 376–377.

Corey, Lewis. 1930. *The House of Morgan: A Social Biography of the Masters of Money*. New York: Grosset and Dunlap.

Coser, Lewis A. 1956. *The Functions of Social Conflict*. Glencoe, IL: Free Press.

Cramton, Peter and Joseph Tracy. 1998. "The Use of Replacement Workers in Union Contract Negotiations: The U.S. Experience, 1980–1989." *Journal of Labor Economics* 16:667–701.

Crouch, Colin. 2011. *The Strange Non-Death of Neo-liberalism*. Cambridge: Polity.

Dahl, Robert A. 1958. "A Critique of the Ruling Elite Model." *American Political Science Review* 52:463–469.

————. 1961. *Who Governs? Democracy and Power in an American City*. New Haven: Yale University Press.

————. 1982. *Dilemmas of Pluralist Democracy: Autonomy vs. Control*. New Haven: Yale University Press.

Dahrendorf, Ralf. 1959. *Class and Class Conflict in Industrial Society*. Stanford: Stanford University Press.

Darman, Richard. 1996. *Who's in Control? Polar Politics and the Sensible Center.* New York: Simon and Schuster.

Datta, Deepak K., James P. Guthrie, Dynah Basuil, and Alankrita Pandey. 2010. "Causes and Effects of Employee Downsizing: A Review and Synthesis." *Journal of Management* 36:281–348.

David, Thomas, Stéphanie Ginalski, Frédéric Rebmann, and Gerhard Schnyder. 2009. "The Swiss Business Elite between 1980–2000: Declining Cohesion, Changing Educational Profile, and Growing Internationalization." Pp. 197–220 in Friederike Sattler and Christoph Boyer (eds.), *European Economic Elites: Between a New Spirit of Capitalism and the "Erosion of State Socialism."* Berlin: Duncker and Humblot.

Davis, Gerald F. 1991. "Agents without Principles? The Spread of the Poison Pill through the Intercorporate Network." *Administrative Science Quarterly* 36:583–613.

———. 2009. *Managed by the Markets: How Finance Re-Shaped America.* New York: Oxford University Press.

Davis, Gerald F., Kristina A. Diekmann, and Catherine H. Tinsley. 1994. "The Decline and Fall of the Conglomerate Firm in the 1980s: The Deinstitutionalization of an Organizational Form." *American Sociological Review* 59:547–570.

Davis, Gerald F. and E. Han Kim. 2007. "Business Ties and Proxy Voting by Mutual Funds." *Journal of Financial Economics* 85:552–570.

Davis, Gerald F. and Mark S. Mizruchi. 1999. "The Money Center Cannot Hold: Commercial Banks in the U.S. System of Corporate Governance." *Administrative Science Quarterly* 44:215–239.

Derthick, Martha. 1979. *Policymaking for Social Security.* Washington, DC: Brookings Institution.

Dobbin, Frank. 1994. *Forging Industrial Policy: The United States, Britain, and France in the Railway Age.* Cambridge: Cambridge University Press.

Domhoff, G. William. 1967. *Who Rules America?* Englewood Cliffs, NJ: Prentice-Hall.

———. 1970. *The Higher Circles: The Governing Class in America.* New York: Vintage.

———. 1990. *The Power Elite and the State: How Policy Is Made in America.* New York: Aldine De Gruyter.

———. 2006. *Who Rules America?* 5th ed. New York: McGraw-Hill.

———. 2011. *Corporate Power and the Resurgence of Inequality: Postwar Liberalism in the Face of a Long Right Turn.* Unpublished book manuscript, Department of Sociology, University of California, Santa Cruz.

Drutman, Lee J. 2010. *The Business of America is Lobbying: The Expansion of Corporate Political Activity and the Future of American Pluralism.* PhD diss., Department of Political Science, University of California, Berkeley.

Dudzik, Mark. 2011. "Why Won't Corporate America Support Single Payer Medicare-for-All?" Physicians for a National Health Program, May 16. http://www.pnhp.org.

Dye, Thomas R. 1983. *Who's Running America?* 3rd ed. Englewood Cliffs, NJ: Prentice-Hall.

Economic Report of the President. 1970. http://www.presidency.ucsb.edu/economic _reports/1970.pdf.

Edsall, Thomas Byrne. 1984. *The New Politics of Inequality.* New York: W. W. Norton.

Ehrbar, A. F. 1979. "Pragmatic Politics Won't Win for Business." *Fortune* (November):76–80.

———. 1982. "The Battle Over Taxes." *Fortune* (April):58–63.

Evans, Michael K. 1980. "The Bankruptcy of Keynesian Econometric Models." *Challenge* 22(6):13–19.

Fairris, David. 1994. "Shopfloor Relations in the Postwar Capital-Labor Accord." Pp. 193–211 in David M. Kotz, Terrence McDonough, and Michael Reich (eds.), *Social Structures of Accumulation.* Cambridge: Cambridge University Press.

Feldstein, Martin. 1994. "American Economic Policy in the 1980s: A Personal View." Pp. 1–79 in Martin Feldstein (ed.), *American Economic Policy in the 1980s.* Chicago: University of Chicago Press.

Ferguson, Thomas and Joel Rogers. 1986. *Right Turn: The Decline of the Democrats and the Future of American Politics.* New York: Hill and Wang.

Fitch, Robert. 1972. "Sweezy and Corporate Fetishism." *Socialist Revolution* 2(6):93–127.

Fitch, Robert and Mary Oppenheimer. 1970a. "Who Rules the Corporations?" *Socialist Revolution* 1(4):73–108.

———. 1970b. "Who Rules the Corporations?" [Part 2.] *Socialist Revolution* 1(5):61–114.

———. 1970c. "Who Rules the Corporations?" [Part 3.] *Socialist Revolution* 1(6):33–94.

Fligstein, Neil. 1990. *The Transformation of Corporate Control.* Cambridge, MA: Harvard University Press.

———. 2001. *The Architecture of Markets: An Economic Sociology of Twenty-First-Century Capitalist Societies.* Princeton: Princeton University Press.

Fones-Wolf, Elizabeth A. 1994. *Selling Free Enterprise: The Business Assault on Labor and Liberalism.* Urbana: University of Illinois Press.

Freeman, Joshua. 1978. "Delivering the Goods: Industrial Unionism during World War II." *Labor History* 19:570–593.

Freeman, Linton C. 1979. "Centrality in Social Networks: Conceptual Clarification." *Social Networks* 1:215–239.

Freeman, Richard B. 1998. "Spurts in Union Growth: Defining Moments and Social Processes." Pp. 265–295 in Michael D. Bordo, Claudia Goldin, and Eugene N. White (eds.), *The Defining Moment: The Great Depression and the American Economy in the Twentieth Century.* Chicago: University of Chicago Press.

———. 2008. *America Works: The Exceptional U.S. Labor Market.* New York: Russell Sage Foundation.

Freitag, Peter J. 1975. "The Cabinet and Big Business: A Study of Interlocks." *Social Problems* 23:137–152.

Friedman, Milton. 1966. "Letter to the Editor." *Time.* February 4. http://www.time.com/time/magazine/article/0,9171,898916,00.html.

Friedman, Thomas. 2005. "CEOs MIA." *New York Times,* May 25, A25.

Frydman, Carola and Dirk Jenter. 2010. "CEO Compensation." *Annual Review of Financial Economics* 2:75–102.

Funk, Russell J. and Daniel Hirschman. 2011. "Endogenous Legal Change: How Organizations Re-shaped Glass-Steagall." Working paper, Department of Sociology, University of Michigan.

Galaskiewicz, Joseph. 1985. *Social Organization of an Urban Grants Economy: A Study of Business Philanthropy and Nonprofit Organizations.* Orlando: Academic Press.

Galbraith, John Kenneth. 1952a. *American Capitalism: The Concept of Countervailing Power.* Boston: Houghton Mifflin.

———. 1952b. "We Can Prosper without Arms Orders." *New York Times Magazine,* June 22.

———. 1967. *The New Industrial State.* Boston: Houghton Mifflin.

Garrett, Geoffrey. 1995. "Capital Mobility, Trade, and the Domestic Politics of Economic Policy." *International Organization* 49:657–687.

Glasberg, Davita Silfen. 1989. *The Power of Collective Purse Strings: The Effect of Bank Hegemony on Corporations and the State.* Berkeley: University of California Press.

Goodrich, Carter. 1960. *Government Promotion of American Canals and Railroads, 1800–1890.* New York: Columbia University Press.

Gordon, Robert Aaron. 1945. *Business Leadership in the Large Corporation.* Washington, DC: The Brookings Institution.

Graetz, Michael J. and Ian Shapiro. 2005. *Death by a Thousand Cuts: The Fight over Taxing Inherited Wealth.* Princeton: Princeton University Press.

Greene, John Robert. 2000. *The Presidency of George Bush.* Lawrence: University Press of Kansas.

Griffith, Robert. 1982. "Dwight D. Eisenhower and the Corporate Commonwealth." *American Historical Review* 87:87–122.

Gross, James A. 1995. *Broken Promise: The Subversion of U.S. Labor Relations Policy, 1947–1994.* Philadelphia: Temple University Press.

Handler, Edward and John R. Mulkern. 1982. *Business in Politics: Campaign Strategies of Corporate Political Action Committees.* Lexington, MA: Lexington Books.

Harbison, Frederick H. 1950. "The General Motors-United Auto Workers Agreement of 1950." *Journal of Political Economy* 58:397–411.

Harris, Howell John. 1982. *The Right to Manage: Industrial Relations Policies of American Business in the 1940s.* Madison: University of Wisconsin Press.

Harrison, Peter. 2009. "Median Wages and Productivity Growth in Canada and the United States." Ottawa: Centre for the Study of Living Standards Research, Note 2009-2. http://www.csls.ca/notes/Note2009-2.pdf.

Hartz, Louis. 1948. *Economic Policy and Democratic Thought: Pennsylvania, 1776–1860.* Cambridge, MA: Harvard University Press.

Harvey, David. 2007. *A Brief History of Neoliberalism.* Oxford: Oxford University Press.

Haunschild, Pamela R. 1993. "Interorganizational Imitation: The Impact of Interlocks on Corporate Acquisition Activity." *Administrative Science Quarterly* 38:564–592.

Hayward, Steven F. 2001. *The Age of Reagan: The Fall of the Old Liberal Order, 1964–1980.* Roseville, CA: Prima Publishing.

Heemskerk, Eelke. 2007. *Decline of the Corporate Community: Network Dynamics of the Dutch Business Elite.* Amsterdam: Amsterdam University Press.

Herman, Edward S. 1973. "Do Bankers Control Corporations?" *Monthly Review* 25(2):12–29.

———. 1979. "Kotz on Banker control." *Monthly Review* 31(3):46–57.

———. 1981a. *Corporate Control, Corporate Power.* New York: Cambridge University Press.

———. 1981b. "Reply to David Kotz." *Monthly Review* 33(1):61–64.

Herman, Edward S. and Carl F. Safanda. 1973. "Proxy Voting by Commercial Bank Trust Departments." *The Banking Law Journal* 90:91–115.

Hilferding, Rudolf. 1981 [1910]. *Finance Capital: A Study of the Latest Phase of Capitalist Development.* London: Routledge and Kegan Paul.

Hillman, Amy J. 2005. "Politicians on the Board of Directors: Do Connections Affect the Bottom Line? *Journal of Management* 31:464–481.

Himmelstein, Jerome L. 1990. *To the Right: The Transformation of American Conservatism.* Berkeley: University of California Press.

Hirschman, Albert O. 1970. *Exit, Voice, and Loyalty: Responses to Decline in Firms, Organizations, and States.* Cambridge, MA: Harvard University Press.

Hoffman, Paul G. 1946. "The Great Challenge to Capitalism." *New York Times,* September 8, SM3.

Hofstadter, Richard. 1965. *The Paranoid Style in American Politics, and Other Essays.* New York: Knopf.

Höpner, Martin and Lothar Krempel. 2003. "The Politics of the German Company Network." MFIfG working paper 03/9. Cologne: Max Planck Institute for the Study of Societies.

Hunter, Floyd. 1953. *Community Power Structure: A Study of Decision Makers.* Chapel Hill: University of North Carolina Press.

Jacoby, Sanford M. 1993. "Employers and the Welfare State: The Role of Marion B. Folsom." *Journal of American History* 80:525–556.

James, Christopher and Joel Houston. 1996. "Evolution or Extinction? Where Are Banks Headed?" *Journal of Applied Corporate Finance* 9(2):8–23.

Jenkins, J. Craig and Teri Shumate. 1985. "Cowboy Capitalists and the Rise of the 'New Right': An Analysis of Contributions to Conservative Policy Formation Organizations." *Social Problems* 33:130–145.

Jensen, Gordon. 1956. *The National Civic Federation: American Business in the Age of Social Change and Social Reform, 1900–1910.* PhD diss., Princeton University.

Jensen, Michael C. and William H. Meckling. 1976. "Theory of the Firm: Managerial Behavior, Agency Costs, and Ownership Structure." *Journal of Financial Economics* 3:305–360.

Johnson, Simon and James Kwak. 2010. *13 Bankers: The Wall Street Takeover and the Next Financial Meltdown.* New York: Pantheon.

Josephson, Matthew. 1962 [1934]. *The Robber Barons: The Great American Capitalists, 1861–1901.* New York: Harcourt Brace Jovanovich.

Judis, John B. 1995. "Abandoned Surgery: Business and the Failure of Health Care Reform." *The American Prospect* 21(Spring):65–73.

———. 2001. *The Paradox of American Democracy: Elites, Special Interests, and the Betrayal of Public Trust.* New York: Routledge.

Kaplan, Steven N. and Bernadette A. Minton. 2008. "How Has CEO Turnover Changed?" Unpublished manuscript, Booth School of Business, University of Chicago.

Keller, Amy. 1997. "GOP Pressures Business Group to Dump Their Dem Lobbyists." *Roll Call,* January 20.

Kelman, Steven. 1980. "Occupational Safety and Health Administration." Pp. 236–266 in James Q. Wilson (ed.), *The Politics of Regulation*. New York: Basic Books.

Kentor, Jeffrey and Yong Suk Jang. 2004. "Yes, There Is a (Growing) Transnational Business Community: A Study of Global Interlocking Directorates, 1983–98." *International Sociology* 19:355–368.

Keynes, John Maynard. 1940. "The United States and the Keynes Plan." *The New Republic* 103(5):156–159.

Keys, C. M. 1910. "The Building of a Money Trust." *World's Work* 19:12618–12625.

Khurana, Rakesh. 2002. *Searching for a Corporate Savior: The Irrational Quest for Charismatic CEOs*. Princeton: Princeton University Press.

———. 2007. *From Higher Aims to Hired Hands: The Social Transformation of American Business Schools and the Unfulfilled Promise of Management as a Profession*. Princeton: Princeton University Press.

Kimeldorf, Howard. 2011. "Disruption and Worker Replacement: Historical Sources of Unionization in the United States." Unpublished manuscript, Department of Sociology, University of Michigan.

Kochan, Thomas A., Harry C. Katz, and Robert B. McKersie. 1994. *The Transformation of American Industrial Relations*. Ithaca, NY: ILR Press.

Kolko, Gabriel. 1965. *Railroads and Regulation, 1877–1916*. Princeton: Princeton University Press.

Kotz, David M. 1978. *Bank Control of Large Corporations in the United States*. Berkeley: University of California Press.

———. 1981. "Reply to Edward Herman." *Monthly Review* 33(1):57–60.

Krippner, Greta R. 2011. *Capitalizing on Crisis: The Political Origins of the Rise of Finance*. Cambridge, MA: Harvard University Press.

Krooss, Herman E. 1970. *Executive Opinion: What Business Leaders Said and Thought on Economic Issues, 1920–1960*. Garden City, NY: Doubleday.

Krugman, Paul. 1995. "Growing World Trade: Causes and Consequences." *Brookings Papers on Economic Activity* 1995(1):327–362, 376–377.

———. 2009. "How Did Economists Get It So Wrong?" *New York Times Magazine,* September 6, SM36.

———. 2010. "That 1937 Feeling." *New York Times,* January 4, A21.

Lachmann, Richard. 2009. "Greed and Contingency: State Fiscal Crises and Imperial Failure in Early Modern Europe." *American Journal of Sociology* 115:39–73.

———. 2011. "The Roots of American Decline." *Contexts* 10(1):43–49.

Lamoreaux, Naomi R. 1985. *The Great Merger Movement in American Business, 1895–1904*. New York: Cambridge University Press.

Lane, Robert E. 1965. "The Politics of Consensus in the Age of Affluence." *American Political Science Review* 59:874–895.

La Porta, Rafael, Florencio Lopez-de-Silanes, and Andrei Shleifer. 1999. "Corporate Ownership around the World." *Journal of Finance* 54:471–517.

Lasser, Karen E., David U. Himmelstein, and Steffie Woolhandler. 2006. "Access to Care, Health Status, and Health Disparities in the United States and Canada: Results of a Cross-National Population-Based Survey." *American Journal of Public Health* 96:1300–1307.

Laumann, Edward O. and David Knoke. *The Organizational State: Social Choice in National Policy Domains.* Madison: University of Wisconsin Press.

Lawrence, Harry. 2004. *Aviation and the Role of Government.* Dubuque, IA: Kendall/Hunt.

Leach, Richard H. 1957. "The Interstate Oil Compact: A Study in Success." *Oklahoma Law Review* 10:274–288.

Lenin, V. I. 1975 [1917]. *Imperialism: The Highest Stage of Capitalism.* Peking (Beijing): Foreign Languages Press.

Lekachman, Robert. 1966. "The Automation Report." *Commentary* 41(5):65–71.

Lester, Richard A. 1958. *As Unions Mature: An Analysis of the Evolution of American Unionism.* Princeton: Princeton University Press.

Levitan, Sar A. and Martha R. Cooper. 1984. *Business Lobbies: The Public Good and the Bottom Line.* Baltimore: Johns Hopkins University Press.

Licht, Walter. 1992. *Getting Work: Philadelphia, 1840–1950.* Cambridge, MA: Harvard University Press.

Lichtenstein, Nelson. 1985. "UAW Bargaining Strategy and Shop-Floor Conflict: 1946–1970." *Industrial Relations* 24:360–381.

———. 1989. "From Corporatism to Collective Bargaining: Organized Labor and the Eclipse of Social Democracy in the Postwar Era." Pp. 122–152 in Steve Fraser and Gary Gerstle (eds.), *The Rise and Fall of the New Deal Order, 1930–1980.* Princeton: Princeton University Press.

———. 1995. *Walter Reuther: The Most Dangerous Man in Detroit.* Urbana: University of Illinois Press.

———. 1997–1998. "Taft-Hartley: A Slave-Labor Law?" *Catholic University Law Review* 47:763–789.

———. 2003. *State of the Union: A Century of American Labor.* Princeton: Princeton University Press.

Lindblom, Charles E. 1977. *Politics and Markets: The World's Political-Economic Systems.* New York: Basic Books.

Linder, Marc. 1999. *Wars of Attrition: Vietnam, the Business Roundtable, and the Decline of Construction Unions.* Iowa City: Fanpihua Press.

Lintner, John. 1966 [1959]. "The Financing of Corporations." Pp. 166–201 in Edward S. Mason (ed.), *The Corporation in Modern Society.* New York: Atheneum.

Lipset, Seymour Martin and William Schneider. 1983. *The Confidence Gap: Business, Labor, and Government in the Public Mind.* New York: Free Press.

———. 1987. "The Confidence Gap during the Reagan Years, 1981–1987." *Political Science Quarterly* 102:1–23.

Lo, Clarence Y. H. 1990. *Small Property versus Big Government: Social Origins of the Property Tax Revolt.* Berkeley: University of California Press.

Loper, Mary Lou. 1987. "Town Hall of California Marks Its 50th Anniversary." *Los Angeles Times,* November 19, F4.

Lowi, Theodore J. 1969. *The End of Liberalism: Ideology, Policy, and the Crisis of Public Authority.* New York: Norton.

Manne, Henry G. 1965. "Mergers and the Market for Corporate Control." *Journal of Political Economy* 73:110–120.

Manza, Jeff. 2000. "Political Sociological Models of the U.S. New Deal." *Annual Review of Sociology* 26:297–322.

Mao Tse-Tung. 1967. *Quotations from Chairman Mao Tse-Tung.* New York: Frederick A. Praeger.

March, James G. 1994. *A Primer on Decision Making: How Decisions Happen.* New York: Free Press.

March, James G. and Herbert A. Simon. 1958. *Organizations.* New York: John Wiley and Sons.

Margolis, Joshua D. and James P. Walsh. 2003. "Misery Loves Companies: Rethinking Social Initiatives by Business." *Administrative Science Quarterly* 48:268–305.

Markovsky, Barry and Edward J. Lawler. 1994. "A New Theory of Social Solidarity." *Advances in Group Processes* 11:113–137.

Marquis, Christopher, Mary Ann Glynn, and Gerald F. Davis. 2007. "Community Isomorphism and Corporate Social Action." *Academy of Management Review* 32:925–945.

Marquis, Christopher and Matthew Lee. 2012. "Who Is Governing Whom? Executives, Governance, and the Structure of Generosity in Large U.S. Firms." *Strategic Management Journal.* In press.

Martin, Cathie Jo. 1991. *Shifting the Burden: The Struggle over Growth and Corporate Taxation.* Chicago: University of Chicago Press.

———. 1994. "Business and the New Economic Activism: The Growth of Corporate Lobbies in the Sixties." *Polity* 27:49–76.

———. 2000. *Stuck in Neutral: Business and the Politics of Human Capital Investment Policy.* Princeton: Princeton University Press.

Mayer, Gerald. 2004. "Union Membership Trends in the United States." Congressional Research Service, Library of Congress. http://digitalcommons .ilr.cornell.edu/cgi/viewcontent.cgi?article=1176&context=key_workplace.

McCartin, Joseph A. 2011a. *Collision Course: Ronald Reagan, the Air Traffic Controllers, and the Strike that Changed America.* New York: Oxford University Press.

————. 2011b. "The Strike that Busted Unions." *New York Times,* August 2, A25.

McConnell, Grant. 1966. *Private Power and American Democracy.* New York: Alfred A. Knopf.

McDonough, Terrence. 1994. "The Construction of Social Structures of Accumulation in US History." Pp. 101–132 in David M. Kotz, Terrence McDonough, and Michael Reich (eds.), *Social Structures of Accumulation.* Cambridge: Cambridge University Press.

McIntyre, Richard and Michael Hillard. 2008. "The 'Limited Capital-Labor Accord': May It Rest in Peace?" *Review of Radical Political Economics* 40:244–249.

McKinley, William, Carol M. Sanchez, and Allen G. Schick. 1995. "Organizational Downsizing: Constraining, Cloning, and Learning." *Academy of Management Executive* 9(3):32–44.

McQuaid, Kim. 1978. "Corporate Liberalism in the American Business Community, 1920–1940." *Business History Review* 52:342–368.

Meyer, Rachel E. 2008. *Perpetual Struggle: Sources of Working-Class Identity and Activism in Collective Action.* PhD diss., Department of Sociology, University of Michigan.

Miliband, Ralph. 1969. *The State in Capitalist Society: An Analysis of the Western System of Power.* New York: Basic Books.

Miller, Matt. 2009. "A Real Employee Free Choice Act." *Wall Street Journal* (online version), October 1. http://online.wsj.com/article/SB1000142405274 8704471504574446921885356260.html.

Mills, C. Wright. 1948. *The New Men of Power: America's Labor Leaders.* New York: Harcourt, Brace, and World.

————. 1956. *The Power Elite.* New York: Oxford University Press.

Milner, Helen V. 1988. *Resisting Protectionism: Global Industries and the Politics of International Trade.* Princeton: Princeton University Press.

Mintz, Beth. 1995. "Business Participation in Health Care Policy Reform: Factors Contributing to Collective Action within the Business Community." *Social Problems* 42:408–428.

————. 1998. "The Failure of Health Care Reform: The Role of Big Business in Policy Formation." Pp. 210–224 in Clarence Lo and Michael Schwartz (eds.), *The Clinton Presidency: The First Term.* Oxford: Basil Blackwell.

Mintz, Beth and Michael Schwartz. 1985. *The Power Structure of American Business.* Chicago: University of Chicago Press.

Mishel, Lawrence, Jared Bernstein, and Sylvia Allegretto. 2007. *The State of Working America 2006/2007.* Ithaca, NY: ILR Press.

Mitchell, Neil J. 1989. *The Generous Corporation: A Political Analysis of Economic Power.* New Haven: Yale University Press.

Mizruchi, Mark S. 1982. *The American Corporate Network, 1904–1974.* Beverly Hills, CA: Sage.

————. 1983. "Who Controls Whom? An Examination of the Relation between Management and Boards of Directors in Large American Corporations." *Academy of Management Review* 8:426–435.

————. 1991. "Urgency, Motivation, and Group Performance: The Effect of Prior Success on Current Success among Professional Basketball Teams." *Social Psychology Quarterly* 54:181–189.

————. 1992. *The Structure of Corporate Political Action: Interfirm Relations and Their Consequences.* Cambridge, MA: Harvard University Press.

————. 1996. "What Do Interlocks Do? An Analysis, Critique, and Assessment of Research on Interlocking Directorates." *Annual Review of Sociology* 22:271–298.

————. 2004. "Berle and Means Revisited: The Governance and Power of Large U.S. Corporations." *Theory and Society* 33:579–617.

Mizruchi, Mark S. and David Bunting. 1981. "Influence in Corporate Networks: An Examination of Four Measures." *Administrative Science Quarterly* 26:475–489.

Mizruchi, Mark S. and Gerald F. Davis. 2004. "The Globalization of American Banking, 1962 to 1981." Pp. 95–126 in Frank Dobbin (ed.), *The Sociology of the Economy.* New York: Russell Sage Foundation.

Mizruchi, Mark S. and Daniel Hirschman. 2010. "*The Modern Corporation* as Social Construction." *Seattle University Law Review* 33:1065–1108.

Mizruchi, Mark S. and Linda Brewster Stearns. 1994. "A Longitudinal Study of Borrowing by Large American Corporations." *Administrative Science Quarterly* 39:118–140.

————. 2001. "Getting Deals Done: The Use of Social Networks in Bank Decision-Making." *American Sociological Review* 66:647–671.

Mizruchi, Mark S., Linda Brewster Stearns, and Christopher Marquis. 2006. "The Conditional Nature of Embeddedness: A Study of Borrowing by Large U.S. Firms, 1973–1994." *American Sociological Review* 71:310–333.

Mizruchi, Susan L. 2008. *The Rise of Multicultural America: Economy and Print Culture, 1865–1915.* Chapel Hill: University of North Carolina Press.

Moody, James and Douglas R. White. 2003. "Structural Cohesion and Embeddedness: A Hierarchical Concept of Social Groups." *American Sociological Review* 68:103–127.

Mosher, Lawrence. 1981a. "Wilderness System Is Under Siege by Oil, Gas, Mineral and Timber Interests." *National Journal* 13:2076–2080.

———. 1981b. "Move Over Jim Watt, Anne Gorsuch Is the Latest Target of Environmentalists." *National Journal* 13:1899–1902.

———. 1983. "Watt's Departure from Interior May Not Mean a Sharp Break with His Policies." *National Journal* 15:2306–2309.

Moynihan, Daniel Patrick. 1985. "Reagan's Inflate-the-Deficit Game." *New York Times,* July 21, E21.

Mullen, Brian and Carolyn Copper. 1994. "The Relation between Group Cohesiveness and Performance: An Integration." *Psychological Bulletin* 115:210–227.

Murray, Shailagh. 2009. " 'Public Option' May Be Highest Hurdle in Senate." *Washington Post,* June 24, A11.

Myers, Gustavus. 1910. *History of the Great American Fortunes,* vol. 2. Chicago: Charles H. Kerr and Co.

National Labor Relations Board. 1935. *Hearings before the Committee on Education and Labor,* United States Senate, Seventy-Fourth Congress, First Session, on S. 1958, March 15, 18, and 19. Washington, DC: U.S. Government Printing Office.

Nelson, Daniel. 1982. "The Company Union Movement, 1900–1937: A Reexamination." *Business History Review* 56:335–357.

Noble, Charles. 1986. *Liberalism at Work: The Rise and Fall of OSHA.* Philadelphia: Temple University Press.

Nordhaus, William D., Nicholas Kaldor, Alan Greenspan, and William Brainard. 1974. "The Falling Share of Profits." *Brookings Papers on Economic Activity* 1974(1):169–208.

Norsworthy, J. R. and Craig A. Zabala. 1985. "Worker Attitudes, Worker Behavior, and Productivity in the U.S. Automobile Industry, 1959–1976." *Industrial and Labor Relations Review* 38:544–557.

Noyes, Alexander Dana. 1909. *Forty Years of American Finance: A Short Financial History of the Government and People of the United States Since the Civil War, 1865–1907.* New York: G. P. Putnam's Sons.

O'Connor, Alice. 2008. "Financing the Counterrevolution." Pp. 148–168, 328–330 in Bruce J. Schulman and Julian E. Zelizer (eds.), *Rightward Bound: Making America Conservative in the 1970s.* Cambridge, MA: Harvard University Press.

O'Connor, James. 1972. "Question: Who Rules the Corporations? Answer: The Ruling Class." *Socialist Revolution* 2(1):117–150.

Page, Benjamin I., Fay Lomax Cook, and Rachel Moskowitz. 2011. "Wealthy Americans, Philanthropy, and the Common Good." Unpublished paper. New York: Russell Sage Foundation. http://www.scribd.com/doc/75022549 /Wealthy-Americans-Philanthropy-and-the-Common-Good.

Page, Scott E. 2007. *The Difference: How the Power of Diversity Creates Better Groups, Firms, Schools, Societies.* Princeton: Princeton University Press.

Paretsky, Nick. 2003. *Policy-Planning Organizations and Capitalist Support for Industrial Policy, 1970–1984.* Unpublished PhD diss., University of Missouri, Columbia.

Perlo, Victor. 1957. *The Empire of High Finance.* New York: International Publishers.

Perrow, Charles. 1986. *Complex Organizations: A Critical Essay.* 3rd ed. New York: Random House.

Peschek, Joseph G. 1987. *Policy-Planning Organizations: Elite Agendas and America's Rightward Turn.* Philadelphia: Temple University Press.

Pfeffer, Jeffrey and Gerald R. Salancik. 1978. *The External Control of Organizations: A Resource Dependence Perspective.* New York: Harper and Row.

Phillips-Fein, Kim. 2009. *Invisible Hands: The Businessmen's Crusade against the New Deal.* New York: Norton.

Piketty, Thomas and Emmanuel Saez. 2003. "Income Inequality in the United States, 1913–1998." *Quarterly Journal of Economics* 118:1–39.

Piore, Michael J. and Charles F. Sabel. 1984. *The Second Industrial Divide: Possibilities for Prosperity.* New York: Basic Books.

Poole, Keith T. and Howard Rosenthal. 1997. *Congress: A Political-Economic History of Roll Call Voting.* New York: Oxford University Press.

Prasad, Monica. 2006. *The Politics of Free Markets: The Rise of Neoliberal Economic Policies in Britain, France, Germany, and the United States.* Chicago: University of Chicago Press.

Pratt, Soreno S. 1904. "Who Owns the United States?" *World's Work* 17:4259–4266.

———. 1905. "Our Financial Oligarchy." *World's Work* 10:6704–6714.

Prechel, Harland. 1990. "Steel and the State: Industry Politics and Business Policy Formation, 1940–1989." *American Sociological Review* 55:648–668.

———. 2000. *Big Business and the State: Historical Transitions and Corporate Transformation, 1880s–1990s.* Albany: State University of New York Press.

Priest, Dana and Michael Weisskopf. 1994. "Health Care Reform: The Collapse of a Quest." *Washington Post,* October 11, A6.

Quadagno, Jill S. 1984. "Welfare Capitalism and the Social Security Act of 1935." *American Sociological Review* 49:632–647.

———. 1985. "Two Models of Welfare State Development: Reply to Skocpol and Amenta." *American Sociological Review* 50:575–578.

———. 1988. *The Transformation of Old Age Security: Class and Politics in the American Welfare State.* Chicago: University of Chicago Press.

Rabern, Susan J. 2009. "Leveraging the Feds: An Assessment of the Effectiveness of Fortune 500 Corporate Political Activities, 2001–2008." Unpublished manuscript, Center for Leadership and Ethics, Virginia Military Institute.

Rajan, Raghuram G. and Luigi Zingales. 2003. *Saving Capitalism from the Capitalists: Unleashing the Power of Financial Markets to Create Wealth and Spread Opportunity.* New York: Crown Business.

Ratcliff, Richard E. 1980. "Banks and Corporate Lending: An Analysis of the Impact of the Internal Structure of the Capitalist Class on the Lending Behavior of Banks." *American Sociological Review* 45:553–570.

Rees, Albert. 1952. "Industrial Conflict and Business Fluctuations." *Journal of Political Economy* 60:371–382.

Riddick, Floyd M. 1961. "The Eighty-Sixth Congress: Second Session." *Western Political Quarterly* 14:415–431.

Rieder, Jonathan. 1985. *Canarsie: The Jews and Italians of Brooklyn against Liberalism.* Cambridge, MA: Harvard University Press.

Rodrik, Dani. 1998. "Why Do Open Economies Have Bigger Governments?" *Journal of Political Economy* 106:997–1032.

Roe, Mark J. 1994. *Strong Managers, Weak Owners: The Political Roots of American Corporate Finance.* Princeton: Princeton University Press.

Rothkopf, David. 2008. *Superclass: The Global Power Elite and the World They Are Making.* New York: Farrar, Straus, and Giroux.

Roy, William G. 1981. "The Process of Bureaucratization in the U.S. State Department and the Vesting of Economic Interests, 1886–1905." *Administrative Science Quarterly* 26:419–433.

———. 1983. "The Unfolding of the Interlocking Directorate Structure of the United States." *American Sociological Review* 48:248–257.

———. 1997. *Socializing Capital: The Rise of the Large Industrial Corporation in America.* Princeton: Princeton University Press.

Sale, Kirkpatrick. 1975. *Power Shift: The Rise of the Southern Rim and Its Challenge to the Eastern Establishment.* New York: Random House.

Saloma, John S., III. 1984. *Ominous Politics: The New Conservative Labyrinth.* New York: Hill and Wang.

Schifeling, Todd. 2011. "Defense against Recession: U.S. Business Mobilization, 1950–1970." Unpublished manuscript, Department of Sociology, University of Michigan.

Schmitt, Mark. 2005. "The Legend of the Powell Memo." *American Prospect,* April 27. http://prospect.org/cs/articles?articleId=9606.

Schriftgiesser, Karl. 1960. *Business Comes of Age: The Story of the Committee for Economic Development and Its Impact upon the Economic Policies of the United States, 1942–1960.* New York: Harper and Brothers.

Scott, John. 1979. *Corporations, Classes, and Capitalism.* New York: St. Martin's Press.

Selznick, Philip. 1949. *TVA and the Grass Roots: A Study in the Sociology of Formal Organization.* Berkeley: University of California Press.

Silk, Leonard and Mark Silk. 1980. *The American Establishment.* New York: Basic Books.

Silk, Leonard and David Vogel. 1976. *Ethics and Profits: The Crisis of Confidence in American Business.* New York: Simon and Schuster.

Sills, David L. 1957. *The Volunteers: Means and Ends in a National Organization.* Glencoe, IL: Free Press.

Simmel, Georg. 1955. *Conflict and The Web of Group Affiliations.* New York: Free Press.

Simon, Herbert A. 1959. "Theories of Decision-Making in Economics and Behavioral Science." *American Economic Review* 49:253–283.

Singer, James W. 1980. "Behind the New Aggressiveness." *National Journal* 12:1367.

Sklair, Leslie. 2001. *The Transnational Capitalist Class.* Oxford: Blackwell.

Skocpol, Theda. 1980. "Political Response to Capitalist Crisis: Neo-Marxist Theories of the State and the Case of the New Deal." *Politics and Society* 10:155–201.

———. 1996. *Boomerang: Clinton's Health Security Effort and the Turn against Government in U.S. Policy.* New York: Norton.

Skocpol, Theda and Edwin Amenta. 1985. "Did Capitalists Shape Social Security?" *American Sociological Review* 50:572–575.

Skocpol, Theda and John Ikenberry. 1983. "The Political Formation of the American Welfare State in Historical and Comparative Perspective." *Comparative Social Research* 6:87–148.

Sobel, Robert. 1965. *The Big Board: A History of the New York Stock Market.* New York: Free Press.

Special Studies Project. 1958. *The Pursuit of Excellence: Education and the Future of America.* Rockefeller Brothers Fund America at Mid-Century Series, Panel Report V of the Special Studies Project. Garden City, NY: Doubleday.

Staples, Clifford L. 2006. "Board Interlocks and the Study of the Transnational Capitalist Class." *Journal of World-Systems Research* 12:309–319.

Starr, Paul. 2011. *Remedy and Reaction: The Peculiar American Struggle over Health Care Reform*. New Haven: Yale University Press.

Stearns, Linda Brewster. 1986. "Capital Market Effects on External Control of Corporations." *Theory and Society* 15:47–75.

Stearns, Linda Brewster and Kenneth D. Allan. 1996. "Economic Behavior in Institutional Environments: The Corporate Merger Wave of the 1980s." *American Sociological Review* 61:699–718.

Stearns, Linda Brewster and Mark S. Mizruchi. 1993. "Corporate Financing: Social and Economic Determinants." Pp. 279–307 in Richard Swedberg (ed.), *Explorations in Economic Sociology*. New York: Russell Sage Foundation.

Stein, Herbert. 1969. *The Fiscal Revolution in America*. Chicago: University of Chicago Press.

Stieber, Jack. 1966. "The President's Committee on Labor-Management Policy." *Industrial Relations* 5(2):1–19.

Stigler, George J. 1971. "The Theory of Economic Regulation." *Bell Journal of Economics and Management Science* 2:3–21.

Stockman, David A. 1986. *The Triumph of Politics: How the Reagan Revolution Failed*. New York: Harper and Row.

Streeck, Wolfgang and Lane Kenworthy. 2005. "Theories and Practices of Neocorporatism." Pp. 441–460 in Thomas Janoski, Robert R. Alford, Alexander M. Hicks, and Mildred A. Schwartz (eds.), *The Handbook of Political Sociology*. New York: Cambridge University Press.

Sutton, Francis X., Seymour E. Harris, Carl Kaysen, and James Tobin. 1956. *The American Business Creed*. Cambridge, MA: Harvard University Press.

Sweezy, Paul M. 1941. "The Decline of the Investment Banker." *Antioch Review* 1:63–68.

———. 1972. "The Resurgence of Financial Control: Fact or Fancy?" Pp. 113–145 in Paul M. Sweezy and Harry Magdoff (eds.), *The Dynamics of U.S. Capitalism*. New York: Monthly Review Press.

Sweezy, Paul M. and Harry Magdoff. 1972. "The End of U.S. Hegemony." Pp. 197–212 in Paul M. Sweezy and Harry Magdoff (eds.), *The Dynamics of U.S. Capitalism*. New York: Monthly Review Press.

Tan, Elaine S. 2008. "Champernowne Model Estimates of Aggregate Concentration in the US, 1931–2000." Social Science Research Network, http://ssrn.com/abstract=1285070.

Tarbell, Ida M. 1905 *The History of the Standard Oil Company*. New York: McClure, Phillips, and Co.

Taylor, Frederick Winslow. 1911. *The Principles of Scientific Management*. New York: Harper and Brothers.

Time. 1965. "The Congress: Ev's Extendalong." October 15. http://www.time
.com/time/magazine/article/0,9171,834479-1,00.html.

———. 1969. "Construction: Roger's Roundtable." August 29. http://www.time
.com/time/magazine/article/0,9171,901319,00.html.

Tomlins, Christopher L. 1985. *The State and the Unions: Labor Relations, Law,
and the Organized Labor Movement in America, 1880–1960.* Cambridge:
Cambridge University Press.

Truman, David B. 1951. *The Governmental Process: Political Interests and Public
Opinion.* New York: Alfred A. Knopf.

U.S. Congress. 1913. House Banking and Currency Committee. *Investigation of
Financial and Monetary Conditions in the United States.* Washington, DC:
U.S. Government Printing Office.

———. 1999. *Congressional Record—Senate.* 106th Congress, October 27,
145(148):26954–26955. Washington, DC: U.S. Government Printing
Office.

U.S. Congress. Senate. 1935. National Labor Relations Board. *Hearings before the
Committee on Education and Labor.* Seventy-Fourth Congress. On S. 1958.
Washington, DC: U.S. Government Printing Office.

———. 1945. *Full Employment Act of 1945. Hearings before a Subcommittee of the
Committee on Banking and Currency.* Seventy-Ninth Congress. First Session
on S. 380. Washington, DC: U.S. Government Printing Office.

Useem, Michael. 1980. "Corporations and the Corporate Elite." *Annual Review
of Sociology* 6:41–77.

———. 1984. *The Inner Circle: Large Corporations and the Rise of Business
Political Activity in the U.S. and U.K.* New York: Oxford University Press.

———. 1993. *Executive Defense: Shareholder Power and Corporate Reorganiza-
tion.* Cambridge, MA: Harvard University Press.

———. 1996. *Investor Capitalism: How Money Managers are Changing the Face of
Corporate America.* New York: Basic Books.

———. 2011. "The Business of Employment: Time to Revise Investor Capitalism's Mantra." *Washington Post,* August 9. http://www.washingtonpost.com
/national/on-leadership/the-business-of-employment-time-to-revise-investor
-capitalisms-mantra/2011/08/09/gIQAh8rs4I_story.html.

Vancil, Richard F. 1987. *Passing the Baton: Managing the Process of CEO Succession.* Boston: Harvard Business School Press.

Vancouver, Jeffrey B., Charles M. Thompson, and Amy A. Williams. 2001. "The
Changing Signs in the Relationships among Self-Efficacy, Personal Goals,
and Performance." *Journal of Applied Psychology* 86:605–620.

Venn, Fiona. 1998. *The New Deal.* Edinburgh: Edinburgh University Press.

Vogel, David. 1989. *Fluctuating Fortunes: The Political Power of Business in America*. New York: Basic Books.

Warren, Edgar L. 1948. "The Conciliation Service: V-J Day to Taft-Hartley." *Industrial and Labor Relations Review* 1:351–362.

Weidenbaum, Murray L. 1979. "The High Cost of Government Regulation." *Challenge* 22(5):32–39.

Weinstein, James. 1968. *The Corporate Ideal in the Liberal State, 1900–1918*. Boston: Beacon Press.

Weisberg, Jacob. 1998. "Happy Birthday, Heritage Foundation." *Slate,* January 9. http://www.slate.com/id/2299/.

Weisman, Jonathan. 2004. "Reagan Policies Gave Green Light to Red Ink." *Washington Post,* June 9, A11.

Weisskopf, Thomas E., Samuel Bowles, and David M. Gordon. 1983. "Hearts and Minds: A Social Model of U.S. Productivity Growth." *Brookings Papers on Economic Activity* 1983(2):381–450.

Welch, Jack with John A. Byrne. 2001. *Jack: Straight from the Gut*. New York: Warner Business Books.

White, Harrison C., Scott A. Boorman, and Ronald L. Breiger. 1976. "Social Structure from Multiple Networks. I. Blockmodels of Roles and Positions." *American Journal of Sociology* 81:730–780.

Whitman, Marina V. N. 1999. *New World, New Rules: The Changing Role of the American Corporation*. Boston: Harvard Business School Press.

Whitt, J. Allen. 1982. *Urban Elites and Mass Transportation: The Dialectics of Power*. Princeton: Princeton University Press.

Wiebe, Robert H. 1958. "Business Disunity and the Progressive Movement, 1901–1914." *Mississippi Valley Historical Review* 44:664–685.

Wilson, Charles E. 1949. "Where Are We Going from Here." Minutes of the UAW-GM Pension Committee, Box 6, United Auto Workers Archives, Wayne State University, November 15.

Wilson, Hugh A. 2009. "President Eisenhower and the Development of Active Labor Market Policy in the United States: A Revisionist View." *Presidential Studies Quarterly* 39:519–548.

Wines, Michael. 1981. "They're Still Telling OSHA Horror Stories, But the 'Victims' Are New." *National Journal* 13:1985–1989.

Winters, Jeffrey A. 2011. *Oligarchy*. New York: Cambridge University Press.

Youngman, Anna. 1907a. "The Tendency of Modern Combination: I." *Journal of Political Economy* 15:193–208.

———. 1907b. "The Tendency of Modern Combination: II." *Journal of Political Economy* 15:284–298.

Zajac, Edward J. and James D. Westphal. 1995. "Accounting for the Explanations of CEO Compensation: Substance and Symbolism." *Administrative Science Quarterly* 40:283–308.

———. 2004. "The Social Construction of Market Value: Institutionalization and Learning Perspectives on Stock Market Reactions." *American Sociological Review* 69:433–457.

Zald, Mayer N. 1970. *Organizational Change: The Political Economy of the YMCA*. Chicago: University of Chicago Press.

Zeitlin, Maurice. 1974. "Corporate Ownership and Control: The Large Corporation and the Capitalist Class." *American Journal of Sociology* 79:1073–1119.

Zuckerman, Ezra W. 1999. "The Categorical Imperative: Securities Analysts and the Illegitimacy Discount." *American Journal of Sociology* 104:1398–1438.

Zweigenhaft, Richard L. and G. William Domhoff. 2006. *Diversity in the Power Elite: How It Happened, Why It Matters.* Lanham, MD: Rowman and Littlefield.

Periodicals Not Listed Above, Noted in Text by Date of Publication

New York Times Articles—Organized Chronologically, Ascending

New York Times. 1913. "Poor Men Best Citizens: A. C. Bartlett Says Millionaires Seldom Undertake the Burden of Betterment." January 19, 1.

Associated Press. 1945. "Proposed Management-Labor Code." *New York Times,* March 29, 16.

Porter, Russell. 1946. "New Life in CED Urged to Stimulate Country." *New York Times,* May 26, S6.

Crider, John H. 1946. "Truman Talks with Snyder on Anti-inflation Policies." *New York Times,* July 3, 1.

Porter, Russell. 1947. "Program Outlined by Hoffman Group." *New York Times,* January 13, 28.

———. 1947. "CED Affirms Faith in Free Enterprise." *New York Times,* January 22, 15.

New York Times. 1947. "Asks Joint Action to End 'Boom-Bust.'" April 11, 33.

———. 1950. "Tobin, Ching Praise New G.M. Compact." May 24, 3.

———. 1950. "Snyder Advocates a 75 Per Cent Tax on Excess Profits." November 16, 1.

Morris, John D. 1951. "Business Unit Asks 10 Billion Tax Rise." *New York Times*. March 30, 1.

Trussell, C. P. 1951. "Senate Bill Eases Income Tax Rises." *New York Times,* August 22, 1.

New York Times. 1953. "Stand-by Controls Approved by C.I.O." March 14, 31.

———. 1953. "Cut of 6.6 Billion in Budget Is Urged." April 8, 23.

Morris, John D. 1953. "Korea Peace Hope Seen Casting Doubt on Tax Extension." *New York Times*, June 6, 1.

New York Times. 1953. "Budget Battle Line." June 10, 28.

———. 1955. "Tax Cut Outlook in '56 Called Good." May 8, 74.

———. 1958. "A.F.L.-C.I.O. Urges Cut in Taxes Now." March 25, 1.

Dale, Edwin L., Jr. 1958. "Unions' Economic Power Is Seen as a Contribution to Inflation." *New York Times*, July 23, 16.

Dale, Edwin L., Jr. 1959. "President's View on Budget Backed." April 8, 28.

Lawrence, W. H. 1961. "President Names Wage-Price Unit." *New York Times*, February 17, 1.

Waggoner, Walter H. 1961. "Labor Policy Study Urges Smaller Government Roles." *New York Times*, December 10, 1.

New York Times. 1962. "Excerpts from Report to Kennedy on Collective Bargaining." May 2, 20.

Hunter, Marjorie. 1963. "Selective U.S. Aid to Schools Urged." *New York Times*, April 10, 24.

Shanahan, Eileen. 1964. "Johnson Gaining Support of Many Traditionally Republican Businessmen in Northeast, Midwest." *New York Times*, September 16, 13.

New York Times. 1964. "President Names 14 to Automation Unit." November 15, 64.

Franklin, Ben A. 1965. "Businessmen Fear Urban Decay Unless Cities Subsidize Rails." *New York Times*, April 19, 1.

Shanahan, Eileen. 1966. "Chamber Opposes Increase in Taxes." *New York Times*, March 19, 1, 12.

Reston, James. 1966. "Washington: The Big Business Progressives." *New York Times*, October 12, 42.

New York Times. 1966. "Businessmen Ask Tax Rise Big Enough to Allow $3-Billion Budget Surplus." December 2, 24.

———. 1967. "U.S. Credit Urged for States' Taxes." June 8, 32.

Shanahan, Eileen. 1967. "113 Business Leaders Back a Temporary Rise in Taxes." *New York Times*, August 25, 1.

Sibley, John. 1968. "State Panel Recommends a 'Negative Income Tax.'" *New York Times*, April 30, 1.

Silk, Leonard. 1972. "A New Battle: Capitalism vs. Socialism." *New York Times*, May 3, 63.

Rosenthal, Jack. 1972. "Research Unit Asks Reform of Laws." *New York Times*, June 29, 20.

Markham, James M. 1972. "New Support for Making It Legal." *New York Times,* December 3, E2.

New York Times. 1975. "$20-Billion Tax Cut Urged by Private Economic Unit." January 10, 53.

Shanahan, Eileen. 1975. "Antitrust Bill Stopped by a Business Lobby: Top Executives United In New Group to Block Plan for Suing a Company." *New York Times,* November 16, 1.

———. 1976. "Ford Now Opposes Damage-Suit Bill: Big Payments Called Needed." *New York Times,* March 17, 59.

Mullaney, Thomas E. 1977. "Olin: Staunch Fighter for Free Enterprise." *New York Times,* April 29, D3.

Shabecoff, Philip. 1978. "Auto Union Head Protests Role of Business, Quits Carter Panel." *New York Times,* July 20, B4.

New York Times. 1982. "Urban-Business Partnerships Urged in Face of Budget Cuts." February 11, A28.

———. 1982. "Bond Traders Exhorted." March 12, D3.

Raines, Howell. 1982. "Executives Bid Reagan Cut Deficit." *New York Times,* March 13, 31, 38.

Cowan, Edward. 1982. "Plans to Lift Taxes Divide Business." *New York Times,* June 21, D1, D4.

Heinemann, H. Erich. 1983. "Group Asks Action to Raise Productivity." *New York Times,* April 30, 31.

Silk, Leonard. 1983. "Economic Scene." *New York Times,* July 1, D2.

Blumenthal, Sidney. 1983. "Drafting a Democratic Industrial Plan." *New York Times,* August 28, SM31.

Lueck, Thomas J. 1985. "Why Jack Welch Is Changing G.E.: Why Welch Says G.E. Must Change to Grow." *New York Times,* May 5, F1.

New York Times. 1985. "Sticking Up for a Low Tax Bill." May 5, F8.

Kilborn, Peter T. 1985. "Stockman Blockbuster." *New York Times,* July 11, A20.

Wicker, Tom. 1985. "A Deliberate Deficit: Stockman Spilled the Beans." *New York Times,* July 19, A27.

Freudenheim, Milt. 1989. "A Health-Care Taboo Is Broken: The Auto Industry Talks of National Medical Insurance." *New York Times,* May 8, D1.

———. 1989. "Calling for a Bigger U.S. Health Role." *New York Times,* May 30, D1, D11.

Uchitelle, Louis. 1991. "Insurance as a Job Benefit Shows Signs of Overwork." *New York Times,* May 1, A1.

Lohr, Steve. 1992. "Pulling Down the Corporate Clubhouse." *New York Times,* April 12, 1, 5.

Clymer, Adam. 1993. "Many Health Plans, One Political Goal." *New York Times*, October 17, 1.

———. 1994. "Powerful Business Group Backs Rival to President's Health Plan." *New York Times,* February 3, A1.

New York Times. 1994. "Storm Warnings on Health Care." February 7, A16.

Toner, Robin. 1994. "Cold Feet: Companies Get Skittish on Altering Health Care." *New York Times,* May 15, E1.

Freudenheim, Milt. 2002. "Coalition Forms to Reverse Trend of Fast-Rising Ranks of Uninsured Americans." *New York Times*, February 9, A12.

Krueger, Alan B. 2003. "Economic Scene." *New York Times,* March 6, C2.

Justice, Glen. 2005. "A New Target for Advisers to Swift Vets." *New York Times,* February 21. http://www.nytimes.com/2005/02/21/politics/21social.html.

New York Times. 2007. Display Ad 9. January 17, A12.

Freudenheim, Milt. 2007. "With Health Care Topic A, Some Sketches for a Solution." *New York Times,* January 25, C1.

Cohn, Jonathan. 2007. "What's the One Thing Big Business and the Left Have in Common?" *New York Times,* April 1, E44.

Pear, Robert. 2009. "Health Care Industry in Talks to Shape Policy." *New York Times,* February 20, A16.

Greenhouse, Steven. 2011. "Union Membership in U.S. Fell to 70-Year Low Last Year." *New York Times,* January 21. http://www.nytimes.com/2011/01/22/business/22union.html.

Kaufman, Michael T. 2011. "Daniel Bell, Ardent Appraiser of Politics, Economics and Culture, Dies at 91." *New York Times,* January 26, A23.

Leonhardt, David. 2011. "Big Business Leaves Deficit to Politicians." *New York Times,* July 5, B1.

New York Times. 2011. "Surely They Can Read a Spreadsheet." August 21, SR10.

Nocera, Joe. 2011. "We Can All Become Job Creators." *New York Times,* October 17, A27.

———. 2012. "The Good, Bad, and Ugly of Capitalism." *New York Times,* March 17, A21.

Calmes, Jackie. 2012. "Business Leaders Urge Deficit Deal with More Taxes." *New York Times*, October 26, A25.

Schwartz, Nelson D. and David Kocieniewski. 2012. "Business Chiefs Step Gingerly into a Thorny Budget Fight." *New York Times*, November 12, B1.

Rubin, Robert E. 2012. "The Fiscal Delusion." *New York Times*, November 13, A27.

Rattner, Steven. 2012. "More Chips for Tax Reform." *New York Times*, November 25, SR12.

Wall Street Journal Articles—Organized Chronologically, Ascending

Wall Street Journal. 1946. "A Report and CED." March 1, 6.

———. 1950. "Excess Profits Tax: House Group to End Hearings Today." November 22, 4.

———. 1951. "Federal Sales Tax: Snyder Goes on Record against General U.S. Levy in Any Form Either at Retail or Manufacturers' Level." July 11, 3.

———. 1953. "Spending Stays High: Folsom Says Taxes Can't Be Cut Now, Even with Korean Truce." June 6, 2.

———. 1954. "Congress at Work." February 18, 4.

———. 1956. "Private Economic Group Says Users Should Pay for Road Modernization." January 16, 4.

———. 1956. Display Ad 58. November 21, 13.

———. 1966. "Income-Tax Increase Early in 1967 Is Urged by Panel of the CED." December 8, 10.

———. 1968. "The Economy after Vietnam." April 18, 18.

———. 1972. "Business Council Panel of Economists Cautions on Monetary Stimulus." February 18, 2.

———. 1973. "What's News." April 12, 1.

———. 1974. "Tax Rise on Gasoline-Guzzling Vehicles Is Urged by CED to Cut U.S. Oil Demand." December 9, 2.

———. 1976. "The Roundtable's Mission." October 6, 22.

———. 1976. "Rehabilitation Project: Once Mighty CED Panel of Executives Seeks a Revival, Offers Advice to Carter." December 17, 38.

Hyatt, James C. 1977. "Business Pushes 'Employee Bill of Rights' to Blunt Labor's Drive for Law Changes." *Wall Street Journal,* June 24, 8.

Conderacci, Greg. 1977. "The Grass-Roots Looks Askance at Tax Reform." *Wall Street Journal,* August 15, 14.

Lublin, Joann S. 1978. "Seeking a Cure: Companies Fight Back against Soaring Cost of Medical Coverage." *Wall Street Journal,* May 10, 1.

Wall Street Journal. 1982. "Limits of Voluntarism." February 9, 30.

Merry, Robert W. 1982. "Parties' Leaders Face Political Hurdles in Efforts to Get Tax Bill Past the House." *Wall Street Journal,* August 18, 4.

Wall Street Journal. 1985. "Business Group Calls for Increase in Taxes." August 1, 23.

Murray, Alan. 1987. "Conflicting Signals: Lobbyists for Business Are Deeply Divided, Reducing Their Clout; Disagreements over Deficit, Trade Could Widen Split." *Wall Street Journal,* March 25, 1.

Woodside, William S. 1987. "Health Care for the Poor: How to Pay for It." *Wall Street Journal,* May 29, 1.

Ingrassia, Paul and Joseph White. 1992. "Determined to Change, General Motors Is Said to Pick New Chairman: It's Expected to Give Smale Stempel's Job and Speed Pace of Its Downsizing." *Wall Street Journal,* October 23, A1, A4.

Rogers, David. 1994. "Business Delivers Another Blow to Health Plan— Chamber of Commerce Calls Mandates Unacceptable." *Wall Street Journal,* February 4, A3.

Wall Street Journal. 1994. "Top-Level Lobbyist Leaves Chamber of Commerce Post." April 6, B9.

Saddler, Jeanne. 1994. "Chamber Poll Finds Opposition to Health-care Mandate." *Wall Street Journal,* April 27, B2.

Cooper, Helene. 1997. "GOP to Rebuke Companies' Bipartisan Donations." *Wall Street Journal.* January 9, 14.

Solomon, Deborah. 2003. "SEC May Boost Holders' Power to Nominate, Elect Directors." *Wall Street Journal,* October 9, A13.

Wessel, David. 2004. "Roundtable Credibility at Risk with Silence on U.S. Budget Deficit." *Wall Street Journal,* April 8, A2.

Hilsenrath, Jon E. 2004. "Companies Appear Optimistic on Hiring, Capital Spending." *Wall Street Journal,* September 2, A2.

Preciphs, Joi. 2005. "CEOs See Negative Katrina Effect." *Wall Street Journal,* September 22, A6.

Wessel, David. 2005. "Capital: Politicians Must Decide How to Raise Taxes." *Wall Street Journal,* October 13, A2.

Adamy, Janet. 2009. "Business Groups Push Hard against the Senate Bill." *Wall Street Journal,* October 29, A4.

Frank, Robert. 2011. "Millionaires Support Warren Buffett's Tax on the Rich." *Wall Street Journal,* October 27. http://blogs.wsj.com/wealth/2011/10/27/most -millionaires-support-warren-buffetts-tax-on-the-rich/.

Fortune—Organized Chronologically, Ascending

Fortune. 1939. "What Business Thinks." (October):52–53, 90–98.

———. 1970a. "Editorial: Reconciling Progress with the Quality of Life." (February):91–93.

———. 1970b. "What Business Thinks: The Fortune 500-Yankelovich Survey." (February):118–119, 171–172.

Kirkpatrick, David. 1989. "CEOs to Bush: Raise Taxes Now." *Fortune* (January 16):95–96.

———. 1997. "The Fallen Giant." (December):156–157.

Vital Speeches of the Day References—Organized by Author

Baldwin, Robert H. B. 1977. "The Frustration in the Formation of Investment Capital." *Vital Speeches of the Day* 43(13):405. Presented February 23, 1977.

Bonner, Z. D. 1975. "The Abuse of Power by Regulatory Agencies." *Vital Speeches of the Day* 41(7):194. Presented November 19, 1974.

Flannery, Joseph P. 1978. "Government Regulation." *Vital Speeches of the Day* 44(24):749. Presented September 11, 1978.

Larry, R. Heath. 1969. "An Inflationary Binge: The Morning After." *Vital Speeches of the Day* 36(4):115. Presented October 18, 1969.

McCoy, Charles B. 1973. "Productivity." *Vital Speeches of the Day* 39(13):401. Presented March 12, 1973.

Sarnoff, Robert W. 1967. "Communications Technology." *Vital Speeches of the Day* 34(3):94. Presented October 10, 1967.

Ylvisaker, William T. 1978. "Regulation and the Public Interest." *Vital Speeches of the Day* 44(19):604. Presented May 9, 1978.

Index